On The Move: The Psychology of Change and Transition

On the Move: The Psychology of Change and Transition

Edited by
Shirley Fisher
Centre for Occupational and Health Psychology, University of Strathclyde, Glasgow, UK

Cary L. Cooper
Manchester School of Management, University of Manchester, Institute of Science and Technology, Manchester, UK

JOHN WILEY & SONS
Chichester · New York · Brisbane · Toronto · Singapore

Other Wiley Editorial Offices

John Wiley & Sons, Inc., 605 Third Avenue,
New York, NY 10158-0012. USA

Jacaranda Wiley Ltd, G.P.O. Box 859, Brisbane,
Queensland 4001, Australia

John Wiley & Sons (Canada) Ltd, 22 Worcester Road,
Rexdale, Ontario M9W 1L1, Canada

John Wiley & Sons (SEA) Pte Ltd, 37 Jalan Pemimpin #05-04,
Block B, Union Industrial Building, Singapore 2057

Library of Congress Cataloging-in-Publication Data:
On the move : the psychology of change and transition / edited by
Shirley Fisher, Cary L. Cooper.
p. cm.
Includes bibliographical references.
Includes index.
ISBN 0 471 92815 1 (cloth)
1. Life change events—Psychological aspects. 2. Change
(Psychology) I. Fisher, S. (Shirley) II. Cooper, Cary L.
[DNLM: 1. Family—psychology. 2. Life Change Events.
3. Psychological Theory. 4. Stress, Psychological. WM 172 058]
BF637.L53052 1991
155.9—dc20
DNLM/DLC
for Library of Congress 90-12488
CIP

British Library Cataloguing in Publication Data:
On the move : the psychology of change and transition.
1. Man. Transitions. Psychological aspects
I. Fisher, Shirley II. Cooper, Cary L. (Cary Lynn), *1940-*
155.24

ISBN 0 471 92815 1

Phototypeset by Dobbie Typesetting Service, Tavistock, Devon
Printed by Biddles Ltd, Guildford, Surrey

Dedication

To Reginald Pittman for his help, guidance and tolerance in the production of this book.

Contents

List of Contributors

John Arnold
Department of Organizational Psychology, UMIST, PO Box 88, Manchester, UK

Arza Churchman
Program in Social Ecology, University of California, Irvine, California 92717, USA

Cary Cooper
Department of Management Science, UMIST, University of Manchester, PO Box 88, Manchester M60 1QD, UK

Carolyn Cutrona
Department of Psychology, Spence Laboratories of Psychology, The University of Iowa, Iowa City, Iowa 52242, USA

Maurice Eisenbruch
Department of Child and Family Psychiatry, Royal Children's Hospital, Flemington Road, Parkville, Melbourne, Victoria 3052, Australia

Tiffany Field
Mailman Center for Child Development, PO Box 248185, Coral Gables, Florida 33124, USA

Shirley Fisher
Centre for Occupational and Health Psychology, Department of Psychology, Marland House, University of Strathclyde, Glasgow, Scotland

Adrian Furnham
Department of Psychology, University College London, Gower Street, London WC1E 6BT, UK

Paul Gilbert
Department of Psychology, Pastures Hospital, Derby, UK

Terence Lee
Department of Psychology, University of St Andrews, St Andrews, Fife, Scotland

George Mandler
Centre for Human Information Processing, University of California, San Diego, La Jolla, California 92093, USA

Nigel Nicholson
Centre for Organizational Behaviour, London Business School, Sussex Place, Regents Park, London NW1 4SA, UK

Keith Oatley
Department of Psychology, University of Glasgow, University Avenue, Glasgow, Scotland

Roy Payne
Department of Organizational Behaviour, Manchester Business School, University of Manchester, Booth Street West, Manchester M15 6PB, UK

Ted Scharf
Program in Social Ecology, University of California, Irvine, California 92717, USA

Daniel Stokols
Program in Social Ecology, University of California, Irvine, California 92717, USA

Julie A. Suhr
Department of Psychology, Spence Laboratories of Psychology, The University of Iowa, Iowa City, Iowa 52242, USA

Eric M. Vernberg
Department of Psychology, University of Miami, PO Box 248185, Coral Gables, Florida 33124, USA

Robert Weiss
Work and Family Research Unit, Downtown Center, University of Massachusetts, Boston, Massachusetts 02125, USA

Steven Wright
Program in Social Ecology, University of California, Irvine, California 92717, USA

Preface

CHANGE, TRANSITION AND HUMAN DEVELOPMENT

Change and transition recur in the lives of people and are part of human development. Although for some people change is positive, for others it is difficult to accomplish without disruption and often distress. For some, distress levels are very high and the effects are profound and enduring. There is anecdotal evidence to suggest that some people will give up the possibility of new ventures and opportunities, simply because they cannot face the idea of major changes. Change is an experience which can be threatening in advance.

Very little is known about why change should be threatening. Evolutionary advantage should surely favour those able to make changes quickly and easily. Adapting to change is part of homeostasis and is essential if the human race is to survive the variety of geographical, climatic and social environments associated with its growth, expansion and development: the human mind should have acquired, by natural selection, the facility for coping with change. It would seem counter-productive to have evolved a system geared to maintaining the present and clinging to the past. Yet it appears that responding adversely to change and transition is characteristic for many people, at least initially.

DIFFICULTIES WITH INVESTIGATIONS OF THE EFFECTS OF CHANGE

One of the main problems with investigations of change is that it is a common denominator of both positive and negative life events. Moves to a new job or winning a prize in a raffle involve changes which may be very profound if the sum of money is large. Equally, losing a much-loved relative or pet, becoming ill, or losing a job also involve change. One useful difference may be whether the change is imposed or voluntarily sought—but then, as argued above, some positive opportunities may not be welcomed by the individual. The 'assumptive world' of a person, or how he/she perceives environmental evidence may be

the most important consideration (see Fisher and Reason, 1989). Positive changes might be perceived as negative and vice-versa.

If events traditionally regarded as positive, including upward social mobility and educational/vocational opportunity, have properties in common with negative conditions this produces a problem for theory, but also for distinguishing events. Yet probably only in extreme conditions of trauma is there likely to be a uniform response.

One acceptable way of distinguishing events which are part of human development and progression, from those which are largely negative, is in terms of stimulus properties. All changes which afford opportunities for growth and development—moving, adapting to new educational or work environments, migration within or between countries—are, for the purpose of this volume, considered to be part of naturally occurring change rather than negative stress. The one concession is that we have included the transition to unemployment. Whilst this is generally regarded as a negative event, it is nevertheless possible that unemployment may be the stimulus for further development and for new personal initiatives. Since this possibility is important, it was felt by the editors that it should be examined as part of the volume.

ORGANIZATION AND CONTENTS OF THE VOLUME

The volume is addressed to the effects of positive events associated with upward social, educational or occupational mobility and with processes of growing up and developing within and across boundaries. It would have been impossible to cover all forms of potentially positive transitions that occur in life, or to devise methods of distinguishing self-created and other-created opportunities.

Section I provides some theoretical understanding of how and why change, even in a positive context, might be stressful and cause distress in some people. There is concentration on four main theoretical approaches. The first, by Robert Weiss, is based on research on separation and loss, and suggests that there are parallels between infant-mother bonds and the bonds between adults. Change to new environments very often involves the temporary or permanent breaking of relationships between people. These relationships may be important to the individual satisfying emotional needs through interdependency. Thus the individual who incurs this kind of separation may be homesick, insecure or lost. In effect this could be like a small bereavement.

The second theoretical approach, which is developed by George Mandler, is that interruption is a common denominator of change. Thus changes of all kinds, whether positive or negative, cause disruption of on-going planned activities. Since there is energy contained in plans, the consequence of interruption is a release of tension which can translate into anxiety. On the interruption hypothesis, change would cause a period of disruption and distress because of

its association with anxiety at the breaking of familiar routines and activities. These ideas are developed in greater detail by Mandler.

The idea that transitions engender loss of control is explored by Fisher. This approach shifts the responsibility for any adverse effects on the new environment, and perhaps more importantly on a person's ability to become committed, to take opportunities which present themselves and to begin to achieve rapid control over aspects of the new environment. There is indication that some people are more likely to react with passivity, and that this is counter-productive as a strategy for coping.

The importance of status in society and role change engendered by moves is explored by Paul Gilbert in a clinical context, and by Keith Oatley, whose socio-cognitive interests are emphasized. These two chapters offer considerable insights into the broader perspectives of transition and the effects on individuals, with particular emphasis on how a person is perceived by others and by himself or herself, as a determinant of response.

Finally, theoretical insights into the dynamics of transition offered by Arnold emphasize the importance of the time-course of events and the nature of the process of adapting to change.

Section II provides a number of different chapters addressed to topics representing the effects of a broad variety of changes. The constraints of a short preface preclude mention of all authors and chapters. Some situations explored are routinely part of the process of development in modern society, such as the transition to school and the transition to taking a job, or becoming a parent. In addition there are chapters which provide a broader overview of the effects of change in terms of moving home, leaving home and the effects on psychological state, homesickness and health.

The form and variety of response to change is potentially large. Alarm, anxiety, depression, absent-mindedness, longing for the past, searching, obsessionality, insecurity, are other features of reaction. Different individuals may react differently, but some environments are associated with specific kinds of reaction. All students undergoing the transition to university are likely to show increased depression (Fisher and Hood, 1987).

Perhaps the tendency of some people to dwell on the past should form the focus for research because, as already stated, it seems such a counter-productive process. However, although it may constrain against adaptation initially, perhaps it functions to protect against the possible new hostile aspects to change by slowing down or attenuating the decision to undertake it.

Section III provides two accounts of possible coping strategies: the first is addressed to strategies for aiding immediate adjustment; the second considers adaptation in the context of more general strategies for coping with stress, and indicates some possibilities for adjustment in the long term.

SHIRLEY FISHER
CARY COOPER

REFERENCES

Fisher, S. and Reason, J. (1988) (eds) *The Handbook of Life Stress Cognition and Health*. Chichester: John Wiley & Sons.

Fisher, S. and Hood, B. (1987) The stress of the transition to university. A longitudinal study of psychological disturbance and vulnerability to homesickness *British Journal of Psychology*, **78**, 309–320.

Section I: Theories of the Effects of Change and Transition

In this section leading researchers were invited to explore the theory of how and why change creates effects in the lives of individuals. There are many different types and levels of explanation in this section, which should be of particular interest to occupational, clinical and health psychologists who wish to develop understanding of the cognitive basis of change. Those with marginal, custodial or care-giving roles in commercial, public sector or health institutions should find that much of what is covered is of interest to the understanding of effects reported in the middle section of the volume and to the development of personnel selection and coping strategies.

1 Losses Associated with Mobility

ROBERT S. WEISS
Work and Family Research Unit, University of Massachusetts, Boston

Moving away from people with whom social bonds had been established, no matter the reason for the move, is likely to produce distress. The form of the distress is dependent on the nature of the interrupted bonds.

We should first distinguish the distress characterized as 'grief' from other forms of distress. Grief is marked, first, by a driving restlessness which is at bottom a striving to regain the lost relationship, accompanied by painful sadness because the relationship is not to be regained. As the driving restlessness fades it is replaced by deep sadness. Grief of this sort results when individuals lose emotional partners and children (Glick, Weiss and Parkes, 1974; Wortman and Silver, 1987). Sometimes it also occurs when individuals lose parents to whom they are unusually close (Horowitz, 1984). Grief, though to a lesser degree, may also be exhibited by some who lose therapists or teachers or other guides (see Weiss, 1973). The class of relationships whose loss triggers grief may be called relationships of attachment.

Severe and persisting distress may also follow the loss of *all* relationships with family, friends and co-workers. Such losses often are associated with geographical mobility but may also accompany a severe conflict among friends or family, or a loss of work through firing or retirement. In any event, it is not the loss of a bond to one particular individual that is persistingly distressing so much as the loss of access to a community of friends, family or workmates. When it is the community of relationships rather than a particular relationship that is emotionally sustaining (although each individual relationship may be cherished) we may speak of relationships of community.

Relationships of community have in common that they provide the individual with a sense of place and of social meaning. They link the individual to valued groups. They provide the individual with events, happenings, that structure life. The complete absence of community, an experience that may be produced by a solitary emigration, fosters feelings of marginality,

On the Move: the Psychology of Change and Transition. Edited by S. Fisher and C. L. Cooper.

valuelessness and exile (Benny, Weiss, Meyersohn and Riesman, 1959; Weiss, 1974).

Relationships of attachment provide individuals with feelings of security, feelings of an augmentation of self, and the sort of interchange that is likely to maintain their morale and sense of self relatively constant. Relationships of community provide, rather, a sense of place, of membership in a valued collectivity, that gives individuals a feeling of meaning to others and of personal worth.

THE CONCOMITANTS OF LOSS

Relationships of attachment and relationships of community have differences that make for differences in the way their losses are experienced.

1. *Relationships of attachment are security-fostering; relationships of community provide a sense of place and support for feelings of worth.*

The inaccessibility of an attachment figure makes the individual vulnerable to feelings of intense insecurity when in situations in which there is reason for feelings of vulnerability. Being alone often is one such situation. The absence of community makes the individual vulnerable to feelings of not belonging, being outside what is going on, being without genuine importance to others, being without social worth.

2. *The need for relationships of attachment is elicited especially by feelings of threat; the need for relationships of community is elicited especially by socially given timing.*

When individuals feel secure, behaviors associated with the attachment system are in abeyance. Energy and attention are instead given to play or work. There may be no indication of the special importance of the attachment figure. Under conditions of threat to the self or to the reliability of the attachment relationship, attachment feelings and behaviors are expressed. If someone feels beleaguered at work, alone in the evening, tense in the middle of the night, the attachment figure becomes of special importance.

Relationships of community become especially important when there is a sense that events are occurring in which social place is recognized or denied: in which people are included or are left out. So the unemployed are especially distressed during the working week, those estranged from family are especially distressed over the Christmas season and those who are far from friends are especially distressed weekend evenings and at the New Year's season.

3. *Attachment behavior displays the aims of establishing proximity to the attachment figure and gaining the attention and investment of the attachment figure. Behavior linked to membership in community is aimed rather at a sense of acceptance and participation, often in relation to shared goals.*

Reassurance of security, as an aim of attachment behavior, seems to be gained by seeing, hearing or touching the attachment figure. In the absence of the attachment figure some reassurance of security can sometimes be achieved through belief that proximity to the attachment figure will be established in the near future. Behavior relevant to membership in communities is rather aimed at establishing acceptance and membership. So an individual can feel a member of a community of work or play when recognized for having contributed in an effective way to the community's goals, whether or not others are emotionally invested in his or her well-being.

4. *Attachment relationships are organized around particular figures. Relationships of community permit substitution of figures.*

Grief follows loss of the particular individuals who have been attachment figures. Attempts to substitute other figures fail, no matter how ideally the other figures behave. It is that one figure to whom the individual was attached whose presence is needed—no other will do. In contrast, one workmate may be replaced by another, one friend by another, with brief sadness, perhaps, but without persisting grief.

In relationships of attachment, distress is not to be assuaged by the substitution of another figure in the same relationship (another spouse, another child); nor is one sort of attachment in any way substitutive for another. In contrast, Gore (1978) suggests that membership in a community of friends and family limits the distress consequent on loss of membership in a community of work. Henderson, Byrne and Duncan-Jones (1981) suggest that membership in any community is as good as membership in any other in supporting resilience at times of crisis.

That attachments are more linked with particular people has, as a corollary:

5. *Attachments to particular figures are persistent over time. Relationships of community are less persistent.*

Continuing separation from an attachment figure produces pining and, often, anger and distrust, but only slowly and incompletely diminution of attachment. On the other hand, continuing separation from community, so long as an alternative community is available, seems to make possible early and effective forgetting.

6. *The persistence of attachment is unaffected by the quality of experience with the attachment figure. Commitment to community seems more dependent on experience.*

Attachment seems to persist even when the attachment figure is neglecting, disparaging or abusive. Commitment to community, in contrast, seems to be much affected by experiences of misuse, neglect, and absence of appropriate recognition.

WHAT DOES IT MEAN TO RECOVER FROM LOSS?

We cannot imagine that people who have suffered a severe loss will return to the identity and emotional organization they maintained before the loss. As widows and widowers sometimes say, 'You don't get over it. You get used to it.' Severe grief, no matter how fully individuals emerge from it, should be expected to produce character change. In what sense, then, can we use the concept of 'recovery?' A relationship of critical significance has been lost; the individual is likely to have been changed. Is 'recovery' an appropriate term? Should not we rather use terms like, 'adaptation,' 'accommodation,' or even 'degree of damage?'

The answer, I believe, is that there is one query for which the term 'recovery' is indispensable; that is the extent to which there is a return of ordinary functioning. Recovery from grieving can be understood as return to previous levels of functioning. With this definition in mind the assessment of extent of recovery is a meaningful question.

We have, however, no universally accepted criteria for ordinary levels of effective functioning. One listing of reasonable expectations is the following. Associated with each expectation are the likely expressions of failure to recover in that particular respect.

1. *The ability to give energy to everyday life.* Effective functioning requires investment in the present, with adequate energy to meet current challenges. Failure to recover in this respect might occur if the individual's energies remained bound by the experience of loss, with thought and effort still absorbed by that experience or, alternatively, absorbed by the effort to repress memories and feelings associated with the experience. Insofar as this is the case, current life would be seen as empty and meaningless.
2. *Psychological comfort, as demonstrated by freedom from pain and distress.* Effective functioning requires freedom from disturbing thoughts and feelings. Failure to recover would be exhibited by vulnerability to intrusions, which may have the character of flashbacks or of memories with associated pain and distress. Failure to recover could also be exhibited by an identification

with the state of grieving, so that freedom from grieving would feel like a foreign, and anxiety-provoking, state.

3. *Ability to experience gratification; the ability to feel pleasure should desirable, hoped-for, or enriching events occur.* Effective functioning requires the ability to experience pleasure as well as to anticipate pleasure should hoped-for events occur. Failure to recover would be demonstrated by an anhedonic state in which potentially pleasurable events are responded to as meaningless. Individuals may even feel regret or remorse when potentially pleasurable events occur because the events feel to them incomplete without the attachment figure or cruelly ironic in the light of their loss.
4. *Hopefulness regarding the future; being able to plan and care about plans.* Effective functioning requires being able to give meaning to activity, and such meaning requires a sense of a future which may have in it something desirable. Failure to recover would be exhibited by a belief that the future is hopeless, pointless or empty, and that life is already over. Alternatively, the individual's conceptual field may narrow so that memories of the past and thoughts of the future are avoided.
5. *The ability to function with reasonable adequacy in social roles as spouse, parent and member of community.* Effective functioning might be held to require meeting social expectations well enough to maintain emotionally significant relationships. Failure to recover might then be displayed, for example, by unpredictable behavior in attachment relationships because of distrust of these relationships, or by so great a preoccupation with loss that energy cannot be invested in new relationships of attachment.

The return of ordinary capacity to function as an adult and as a member of the society would seem to require that each of these five abilities return in at least some degree. Identifying them as aspects of recovery is based on the idea that recovery means the return of various aspects of personal and social functioning, and also implies that recovery may be partial or incomplete.

MOVEMENT TO RECOVERY

The process of recovery from grief—the condition into which individuals are cast by loss of attachment figures—has been given much more attention than the process of recovery from the sense of marginality and pointlessness associated with loss of relationships of community. At this point we may surmise that the processes in the two cases are similar, but we do not really know this.

Recovery from loss of attachment figures seems to involve phases in which different ways of relating to loss are dominant, although there is much intermeshing of these phases. The phases seem to follow a sequence in which the loss is first emotionally denied, even though it may be consciously accepted,

then accepted but not accepted as permanent, with attempts made to end it, then accepted as permanent, with hopelessness giving rise to depression, and finally accepted as permanent, but with hope of satisfactory life nevertheless. Judging from studies of the unemployed, recovery from loss of community seems to involve the same sequence.

Phases of grieving following loss of attachment figures have been reported to occur with some reliability in all grieving that eventually moves to recovery, although the phases are best documented in connection with the loss of pair bonds (Bowlby and Parkes, 1970; Glick, Weiss and Parkes, 1974). However, survey studies of individuals who have suffered losses have led some investigators to question whether there may not be a substantial minority of individuals who do not experience deep grief and so do not move through phases of recovery (Wortman and Silver, 1988). However, insofar as individuals move from grief to recovery, some sequence of phases seems likely.

The phases of recovery that have regularly been identified may be named, to follow Bowlby, as shock, protest, despair and then a long interval of adaptation (Bowlby, 1980).

1. The phase of *shock* is a numbed refusal to credit the reality of the loss event which precedes actual grief. Shock tends especially to be seen where loss is not forewarned. Shock seems to be a defensive, perhaps emotionally necessary, temporary refusal to accept that loss has occurred.
2. The first phase of grief itself, Bowlby's phase of *protest*, is one in which effort is devoted to undoing the loss, even though there can be awareness that this is impossible. In this phase the individual is agitated and fearful, oppressed by intense pain and subject to bouts of anxiety mounting to panic. When it is an attachment figure that has been lost there is a vigilant scanning of the environment for sights or sounds that would indicate the return of the attachment figure. Pain and panic are heightened by awareness that the search is in vain.
3. With continuing frustration of the attempt to undo loss emotional conviction develops that further attempts are hopeless. Now the individual withdraws into despairing lethargic depression: Bowlby's phase of *despair*.
4. The two phases of grief proper, the phase of search and protest, and the phase of depressive withdrawal, may overlap, or intervals of the one may occur at a time when the other is predominant. But by and large protest and search characterize an earlier phase of grieving, depressive withdrawal a later phase.

A final phase of recovery may be identified, that of 'adaptation,' in which the individual gives energy to establishing a new way of life with new potentials for satisfaction and goal attainment. In response to loss of an attachment figure, as long as four years or more may be needed for adaptation to occur (Glick, Weiss and Parkes, 1974). Recovery from loss of community seems much more

rapid. In one study newcomers were found to feel themselves a part of a new community within six months of arrival (Weiss, 1974).

At least three processes appear to be involved in movement to recovery. These might be characterized as cognitive acceptance, emotional acceptance and identity change.

COGNITIVE ACCEPTANCE

Individuals moving well toward recovery appear to develop a satisfactory account of the causes of the loss event. The objective validity of the account is less important than its subjectively felt validity.

Ordinarily, it appears, satisfactory accounts can be developed rather quickly, if they can be developed at all. The absence of a satisfactory account seems to leave individuals anxiously perplexed, searching their cognitive field for contributions to the loss they may have made themselves, or that may have been made by enemies or other third parties.

EMOTIONAL ACCEPTANCE

Recovery seems to require individuals to achieve a neutralization of memories and associations so that recall does not paralyze functioning. This process of neutralization requires the confrontation of emotion-laden memories and associations one by one and, with each, the reduction of associated pain so that there develops tolerance for the memory. Until this happens to an adequate extent there is continued vulnerability to pain. Also part of the process of emotional acceptance is the diminishing of the importance of examination of alternative scenarios; scenarios that would have avoided loss. These 'If only's', though they may be less painful than memories and associations, represent another way in which thoughts and feelings remain anchored in the past.

The process of neutralization seems to require variable amounts of time, depending on the nature of the loss, but may require several months for progress to be observable when it is an attachment figure that has been lost. In relation to loss of community and intentional loss of an attachment figure (through marital separation) there may be persisting feelings of anger that are entirely acceptable to the self. No effort is made to 'recover' from them.

IDENTITY CHANGE

Finally, it seems to be necessary for individuals to develop a new image of themselves, in which their connection to unavailable figures is seen as associated with a past self rather than a present self. For this to be fully accomplished, the individual must make new commitments to new relationships.

This appears to be much more easily accomplished in relation to losses of community than in relation to losses of attachments.

THE FORMS OF FAILURES TO RECOVER

Most frequently, failure to recover is marked by *chronicity*. This is the unmoving persistence of one or both of the phases of grief proper: the attempt to undo the loss, or depression because of inability to undo the loss and inability to withdraw investment in the relationship. In chronic distress there continues to be identification of self with the relationship to the inaccessible figures; there may be refusal to acknowledge the reality or the permanence of loss. Anhedonia will be marked, as will be estrangement from others, since the individual's picture of reality will be discordant with that of others.

Failure to recover may also be marked by *compartmentalization*. This is the defensive posture expressed as 'I don't care; there are other things I'm giving my attention to.' Here the feelings associated with the loss are fended off, and energy is given to weakening the stimulus value of any observation or memory that might trigger awareness of the loss. At the same time there may be heightening of the stimulus value of other emotional commitments.

Compartmentalization is not the same as repression or denial; there is no refusal to recognize reality, only a refusal to attend to it. The event of loss is 'put out of one's mind', 'walled away,' to use terms offered by respondents. Compartmentalization is easily interrupted; for example, learning from a neighbor that there is to be a neighborhood activity to which one has not been invited can permit a breakthrough of massive feelings of marginality.

It is difficult to judge the cost of compartmentalization. It may make for a guardedness in interaction, as though a part of the self was being withheld—as, indeed, it is. It certainly will make it difficult for the individual to neutralize painful memories, insofar as such neutralization depends on the acceptance of loss. The most apparent cost is that the vigilance necessary to prevent compartmentalization from being breached may overgeneralize and lead to the exclusion from awareness of a good deal that is emotionally important. Insofar as there is defensive inattention, the result would seem likely to be impoverishment of the individual's emotional life. And it may be that in new relationships which in some way duplicate the relationship whose associations are compartmentalized selective inattention will result in a failure to recognize the individuality of this new other. This would permit replacement relationships, but at a cost in relational sensitivity.

Observation suggests that compartmentalization as a form of failure to recover is not necessarily consuming of energy. There can, indeed, be a great deal of energy expended in pursuit of goals distant from the loss despite the devotion of energy to vigilant refusal to attend to the loss. Whether there is anhedonia

is difficult to say (Lindemann, 1949, seems to believe there is). It may be in their ability to function in new emotional relationships that those who have dealt with loss by compartmentalization will experience most cost. Vigilance against re-experiencing the pain of loss may make for the avoidance of new experiences that could elicit memories.

In most failures to recover a mix of chronicity and compartmentalization can be observed. Horowitz *et al.* (1979) report that post-traumatic stress disorder gives rise to two classes of symptoms: 'intrusion' symptoms such as thinking about the traumatic event despite wishing not to (suggestive of chronicity) and 'avoidance' symptoms such as trying to remove the event from memory (suggestive of compartmentalization).

The mix of chronicity and compartmentalization may take many forms. There may be partial withdrawal from social life and the relinquishing of hopes for the future, both suggestive of chronicity, together with a blank absence of interest in the past, suggestive of compartmentalization. There may be constant awareness that a critical figure has died, suggestive of chronicity, together with refusal to talk about the death, suggestive of compartmentalization. There may be immersion in exciting activity, suggestive of compartmentalization, together with regular episodes of alcohol-facilitated sorrow, suggestive of chronicity.

A CONCLUDING STATEMENT

Change, like crisis, provides both opportunity and risk. There is opportunity for growth and development and for the formation of new selves with new perspectives. And there is risk of all the distress associated with loss and of that distress becoming chronic. Especially is there risk when the relationships which are lost are relationships of attachment. Then it may require resilience and patience to achieve a recovery in which it is possible to become fully engaged in the new situation.

REFERENCES AND BIBLIOGRAPHY

Benny, M., Weiss, R. S., Meyersohn, R. and Riesman, D. (1959) Christmas in an apartment hotel. *American Journal of Sociology*, November, pp. 233-240.

Bowlby, J. (1969) *Attachment and Loss*, Vol. I: *Attachment.* New York: Basic Books.

Bowlby, J. (1973) *Attachment and Loss*, Vol. II: *Separation: Anxiety and Anger*. New York: Basic Books.

Bowlby, J. (1980) *Attachment and Loss*, Vol. III: *Loss: Sadness and Depression*. New York: Basic Books.

Bowlby, J. and Parkes, C. M. (1970) Separation and loss. In E. J. Anthony and C. Koupernik (eds), *The Child and His Family*. Vol. 1 of *International Yearbook of Child Psychiatry and Allied Professions* (Anthony E. J. and Koupernik C., eds). New York: John Wiley & Sons.

Ekerdt, D. J., Boss, R. and Levkoff, S. (1985) An empirical test for phases of retirement: findings from the normative aging study. *Journal of Gerontology*, **40**(1), 95-101.
Fried, M (1963) Grieving for a lost home. In L. J. Duhl (ed.), *The Urban Condition*. New York: Basic Books, pp. 151-171.
Glick, I., Weiss, R. S. and Parkes, C. M. (1974) *The First Year of Bereavement*. New York: Wiley-Interscience.
Gore, S. (1978) The effect of social support in moderating the health consequences of unemployment. *Journal of Health and Social Behavior*, **19**, 157-165.
Henderson, S., Byrne, D. and Duncan-Jones, P. (1981) *Neurosis and the Social Environment*. New York: Academic Press.
Horowitz, M. J., Weiss, D., Kaltreider, N., Krupnick J., Wilner N., Marmar C. and DeWitt, K. (1984) Reactions to the death of a parent: results from patients and field subjects. *The Journal of Nervous and Mental Diseases*, **172**, 383-392.
Horowitz, M. J., Wilner, N. and Alvarez, A. (1979) Impact of event scale: a measure of subjective stress. *Psychosomatic Medicine*, **41**, 209-218.
Kitson, G. C. and Zyzanski, S. J. (1987) Grief in widowhood and divorce. *Psychiatric Clinics of North America*, **10**, 369-385.
Lehman, D. R., Wortman, C. B. and Williams, A. F. (1987) Long-term effects of losing a spouse or child in a motor vehicle crash. *Journal of Personality and Social Psychology*, **52**, 218–231.
Lindemann, E. (1949) Symptomatology and management of acute grief. *American Journal of Psychiatry*, **101**, 141-149.
Marris, P. (1974) *Loss and Change*. New York: Pantheon.
Parkes, C. M. (1972) *Bereavement*. New York: International Universities Press.
Parkes, C. M. (1971) Psycho-social transitions: a field for study. *Social Science and Medicine*, **5**, 101-115.
Parkes, C. M. and Weiss, R. S. (1983) *Recovery From Bereavement*. New York: Basic Books.
Weiss, R. S. (1973a) *Loneliness: the Experience of Emotional and Social Isolation*. Cambridge, MA: MIT Press.
Weiss, R. S. (1973b) Helping relationships: relationships with physicians, social workers, priests and others. *Social Problems*, **20**, 319-328.
Weiss, R. S. (1974) The provisions of social relationships. In Z. Rubin (ed.), *Doing Unto Others: Joining, Molding, Conforming, Helping, Loving*. Englewood Cliffs, NJ: Prentice-Hall/Spectrum Books, pp. 17-26.
Weiss, R. S. (1975) *Marital Separation*. New York: Basic Books.
Weiss, R. S. (1982) Attachment in adults. In C. M. Parkes and J. Stevenson-Hinde (eds), *The Place of Attachment in Human Behavior*. New York: Basic Books, pp. 171-184.
Weiss, R. S. (1987) Principles underlying a manual for parents whose children were killed by a drunk driver. *American Journal of Orthopsychiatry*, **57**(3), 431-440.
Wortman, C. B. and Silver, R. C. (1987) Coping with irrevocable loss. In *Cataclysms, Crises and Catastrophes: Psychology in action* (Master Lecture Series, Vol. 6), Washington, DC: American Psychological Association.
Wortman, C. B. and Silver, R. C. (1988) The myths of coping with loss. Unpublished paper. Survey Research Center, University of Michigan.

2 Interruption (Discrepancy) Theory: Review and Extensions

GEORGE MANDLER
Center for Human Information Processing, University of California, San Diego

INTRODUCTION

In 1964 I presented 'The interruption of behavior' (Mandler, 1964)—the initial statement of interruption theory. Since then the theory has become one of the mainstays of a general theory of emotional experience (Mandler, 1975, 1984, 1990), and it also has incorporated the major changes in psychology that have come about with the advent of the theoretically oriented 'new' cognitive psychology. In the process the notion of interruption was generalized under the rubrics of discrepancy and inconsistency, and its applicability was extended to problems of stress at one extreme and the development of human values at the other. In the context of the present volume interruptions are a significant aspect of moves and transitions, which interrupt previously predictable situations and life sequences. In the following I shall describe the development of interruption/discrepancy theory and its various applications. The original statement of the interruption hypothesis read:

> *The interruption of an integrated or organized response sequence produces a state of arousal which will be followed by emotional behavior.*

Over 25 years later the statement would have to be expanded and amplified and might read:

> Visceral arousal follows perceptual or cognitive discrepancies and the interruption or blocking of ongoing actions. Discrepancies occur when the expectations generated by some schema (whether determining thought or action) are violated. This is the case whether the violating event is worse or better than the expected one—and accounts for visceral arousal in both unhappy and joyful occasions

On the Move: the Psychology of Change and Transition. Edited by S. Fisher and C. L. Cooper

> Most emotions follow such discrepancies. It is the combination of arousal with an on-going evaluative cognition that produces the subjective experience of an emotion.

I will return to this more recent version of the hypothesis after briefly delineating some of its theoretical fathers and cousins.

A BRIEF HISTORY OF THE INTERRUPTION/DISCREPANCY HYPOTHESIS

Earlier notions related to interruption theory can be found in theoretical speculations about emotion in the nineteenth century. The major proponents were Frédéric Paulhan (1887) and John Dewey (1894, 1895).[1] Paulhan ascribed emotional phenomena to the occurrence of arrested tendencies, essentially conditions other than what has usually been the case in the past or what would be expected to occur. Some themes like this had been heard before, but Paulhan's most important contribution was to assign both positive and negative emotions to the sequelae of arrested tendencies, and also to insist that the nature of the particular emotion that is generated depended on the tendency arrested, as well as on the conditions under which the 'arrest' occurs. Within 10 years Dewey noted that emotions arise when the organism's current actions (reactions) cannot be integrated with other implicit or overt reactions. When there is conflict, emotion ensues; without conflict there is no emotion. However, neither of these formulations ever enjoyed wide popularity (see Angier, 1927).

More recent theoretical speculations in psychology relevant to the hypothesis are found in Kurt Lewin's and Sigmund Freud's work. Lewin (1935, 1940) suggested that any intention to reach a goal generates a tension system which is released when the goal is reached, and which is preserved if the goal is blocked. The major differences between Lewin's formulation and mine are that I invoke a tendency/attempt to complete a particular action sequence, rather than a tension system which maintains such a tendency, and that I invoke a tension/arousal system that becomes active only *after* the action sequence has been blocked or interrupted.

Propositions more closely related to emotional reactions can be found in Freud and D. O. Hebb. Freud related anxiety to an inability to reach a goal when he described anxiety as a reaction to the perception of the absence of the object (Freud, 1926). Hebb suggested that 'fear originates in the disruption of temporally and spatially organized cerebral activities' (Hebb, 1946, p. 274).[2]

One other tradition has been concerned with emotional effects of inconsistent or discrepant events, namely the behaviorist treatment of extinction phenomena. For example, Skinner, (1938, p. 409) noted that the absence of a previously

produced reinforcement has emotional consequences. The most extensive treatment can be found in Amsel's (1962) frustration effect, which postulated (and showed) that the withdrawal of reward has motivational (and emotional) consequences. Finally, Berkowitz (1964) suggested not only that aggressive acts are a function of visceral arousal and appropriate environmental cues, but also that preventing the completion of an aggressive sequence produces internal tensions that energize other available responses.[3]

All the previous forays into the problem of interruption—with the exception of Paulhan and Dewey—postulated that the consequences of the tension/arousal following interruption or disruption were noxious or negative. For Freud it was anxiety, for Hebb it was fear, for Amsel—frustration. This is quite different from a position which only postulates the occurrence of arousal, but leaves open the question whether the arousal will potentiate positive or negative states of the organism.

At the heart of interruption theory is a theory of emotional experience, and I shall give a brief description of that theory before discussing more general effects of interruptions and discrepancies in social contexts.

INTERRUPTION THEORY AND EMOTIONAL EXPERIENCE

Central to the development of interruption theory after 1964 has been the emergence of cognitive theory and particularly the development of the schema concept which needs an introduction before turning to a discussion of discrepancies.

THE NATURE OF SCHEMAS

A schema is a coherent unit of structured representation that organizes experience. Schemas are not carbon copies of experience, but abstract representations of experiential regularities. Schemas range from the very concrete, involving the most primitive categorization of perceptual experience, to the abstract. Abstract schemas subsume more concrete schemas; the resulting structure is hierarchical. Schemas are built up in the course of experience and interaction with the social and physical environment. They organize and interpret our world, and they organize experience in that current encounters are defined and interpreted in terms of the schemas laid down by past similar and cognate experiences. Currently active schemas define what we are likely to see, hear and remember, and new information activates relevant schemas that in turn organize our experience of the world.

The activation of schemas proceeds automatically from the most concrete to the most abstract relevant schemas. At the same time, and also automatically, activated high-level schemas pass activation to lower schemas (top-down

processing) which constrain further perception. Expectations are those elements of schemas activated by top-down processing that are not directly supported by input evidence. Expectations influence what will be attended by influencing the ease with which new evidence may be interpreted. Expectations are not met when evidence is not found for all or part of an activated schema; the result is a lack of congruity in schematic processing. This discrepancy is one of the causes of autonomic (sympathetic) nervous system arousal, in part to prepare the organism to cope with a changing environment.

Schemas are not rigidly bounded representations but are best seen as dispositional. Currently available information constructs (out of distributed features of previously developed schemas) a particular representation that responds both to the immediate information and to the regularities (schemas) generated by past events. Since schemas develop through experience, it is important to consider how they change. The single most important description of such a development has been provided by Jean Piaget, who analyzed the process of schema development in terms of *assimilation*, the integration of new elements or input into existing schemas, and *accommodation*, the change in schemas caused by input that cannot be assimilated.

AN APPROACH TO SUBJECTIVE EMOTIONAL EXPERIENCES

The theory of emotion based on the interruption concept addresses the subjective experience of emotion. It is not a theory of emotional behavior, which may or may not be accompanied or followed by positive or negative emotional experience. The theory is constructivist and views the construction of emotion as consisting of the concatenation of a cognitive evaluative schema together with the perception of visceral arousal. This construction is a unitary conscious experience, even though it may derive from separate and even independent schematic representations (Mandler, 1985; Marcel, 1983). Such a view of emotion only approximates the commonsense meaning of the term. To ask 'what is emotion?' is not—in principle—answerable. The term is a natural language expression which has all the advantages (communicative and inclusive) and disadvantages (imprecise and vague) of the common language. However, it is exactly for communicative purposes that one needs to approximate the common meaning as a first step.

I have focused on two dimensions out of the many available from analyses of common language 'emotions': the notion that emotions express some aspect of value, and the assertion that emotions are 'hot'—they imply a gut reaction, a visceral response. The cognition of values—what is good or bad—provides the quality of the emotional experience, and the visceral reaction generates its quantitative aspect. Given the many different possible evaluative states, one of the consequences of such a position is that it leads to the postulation of a

potentially innumerable number of different emotional states. There are of course regularities in human thought and action that produce general categories of these constructions, categories that have family resemblances and overlap in the features that are selected for analysis (whether it is the simple dichotomy of good and bad, or the appreciation of beauty, or the perception of evil). These families of occasions and meanings construct the categories of emotions found in the natural language (and psychology).[4] The emotion categories are fuzzily defined by external and internal situations.

The common themes found within the categories of emotions vary from case to case, and they have different bases for their occurrence. Sometimes an emotional category is based on the similarity of external conditions (as in the case of some fears and environmental threats). Sometimes an emotional category may be based on a collection of similar behaviors (in the subjective feelings of fear related to avoidance and flight). Sometimes a common category arises from a class of incipient actions (as in hostility and destructive action). Sometimes hormonal and physiological reactions provide a common basis (as in the case of lust), and sometimes purely cognitive evaluations constitute an emotional category (as in judgements of helplessness that eventuate in anxiety). Others, such as guilt and grief, depend on individual evaluations of having committed undesirable acts or trying to recover the presence/comfort of a lost person or object. All of these emotional states involve evaluative cognitions, and their common properties give rise to the appearance of discrete categories of emotions.

If evaluative cognitions provide the quality of an emotional experience, then visceral activity provides its intensity and peculiar 'emotional' feel. As a first approximation I assume that degree of automatic (sympathetic) arousal can be mapped into the felt intensity of an emotion. Affective judgements can obviously occur without visceral involvement. To say that something is pretty or fine or awful or even disgusting may be said quite dispassionately and unemotionally. What we need to understand are the occasions where visceral activity (however slight) co-occurs with these judgements or affects.

In one version of the common understanding of emotion, the occurrence of some visceral or gut reaction is generally assumed. Emotions are said to occur when we feel 'aroused', 'agitated', when our 'guts are in an uproar', etc. The reference is almost invariably to some autonomic nervous system activity, such as increased heart rate, sweating, or gastrointestinal upheavals. However, if one looks at the literature on the ANS, one is faced with a lack of any principled account of the sources of ANS activation. It is at this point that interruption theory made its major contribution.

To repeat—visceral (sympathetic nervous system) arousal follows perceptual or cognitive discrepancies and the interruption or blocking of on-going actions.[5]

The construction of emotions requires conscious capacity. The experience of emotion pre-empts limited capacity. Limited capacity refers to the fact that

conscious contents are highly restricted and limited at any one point in time. Whenever some particular construction pre-empts conscious capacity, then other processes that require such capacity will be impaired. The best example is found in stress and panic reactions when emotional reactions prevent adequate problem-solving activities.[6] Emotional experiences may inhibit the full utilization of our cognitive apparatus, thoughts may become stereotyped and canalized, and tend to revert to simpler modes of problem-solving. However, the effects of emotion are not necessarily intrusive and deleterious. In part, it will depend on other mental contents and mechanisms that are activated by the emotional experience and that may become available for dealing with stressful situations. For example, stress tends to focus attention on the perceived central aspects of a situation, and such focusing may be useful. The relationship of 'emotions' to discrepancies and autonomic nervous system recruitment also points to their adaptive function; emotions occur at important times in the life of the organism and may serve to prepare it for more effective thought and action when focused attention is needed.

EXPERIMENTAL STUDIES OF INTERRUPTION

I will summarize a representative sample of experimental studies of interruption, primarily in order to demonstrate some specific consequences of the theory.

In 1964 I reported an animal experiment which extended the well-known effect of extinction on emotionality. Extinction involves the absence of a previously present reinforcement and is therefore an excellent example of an interruption or discrepancy—the expected reinforcement is not available. In the 1964 experiment it was suggested that a similar phenomenon should be demonstrable when animals expect to find food even though they are not hungry. In other words, it is not just the reinforcement that is absent in extinction (i.e. the availability of food for a hungry animal), but the situation itself is defined as the condition when eating (just the consummatory response) is appropriate. Animals (rats) were trained in a Y-maze on a black-white discrimination on a 24-hour maintenance schedule. After reaching criterion on the discrimination, half of the animals were fully satiated before returning to the Y-maze discrimination; the other half were maintained on the deprivation schedule. The satiated animals showed extreme signs of distress, manifested in jerky and convulsive movements after finding no food in the goal box. Relatively little such extreme behavior was found in the other deprived group who were on regular extinction, i.e. hungry with no food reinforcement present. In Mandler and Watson (1966) I extended this observation by giving a subgroup of the animals experience in the negative goal box which was to serve as substitute behaviour. These data are

shown in Figure 2.1. Between training trials animals were placed in the negative goal box with another animal. After such experience had been given and criterion reached in the Y-maze discrimination, the animals were again either satiated or continued on the deprivation schedule. For some of the animals the previously experienced companion was now placed in the negative goal box. In brief the results showed that the availability of an alternate organized response—spending time with their companion—successfully suppressed the extreme distressed behavior (jerky and convulsive movements) for the first four days of this 'extinction' training

In summary these experiments show that interrupting an organized response (not just extinction in the presence of appropriate hunger motivation) produces extreme emotional behavior. Such behavior can be controlled and suppressed—

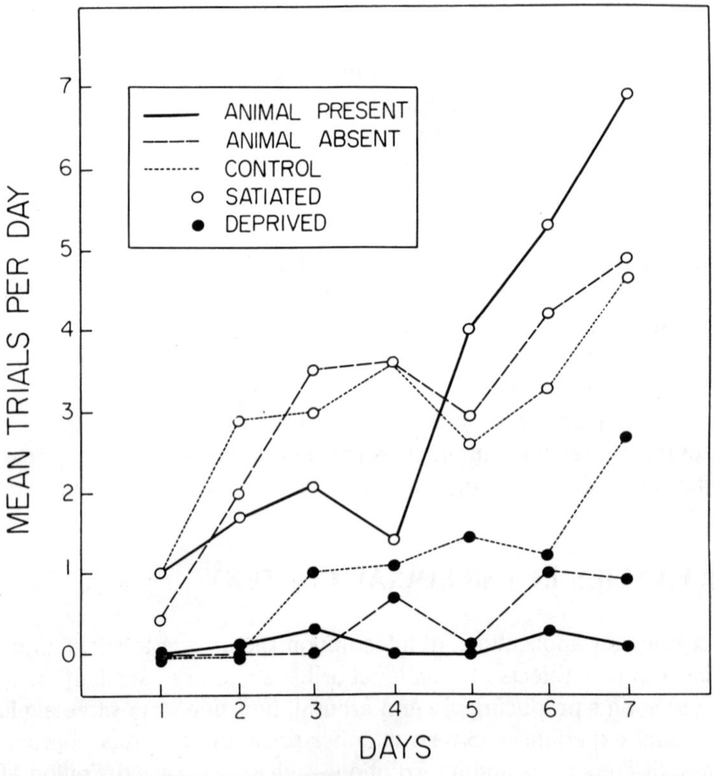

Figure 2.1. Number of trials (out of 10) per day on which jerky and convulsive behavior was observed for six experimental groups. Subjects were either deprived or satiated prior to test. Some of the animals had also been given experience in the negative goal box with another animal. There were three subgroups (a) an animal present in negative goal box, (b) prior experience with negative goal box but no animal present, or (c) a control group with no alternate, negative goal box experience.

at least for a short time—by the availability of another organized substitute response—the presence and interaction with another animal.

In Mandler (1964) I also reported the initial series of studies of the effects of interruption in human subjects. The experiments were concerned with series of sentences the subjects heard and learned to anticipate or a list of conceptually related items that subjects learned to anticipate. Interruptions were created by giving subjects erroneous feedback during these anticipations. The main results showed that autonomic response (GSR) varied directly as a function of the degree of prior organization of the material. The more organized a list the less lasting the disruption on subsequent behavior, and a 'relevant' interruption produced less disruption than an irrelevant one.

More recently a study by Yoshio Nakamura in our laboratory presented subjects with very simple—deliberately boring—stories and asked subjects to imagine how the stories would end. The stories were presented one sentence at a time and the last sentence was either consistent or discrepant with the preceding context. One story, for example, was about a little girl building sand castles. The tide threatens to wipe out her castle, but eventually the tide recedes. In the consistent ending she was happy that her castle was saved; in the discrepant one she was happy that her castle was ruined. In all cases we obtained significant increases in heart rate variability following discrepancy.

More evidence was accumulated in a study with an interactive computer game (MacDowell and Mandler, 1989). Here we obtained consistent increases in heart rate of the order of 10-20 beats per minute, and equally so to positive and negative discrepant events. We also obtained significant correlations between sympathetic arousal and intensity of emotional experience reported by our subjects. In addition, subjective intensity seems to depend, in some interactive fashion, on both the autonomic response to the discrepancy and the evaluation of the salience of the discrepancy. In other words, autonomic arousal is a necessary but not a sufficient condition for determining the intensity of an emotional experience.

DISCREPANCIES IN THE SOCIAL CONTEXT

The most relevant applications of interruption theory are to social interactions and social contexts. Effects of situational or life stress are excellent examples of unexpected events producing visceral arousal, negative or positive evaluations, and emotional experiences. Stress, whether social or individual, occurs on the occasion of discrepancies and interruptions—whatever one's definition of stress, but a detailed discussion of stress in general is out of place here.[7] I will be concerned here specifically with social stresses.

In recent years the interest in life stress and its psychological and physiological consequences has occasioned the appearance of rating scales that have been reasonably successful in retrospective studies of life stress and illness (e.g. Holmes

and Rahe, 1967; Dohrenwend, Krasnoff, Askenasy and Dohrenwend, 1978). The life stresses surveyed in these various scales and questionnaires are generally consistent with interruption theory. They typically refer to life situations in which change is encountered, and such change can be either negative or positive in value. Frankenhaeuser (1979) has noted that psychosocial conditions that are 'perceived as deviating from those to which the person is accustomed will induce a change in adrenalin output'. Whether it is the loss of a loved one or marriage, the birth of a child or the loss of a job, all such events generate interruption and discrepancy for the individual. The ensuing unusual autonomic nervous system activity and other physiological events all contribute to stress and systemic malfunctioning (see, for example, Fisher, 1988; Solomon and Amkraut, 1983).

In a general analysis of close relationships, Berscheid (e.g. 1983) has imaginatively described the conditions of interpersonal interactions that lead to interruptions and discrepancies and therefore to emotional reactions. When a relationship is meshed, when one individual's actions depend on the actions of the other, then the two people involved may become occasions for each other's interruptions. The actions of the other are essential for one's own action. Thus, emotional reactions are more likely in such meshed relationships than they are when the two lives are—in effect—parallel, when the actions of the two are not interdependent. This analysis can be extended to a variety of different social relationships and life situations. The extent to which a change in work, status, involvement, conditions and situations will be experienced emotionally, either by the actor or by colleagues and friends, will depend on the degree to which actions and behaviors are meshed, i.e. the degree to which actions depend on other actions, and people's behavior and thoughts depend on the presence and actions of another. As Berscheid has noted, the potential emotionality of a situation should not be evaluated in terms of its surface characteristics, but rather in terms of the interdependence of actions and people.

David Watson and I (Mandler and Watson, 1966) have discussed the effects of social structures and social policy on individual emotional reactions. Specifically, we were concerned with the expectations that a society generates, but for which it often fails to provide adequate opportunities for their realization. If, for example, all members of a society are led to believe that they can expect to achieve economic success—but few do, then the conditions for emotional reactions are rife. Specifically, the discrepancy sets off arousal and the sense of failure and resentment gives the emotional reaction the qualitative contents of anger and hostility. At a more restricted level, lack of communication, inefficient work flow, and vague power structures produce social disorganization which interrupts organized action and behavior and fails to provide alternative ways of coping. We suggested that a social system might fruitfully be analyzed in terms of the way it encourages actions that are in fact interrupted and necessarily left incomplete, the degree of control it permits the individual over actual and potential discrepancies and interruptions, and the range and

availability of alternative actions that are offered. The fact that societies generate interruptions and discrepancies leads to a more general analysis, namely the way in which such discrepancies and contradictions are the occasions for the emergence and change of social values.

INTERRUPTION/DISCREPANCY AND VALUES

In previous discussions (Mandler, 1984) I have distinguished three general classes of values—those arising out of actions and behaviors, socially acquired values, and structurally determined values. In the present context I shall focus on structural sources of values which are primarily responsible for the persistence as well as the change of values.

I shall address three different structural contributions to the emergence of values: patterning, consistency, and discrepancy. The patterning aspect of value resides in the cognitive structure of objects, in the relations among features, as in the appreciation of an object seen as beautiful or abhorrent as a function of a particular structural concatenation. Structural value, which differentiates *patterns* of features rather than the mere *presence* of features, arises out of our experience with objects and our analyses of their constituent features. It is of course the social context that defines which pattern will be judged as positive or negative. Thus, it is the patterning of sounds that describes acceptable music for a particular culture, and it is the pattern of the features of the human body that determines local standards of beauty. I shall be more concerned with the two other aspects of structure: consistency and discrepancy.

FAMILIARITY, DISCREPANCIES AND CONTRADICTIONS

One of the factors that influences judgements arising out of structural consideration is the frequency of occurrences and encounters. The more frequently an object or event has been encountered, the more consistent the representational schema. If an experience fits an existing schema it is—*ceteris paribus*—an acceptable/expected event. In most cases it is the preferred state of the world. We generally prefer the known to the unknown. If we see a building that conforms to our acquired views of what such a building should look like, we tend to like it.

Schema theory generates a psychological picture of humans that makes comprehensible both their conservatism and their acceptance and generation of change. Order arises out of repeated experiences with our personal world, giving rise to a conservative organism who prefers the known to the novel, the old to the new. However, the world is not constant—it presents us with changed conditions, with reordered social relations, power positions and dependencies. Change is often inherent in the structure of a society that generates inconsistent expectations and contrasting values and requirements. Such social inconsistencies are often referred to as social contradictions. Contradictions imply change and

emotional upheaval. Such discrepancies and disorders are an inherent aspect of our world; we attempt to impose structure and order on the disorder, and the attempted resolutions of contradictions in our lives lead to new discrepancies.

Schemas change in the course of one's interactions with the world, and do so dramatically in early life. For the adult, schemas become powerful organizers of expectations, beliefs, opinions and actions. Eventually, little change occurs in our perception of the social environment and even less of the physical environment. Normally the world changes relatively slowly and schemas easily assimilate changes in our world of communication, production, transportation, etc. Television did not suddenly replace radio, and automobiles only slowly displaced horses. The social world is somewhat more changeable, we encounter new people, make new friends, construct new conditions of work and play. Accommodation and assimilation describe the major agents of schematic change. Assimilation refers to one end of a continuum where new information and new events are assimilated into existing schemas without generating any important changes in the prototypical relevant schema. When the new information cannot be assimilated we refer to the other end of the continuum—accommodation—which implies a change in a schema in order to integrate information that could not be assimilated to its current variables.

Our species operates on a principle of least effort when it comes to schematic change. Current schemas—our current view of the world and ourselves—are changed only with effort, and whenever possible the organism stays with what it knows and with past actions and beliefs. The degree to which an existing schematic view of the world will change will depend on the degree of consistency and integration of the schema on the one hand, and the challenge that new information provides on the other. Accommodation requires cognitive effort, and in the absence of some motive for change, we stay with current conceptions and perceptions. The motives for change may be the availability of alternative views of the world that promise better conditions of existence or intolerable current conditions that require change. Habitual ways of knowing and perceiving are typically preferred to novel constructions that require mental—and often physical—effort. Assimilation is the preferred mode of dealing with the world and, I shall argue, is in fact one of the basic values that informs human thought and action. What is known and expected is—*ceteris paribus*—preferred to what is unknown and unexpected. The more experiences we have had with a particular event (be it a person, a home, a career, or a food) the more likely it is that we will find it acceptable. An extensive experimental literature has shown that repeated encounters (development of stable schemas) increase the acceptability of and preference for the repeated event (see, for example, Gaver and Mandler, 1987; Mandler and Shebo, 1983; Zajonc, 1968).

I have struggled with the problem of defining, i.e of finding just the right expression for, the sense of preference or liking that arises out of the familiar. We really do not have the right words for it—but it seems to be related to a sense of comfort, nostalgia, a sense of belonging and similar 'sentiments'. It is a

sense of avoiding cognitive effort, i.e. the cognitive structures do not need to be changed, and we passively accept their familiar contents.[8]

So much for the conservative, *status quo*-maintaining aspect of human nature. But our social world in particular is often a world of discrepancies. What we have experienced and expect is contradicted by new social conditions, by changes in the social order. The contradictions introduced by the economic, social and interpersonal world are the very discrepancies that generate arousal.

If we accept that discrepancies and contradictions abound in our world, then we need to consider how these discrepancies are resolved. The dominant model in psychology has been one based on simple tension reduction and the achievement of orderliness and quietude, as in Freud. Another approach has been to borrow Walter Cannon's model of the homeostatic resolution of imbalance and to apply it to psychological states. In an important essay on disorder and order, Rudolf Arnheim tackles the problem from the point of view of Gestalt psychology. He rejects simple tension reduction and homeostatic models of disorder resolution and opts for the achievement of a new structure. He notes that, in contrast to mere orderliness, the imposition of order in the face of disorder (and tension) requires active processes; the individual must effortfully find and impose a new ordering on percepts and concepts. Disorder 'is not the absence of all order but rather the clash of uncoordinated orders' (Arnheim, 1966, p. 125). In terms of the present discussion, disorder implies contradictions. Discrepancy and contradictions require accommodation, i.e. the establishment of new schematic structures.

Within the context of emotional reactions, I have described the various possible resolutions that may follow different degrees of discrepancy or discontinuity. Figure 2.2 shows increasing discrepancy from left to right (congruity to severe

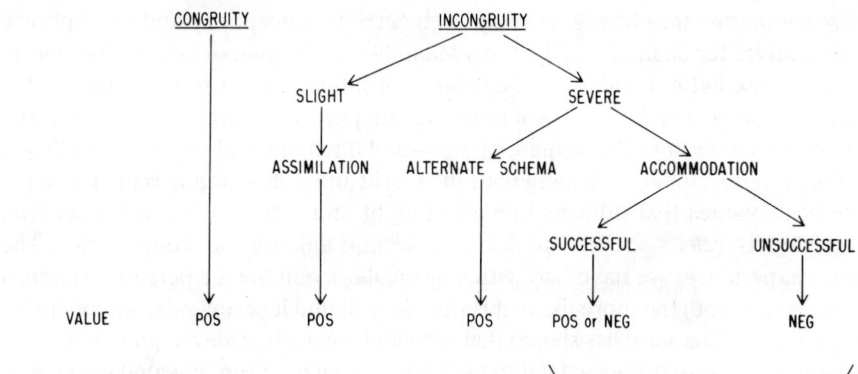

Figure 2.2. Several possible outcomes of schema congruity and incongruity in terms of both values and affective intensity. The resultant value is shown as either positive (pos) or negative (neg). Degree of affective intensity is shown to vary from zero to +++. Reproduced from Mandler (1984).

incongruity). Starting at the right of the figure, it is assumed that for severe incongruity assimilation is not possible and accommodation (change of schema) is necessary. Such a change can be successful when the new schema 'fits' the new experience. If successful, the very fact of successful accommodation may produce a positive value and, in addition, tension/arousal is presumably ameliorated and the value will be positive. On the other hand, the incongruity may produce a negative tone, and in some cases intensely so; for example if the accommodation requires the forceful removal of a disruptive event (aggression). Conversely, such events as unexpected praise or recovering a lost person or object would lead to a positive evaluation. In the case of unsuccessful accommodation, I assume that the sign of the subjective value will be negative. What the specific negative value will be depends on the context of the event and past experience with the event itself. If, however, a previously established alternate way of handling the situation is found (e.g. as in denial) arousal is attenuated and the value of the event is likely to be positive. In the case of assimilation, on the other hand, I assume that all outcomes involve no further mental effort and the values are all positive. The positive value arises at least in part out of the fact of successful assimilation—the very act of assimilating an experience may well be positively valued. I have also suggested (Mandler, 1984) that a parallel of such assimilation, i.e. successfully completing an intended action or thought sequence, has positive value—resulting in what might be called the 'joy of completion'.

The preceding discussion suggests that accommodation involves the generation of a new structure, a new ordering of experience. However, we should note that the imposition of structure (and order) on an event or experience does not necessarily produce a state of quiescence. The newly imposed or discovered order will bring with it its own discrepancies and contradictions. For example, Arnheim notes that '[o]rder and complexity are antagonistic, in that order tends to reduce complexity while complexity tends to reduce order' (Arnheim, 1966, p. 124). Complexity requires coping with a variety of different attributes and relations among them, and as a result structures may change and reduce the ability to cope with the event. New structures may also bring with them values of their own. The affective state following a state of discrepancy depends on the evaluation of the new, changed state. It is only rarely that the perceiver discovers the optimal order with a structure and complexity that can be accepted unchanged and unchallenged. Depending on the particular context and the person's preparation for the new situation, a variety of different reactions is possible. If past experience predisposes one to deal effectively with new complexities, then positive values are generated. If one feels helpless in the face of changing conditions, the values will be negative. In some cases the complex structure may be preferred just because it invites new explorations, new tension and new contradictions to be resolved in ever new perceptions of the world.

THE CHALLENGE OF NOVELTY

Novelty is not an all-or-none concept; an event may be novel because some well-known evidence is encountered which has not been encountered in a particular context before, or it may be novel because it is entirely 'new', and a number of variations of these themes all deserve the label of novelty. Frequently the novel produces negative affect—it does not fit and there is no way in which we can accommodate to its demands. New styles of music and painting, new ways of structuring our social world, new modes of organization are usually greeted with negative evaluations. When is the novel positively valued—as it often is? The most likely candidate for coloring the novel positive is some other evaluative structure that interacts with the novel event. Such structures may be social, e.g. when a novel aspect of a difficult problem is seen as a possible solution, or it may be individual, i.e. for people who seek the novel and find positive value in problem-solving, whether cognitive or aesthetic (e.g. the creative individual who seeks out complexity; see Dellas and Gaier, 1970). The creative artist and scientist both are part of a cultural tradition that values the novel construction and that seeks out novelty. On the other hand, there are social and cultural conditions in which the novel is avoided and considered inappropriate (e.g. in authoritarian societies).

The novel and particularly the creative event produces discrepancies and discontinuities. New ways of doing and seeing are by definition of this order, but the creative act is often seen as destructive and alien. This is usually the case in social action, but it is most easily demonstrated in the arts where the new way of seeing or hearing creates strong dissonances in the viewer and hearer. Beethoven's music provides one of many examples. A contemporary critic of the *Eroica* symphony noted that one left the concert hall 'crushed by the mass of unconnected and overloaded ideas and a continuing tumult by all the instruments' (cited by Rosen, 1971, p. 393).

There are reasons other than structural change why discrepancy and contradiction foster value-laden reactions. I have previously suggested one other possibility, i.e. that sympathetic nervous system arousal may have an additional (adaptive) function of alerting the organism to examine the environment, to discern what it is that has changed that has brought about the autonomic alerting reaction. Any such renewed analysis of the world would bring with it some evaluative reaction. A parallel argument can be developed out of considerations of the role of consciousness in human thought and action. One occasion that produces new states of consciousness—new conscious mental contents—is a change in currently active schemas and structures. Any change in current mental contents—independent of its effect on the sympathetic nervous system—would bring with it some evaluation of the new state of affairs.

The import of the preceding is that discrepancies and contradictions are the occasion for the development or imposition of new values, that changes in values

are most likely to occur when contradictions have to be faced. This is to be contrasted with the conservatism of holding to the familiarity and comfort of well-established, habitual schemas. Which of these two roads will dominate in a situation depends on the general system of schemas that characterize the individual's value system. The outcome of the dialectic between conservatism and change is in turn determined by historical and social aspects of the society and the personal history of the individual within that society.

The most intense interest in the role of discrepancy and discontinuity and their effect on value has developed in the arts, both in visual arts and in music. I have already had occasion to refer to the work of Rudolf Arnheim. Still in the visual arts, the art critic John Berger (1988) suggested a pervasive disjunction or discrepancy in art:

> Before any impressive painting one discovers the same enigma. The continuity of space (the logic of the whereabouts) will somewhere on the canvas be broken and replaced by a haunting discontinuity. This is true of a Caravaggio or a Rubens as of a Juan Gris or a Beckmann. The painted images are always held within a broken space. Each historical period has its particular system of breaking. Tintoretto typically breaks between foreground and background. Cezanne miraculously exchanges the far for the near. Yet always one is forced to ask: What I'm being shown, what I'm being made to believe in, is exactly where? Perspective cannot provide the answer. The question is both material and symbolic, for every painted image of something is also about the absence of the real thing. All painting is about the presence of absence. This is why man paints. The broken pictorial space confesses the art's wishfulness.

In the analysis of musical aesthetics, Leonard Meyer (1956) is the most emphatic modern writer in tying affect *directly* to the interruption or inhibition of expectations. Meyer's discussion is concerned almost exclusively with affect as it is found in music—its composition and performance. Starting with principles of Gestalt psychology, he has described in depth how expectations, their products and their violations, produce meaning and emotion in music. A couple of quotes from the eminent musicologist, Charles Rosen, will provide a final illustration: '[W]hat is important is the periodic breaking of continuity' (1971, p. 58); 'The emotional force of the classical style is clearly bound up with [the] contrast between dramatic tension and stability' (p. 74) 'I do not want to turn Haydn, Mozart, and Beethoven into Hegelians, but the simplest way to summarize classical form is as the symmetrical resolution of opposing forces' (p. 83).

I cite these instances in order to draw attention to the fact that problems of value, in this case of aesthetic value, have not been unattended, and that when they are analyzed phenomena of contradiction and discrepancy appear just as they do in the analysis of the social order.

INTERRUPTION, CHANGE AND TRANSITION

I now turn to the topic of this volume—the general effects of transition, and in particular the transition of place. The notion that moving one's home is an emotional experience is, of course, not new. But why should a transition that is welcomed and eagerly anticipated produce stress and vulnerability to both physical and psychological distress? The answer from the vantage of interruption theory should be obvious—any change which is not anticipated or which cannot be adequately handled will produce arousal and possible emotional consequences, whether that change occurs in the environment or in the individual's internal apparatus. The question which must always be raised is whether the new environment produces demands and situations which are different from what the individual expects.

Consider the transition to university. The number of discrepancies is numerous and ranges from very simple everyday events of waking up in a strange bed, eating different (worse?) food, to more complex social discrepancies such as meeting new people and coping with their differential demands and expectations. In addition, the degree of emotional reaction will depend on the availability of alternate ways of acting, i.e. the likelihood that new experiences can be assimilated and do not require extensive accommodation. For example, Fisher and Hood (1988) note that students who do not report homesickness after moving to university were more likely to have been previously away from home. Homesickness is the emotion that is generated by the arousal due to interruptions and discrepancies on the one hand, and the quality of the cognitive evaluation on the other. The latter consists presumably of feelings of loss, preferences for home over the new environment, and general negative experiences with the new home. Fisher, Murray and Frazer (1985) reported that one of the major factors in homesickness was the desire to visit the old home. Ruminations about a goal that is practically unattainable is a frequent characteristic of many emotional states. In grief, for example, it is the wish for being with the lost person; in guilt it is the desire to undo a previous action.

A word about the question of control. Fisher and her co-workers report the importance of the individual having a sense of control in alleviating the effects of change and transition. What does it mean for an individual to have control over a situation? Essentially, it involves structuring the situation in such a way that one can know what is likely to happen and can determine what one will encounter. If somebody decides to go to university and selects which university to attend, then they are likely to know much more about what they are likely to encounter and how they can cope with it or how others have successfully coped with it. In contrast, if the desire to go to university is relatively weak and one goes primarily because of parental and/or peer pressure, and if in addition the choice of a university is made by others (or by chance), then many more events are likely to be unanticipated and discrepant. Control involves

planning and the development of action-relevant schemas; the absence of control puts the planning into the hands of others or providence. And providence frequently is interruptive.

How is the reaction to change and transition ameliorated? How does homesickness abate? The most obvious step is to change the values associated with the new environment, to experience it as positive and manageable. With time and experience, as one learns the new ways of acting and perceiving, the new situation becomes less discrepant, fewer interruptions will occur and arousal (and the intensity of the emotional reaction) will dissipate. At the same time the quality of any remaining emotional experience will change as the new environment is no longer interpreted as unpleasant. With experience, and with the establishment of new stable schemas, the new home becomes familiar and positively valued. Under some circumstances this process will be short-circuited by significant new positive experiences. A love affair in the new environment may change the evaluative reactions to the new home quite radically.

Finally, a word about nostalgia. The reactions to and schemas about the old, familiar home are not replaced by the new situation—to a large extent they become quiescent, to some extent they may be subtly changed. When we return to the home of our early years there are discrepancies, i.e. our memories have changed and the old is not quite what we thought it was, it is larger, smaller, duller, brighter than we remember or expect. But the evaluations are to a large extent the old ones—they are positive. And these discrepancies and evaluations generate a new experience—the low-intensity, mostly positive emotion of nostalgia.

I have tried to present as complete a picture of interruption/discrepancy theory as is feasible within the context of this chapter. The parameters of emotional experience, and their positive and negative aspects, are obviously complex and subtle functions of situations and of people. However, the utility of the theory for a variety of applications should be apparent, and the approach should help to bring many different phenomena under a common point of view.

SUMMARY

I started with the history of interruption/discrepancy theory and its relation to current and historical cognate notions. The relation between discrepancies and the construction of emotional experiences was elaborated, with special stress on the role of discrepancies in generating the intensity aspect of emotional experience. Human and animal experiments motivated by the theory were then cited in support. The major part of the chapter considered interruptions and discrepancies in the social context, and their effect on the development of human values. Scheme theory was invoked to discuss the experience of familiarity and its juxtaposition with novelty and discrepancy. Finally, interruption theory was applied to problems of transition and particularly transitions of place.

ACKNOWLEDGEMENT

Preparation of this chapter was supported in part by a grant from the Spencer Foundation.

NOTES

1. I should confess that I was unaware of these antecedents until I wrote a chapter on the history of research on emotion (Mandler, 1979)
2. A variety of suggestions can be found in the literature on psychopathology about the function of interruption and frustration (e.g. Rosenzweig, 1944; Maier, 1949; and Lindemann (1944), who was one of first to note the importance of interrupted social intercourse as a precursor of grief).
3. For a more detailed discussion of the earlier (behaviorist) literature and its bearing on questions of completion, frustration and the consequences of interruption see Mandler (1964).
4. For an extensive analysis of these various evaluative states from a somewhat different point of view, see Ortony, Clore and Collins (1988).
5. Discrepancies are only a sufficient, not necessary, condition of sympathetic arousal. Other sources of sympathetic nervous system arousal can and do also play a role in emotional experience.
6. For a discussion of intellective stress and the interruptive effects of errors on mathematical problem solving see Mandler (1989).
7. For more discussion see Mandler (1984, Ch. 11) and Mandler (1983).
8. I have not discussed the complex and interesting problem of repeated exposures to unpleasant events, as well as other aspects of repeated exposures, such as boredom. These issues will be discussed in a forthcoming paper on 'Approaches to a psychology of value'.

REFERENCES

Amsel, A. (1962) Frustrative nonreward in partial reinforcement and discrimination learning. *Psychological Review*, **69**, 306–328.

Angier, R. P. (1927) The conflict theory of emotion. *American Journal of Psychology*, **39**, 390–401.

Arnheim, R. (1966) *Toward a Psychology of Art*. Berkeley, CA: University of California Press.

Berger, J. (1988) The art of the interior. *New Statesman and Society*, **116**, 32–34.

Berkowitz, L. (1964) Aggressive cues in aggressive behavior and hostility catharsis. *Psychological Review*, **71**, 104–122.

Berscheid, E. (1983) Emotion. In H. H. Kelley, E. Berscheid, A. Christensen, J. H. Harvey, T. L. Hudson, G. Levinger, E. McClintock, L. A. Peplau and D. R. Peterson (eds) *Close Relationships*. San Francisco, CA: Freeman.

Dellas, M. and Gaier, E. L. (1970) Identification of creativity. *Psychological Bulletin*, **73**, 55–73.

Dewey, J. (1894) The theory of emotion, I. Emotional attitudes. *Psychological Review*, **1**, 553–569.
Dewey, J. (1895) The theory of emotion, II. The significance of emotions. *Psychological Review*, **2**, 13–32.
Dohrenwend, B. S., Krasnoff, L., Askenasy, A. R. and Dohrenwend, B. P. (1978) Exemplification of a method for scaling life events: The PERI life events scale. *Journal of Health and Social Behavior*, **19**, 205–229.
Fisher, S. (1988) Leaving home: homesickness and the psychological effects of change and transition. In S. Fisher and J. Reason (eds), *Handbook of Life Stress, Cognition and Health*. Chichester: John Wiley & Sons.
Fisher, S. and Hood, B. (1988) Vulnerability factors in the transition to university: self-reported mobility history and sex differences as factors in psychological disturbance. *British Journal of Psychology*, **79**, 309–320.
Fisher, S., Murray, K. and Frazer, N. A. (1985) Homesickness, health and efficiency in first year students. *Journal of Environmental Psychology*, **5**, 181–195.
Frankenhaeuser, M. (1979) Psychoneuroendocrine approaches to the study of emotion as related to stress and coping. In H. E. Howe and R. A. Dienstbier (eds), *Nebraska Symposium on Motivation, 1978*. Lincoln, NB: University of Nebraska Press.
Freud, S. (1926/1975) Inhibitions, symptoms, and anxiety. In *The Standad Edition of the Complete Psychological Works of Sigmund Freud*, Vol. 20. London: Hogarth Press.
Gaver, W. and Mandler, G. (1987) Play it again, Sam: on liking music. *Cognition and Emotion*, **1**, 259–282.
Hebb, D. O. (1946) On the nature of fear. *Psychological Review*, **53**, 259–276.
Holmes, T. H. and Rahe, R. H. (1967) The social readjustment rating scale. *Journal for psychosomatic Research*, **11**, 213–219.
Lewin, K. (1935) *A Dynamic Theory of Personality*. New York: McGraw-Hill.
Lewin, K. (1940) Formalization and progress in psychology. *University of Iowa Studies in Child Welfare*, **16**(3), 9–42.
Lindemann, E. (1944) Symptomatology and management of acute grief. *American Journal of Psychiatry*, **101**, 141–148.
MacDowell, K. and Mandler, G. (1989) Constructions of emotion: discrepancy, arousal and mood. *Motivation and Emotion*, **13**, 105–124.
Maier, N. R. F. (1949) *Frustration: The study of behaviour without a goal*. New York: McGraw-Hill.
Mandler, G. (1964) The interruption of behavior. In E. Levine (ed.), *Nebraska Symposium on Motivation 1964*. Lincoln, NB: University of Nebraska Press.
Mandler, G. (1975) *Mind and Emotion*. New York: John Wiley & Sons.
Mandler, G. (1979) Emotion. In E. Hearst (ed.), *The First Century of Experimental Psychology*. Hillsdale, NJ: Lawrence Erlbaum.
Mandler, G. (1983) Emotion and stress: a view from cognitive psychology. In L. Temoshok, C. VanDyke, and L. S. Zegans (eds), *Emotions in Health and Illness: theoretical and research foundations*. New York: Grune & Stratton.
Mandler, G. (1984) *Mind and Body: psychology of emotion and stress*. New York: Norton.
Mandler, G. (1985) *Cognitive Psychology: an essay in cognitive science*. Hillsdale, NJ: Lawrence Erlbaum.
Mandler, G. (1989) Affect and learning: causes and consequences of emotional interactions. In D. B. McLeod and V. M. Adams (eds), *Affect and Mathematical Problem Solving: a new perspective*. New York: Springer.
Mandler, G. (1990) A constructivist theory of emotion. In N. S. Stein, B. L. Leventhal and T. Trabasso (eds), *Psychological and Biological Approaches to Emotion*. Hillsdale, NJ: Lawrence Erlbaum.

Mandler, G. and Shebo, B. J. (1983) Knowing and liking. *Motivation and Emotion*, **7**, 125–144.
Mandler, G. and Watson, D. L. (1966) Anxiety and the interruption of behavior. In C. D. Spielberger (ed.), *Anxiety and Behaviour*. New York: Academic Press.
Marcel, A. J. (1983) Conscious and unconscious perception: an approach to the relations between phenomenal experience and perceptual processes. *Cognitive Psychology*, **15**, 238–300.
Meyer, L. B. (1956) *Emotion and Meaning in Music*. Chicago, IL: University of Chicago Press.
Ortony, A., Clore, G. L. and Collins, A. (1988) *The Cognitive Structure of Emotions*. New York: Cambridge University Press.
Paulhan, F. (1887) *Les phénomènes affectifs et les lois de leur apparition*. Paris: F. Alcan.
Rosen, C. (1971) *The Classical Style*. New York: Viking Press.
Rosenzweig, S. (1944) An outline of frustration theory. In J. McV. Hunt (ed.), *Personality and the Behavior Disorders*. New York: Ronald.
Skinner, B. F. (1938) *The Behavior of Organisms*. New York: Appleton-Century-Crofts.
Solomon, G. F. and Amkraut, A. F. (1983) Emotions, immunity and disease. In L. Temoshok, C. VanDyke and L. S. Zegans (eds), *Emotions in Health and Illness: theoretical and research foundations*. New York: Grune & Stratton.
Zajonc, R. B. (1968) Attitudinal effects of mere exposure. *Journal of Personality and Social Psychology Monograph*, **9**, 1–28.

3 Changes: Rank, Status and Mood

PAUL GILBERT
Department of Clinical Psychology, Pastures Hospital, Derby

This chapter explores the way evaluations of rank and status underpin much of our behaviour, making us highly susceptible to changes in our evaluated social rank. Status, however, is a difficult concept to define because it has such wide usage in normal language that it can mean different things. We can talk about status in both social (e.g. the status of an individual, professional group or country) and non-social terms (e.g. the status of an academic theory). Objects (e.g. cars) can be also seen as symbols of status. But perhaps what all the different uses of the word 'status' have in common is that they pertain to an evaluation of position in some relative rank order. That is to say, status is a concept that is concerned with ranking evaluations. Furthermore, there are often important consequences to the position held within the rank; i.e. those higher in status are regarded as better or superior in some way to those individuals, groups or objects that are associated with lower status.

STATUS, POWER AND DOMINANCE

There are various terms that relate to ranking behaviour. For example Harper (1985) discriminates between power, dominance and status in the following way:

> While power and dominance are undeniably overlapping phenomena power does not necessarily imply dominance as in the case of the 'Gentle Giant' or the 'benevolent despot'. Power is generally considered the ability to influence others to do what one wants. Dominance, however, probably always involves some component manifestation of power, especially as it is based on coercive, expert, legitimate, and referent aspects of power. . . . Finally, status refers to the position assigned or accorded a person in a hierarchy by other members of that social organization. Again, while status, dominance, and power are all strongly correlated, there are exceptions such instance of the titular king or queen who may have great status without power or dominance except in a social sense. Thus, status is at least the appearance of power (p. 33).

On the Move: the Psychology of Change and Transition. Edited by S. Fisher and C. L. Cooper.

What Harper is describing here is a distinction between what an individual may do to others (e.g. use or exert power) and what others do to an object or person of status, that is to bestow value and a position in a relative rank. Kemper (1988) has made a similar point, and argues that power (representing compelling, forcing, coercing) and status (representing freely given value to another) are two dimensions of human social behaviour. He notes Hegel's distinction of noble (status) and base (power) causes or action.

When a person(s), object or theory 'loses' status, the immediate cause and consequence is that others reduce the amount of value or attention that they bestow on them or it. To understand why mood changes are often involved with changes of status (rank) requires consideration of the implications of this loss or gain of 'bestowed value and attention'. To explore this area it is useful to consider briefly the issues of status, dominance and power (that is the importance of ranking behaviour) form an evolutionary perspective.

EVOLUTION

Darwin (1871) suggested that the mechanisms by which organisms are transformed over time is via the operation of three forms of selection. The first was natural selection, which relates to the inheritance of attributes that help in the battle against the natural forces of the environment (e.g. climate, predators). The second form of selection was called sexual selection. There are two forms of sexual selection: intra- and intersexual selection. Intrasexual selection works through the inheritance of comparative skills that confer advantage in competition with members of one's own gender (e.g. size, strength, fighting ability). In other words the 'power' to beat one's potential opponents or impede them in contests for access and control over breeding resources. Intersexual selection, on the other hand, refers to the ability to present self as attractive to members of the opposite sex (e.g. plumage, and other various displays which have attracting qualities).

In phylogenetic terms dominance hierarchies are usually developed from intrasexual interactions and are concerned with the organization of breeding behaviour and access to resources. There appear to be two basic forms to these organizations: territorial and group. In the territorial situation animals of the same gender display to each other their ability to obtain and defend a territory. This is often via ritualistic displays, referred to as ritualistic agonistic behaviour. In other words these animals usually face each other or engage in side-on movements which are designed to advertise their fighting ability and strength. This had been called display of resource-holding potential (RHP) (Parker, 1974; Price and Sloman, 1987; Archer, 1988).

During these 'dances' each animal is able to weigh the other up. Those that evaluate that they have inferior or unfavourable RHP to a potential contestant

(i.e. they are weaker or unlikely to win if it came to a fight) will back down or flee. Only if animals evaluate that they are of relatively equal strength will fighting break out. However, the territory-holder is usually at an advantage in such situations and will win. The factors controlling fighting are complex and depend (in addition to estimates of relative RHP) on things such as the value of the resource contested, season, the costs involved in fighting versus the benefits and so on (Archer, 1988; Bailey, 1987). However, from our point of view the most important aspect to stress here is that contesting rank and pursuing resources depends in part on a social comparative evaluation, i.e. one animal matching its ability against another.

Hence the first clues of the relation of rank to mood might be found in this sexual selection process. Losers and those that evaluate that they are (compared to a potential contestant) inferior or have unfavourable relative RHP, must leave the desired territory and consequently lose access to those resources (e.g. food and mates) that gaining that territory would confer. Put another way, losers may lose control (access) over important reproduction opportunities.

The above might be viewed as a principally masculine form of behaviour. However, rank is a very important component of female social behaviour. For females, rank is more closely related to kin (genetic) line, i.e. the daughters of dominants tend to become dominant themselves. However, subordinate females can be significantly harassed, biologically inhibited from breeding, and have their young attacked or even killed by more dominant females. Hence rank is as important for females as males (Kevles, 1986).

The two aspects that flow from this analysis are;.

1. Competing for access to resources depends on a particular kind of social comparative evaluation (is the other stronger or weaker than me?). The evaluation is called relative RHP. The behaviours that flow in the wake of this estimate give rise to dominance hierarchies, and facilitate the development of ranked social structures.
2. As a result of these types of evaluation an animal makes about itself in relation to another, it will either attack, flee or submit in the context of competing for breeding resources.

DOMINANCE

Before we proceed further it is important to notice some potentially confusing points concerning dominance. A concise discussion of these issues can be found in Dunbar (1988, especially, chapter 10). Here I will only summarize the main points: (a) dominance is a description of a relationship and is not of itself a quality of an individual; (b) dominance is not an end in itself, only the rewards (e.g. access to resources) that it leads to; (c) dominance in one domain does not necessarily imply dominance in other domains—for example an academic who

is dominant or is accorded high status in his department would not necessarily enjoy the same relationship in his local cricket team; (e) aggression is important but by no means the only way an animal can come to gain dominance over others; for example, the capacity for alliance formation and the ability to elicit valuing from others, i.e. to appear attractive to others, is also most important.

In general, then, we should separate the preparedness for individuals to pursue resources and attempt to control access to resources (and gain rank) from the tactics that are used to secure this end. Type A personalities, for example, appear to pursue very individualistic and task-focused strategies for control, and are often hostile, especially in the face of frustration or conflict (V Price, 1982; Gilbert, 1989). In part it is the social structure which may have a significant influence on the tactics of ranking that any one individual uses.

THE SOCIAL STRUCTURE

The structure of the social organization plays an important role in the behaviour of members of the group; for example who pays attention to whom and who can control decision-making within the organization. Chance (1980, 1984, 1988) has suggested that the social organizations of primates fall into two distinguishable types, called the agonic mode and the hedonic mode. The agonic mode represents a pattern of social behaviour within the social structure such that the dominants gain and maintain their rank by threat. The subordinates are attentive to the dominant and express various repertoires of submission and appeasement behaviours to him/her. The subordinates in agonic groups show inhibition of aggressive behaviour and the vigorous pursuit of control over resources. Even in human groups subordinates are less explorative, initiate less and are more timid (Kennedy and McKenzie, 1986; Wedgewood-Oppenheim, 1988). The propensity to submit and not challenge, acts to reduce the level of actual fighting in groups. However, the occupancy of low rank (and loss of rank) is not cost-free. The occupancy of low rank can, under certain conditions, have significant moderating effects on the biological state of the animal (e.g. on various neurotransmitters, hormones and state of arousal; Bailey, 1987; Gilbert, 1989; Henry and Stephens, 1977).

The hedonic mode, on the other hand, is noted by a more relaxed social style, a high level of reassurance behaviour between members and a relative absence of threat-derived hierarchical structures. As Chance (1980, 1984, 1988) points out, this social organization has the effect of liberating attention away from self-protection, since the social environment is not a source of continual or potential threat. The behaviour of conspecifics in these groups is more explorative, open and free, and less spaced out (except when foraging). This classification of group structure has been explored with regard to various human organizational structures (Wedgewood-Oppenheim, 1988).

SOCIAL ATTENTION-HOLDING POTENTIAL

In primitive species we noted that animals are able to evaluate their relative resource-holding potential. This arises from a socially comparative evaluation of their estimated ability to fight and win contests with others. Perhaps one of the most important changes which has taken place in the evolution of humans has been the switch from asymmetries and rank based on threat and coercion (characteristics of the agonic mode) to asymmetries and rank based on conferral from others. That is, rank and social asymmetries are derived from attractiveness and are conferred by some kind of consensus about what warrants a high rank position (Kemper, 1988).

Elsewhere (Gilbert, 1989) it has been suggested that RHP has been adapted to social attention-holding potential (SAHP). SAHP refers to the quality and quantity of attention that people pay to each other. Hence in humans there is competition for social attention and the bestowing of value. It is the bestowing of value that leads to status. Furthermore, we can hypothesize that just as relative RHP arises from a social comparison, similarly relative SAHP arises from a comparison of the SAHP one is receiving compared to others. In other words, any ranking evaluation depends on a social comparative analysis. The less attention, value and control that is bestowed on an individual the lower the rank.

This change has occurred against a background of increasing capabilities for affiliative behaviour, reconciliation and cooperation. The ability to win allies can significantly increase RHP and access to resources (Crook, 1980; Archer, 1988; Dunbar, 1988). Furthermore humans are probably the primate species that are the most motivated and skilful hunters. Hence the effect of hunting on the social structures (in contrast to foragers) needs consideration. Successful human hunting probably involves a good deal of cooperative behaviour and a willingness to ascribe roles (status) to the more competent and to follow the higher ranks into a hunt. Also the sharing of information/knowledge and the ability to share and coordinate a plan for a hunt would bestow advantage.

SAHP is often bestowed by the demonstration of competence to perform some function or role (e.g. doctor, psychologist, actor) which is valued by the bestowers. SAHP is therefore not something that can be obtained by force or coercion because it requires validation by a number of others. Consequently, to gain SAHP individuals have to display their ability to perform those roles that are bestowed value by others. In this way a person integrates him/herself into the group and ensures that by making a contribution which others value he/she has access to resources (Hill, 1984). Those that are not able to behave in this way are often cut off from resources. In the more hostile and primitive situation (the agonic mode; Chance, 1988) this is not necessary, since by strength and gaining RHP the individual takes what she/he wants and inhibits others from doing likewise by threatening them.

It is also unclear how far intersexual selection has had an important effect on the switch from tactics of coercion to tactics of attractiveness as a means of acquiring rank. In chimpanzees, for example, hostile males are shunned by females and often by other members of the group (Chance, personal communication; Power, 1988). Also the attention that females show males can have a significant effect on the male's rank and reproductive success (Shively, 1985; Kevles, 1986).

OVERVIEW

So far we have suggested, first, that rank and social asymmetries are important characteristics of all animal organizations; second, that the rank an individual gains has significant effects on access and control over resources or reinforcers (including the amount of attention and bestowed value that others will accord him/her); third, that rank and loss of rank have important effects on psychobiological state and mood; fourth, that the acquisition of rank (i.e. control over resources) can be carried out in different ways and with different tactics (e.g. hostile–friendly); fifth, that the social structure plays an important role in how the tactics of ranking are played out and reinforced.

CONSEQUENCES OF CHANGES IN RANK: GOING OR BEING UP

Whatever the evolutionary pressure to increase the importance of ranking by attractiveness, it seems that humans compete to be seen as more attractive or talented than their fellows. Hence human methods of ranking each other (and themselves) are now highly ritualized; in the examination rooms, work assessments, the staged contests of talent and beauty and so on. Many arenas of life are designed to provide opportunities to display qualities that may be desired, valued or admired by others. By our public observation of these 'contests' we have all become familiar with sports personalities who break down or withdraw if they lose, or who strut proudly around the arena if they win. However, it should be remembered that because it is social attention that is at stake then cultures may vary in the degree to which they will applaud the winner and ignore the loser. This will have effects on the individual's experience and behaviour to winning and losing (i.e. modesty versus gloating and acceptance of defeat versus vengeful retaliation, etc.).

PRESTIGE AND THE HERO/HEROINE

Prestige increases the chance of being able to direct attention in a way that is beneficial or in accord with the desires of the person who has it (e.g. Christ, Buddha) and it elicits voluntary following (in contrast to involuntary, submissive)

behaviour. Hence high-status individuals may have a significant impact on shaping public opinion, setting models and so on. The point about these ways of gaining prestige and status is that they increase attention-holding from the target audience to whom they are displayed. Further, they open up various avenues for the access to resources because the target audience bestows value on them. For this reason we may understand many aspects of human competition and ranking as relating to the pursuit of 'social attention-holding potential' (SAHP) and relative SAHP.

Among the many psychological processes related to rank are the phenomena of the hero/heroine, hero worship and idealizing. Individuals who function as heroes and who are idealized are usually accorded high rank in some domain of human activities. It is unusual, if at all, for the person who is idealized to be perceived by the idealizers to be of lower rank than themselves, at least in the dimension of comparison. Hence the phenomena of heroes, hero worship and idealizing only make sense when we recognize them as relationships derived from ranking. Individuals who desire to be heroes are in fact attempting to increase their rank and relative SAHP. Similarly the power of approval is related to rank. Under most conditions approval from another is more powerful in giving us a sense of increased SAHP if the person giving the approval is evaluated to be of higher rank than ourselves. As we change, therefore, we will also change those we seek approval from.

A variation on this may be the way prestige and status can be gained by being associated with certain other individuals. At the human level we may seek to be employed by the more prestigious institutions and universities, or be associated with (support) the more prestigious teams. In this context we experience a kind of reflected status by their success. If they change their rank (i.e. the team we identify with wins or loses) we may experience a kind of reflected increase in positive mood or dysphoria.

ELATION

The consequences of winning an encounter which has ranking implications is often associated with a positive change in mood. We might call this winner's elation. Some individuals would seem to deliberately seek out competitive contests in order to get a 'buzz' from winner's elation. Gardner (1982, 1988) has suggested that it may be dysfunctional control in these brain mechanisms that lies behind hypomania and mania. Generally, however, as witnessed from our own personal contests, and those displayed in the media, going up in rank/status is associated with positive mood.

ALTRUISM

Altruistic and friendly behaviour may not be independent of rank position. Those with status may be more likely to behave in a friendly or altruistic manner

compared with those without status or of low rank. To put this another way, the positive mood associated with winning or acquiring a high rank (in some contexts) may be more likely to produce friendly and altruistic behaviour than the negative mood associated with losing and low rank. Whether this effect works through mood is not known, and the relation between helping behaviour, rank and self-esteem is complex (Eisenberg, 1986). How, and in what contexts, major differences in rank facilitate helping versus not helping, and under what conditions, remains to be researched. In some cases receiving help can be regarded as a rank or status issue and some may refrain from seeking help because of negative effects on their perceived status (Fisher, Nadler and Whitcher-Alagna, 1982).

On the other hand, Brewin (1988) cites research that has shown that the help given to others (e.g. in a hospital accident department) may relate to the perceived status of the person in need of help. Those evaluated to be of low status may be given less help than those perceived to be of high status.

RECONCILIATION

In regard to changes in rank and status the importance of reconciliation cannot be overemphasized. De Waal (1988) has pointed out that reconciliation from a winner to a loser (often in the form of grooming or close physical contact) is an important behaviour in certain species. In this situation the winner or higher rank animal displays conciliatory behaviour to the lower rank, which has the effect of actually increasing affiliative behaviour between previous adversaries. Hence, as De Waal points out, any aggressive behaviour between conspecifics for rank needs to be understood in terms of both the pre- and post-relational behaviours. It is not the case that losers are always harassed or pushed into some peripheral position. In fact adversaries can become allies.

Although caution must be exercised in translating relational styles from the individual to the group level, there are some important considerations to the phenomena of reconciliation that might apply to group conflicts. It has been suggested that it was a combination of shame–rage and envy, that unleashed the horror of the Second World War (Nathanson, 1987b). After the First World War, Germany was held responsible and made to pay crippling reparations to the allies. Allied troops and workers occupied the factories and coalfields of Germany. Hitler's appeal was to those who felt particular shame–rage (see below) and a sense of grieved inferiority. Such experiences go with desires for revenge. In his narcissistic ideals for Germany he offered to rebuild pride and turn their perception of themselves around from shamed losers to mighty superiors.

After the Second World War the allies, especially America, poured vast resources into both Germany and Japan, having learned the lesson that one should never humiliate a defeated adversary, for here lay the seeds of the next war: vengeful retaliation. Hence quick reconciliation and efforts to avoid

humiliating a previous adversary may well reduce the chances of subsequent conflict and desires for revenge and 'table-turning'. It follows, then, that in understanding the consequences of changes in status it is important to understand how the new winners relate to those that have lost. Efforts to humiliate losers, or ignore them, may set the seeds for vengeful retaliation. One major problem for humans is that a loser's efforts to obtain reassurance or reconciliation from a winner may be taken to be yet a further sign of weakness, rather than something of importance for subsequent relationships (Gilbert and Trower, 1990).

GOING OR BEING DOWN

If it is true that the tactics and contexts of ranking have changed and complexified in humans, then what about the consequences of losing status or having low status? Here things appear to have changed little. First, as a general principle, however a rank is formed, those at the bottom of the rank are accorded far less attention, and have reduced access to various resources, than those at the top. Second, and perhaps more important for our concern here, the loss of rank seems to be a generally dysphoric experience.

SOCIAL ANXIETY

Like the subordinates of most species the subordinates in human groups are generally more tense and anxious, especially if called on to 'display' to the more high-ranking individuals. For example, public speaking seems to be far more anxiety-provoking in the context of others who have higher status than the speaker, than it is in contexts where the speaker is of equal or higher status. Giving a talk to a group of new students may be far less anxiety-provoking than giving the same talk at a world conference. Indeed social anxiety relates to the degree to which individuals see situations as a ranking encounter where others (evaluators) can add or subtract from status, i.e. they have the potential to 'spoil' the display of the speaker and hence reduce SAHP. In fact ranking evaluations seem to lie at the heart of social anxiety (Beck, Emery and Greenberg, 1985; Trower and Gilbert, 1989; Gilbert and Trower, 1990).

Asendorpf (1990, and personal communication) points out that one aspect marking the shy and socially anxious individual is an inhibition of initiation behaviour (i.e. such people are slower to initiate contact with a stranger or in socially evaluative situations). He relates this inhibition to activity in an internal behaviour inhibitory system suggested by Gray (1982). Hence it is possible that in some manner, yet to be understood, evaluations of rank have an effect on the internal behavioural inhibition system. Of course it could also work the other way around, in that the greater the inhibition the more anxious and less able the individual is to be able to display and initiate behaviours that would gain

rank (SAHP). However, in general it does appear as if those lower in rank are more inhibited (make fewer initiations) than those of higher rank (Gilbert, 1989).

Understanding the role of inhibition in rank is important as people move up and down social hierarchies. For example, changes in rank within a social organization may mean that people who behaved competently with one group might feel inhibited if promoted to a group they perceived to be of higher status. Under such conditions, and in line with evolutionary theory, this would require a period of time where those of higher rank help to reassure the new or more junior member. People express themselves in different ways (e.g. free or inhibited), depending on the social structure.

Yet another human behaviour that relates to perceived rank and status is obedience to authority. Milgram (1974) demonstrated that individuals can be made to behave in harmful ways (e.g. delivering apparently painful electric shocks) to others, and the only factor that seemed to be responsible for such acts was our human preparedness to ascribe rank to others (i.e. endow them with authority) and then to obey them. It would seem that the presence of an authority figure acted to inhibit more prosocial moral behaviour (Sabini and Silver, 1982).

SHAME

Shame, or the potential for shame, is closely related to social anxiety (Beck, Emery and Greenberg, 1985; Gilbert and Trower, 1990). Whereas anxiety usually declines after exposure, shame may become more intense after the exposure as the anxiety declines (Beck, Emery and Greenberg, 1985). We may in fact feel more ashamed and dysphoric when reflecting on a performance that provoked negative responses from another(s) and the potential loss of rank (and SAHP) that might be involved. Shame then relates to stigma (Goffman, 1963); the consequences being that the stigmatized are accorded very low rank and may become the objects of scorn and disdain.

Shame appears to be an experience that is significantly related to appraisals of rank (Lewis, 1987a, Nathanson, 1987a; Gilbert, 1988, 1989; Gilbert and Trower, 1990). In shame the self is seen as the object of scorn by another, as inferior, contemptible or smaller (Lewis, 1987b; Wicker, Payne and Morgan 1983). Shame provokes behaviour not dissimilar to that seen in submission, e.g. gaze avoidance, lowering of the chin, and stooping body posture. Efforts to hide and conceal are also noticed (Wicker, Payne and Morgan, 1983) and these efforts at hiding and concealing can have psychobiological effects (Pennebaker and Becall, 1986). Shame seems to inhibit sharing for fear of inducing contempt and injury to the self (Mollon and Parry, 1984; Brewin and Furnham, 1986).

RAGE

Associated with shame is rage. It has long been argued that a sense of inferiority can (especially in narcissistically damaged people) induce shame and rage (Nathanson, 1987a; Scheff, 1987). Rage may relate to the desire for revenge. In some individuals this rage or hostility may be expressed directly (e.g. type A personalities—V. Price, 1982). In the definition of narcissistic personality disorder the DSM III-R suggests two criteria that are clearly related to the evaluations of ranking. Item 5 is: 'is preoccupied with fantasies of unlimited success, power, brilliance, beauty, or ideal love'; while item 1 is: 'reacts to criticism with feelings of rage, shame or humiliation (even if not expressed)'.

It was for these reasons that Gilbert (1989) suggested that narcissistic disorders are related to distortions in how individuals evaluate their relative rank, and their tendency to see many interpersonal situations as related to ranking issues.

It has also been suggested that in response to the experience of shame individuals can experience a shame–rage spiral (Scheff, 1987). In such a situation a person may fear the strength of his/her own rage, for if it became known it might induce further attacks or scorn from more diminant others. Alternatively rage can be expressed towards those seen as subordinate (e.g. children or workers lower in the hierarchy). This is called displaced aggression and is probably quite common: 'the boss kicks the man, the man kicks his wife, the wife kicks the child, the child kicks the cat'. Such folk-stories speak volumes about how aggression can flow downwards (but rarely upwards) through a ranked social system and although it has a humorous side its effects are often serious and distressing. Furthermore such behaviour does not exclude the possibility of the desire for revenge at a later date.

It can also be noted that in western fantasy (e.g. films and videos) there appears a continued fascination with the hero who is capable of a good deal of agressive behaviour to beat the 'baddies' (for example, Rambo). It may be that this form of aggressive behaviour is conferred SAHP because it is also associated with the capacity to protect or to be seen in the service of revenge. Probably the most quoted remark here is 'no-one makes me look stupid', or whatever. Such thinking, which is essentially a statement about rank, is used to justify retaliatory aggression.

ENVY

Envy is another one of our primitive affective responses which makes sense when we think about it in terms of a social ranked hierarchy. Klein (1957) made envy an important aspect of object relations theory but confused frustrative aggression with envy. (For a review of the psychoanalytic concept of envy see Joffe, 1969.) There is no ethological account of envy, yet it is perhaps one of the most significant unresearched areas of human life.

Generally, envy relates to rank and the recognition that someone has resources or qualities (e.g. social attention via beauty, competence) that one wants for oneself. We do not envy the painting but the person who owns it. Envy can have positive and negative consequences. Envy may lead us to aspire to be like someone else that we admire or idealize (our heroes). Indeed, it may be our admiration that turns envy into something positive.

Often, however, envy has negative effects. The aggressive 'fight' for a more dominant position to that of the envied may not be expressed directly, but can be expressed indirectly. It may be envy that motivates us to go behind someone's back and attempt to spoil their display and achievements in the eyes of others (i.e. reduce their relative SAHP). 'Fancy him getting the prize; of course he is only an upstart, more mouth than brains; personally I wouldn't trust him to mow the lawn let alone be in charge of the team', etc.

The envious person begrudges the success, rank and status (attention) accorded to the other. He or she may fail to offer assistance to those that succeed and be undermining of their efforts. Such behaviour has been noted in Type A characters (V. Price, 1982) but often the role of envy is only mentioned in passing. According to DSM III-R the narcissistic personalities are also prone to significant envy. It should also be noted that it is not necessarily the case that the negative (anger and efforts to spoil the SAHP of the envied) and positive (idealizing) aspects of envy are mutually exclusive. Indeed, in therapy both the positive and negative components of envy can be directed at the therapist.

Envy and attempts to maintain the rank order in marriage can also be the source of a spouse (usually the husband) belittling and undermining changes in achievement of the other spouse (usually the wife), especially if these appear to raise her status position or facilitate more control (Horung, McCullough and Sugimoto, 1981). Sometimes these 'battles' over rank/dominance and the subtle signals aimed at maintaining the wife in a subordinate and compliant position can lead to significant hostility and depression in the wife (Price, 1988).

Another side to envy relates to stealing. There is no research evidence to support this view but it seems likely that envious people are more prone to stealing (e.g. other people's ideas) in an effort to increase their relative rank. It is likely that envy increases as a function of the size of rank differentials and shortage of resources, but such a view awaits research validation. Nevertheless, at both the individual and group level, anecdotal evidence suggests that the greater the potential rewards (e.g. Nobel Prize, research funds and the more these rewards are idealized) the greater the potential for envy between competitors. Those concerned with changes within organizations would do well to pay attention to envy within the organization since its effects can be highly destructive. Envy may be involved in the way a manager actually inhibits or undermines the efforts of people in his/her department if they threaten to outshine him/her.

Envious stealing can also have an even more offensive side. Berke (1987) has made a distinction between the greedy thief and the envious thief. He suggests

that the greedy thief breaks into a house carefully and takes only the most precious and valuable items. The envious thief, however, usually smashes his way in, leaves the most valuable items but is intent on messing the place up, even defaecating and urinating about the place. In academic contests things rarely go this far, but individuals often talk of 'rubbishing' the contestant, etc, and undermining his/her efforts.

DEPRESSION

We have mentioned that winning or gaining/increasing rank may be the source of a shift to positive mood; winner's elation. Individuals that lose rank, however, rarely if ever experience positive mood (unless defeat allows them to leave a battle they never had desire for). We have mentioned that losing rank has significant effects on psychobiological state (Henry and Stephens, 1977). However, in humans it may be that the dysphoric effects of a loss of rank may be very indirectly related to resources as such. For example, a religious person may give up access to resources, but gains prestige in so doing. The issue here may be whether it is a voluntary giving up of resources or an involuntary one. It seems unlikely that individuals would be motivated to give up resources if there were not some rank gains to be made (even in heaven or a sense of moral/spiritual superiority).

Elsewhere (Gilbert 1984, 1988) it has been suggested that depression can arise from at least two sources: loss of attachment bonds and loss of rank. Loss of rank can take various forms; for example the person may believe that he/she has lost value and may see him/herself as a burden to others, i.e. he/she is no longer attractive. In behavioural terms this was described as losing reinforcing qualities to others. However, it is the rank perception that is important. It should be noted that research evidence suggests that depressives are much more likely to behave submissively with efforts to appease in the face of a confederate threat (Forrest and Hokanson, 1975).

In a different approach Oatley and Boulton (1985) have suggested that depression can arise from a loss or invalidation of social roles. In this presentation it would be the manner by which a role provided information about rank, social comparative information and self-worth (Swallow and Kuiper, 1988) that would have the most dysphoric effect. Furthermore, it may be that for some the opportunity to display socially valued roles is seriously reduced. In other words these individuals are unable to gain much SAHP from their fellows. Prime candidates may be women who have no outside employment and have young children living at home (Brown and Harris, 1978). These individuals may have few sources from which to gain a sense of value from other adults, especially in a society where other women have invested their self-esteem in work rather than mothering. Hence the roles that society bestows value on is an important factor.

As suggested elsewhere (Gilbert, 1989) it is not only that people desire support, but that they need to have a sense of their value to others (SAHP). Once it is recognized that SAHP is an important component of rank, and a sense of integration in a group or relationship, then we might begin to understand why loss of the opportunity to perform certain roles (gain SAHP) can have such a devastating effect for some people. Clinical anecdotal evidence suggests that depressions and other conditions can remit when the patient finds employment or is able to function in some role that others bestow value on.

OVERVIEW

In general, then, it is argued that the predisposition to evaluate ourselves and to organize ourselves in relation to rank is an innate predisposition. Furthermore, various motivational states, moods and emotions are related to the evaluation of rank, e.g. elation, aggression, submission, shame, social anxiety, envy and depression. The role rank plays in our emotional life has yet to be fully researched in spite of the fact that many forms of mental disorder are associated with (perceived) low rank and evaluations of inferiority. However, because human ranks depend in large measure on social validation, this means that the roles or attributes that will lead to status are culturally varied.

INTERNAL EVALUATIONS: SOCIAL COMPARISON AND SELF-ESTEEM

SOCIAL COMPARISON

Much of what has been discussed relates to social comparison. The role of social comparison has been an important research area since Festinger (1954) wrote his paper on a theory of social comparison processes. More recently Swallow and Kuiper (1988) have given an excellent review of the role of social comparison in relation to self-esteem and mood. They point out that social comparison has two major effects: self-evaluation and self-enhancement. It appears that people usually desire social comparison especially at times of uncertainty (Festinger, 1954; Swallow and Kuiper, 1988). As discussed, much of our social and work life, in examinations and entertainments, provide numerous opportunities for comparing the self with others. Furthermore, social comparison conveys information about the control over resources one can expect (e.g. the lower one's rank the less SAHP one will have, the worse the employment prospects, the selection of mate and friends and so on). Some of the issues that pertain to social comparison, self-esteem and mood include the following.

First, the quality that one compares is important. For example people may experience little impact in knowing that others are better at gardening, but be

more upset if they believe that others are better as parents, or psychologists, especially if these are core-attributes of self-esteem and the sense of personal worth.

However, again it is not inevitable that this would produce a serious dysphoric effect. For example the individual may say 'I'm glad I see that they are better. Now I can learn from them and become better myself.' In other words the attribution of effort (I can do better if I try, behavioural attribution) versus the attribution of ability or character attribution (I am just inferior to them) is important. In the former case the individual perceives the rank to be fluid, and gains can be made. In the later case the rank is perceived to be rigid, and it is unlikely that gains can be made. This may relate to previous history in relating to parents or peers, where a setback resulted in withdrawal rather than effort.

Second, House (1983) found that negative self-attribution in students varied according to whether the attribution was made publicly or privately. As Brewin (1988) points out, negative self-attribution may serve to warn the target audience not to expect too much of them in the future, thus avoiding loss of SAHP in the future. It may also be that by making a negative self-attribution, not only is the person trying to appear more attractive (e.g. displaying modesty) but also is attempting to reduce the chances of others seeing him or her as a competitive target. That is, these kinds of attribution may be an attempt to reduce the chances of invoking an envious or status-related attack. In other words it is a self-protective self-presentation (Arkin, 1981; Trower and Gilbert, 1989).

Related to envy, perhaps, is the fact that we may select inappropriate targets to compare ourselves with (e.g. because we would like to be highly valued or respected like the target). This can lead one to fail to discount certain information about the target (e.g. the target is older/younger, more experienced, etc.). Interestingly, Swallow and Kuiper (1988) suggest that in depression there may be a failure to employ this discounting principle. Much may depend then on why a person chooses an inappropriate target to compare with. Certainly some believe that depression vulnerability arises from setting unrealistic targets and goals, which if they are achieved are believed to bring a major increase in social attention, love and approval (Arieti and Bemporad, 1980).

Third, some individuals may fail to compare and gain validation for beliefs or experiences because they assume that they are different from others, and that revealing their beliefs or experiences would result in further shame or scorn (Brewin and Furnham, 1986).

Fourth the individual may live within a social context where social comparisons are made directly or indirectly. For example a person may be told explicitly that he/she is not as good or competent as John or Mary. This kind of information may be given by parents, teachers, bosses or spouses. Indeed in depressed women it is not unusual to find a significant other (e.g. spouse or mother) giving direct information of this kind. The more indirect way is by individuals showing 'favouritism', i.e. differential social attention and approval. Another indirect way

is by the preparedness of another to take control in certain situations; e.g. a mother after her daughter has given birth, and in this way imply indirectly that the daughter is not competent to be a mother (Arieti and Bemporad, 1980).

THE ROLE OF THE SOCIAL STRUCTURE

It is important that rank is recognized as a social concept. Therefore rank and status can exert effect only when understood interactionally. Problems can arise when we discover that the evaluations of our rank or worth are not shared by others. In other words we need to have an idea of the esteem 'the other' has of us. Whether this is an adaptation that occurs in the change from RHP to SAHP ranking systems is unknown. Lasch (1985), in his social critique of modern society, puts it this way:

> Both as worker and as consumer, the individual learns not merely to measure himself against others but to see himself through others' eyes. He learns that the image he projects counts more than accumulated skills and experience. Since he will be judged, both by his colleagues and superiors at work and by the strangers he encounters on the street, according to his possessions, his clothes, and his 'personality'—not, as in the nineteenth century, by his 'character'—he adopts a theatrical view of his 'performance' on and off his job. . . . When people complain of feeling inauthentic or rebel against 'role-playing', they testify to the prevailing pressure to see themselves with the eyes of strangers and to shape the self as another commodity offered up for consumption on the open market (pp. 29–30).

Lasch argues that the means of production and socioeconomic structures have a significant effect on who gets what, and who controls whom in the pursuit of who gets what. It is no longer the case that a personal evaluation of rank will suffice in understanding the complexities of mood and behavioural changes associated with rank. We must also understand the role of social groups and relationships in which we operate, since it is in relationships that status is conferred or withheld. It is for and from relationships that determined the vigour and type of our status-seeking behaviours. Further, it is in the social domain that the qualities or behaviours that are bestowed status are decided.

CONCLUSION

This chapter has discussed the evolutionary origins of rank. It has explored the role of aggression in acquiring dominance and control over resources and shown how, over time, rank has become increasingly centred on the display of attractiveness leading to social attention-holding potential (SAHP); i.e. human ranks are often derived from a voluntary bestowing of value and status. However, rank is first and foremost about social control.

It is difficult to imagine a society or any group that was not organized around some form or ranking (by talents, age, sex, etc.) However, because humans can acquire rank by attractiveness we are quite flexible as to the actual qualities that rank and status can be bestowed upon. Hence we can bestow rank and status on money-making, on presenting self as powerful and the so-called masculine traits, on intelligence and scientific endeavour and/or on moral stances. Within our culture we may amplify the values of strong versus weak; winner versus loser and individualism in our economic structures. We may belittle the attempts of those that have different values (e.g. ecological movements), label them as eccentric and not pay their concerns much attention or provide resources. These social exchanges, on what should and should not be valued, have significant impact on how a group or society conducts itself. This is in part because what a group values will have a significant effect on how people come to judge themselves, their social relationships and the models they aspire to (copy) and those that produce shame, anxiety and envy.

Ritualized and unritualized aggression is not now the normal way in which status is won or control exercised. This is partly because the use of law prohibits such contests, and partly because it is a culturally agreed that the most aggressive or threatening individuals are not (usually) the best people to confer status on. Hence there can be conflict over presenting self as confident and assertive yet not aggressive (Baumeister, 1982).

It remains true, however, that nations and other groups (e.g. criminal groups) still settle disputes and form hierarchies by fighting and/or threatening each other. Furthermore where the rule of law seems weakly represented, as in marriage or parental behaviour perhaps, aggressive fights for control, dominance and power still exist (Andrews and Brown, 1988; Gilbert, 1989). However, individuals vary in their preparedness to engage others in a hostile or threatening manner (tactic of coercion) to secure what they want and their position in a ranked social system. When acting in groups, inhibitions to aggressive fights for power and rank may break down for various reasons (e.g. loyalty and group identification). Hence although we are to some degree liberated from having to form our ranks according to the most threatening, this is a thin veneer in some situations. When it comes to group conflict and war, ritualized and unritualized aggressive contests still seem the preferred tactics.

This brings us to our last point about rank. That is, ranking can also be used to identify those that need more help and more resources or opportunities. In the early days of IQ testing the purpose was to identify those that needed extra help. Unfortunately over time it has often become a way of targeting the talented and giving them the extra resources, thus amplifying, rather than reducing, rank differentials. This in turn increases the likely activation of envy and greed, fear and depression, since these are inevitable consequences of a highly ranked system where those at the top have much more of everything. There is no easy solution to this, since presumably it is important to

distribute scarce resources to those who can make the best use of them (e.g. researchers, etc).

While it is true that we can gain rank and status by numerous means, evolution does not seem to have changed very much what happens to those that lose rank or are rendered subordinates. Here we see various anxieties, depressions and envious–aggressive responses. If we are serious in learning from psychology (which often we are not) then we would be extremely cautious over endorsing social systems that have at their heart the manufacture of rank differentials. Such a system may end up divisive unless it is recognized that those who are talented and have SAHP need to make available resources, SAHP and opportunities to those that are less talented or able. In other words, although we cannot abandon ranking (and in a sense nor should we try, since we do need the more competent to be our doctors, scientists, etc., rather than the less competent), we must concern ourselves with those that need extra help. In other words we need to think more clearly about how ranks work and how we can overcome the more distressing and destructive aspects of ranking. In part this may come from greater recognition of our mutal dependence on each other (Power, 1988). Maybe if we gave SAHP to these efforts, things might change for the better—on our streets, in our psychiatric hospitals and at our places of work.

REFERENCES

Andrews, B. and Brown, G. W. (1988) Marital violence in the community: a biographical approach. *British Journal of Psychiatry*, **153**, 305–312.

Archer, J. (1988) *The Behavioural Biology of Aggression*. Cambridge: Cambridge University Press.

Arieti, S. and Bemporad, J. (1980) The psychological organisation of depression. *American Journal of Psychiatry*, **137**, 1360–1365.

Arkin, R. M. (1981) Self-presentation styles. In J. T. Tedeschi (ed.), *Impression Management Theory and Social Psychological Research*. New York: Academic Press.

Asendorpf, J. (1990) Shyness as a common pathway for two different kinds of inhibition. *Journal of Personality and Social Psychology* (In press).

Bailey, K. (1987) *Human Paleopsychology: Applications to Aggression and Pathological Processes*. Hillsdale, NJ: Lawrence Erlbaum.

Baumeister, R. F. (1982) A self-presentational view of social phenomena. *Psychological Bulletin*, **91**, 3–26.

Beck, A. T., Emery, G. and Greenberg, R. (1985) *Anxiety Disorders and Phobias: A Cognitive Perspective*. New York: Basic Books.

Berke, J. E. (1987) Shame and envy. In D. L. Nathanson (ed.). *The Many Faces of Shame*. New York: Guildford Press.

Brewin, C. R. (1988) *Cognitive Foundations of Clinical Psychology*, London: Lawrence Erlbaum Associates.

Brewin, C. R. and Furnham, A. (1986) Attributional verus preattributional variables in self-esteem and depression. *Journal of Personality and Social Psychology*, **50**, 1013–1020.

Brown, G. W. and Harris, T. (1978) *Social Origins of Depression*. London: Tavistock.

Chance, M. R. A. (1980) An ethological assessment of emotion. In R. Plutchik and H. Kellerman (eds), *Emotion: Theory Research and Experience*, Vol. 1. New York: Academic Press.

Chance, M. R. A. (1984) Biological systems synthesis of mentality and the nature of the two modes of mental operation: hedonic and agonic. *Man–Environment Systems*, **14**, 143–157.

Chance, M. R. A. (1988) Introduction. In M. R. A. Chance (ed.) *Social Fabrics of the Mind*. Hove, Sussex: Lawrence Erlbaum

Crook, J. H. (1980) *The Evolution of Human Conscious*. Oxford: Clarendon Press.

Darwin, C. (1871) *The Descent of Man and Selection in Relation to Sex*. London: Murray.

De Waal, F. (1988) The reconciled hierarchy. In M. R. A. Chance (ed.), *Social Fabrics of the Mind*. Hove, Sussex: Lawrence Erlbaum.

Dunbar, R. I. M. (1988) *Primate Social Systems*. London: Croom Helm.

Eisenberg, N. (1986) *Altruistic Emotion, Cognition and Behavior*. Hillsdale, NJ: Lawrence Erlbaum.

Festinger, L. (1954) A theory of social comparison processes. *Human Relations*, **7**, 117–140.

Fisher, J. D., Nadler, A. and Whitcher-Alagna, S. (1982) Recipient reactions to aid, *Psychological Bulletin*, **91**, 27–54.

Forrest, M. S. and Hokanson, J. E. (1975) Depression and autonomic arousal reduction accompanying self-punitive behavior. *Journal of Abnormal Psychology*, **84**, 346–357.

Gardner, R. (1982) Mechanisms in manic-depressive disorder: an evolutionary approach. *Archives of General Psychiatry*, **39**, 1436–1441.

Gardner, R. (1988) Psychiatry syndromes as infrastructure for intra-specific communication. In M. R. A. Chance (ed.), *Social Fabrics of the Mind*. Hove, Sussex: Lawrence Erlbaum.

Gilbert, P. (1984) *Depression: From Psychology to Brain State*. Hove, Sussex: Lawrence Erlbaum.

Gilbert, P. (1988) Psychobiological interaction in depression. In S. Fisher and J. Reason (eds), *Handbook of Life Stress, Cognition and Health*. Chichester, Sussex: John Wiley & Sons.

Gilbert, P. (1989) *Human Nature and Suffering*. Hove, Sussex: Lawrence Erlbaum.

Gilbert, P. and Trower, P. (1990) The evolution and manifestation of social anxiety. In R. Crozier (ed.), *Shyness and Embarrassment: Perspectives from Social Psychology*. Cambridge: Cambridge University Press.

Goffman, E. (1963) *Stigma: Notes on the Management of a Spoiled Identity*. Harmondsworth: Penguin.

Gray, J. A. (1982) *The Neuropsychology of Anxiety*. Oxford: Oxford University Press.

Harper, R. C. (1985) Power, dominance and nonverbal communication. In S. C. Ellyson and J. F. Dovidio (eds), *Power, Dominance and Nonverbal Behaviour*. New York: Springer.

Henry, J. P. and Stephens, P. M. (1977) *Stress, Health and the Social Environment*. New York: Springer.

Hill, D. (1984) Human altruism and sociocultural fitness. *Journal of Social and Biological Structures*, **7**, 17–35.

Horung, C. A., McCullough, C. B. and Sugimoto, T. (1981) Status relationships in marriage: Risk factors in spouse abuse. *Journal of Marriage and the Family*, August, pp. 675–692.

House, W. C. (1983) Variables affecting the relationship between depression and attribution of outcomes. *Journal of Genetic Psychology*, **142**, 293–300.

Joffe, W. E. (1969) A critical review of the status of the envy concept. *International Journal of Psychoanalysis*, **50**, 533–545.

Kemper, T. D. (1988) The two dimensions of sociality. In M. R. A. Chance (ed.), *Social Fabrics of the Mind*. London: Lawrence Erlbaum.

Kennedy, J. L. and McKenzie, K. R. (1986) Dominance Hierarchies in Psychotherapy groups. *British Journal of Psychiatry*, **148**, 625–631.

Kevles, B. (1986) *Females of the Species: Sex and Survival in the Animal Kingdom.* Cambridge, MA: Harvard University Press.

Klein, M. (1975) Envy and Gratitude. In *Envy and Gratitude and Other Works (1946–1963).* London: Hogarth Press.

Lasch, C. (1985) *The Minimal Self.* London: Picador/Pan.

Lewis, H. B. (ed.) (1987a). *The Role of Shame in Symptom Formation.* Hillsdale, NJ: Lawrence Erlbaum.

Lewis, H. B. (1987b) Introduction: Shame—the 'sleeper' in psychopathology. In H. B. Lewis (ed.), *The Role of Shame in Symptom Formation.* Hillsdale NJ: Lawrence Erlbaum.

Milgram, S. (1974) *Obedience to Authority.* New York: Harper & Row.

Mollon, P. Parry, G. (1984) The fragile self: narcissistic disturbance and the protective function of depression. *British Journal of Depression*, **57**, 137–145.

Morris, D. (1977) *Manwatching: A Field Guide to Human Behaviour.* London: Triad Granada.

Nathanson, D. L. (ed.) (1987a) *The Many Faces of Shame.* New York: Guildford Press.

Nathanson, D. L. (1987b) Shaming systems in couples, families, and institutions. In D. L. Nathanson (ed.), *The Many Faces of Shame.* New York: Guildford Press.

Oatley, K. and Boulton, W. (1985) A social-cognitive theory of depression in reaction to life events. *Psychological Review*, **92**, 372–388.

Parker, G. A. (1974) Assessment strategy and the evolution of fighting behaviour. *Journal of Theoretical Biology*, **47**, 223–243.

Pennebaker, J. W. and Becall, S. K. (1986) Confronting a traumatic event: toward an understanding of inhibition and disease. *Journal of Abnormal Psychology*, **95**, 274–287.

Power, M. (1988) The cohesive foragers: In M. R. A. Chance (ed.), *Social Fabrics of the Mind.* Hove, Sussex: Lawrence Erlbaum.

Price, J. S. (1988) Alternative channels for negotiating assymmetry in social relationships. In M. R. A. Chance (ed.), *Social Fabrics of the Mind.* Hove, Sussex: Lawrence Erlbaum.

Price, J. S. and Sloman, L. (1987) Depression as yielding behavior; an animal model based on Schjelderup-Ebb's pecking order. *Ethology and Sociobiology*, **8**, 85–98.

Price, V. A. (1982) *Type A Behavior Pattern: A Model for Research and Practice.* New York: Academic Press.

Sabini, J. and Silver, M. (1982) *The Moralities of Everyday Life.* New York: Oxford University Press.

Scheff, T. J. (1987) The shame–rage spiral: a case study of an interminable quarrel. In H. B. Lewis (ed.), *The Role of Shame in Symptom Formation.* Hillsdale, NJ: Lawrence Erlbaum.

Shively, C. (1985) The evolution of dominance hierarchies in non-human primates. In S. L. Ellyson and J. F. Dovidio (eds), *Power, Dominance and Non-verbal Behavior.* New York: Springer-Verlag.

Swallow, S. R. and Kuiper, N. A. (1988) Social comparison and negative self-evaluation: an application to depression. *Clinical Psychology Review*, **8**, 55–76.

Trower, P. and Gilbert, P. (1989) New theoretical conceptions of social phobia. *Clinical Psychology Review*, **9**, 19–35.

Wedgewood-Oppenheim, F. (1988) Organisational culture and the agonic/hedonic bimodality. In M. R. A. Chance (ed.), *Social Fabrics of the Mind.* London: Lawrence Erlbaum.

Wicker, F. W., Payne, G. C. and Morgan, R. D. (1983) Participant descriptions of guilt and shame. *Motivation and Emotion*, **7**, 25–39.

4 Environmental Change, Control and Vulnerability

SHIRLEY FISHER
Centre for Occupational & Health Psychology, Strathclyde University, Glasgow, Scotland

INTRODUCTION

In a developmental perspective, change and transition are recurring features of life history. A child who leaves home for school may even become resident at school at a young age, takes up secondary and then perhaps tertiary education or vocational training and employment. At some stage, there will probably be a change from single to married status, the beginning of a family, job changes and changes within the job brought about by new technology, new office designs, new status. Moving home is often a recurring feature of adult life.

These changes are mostly positive, often characterized by upward social or economic mobility. However they may still be accompanied by disorganization and distress in the short term, and for some people these apparently positive changes may be accompanied by long-term debility and emotional reaction. Refusing to change in the first place may represent anticipatory recognition of this by a person. Running away, or returning home, may be a manifestation of post-change trauma.

This book focuses largely on positive changes associated with life history. However, change is also a common denominator of most negative life experiences such as bereavement, marital separation or divorce, loss of employment, going to prison, being ill or incapacitated. These are the traditional life stresses now widely believed to be risk factors in health and daily efficiency (see Fisher, 1989; Rahe, 1989; Cox, 1989). Once thought to be the domain of modern medical science, this topic area is now increasingly regarded as a central aspect of modern medicine.

Some readers may well decide that this is an artificial separation, that a book purporting to be about change and transition should include negative as well as positive change, and that in any case the criteria for separation are insecure in that what is positive for some people may be highly negative for others.

On the Move: the Psychology of Change and Transition. Edited by S. Fisher and C. L. Cooper.

Personal meanings are important determinants of the impact of change. Whilst the force of such arguments is obvious, if we were to address all the major negative stresses in people's life histories this volume would be substantial (see Fisher and Reason, 1988). As indicated in the Preface, this volume is restricted to the types of positive moves and progressions that are part of growing up and functioning in a modern technological society.

Change is actually an abstract representation of a situation where there is removal of the known, familiar, predictable or secure, and replacement by the new and the different. This conceptualization encompasses routines, objects and, of course, people and social relationships. Yet even such an all-embracing formulation may not adequately represent the essence of change; it is possible, for example, for change to involve return to the old and familiar, after experience of a new environment. Little is known about the level of symmetry associated with aspects of the effects of changes of different kinds.

These issues are important because one of the effects of change to be considered in this chapter is perceived loss of control. Loss of control could be seen as a natural correlate of change; a person leaves the familiar and the secure to be confronted by the new and the insecure. The perception of low control over the psychosocial environment might be expected to account for much of the short-term or long-term distress effects which occur.

Before considering the control hypothesis in detail it is necessary to provide some indication of the nature of the concept and its effects in precipitating or maintaining stress. The effects of control have been found to be greater for negative situations than for positive; being able to reverse unpleasant conditions is an important moderating factor in stress (see Fisher, 1986).

THE CONCEPT OF STRESS

Stress is best described as an umbrella concept embracing a wide variety of circumstances and reactions. In historical perspective, early research on stress tended to focus on environmental conditions such as noise, heat, glare, vibration or internal conditions such as circadian rhythm changes, fatigue and sleep deprivation in terms of the effects on behaviour and performance. Collectively these stresses arise as a function of environmental extremes. The organism might be regarded as operating within a relatively narrow band of optimum conditions. Outside these conditions the environment is perceived as unpleasant or hostile, and the individual will try to avoid prolonged exposure to it.

This rather simple 'tolerance' definition does not, however, take into account the plethora of stresses concerned with issues such as loss, failure, status change, examinations and tests or public speaking. These stresses depend partly on the aims and ambitions of a person. For this reason the cognition of an individual is an intrinsic aspect of the stress encountered, because it is the beliefs and

attitudes which determine what is to be achieved and what is to be avoided. Failing an examination is successful only if there is high personal value placed on success. Fisher (1984) defined 'internally derived' stresses as those stresses which depend on values held by individuals. These values may translate into the major directives for daily behaviour. Preventing, interrupting or changing events may violate codes in the values people hold, thus producing a mismatch between what is desired and perceived reality.

It is important to understand that people have different motives. Work on achievement motivation (McClelland, Atkinson, Clarke and Lowell, 1953; Atkinson, 1957) has identified two fundamentally different motives in the performance of tasks. The first motive is achievement-oriented; the individual seeks success and generally will not undertake either very complex tasks or very simple tasks in which success could be regarded as inevitable.

A second identifiable motive is the need to avoid failure. Fear-of-failure individuals, as defined by scores on a validated questionnaire, typically avoid moderate and challenging tasks and seek very simple or complex tasks. In the former case success is inevitable, and the individual is protected from failure. In the latter case the task is perceived by others as so difficult that success is unlikely. He or she can thus fail in safety.

These motives may determine the context in which a person operates, and hence the types of stress encountered. When a person moves, or there is a major change at home or work, these two different directives (need achievement, and fear of failure) may influence the outcome because of the level of commitment that operates. The need-achiever would be expected to make the most of the opportunities of the new environment, whereas the fear-of-failure individual might be expected to avoid challenge or to generate an impossible set of tasks experiencing low control in the process.

THE CONCEPT OF CONTROL

Control is often defined as power or mastery over the environment. An individual with control can act to change or reverse situations which are disliked. Control has been found to be one of the more interesting issues concerning change of all kinds, including geographical moves, office changes and the introduction of new technology. Perceived loss of control may create negative responses.

However, before this can be considered in any detail the difficulties with the concept need to be evaluated. First, it is not clear that what appears to an outsider as loss of personal control is valid. Animal studies generally confirm the importance of the availability of the means for escape as a factor which ameliorates the damaging effect of electric shock (Mowrer and Viek, 1948; Weiss, 1971). Human studies involving either self-presentation or experimenter-presentation of electric shock have been rather less clear. Generally, biological

responses to shock are minimally affected (see Haggard, 1943). What seems to reflect the level of available control and predictability in self-shock conditions is tolerance, perceived anxiety level and willingness to take part in the study (see Pervin, 1963).

Human studies have indicated that the means for control does not have to be present, and that the effects may be delayed. Studies by Glass and colleagues demonstrated the importance of providing a means for control over adverse levels of noise as a determinant of the effects on performance, even for tasks presented after the noise was terminated. For example, on a subsequent proofreading task, fewer errors were reported. The effect occurred even when subjects did not personally operate the switch (Glass, Rheim and Singer, 1971).

However, situations of apparent low control might be defined differently as a function of underlying motives. What appears as low control may be a powerful form of control. Ball and Vogler (1971) examined human motives for the choice of whether to accept machine-delivered or self-delivered shock. Subjects were given an initial choice of being self-shocked or machine-shocked, but half-way through the trials they were instructed to change to a different mode or accept a penalty of double shock. Of the 36 subjects, 25 chose self-shock and 21 claimed that this reduced uncertainty. Of those who chose machine-shock, four were prepared to stay with the decision in spite of incurring a double shock penalty. However, when each subject was interviewed, the reason given for the decision implied that a form of control was being operated. For example, one subject said that he accepted double machine shock in order to foil the investigators; another indicated that acceptance of pain was a form of acquiescence to God's will.

This illustrates a fundamental difficulty in the judgement of control by external observers. A person who appears to be helpless may actually be operating a very powerful form of control, but in another domain. Choosing machine shock may provide a very potent means of controlling a situation by presenting a challenge, enhancing self-esteem or even achieving an ultimate goal such as a pleasant life after death!

Work on 'locus of control', where people are asked to decide how much control they generally expect to have in life, is addressed to the issue of controllability at the level of an ideology; it is argued that people have enduring beliefs in this respect. The locus of control scale designed by Rotter (1954) assumed that a single dimension of beliefs about control could be identified; at one end was 'externality' characterized by the belief that change of any kind was likely to be determined by chance, luck or fate; at the other end was 'internality' characterized by the belief that personal endeavour could create change and reverse unpleasant conditions. Taken literally, the proposal of different beliefs about control would indicate different attitudes to the new environment created by moving; internalizers should expect and achieve higher control over aspects of the move than externalizers. In fact this has not generally been found to be

the case, although there is evidence to suggest that internalizers collect more information than externalizers about what is happening to them (see Fisher, 1984; Fisher, Murray and Frazer, 1985).

One of the problems may be that, as indicated above, domains for control differ between situations and between individuals. Rotter's assumption of a single dimension of beliefs about control has been challenged by analyses of the factors involved. Estimates of the number of factors vary from three to 100, but there is broad agreement that different domains of control exist; personal, interpersonal and sociopolitical domains of control have, for example, been identified by Paulhaus and Christie (1981). A person might have low personal control but high interpersonal control. A helpless invalid may use interpersonal means to gain control over other people, even exploiting compassion. The fact that Machiavellianism scores generally correlate negatively with scores for personal control could be explained in this way.

In terms of the response to change and transition, it might be important therefore to identify a person's characteristic *domain of controllability* (personal, interpersonal, sociopolitical) and then assess the likelihood of achieving that degree of control in the new environment. For example, a child used to being looked after at home by devoted parents might have evolved a means of ensuring comfort and progress by exerting interpersonal control over the parents. This form of control would be less appropriate in an environment of strangers. Thus an overprotected child might have learned to rely on a specific domain of control which later becomes inappropriate because of the new environment. A self-sufficient child, by contrast, might have skills readily adaptable to coping with an environment no longer dominated by parents. This may account for the findings of Fisher, Frazer and Murray (1986) and Fisher and Hood (1988), indicating that previous moves away from home benefit a child in terms of reducing homesickness for a current move; the child may have learned to have specific control skills suitable for coping with moves to new environments.

On the above analysis it would be suggested that a person may be advantaged by a profile of domain of control for certain kinds of changes. A person most advantaged would be one with personal control skills suitable for coping with the demands of a new environment or interpersonal skills which enable the benefits of help from other people to be readily accessed. Stokols, Schumaker and Martinez (1983) consider people with 'low exploratory tendency' to be most likely to adapt badly following a move to a new job. It is possible that these individuals are lacking the necessary skills to exert control over the new environment.

The *target* for control may be related to domain of control, but provides a more specific directive for the exercise of control. The target is defined as what it is the individual seeks to achieve—personal comforts, wealth, leisure pursuits, satisfaction, personal relationships. An individual who needs a certain level of exercise, or enjoys a particular sport, would be expected to seek the means for

continuing with this in the new environment. If the environment is restricted and cannot offer those facilities, the individual would be expected to experience low control. Thus congruence between what an individual expects and what the new environment can provide is hypothesized to be a critical factor in the success of moving. Expectancies of university students with regard to (or concerning) life in residence at a university for the first time have been found to be a factor in the incidence and level of homesickness. Those who are homesick have higher expectancies of friendship, residential and institutional factors than those who are not (Fisher, Murray and Frazer, 1985). Disappointment on arrival may be associated with perceived loss of control if the circumstances cannot easily be reversed. Matching the features of the new environment with expectancies of those proposing to make a transition might be a practical step of importance. Also pre-move exposure to the new environment should be beneficial in enabling the individual to assess its psychosocial features, and to consider ways of establishing desired conditions following the move.

THE PERCEPTION OF CONTROL BY NEW STUDENTS AT UNIVERSITY

From all the preceding remarks it would be expected that the decision about whether or not there is control over the new environment is multifaceted, and that if people are asked to assess control relative to the old environment the precise wording of the question would be important. A study where university students newly arrived in residence were asked to assess how much control they felt they had over their lives, illustrates the problem very well (see Fisher, 1989, and to be published). The purpose of the study was to see whether those who were homesick were experiencing a form of 'job strain' in the new environment, more intensely than those who were not homesick. The assessment of homesickness was based on self-report on a five-category rating scale from 'no homesickness' through to 'extremely homesick'. The job strain model proposed by Karasek (1979) assumes that strain occurs when perceived demand imposed on a person is high and personal control is low. It was therefore hypothesized that homesick students (defined as those indicating some form of homesickness on the scale outlined above) should indicate high demand and low control. 'Demand' was defined as personally perceived level of threat or requirement for action; 'control' was defined as personal jurisdiction or discretion over the environment. Both demand and control were independently assessed on five-category rating scales from 'very high' through a neutral point to 'very low'.

The study showed that both homesick and non-homesick students reported high demand, but that the homesick group produced significantly higher scores. The expected result was that both groups indicated that they had high level

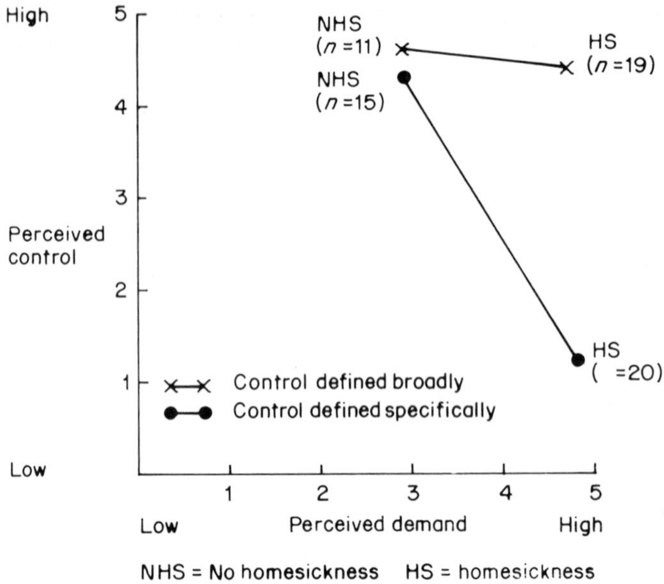

Figure 4.1. From Fisher (1990) by permission of Lawrence Erlbaum Ass.

of control over their lives, and there were no significant differences between the homesick and non-homesick in ratings of control. The result makes intuitive sense because university students do have a great deal of control over their daily lives. They can choose which lectures to attend, when to study or to socialize, when to get out of bed in the morning, etc.

It was decided that a more specific definition of control was needed. The study was repeated using a different group of students, but this time the definition of control was defined more narrowly. Previous work had established that the most commonly reported set of problems for students concerned academic matters such as understanding lecturers, feeling unsure about standards, finding books, how much work was needed, failing examinations, writing essays (see Fisher, Murray and Frazer, 1985). It was decided that the important feature of control should be that it was geared to daily problems. There is evidence that the effects of lack of control are greater for *negative* life events (see review by Fisher, 1986). Accordingly, control was redefined as jurisdiction over academic aspects of university life and assessed on a five-category scale (as described for the previous study).

Figure 4.1 shows the main result of interest. The results for 'demand' were similar in character to those in the first study, but the results for 'control' were different in that the homesick group reported significantly lower control over academic aspects of university. Thus there was evidence to suggest that the distressed group perceived significantly lower control over a specific aspect of the new environment.

The problem of interpretation arises because there is no way of knowing whether personally perceived low control is cause or consequence of distress, or specifically of homesickness. The homesick tend to withdraw and socialize relatively little, hence they may find out less about what is going on around them and perceive lower 'informational' control as a result. The results of the study (described above) where control was assessed as a general concept (control over life) indicate that being homesick does not necessarily distort the perception of control. This would suggest that the effect is not therefore due to the perception of control. Perhaps the homesick behave differently and thus create reduced control as a consequence. Being withdrawn or having lack of interest and commitment in the new environment would be expected to create lack of knowledge about the new environment. This would be logically consistent with the experience of low control.

THE VULNERABILITY OF THE DEPRESSED TO MOVES

The reaction to stressful life events is now of considerable interest in the research literature. Epidemiological evidence increasingly suggests that there is an association between the experience of life events and the risk of ill-health (see Fisher and Reason, 1988). One of the most important issues concerns personal meanings. The death of a pet for a lonely person may be as significant as a major bereavement, yet most attempts to measure life events have failed to take adequate note of this.

Computation of a measure of life change based on readjustment scores as developed by Holmes and Rahe (1967) involved judgements of normal healthy Americans. An arithmetic weighting was introduced by requiring judges to score the adjustment required to a list of life events relative to marriage which was given the value of 50. The resulting scale gave some prediction of the risk of illness both prospectively and retrospectively, but the power to predict was relatively low (see Connolly, 1975). In the case of cardiovascular disease, Rahe (1989) provides evidence of better power of prediction.

However, as already argued, this scale takes no account of personal meanings. Some attempt to rectify this was made by Brown (1974) who developed the Bedford College instrument in which contextual aspects were used to weight the level of threat likely to be associated with a particular event. An element of subjectivity is perhaps inevitable, and replacement with an approach based on self-reported problems has been proposed by Fisher and Elder (1989). At least problems which are reported by individuals, implicitly involve personal meanings and contexts; if a person reports the death of a pet as a major event, the attitude to the pet is implicitly taken account of. One implication is that those psychologists wishing to investigate the effects of change and transition, in terms of the health and welfare of participants, might be advised to concentrate on a problem-oriented approach.

There is now evidence of a large number of attempts to consider various personality traits as determinants of the reaction to life events. Concepts such as 'self-esteem', 'hardiness', 'learned resourcefulness', 'blunting and monitoring' and 'helplessness' have proliferated in the research literature (see Fisher, 1984, 1986; Brewin, 1988; Rosenbaum, 1988; Miller and Birnbaum, 1988; Seligman, 1975). The individual level of analysis may provide important evidence concerning the reaction to a variety of life events including major moves.

Depressed mood has not often been examined in the context of the reaction to life events, and yet there is evidence to suggest that the depressed are vulnerable to change. First, clinically depressed patients report moves and relocations as the third most important precipitants (after major loss and bereavement), in the occurrence of their depression (Leff *et al.*, 1970). This in itself is not strong evidence that the depressed are particularly sensitive to moves; merely that they may have happened to have experienced one recently. Also it cannot be assumed that the depressed have not self-selected themselves into events such as moves, and so the direction of causation is not clearly established.

In historical perspective, the research literature on migration has indicated the vulnerability of migrant groups to hospitalization for depression, as well as for schizophrenia and chronic or acute illness. However, the self-selection argument is still relevant, and it is possible that the depressed are more likely to move or that they drift downwards towards certain poor areas of countries or cities due to failure to cope effectively with life.

There is evidence that the effect of moves often involves grief-like responses characteristic of depression (Fried, 1963), but this in itself does not support the hypothesis that the depressed are vulnerable to moves. More convincing evidence comes from longitudinal studies. Fisher and Hood (1988) showed that those university students who suffer from homesickness following the transition into residence at university are more likely to show signs of raised depression prior to leaving home (two months prior to university). Whilst this may be an anticipatory stress response, it may also be the manifestation of a vulnerability factor. It is possible that those who are mildly depressed lack the resources or capacity to adjust to the demands of the new environment.

Kuhl and Kazen-Sadd (1988) argue that the depressed lack 'planfulness' because of the failure to become committed to new ideas or to transition and change. They argue that the reason is that the depressed find it difficult to disengage an existing commitment in order to form new commitments. Fisher (1986) argues that mild depression might create vulnerability because of displaced beliefs about the ability to exercise control. The depressed would, if they believed that the chances of exerting an influence were low, logically discontinue trying to exercise power. Thus, a belief in lack of personal effectiveness could create a logical tendency to withdraw effort.

Vulnerability to change and transition may thus arise because of reluctance to undertake commitment and to struggle with the new environment. Lack of

commitment either implies lack of planfulness or may be manifest more intensely as phobic avoidance. In either case the new environment will be associated with low personal control and will remain as a source of threat to individuals. This is consistent with Stokols' findings that those with 'low exploratory tendency' are more likely to be distressed or even physically ill following moves (see Stokols *et al.*, 1963).

However, recent work by Fisher (1989) has indicated that the depressed in the early stages of the disorder may be operating functional strategies. The lack of ability to move or undergo change may be a method of responding to life events and to a social world, which prevents or protects against the experience of challenge. Evidence which supports this view comes from the finding of a mismatch between what a depressed person says and what task-oriented judgements he or she makes.

The idea that the depressed are inappropriately helpless was encouraged by experiments with dogs by Seligman (1975) in which dogs pretreated with inescapable shock were found to be slow to learn avoidance as a response to shock on a subsequent task. The hypothesis which follows from the learned helplessness model is that the depressed should underestimate level of contingency (or control) in a variety of situations. Seligman, at the time of reporting the results of the studies, indicated his concern at the applicability of the findings to human studies (why are we not all helpless?).

The hypothesis was formally tested by Alloy and Abramson (1979) in the context of a computer-based task in which depressed and non-depressed subjects were required to judge the level of contingency between action and outcome. The depressed group should always underestimate control on the learned helplessness model. Results showed that, contrary to the learned helplessness hypothesis, the depressed did not underestimate control relative to the non-depressed. This raises doubts about bias in the cognitive basis of depression. Certainly it would be wrong to conclude that the depressed will necessarily perceive the new environment, following a move, more negatively than their non-depressed counterparts.

However, one criticism of the Alloy and Abramson study is that it did not involve judgements of *personal performance*, only of the relationship between action and outcome where subjects might imagine that they were judging the computer system. It might be the case that the depressed perceive low control when they are judging their own performance. This would follow from the statements made by the depressed which generally focus on profound pessimism concerning the self and personal abilities, and are characterized by self-blaming tendencies.

A study by Fisher (1989), in which depressed and non-depressed students were asked to type an overlearned word and then without seeing the results indicate whether the word had been typed correctly or not, showed no differences in typing ability and typing time, but more importantly no differences in the way personal

performance was perceived. The depressed did not report more correctly typed words as errors. They did not therefore show a tendency to underestimate their performance. There was no evidence of profound personal pessimism in the depressed group. This finding would suggest that the depressed should be no more likely than the non-depressed to underestimate personal ability in real-life contexts. However, this brings us back to the point that public statements made by the depressed concerning their own performance are generally negative. In fact the study described previously showed that if after 100 word-typing trials individuals are required to provide a global estimate of abilities on the task in terms of percentage of errors produced, the depressed provide a grossly pessimistic estimate.

This reinforces the notion that the depressed make pessimistic statements about themselves. An obvious question of interest is whether this is a mechanical effect or part of a functional strategy. In other words do the depressed believe what they say or is it part of a protective strategy? If the former is true then the evidence on the above study should have indicated more correctly typed words as errors—and as already reported this is not the case.

Perhaps the notion that the depressed have a tendency to provide negative statements about themselves can be explained as functional in keeping the rest of the world at bay. It implies social defeat and perhaps is treated like that by other people. A statement of social defeat can therefore be self-confirming. A statement such as 'I am no good' can be advantageous only initially.

Translating these ideas into the context of the effects of transition and change, it may be the case that the depressed see these events as potentially threatening and seek to avoid challenge. It is part of the same mechanism as social defeat strategy. Avoiding challenge reduces the effects of public failure by pre-empting it. The depressed are likely to want to avoid moves and to cling to the security of the past because not to do so would expose them to threat. In other words there may be personal dispositions which are non-confrontational and where challenge is feared and avoided. Moves and changes of all kinds may not therefore be advisable for all individuals, and the results of moving will be catastrophic for some individuals.

This might suggest that certain personality dispositions favour the perception of low personal control following change, and that therefore considerable energy will be put into not changing. Enforced change will be likely to create the perception of low control and personal distress.

SUMMARY AND CONCLUSIONS

Change and transition may be associated with short-lived periods of low control, but for some people the low control experience will be inevitable. Dispositions which favour the avoidance of challenge will mean that these people are more

at risk. It is also possible that the 'no-move' individuals exert a powerful form of control over keeping the environment free of challenge. Enforced moves will be associated with distress and low control.

REFERENCES

Alloy, L. B. and Abramson, L. Y. (1979) Judgements of contingency in depressed or non-depressed students: sadder but wiser? *Journal of Experimental Psychology (General)*, **108**, 441-485.

Atkinson, J. W. (1957) Motivational determinants of risk taking behaviour. *Psychological Review*, **64**, 359-327.

Ball, T. S. and Vogler, R. E. (1971) Uncertain pain and the pain of uncertainty. *Perceptual Motor Skills*, **33**, 1195-1203.

Brewin, C. R. (1988) Explanation and adaptation in adversity. In Fisher, S. and Reason, R. (eds), *Handbook of Life Stress, Cognitive and Health*. Chichester: John Wiley & Sons.

Brown, G. (1974) Meaning, measurement and stress of life events. In B. S. Dohrenwend and B. P. Dohrenwend (eds), *Stressful Life Events: Their Nature and Effects*. New York: Wiley.

Connolly, J. (1975) Circumstances, events and illness. *Medicine*, **2**, 454-458.

Cox, T. (1989) Psychobiological reactions in stress and health. In S. Fisher and R. Reason (eds), *Handbook of Life Stress, Cognition and Health*. Chichester: John Wiley & Sons.

Fisher, S. (1984) *Stress and the Perception of Control*. London: Lawrence Erlbaum.

Fisher, S. (1986) *Stress and Strategy*. London: Lawrence Erlbaum.

Fisher, S. (1989) *Homesickness, Cognition and Health*. London and Hillsdale, NJ: Lawrence Erlbaum.

Fisher, S. and Elder, L. (1989) Epidemiological problem analysis: a new approach to the measurement of stress. *Stress Medicine*, (Special Edition), **10**, 1-16.

Fisher, S. and Hood, B. (1987) The stress of the transition to university: A longitudinal study of psychological disturbance and vulnerability to homesickness. *British Journal of Psychology*, **78**, 425-442.

Fisher, S. and Hood, B. (1988) Vulnerability factors in the transition to university: self-reported mobility history and sex differences as factors in psychological disturbance. *British Journal of Psychology*, **79**, 309-320.

Fisher, S. and Reason, R. (eds) (1988) *Handbook of Life Stress, Cognition and Health*. Chichester: John Wiley & Sons.

Fisher, S., Murray, K. and Frazer, N. (1985) Homesickness, health and efficiency in first year students. *Journal of Environmental Psychology*, **5**, 181-195.

Fisher, S., Frazer, N. and Murray, K. (1986) Homesickness and health in boarding school children. *Journal of Environmental Psychology*, **6**, 35-47.

Fried, M. (1962) Grieving for a lost home, In L. J. Duhl (ed.), *The Environment of The Metropolis*. New York: Basic Books.

Glass, D. C., Rheim, B. and Singer, J. E. (1971) Behaviour consequences of adaptation to controllable and uncontrollable noise. *Journal of Experimental Social Psychology*, **7**, 244-257.

Haggard, E. A. (1943) Experimental studies in affective processes: I. Some effects of cognitive structure and active participation in certain autonomic reactions during and following experimentally induced stress. *Journal of Experimental Psychology*, **33**, 257-284.

Holmes, T. H. and Rahe, R. H. (1967) The social readjustment scale. *Journal of Psychosomatic Research*, **11**, 213-218.

Karasek, R. A. (1979) Job demands, job description lassitude and mental strain: implication for job redesign. *Administrative Science Quarterly*, **24**, 285-309.

Kuhl, J. and Kazen-Sadd, M. (1988) A motivational approach to cognition: activation and deactivation of memory representations related to uncompleted intentions. In V. Hamilton, G. Bower and N. Frijda (eds), *Cognition, Emotion and Affect: A Cognitive Science View*, Dordrecht: Martinus Nijhoff Publishing.

Leff, M. J., Roatch, J. F. and Bunney, W. E. (1970) Environmental factors preceding the onset of severe depression. *Psychiatry*, **33**, 293-311.

McClelland, D. C., Atkinson, J. W., Clarke, R. W. and Lowell, E. L. (1953) *The Achievement Motive*. New York: Appleton-Century-Crofts.

Miller, S. and Birnbaum, A. (1988) Putting the life back into life events; toward a cognitive social learning analysis of the coping process. In S. Fisher and J. Reason (eds), *Handbook of Life Stress, Cognition and Health*. Chichester: John Wiley & Sons.

Mowrer, O. H. and Viek, P. (1948) An experimental analogue of fear from a sense of helplessness. *Journal of Abnormal Social Psychology*, **43**, 193-200.

Paulhus, D. L. and Christie, R. (1981) Spheres of control: an interactionist approach to the assessment of perceived control. In H. Lefcourt (ed.), *Research with the Locus of Control Construct*. New York, London: Academic Press.

Pervin, L. A. (1963) The need to predict and control under conditions of threat. *Journal of Personality*, **31**, 570-587.

Rahe, R. (1989) Recent life changes and coronary heart disease. In S. Fisher and R. Reason (eds), *Handbook of Life Stress Cognition and Health*. Chichester: John Wiley & Sons.

Rosenbaum M. (1988) Learned resourcefulness and self-regulation. In S. Fisher and J. Reason (eds), *Handbook of Life Stress, Cognition and Health*. Chichester: John Wiley & Sons.

Rotter, J. B. (1954) *Social Learning and Clinical Psychology*. Englewood Cliffs: Prentice Hall.

Rotter, J. B. (1975) Some problems and misconceptions related to the construct of internal versus external control of reinforcement. *Psychological Monographs*, **48**, 56-67.

Seligman, M. E. P. (1975) *Helplessness: On Depression Development and Death*. San Francisco: Freshman.

Stokols, D., Shumaker, S. A. and Martinez, J. (1983) Residential mobility and personal well being. *Journal of Environmental Psychology*, **3**, 5-19.

Weiss, J. M. (1971) Effects of coping behaviour with and without a feedback signal on stress pathology in rats. *Journal of Comparative and Physiological Psychology*, **77**, 22-30.

5 Role Transitions and the Emotional Structure of Everyday Life

KEITH OATLEY
Department of Psychology, University of Glasgow

INTRODUCTION

> Next my fingers bunched together into a hard lump so that my hands became hooves. . . . I was obliged to face the mortifying fact that I had been transformed . . . into a plain jackass (Apuleius, 2nd century AD, *The Golden Ass*).

> Then these agonies began swiftly to subside, and I came to myself as if out of a great sickness. There was something strange in my sensations, something indescribably new and, from its very novelty, incredibly sweet. I felt younger, lighter, happier in body; within I was conscious of a heady recklessness, a current of disordered sensual images running like a mill race in my fancy, a solution of the bonds of obligation, an unknown but not an innocent freedom of the soul (R. L. Stevenson, 1886, *Dr Jekyll and Mr Hyde*).

> 'He has gone! It is over!' Anna said to herself, standing at the window, and in answer to this question the impressions of the darkness when the candle had flickered out, and her fateful dream mingling into one, filled her heart with cold terror (Leo Tolstoy, 1877, *Anna Karenina*).

> Part of our existence lies in the feelings of those near to us. This is why the experience of someone who has lived for days during which man was merely a thing in the eyes of man is non-human (Primo Levi, 1958, *If This is a Man*)

Robert Louis Stevenson's tale of *Dr Jekyll and Mr Hyde* is science fiction and a melodrama. Having discovered a chemical method of fractionating out the evil part of his personality into the bodily and mental form of Mr Hyde, Dr Jekyll discovers how liberating the single-mindedness of this embodiment is, as compared with the conflicts and obligations of his socially adjusting self. Too late he finds that Dr Jekyll's transitions to Mr Hyde begin to occur involuntarily. Now the personality of Dr Jekyll could no longer be maintained.

On the Move: the Psychology of Change and Transition. Edited by S. Fisher and C. L. Cooper.

Stevenson's story looks back, as it were, into the Victorian world of what are now called 'Gothic tales', and to the Romantic era of biological and moral determinism of the individual. By contrast, though written 10 years earlier, and not melodrama but tragedy, *Anna Karenina* looks forward to our own era. Anna gives up her role of marriage and respectability for love. She places everything in a single relationship with Vronsky. Having vested her whole self into the role of mistress, she finds she has no sense of autonomy. She becomes clinging and jealous of the time Vronsky spends away from her, and thus begins to destroy the love he had for her.

Stevenson's story was on the question of whether each of us has within us a good and an evil part in balance—and it is this conception that contributes to making the story a melodrama. Tolstoy's novel, on the other hand, is in the proper Aristotelian sense a tragedy. Anna is in many ways an admirable woman of strong and vital affections. Her respectable but cold marriage leaves her with a longing for love and intimacy. This, together with the fact of her sexual attractiveness which is not in itself evil, is the seed of an affair with Vronsky. She starts on a path with an end she cannot see. The self that she experiences changes in its course, and is determined not biologically but socially. Her new role as mistress is not one that can sustain her.

It is this difference, I think, between a biological determinism of Stevenson and the social influences that Tolstoy portrays, that makes the one an old-fashioned story and the other a modern one.

From ancient times to the present, the theme of transition has been explored, and continues to fascinate readers and audiences. Its most recent popular embodiment seems to be in stories of spies and double-agents, where the protagonist both is and is not who he seems to be in the eyes of representatives of both hostile and friendly factions, who may or may not care much about him. The persistence of this theme, and its capacity for renewal, indicates that here is something profoundly important for us; something just beyond the edge of our ordinary understanding that needs continuously to be pondered upon.

Dr Jekyll and *Anna Karenina* both appeared about 100 years ago. If we move backward and forward from that time, we can see more clearly that although the theme of transformation has persisted, its implications have changed. In former times when there were transitions a new outer form allowed certain possibilities of action and experience not available to the original person. When Greek gods took on human forms their personalities persisted. And the prince who has been turned into a frog has not changed in any inner way—merely he has been unfortunate enough to be imprisoned in a repellent body, as compared with the good fortune we would like to identify with.

In one of the most famous ancient tales of transformation, Lucius Apuleius's story *The Golden Ass*, written some 1800 years ago, the narrator is turned into a donkey. He has picaresque adventures, before the story culminates in a religious transformation. Lucius is affected by what happens, and his

transformations form the stages in a spiritual autobiography, but nevertheless his personality is maintained. The narrator's voice continues to speak from a largely immutable kernel of self, climbing the stairs, as it were, from bestiality towards a spiritual home.

And in Stevenson's tale the voice of Dr Jekyll is maintained. Evil takes over Jekyll's body and mind, for more and more of the time, but when Mr Hyde is not in residence the same self is there, just as usual, speaking and feeling as before. Evil steals time and controls action. Good is displaced, but not really vanquished.

Modern themes can be much more sombre. They imply that the very core of who we are is affected by our social experience. So as Anna's life closes in, her warmth and generosity of spirit are dimmed. Towards the end of the book is a scene in which her brother, with his friend Levin, one of the central male figures in the book, come to visit her. As a woman without position Anna receives visits from hardly anyone. She turns her charm on Levin, and he leaves her feeling what a marvellous woman she is. But she, 'unconsciously the whole evening had done her utmost to arouse in Levin a feeling of love. . . . and she knew she had attained her aim, as far as was possible in one evening with a married and conscientious man.' She was attempting to show herself that she was still lovable, and was using Levin as an object for this purpose, and to question why her lover Vronsky had become cold towards her. When Levin left she forgot all about him. A kernel of ruthlessness in the use of her sexual attractiveness, which enabled her to begin her affair with Vronsky early in the book, has expanded as the role of 'mistress' has squeezed her into an intolerable position.

As we time-travel from Apuleius's rather bawdy tale to our own era, we can perhaps discern an increase in self-consciousness. We move, for instance, from a society in which the role of slavery was unthinkingly accepted as part of the natural order, to one in which the consciousness of being a slave is reflected upon. Primo Levi's autobiographical book begins: 'It was my good fortune to be deported to Auschwitz only in 1944 . . .'. After that time the Nazis had decided to lengthen the span of life for prisoners before elimination, because of a scarcity of labour.

In *If This is a Man* we confront the modern view of role, and role transitions, in its starkest form. In the camps, people were turned from people into objects to be discarded into the gas chambers when they grew too weak to work. Transition was accomplished quite simply: merely by starvation, cold and the elimination of anything personal. It brought despair and death within days or weeks of arrival. Levi shows that long before they died, almost all the inmates of the camps had ceased to be human. They were treated as things, and before long came to exist merely as things. They could think only of how to steal the next piece of bread, or how to avoid the next blow. In these conditions all sense of themselves as people in relation to other people was extinguished. Their

condition even apparently justified their captors' view of them. The human spark was not too hard to snuff out by privation, bureaucracy and indifference. The Nazis did accomplish a triumph of evil. And, unlike transitions in stories that are perhaps more simple, or less thoughtful, we know that this triumph was not a superficial thing. Even for those few who survived it left effects that could not be erased.

A thread runs through the whole literature of transition of personality from the ancient to modern. It is of the relation between our sense of self as persisting throughout personal history, and of that sense being changeable, dependent on matters outside personal control.

I have started with four classic texts in literature on the theme of role transitions. My objective in the main part of this chapter is to describe the concept of role in social science, and in particular its relation to emotional life. I shall go on to discuss psychological effects, both encouraging and discouraging, of transitions between roles. Here too the same theme is salient; of the relation between the experience of a persisting self and the changes wrought by transitions in this experience. In social science too there are some classical texts, and I will discuss four of these.

WHAT IS A ROLE?

A role is a dynamic conception, a pattern that articulates one person's actions with those of others, like keeping goal in a hockey or soccer team. As Linton (1936) argued, the term 'role' is to be distinguished from 'status', which designates a position in an organization or community, but without explicit reference to action. Role is necessarily dynamic. One enacts a role. The term carries with it, moreover, the implication not just of action but of interaction of the self in relation to one or more others.

The term 'role' derives simultaneously from the metaphor of social interaction as theatre, and as a kind of game. These metaphors are old. But just as the themes of *Anna Karenina* are modern, so the technical term 'role' has only become common in social science during the twentieth century. Indeed one can almost sense the social scientists and economists of the eighteenth and nineteenth centuries, for all their ingenuity and insight, struggling for the lack of this concept.

The way of thinking from which sprang the modern social scientific idea of role derives from American turn-of-the-century pragmatist philosophers and psychologists, who included William James, John Dewey and George Herbert Mead. The basic concept is of a script, and an outline set of social rules which guide a person's actions in relation to others in a defined context.

A person with certain minimal personal characteristics can take on a role by practising the script, and being guided by the rules of interaction. So perhaps one reason why the concept of role is so modern is that the idea of the interchangeability of persons is a characteristically twentieth-century notion.

Role in this sense is not just the Shakespearian notion of one person playing many parts in turn, from the infant mewling and puking, to adulthood and finally to second childishness, sans teeth, sans everything. Shakespeare's image stresses the continuity of the person through its transformations. Indeed it is this continuity of personal history and experience which gives the image such poignancy, as we advance from inability and unconsciousness to achievement and finally back again to impotence.

No—though change through the lifespan has itself become the focus of attention in developmental psychology, the social scientific concept of role is different. It is the almost shocking notion that one takes the very sense of who one is from immediate role-based structures of interaction. It even implies that roles are the primary sources of our selfhood, that any sense of personal history that we have is secondary, and may be insubstantial. Anna Karenina does not merely find love with Vronsky, as she had hoped—she becomes a different person, a 'mistress'.

Each of us may experience ourselves as economically worthwhile and respectworthy by working at a job and fulfilling its demands. Or we can experience ourselves as amiable and trustworthy by taking part in the role of friendship. The obverse is that it is hard to experience ourselves as economically worthwhile without a job, or as socially desirable without friends or a lover.

ROLE CHANGE

The social scientific concept of role is of an outline script. Anyone with certain minimal qualifications can derive the experience of occupying many kinds of role, by learning the lines, and giving a plausible performance in relation to others who will play opposite to one. If you want the sense of being a person capable of controlling other people, perhaps consider joining the police. If you want to be admired, and can acquire the necessary skills, then perhaps become a pop musician, or take up a sport. If you want the experience of being a person both loved and loving, then parenthood might be a good plan.

None of this is to deny that there are continuities in personality. What is perhaps distinctive to this modern idea is that personal identity is not necessarily given either by a germ of indestructible internal selfhood, or primarily by biology; not even by a history of actions done or left undone. Now as we move in the world socially, economically and geographically, roles provide outlines so that a person can slip into new relationships, personal and commercial, by giving the kind of performance that is demanded. The sense of self that we derive is that reflected in the eyes of those with whom we interact.

So what are role transitions, and what is it about them that is either enlivening or stressful? Most of us slip relatively effortlessly from one role to another several times each day, perhaps from being an employee to being a spouse, or from being a parent of young children to being a friend of another adult. Moreover,

when we set out to enjoy ourselves in a game or sport, the enjoyment derives from being able to make the transition to the role that the game or sport allows, perhaps of being the centre of attention in hide-and-seek, of being competitive in chess or tennis, of being a courageous adventurer leaving one's friends to go on a frightening roller-coaster. We may find such transitions to be recreational. Without their possibility, in a life in which there were no role transitions, we might become dull indeed. But some kinds of transition are stressful—indeed the most common definition of stress is the challenge caused by role transitions. I will here describe which kinds of transitions are recreational and which are stressful.

The first classical text that I will discuss is one of the most important in social psychology. It is Goffman's (1961) short book *Encounters*, which contains two essays, 'Fun in games', and 'Role distance'. In these essays Goffman defines the properties of roles, and the effects of taking part in them on the participants' sense of selfhood.

First, as Goffman explains, a role involves a set of rules. These give structure to an interaction. The rules define what is relevant, and what is irrelevant. It is these rules that give an action meaning. So a spherical container of air rolling northwards accross a chalk mark on a muddy field is not just a physical event. Within the rules of football it is the meaningful event of a goal, perhaps a vital goal, being scored.

Moreover, Goffman points out that when we enter any interaction with another person that has some purpose or focus, it is as if we enter through a semi-permeable membrane that encloses that particular kind of interaction with its own rules. So I can pick up something from my house, put it in my pocket, and walk outside with it. But once having passed through the semi-permeable membrane of a shop, the rules are quite different. In a shop, if I pick up something I must pay for it before putting it in my pocket or going outside—indeed the official focus of all interactions in a shop is the purchase of goods according to certain rules. Inside the shop one takes on the role and obligations of customer in relation to others who have the roles and obligations of salespeople.

It is the same, argues Goffman, when one joins a game. One enters through a kind of membrane. Within it certain rules apply. But—and this is where Goffman is more illuminating than many of his contemporaries—occupying a role is not just a matter of fulfilling the rules. It is by becoming engaged in the micro-world that one can derive a sense of who one is. One can experience oneself as athletic at tennis, thoughtful at chess, cool at poker. Then a whole world of meaning comes into being: 'A matrix of possible events and a cast of roles through whose enactment the events occur constitute together a field for fateful dramatic action, a plane of being, an engine of meaning' (p. 26).

The alternative to engrossing oneself in roles is not a matter of having a hard, indivisible personality, maintained against the vagaries of life. The alternative of entering into roles, but not being affected by them, is of being disengaged

from what one is doing. It is just to go through the motions, to suffer a peculiar form of empty meaninglessness, which in psychopathology is called being schizoid.

So the reason why we might be interested in games is not that they are trivial, but because they are like ordinary life, except that their rules are more codified. Games bear the same relation to real social life, as a computer simulation bears to the aspect of the world that it represents. It is a simplification, of course. But if the simulation is a good one, then it captures something of the essence.

ENGAGEMENT IN ROLES

Goffman asks why we can expect to have fun when playing a game. His answer is that fun comes from becoming fully engaged in a role. Fun is a lesser relative of joy. Joy occurs when we are fully immersed in what we are doing, walking in the hills, engrossed in conversation, wrapped up in something we find creative.

So what a game offers principally is a cast of roles, into which almost any of us can make an easy transition. We pass through the semi-permeable membrane of the game into the world in which the rules allow just this set of meanings. Then, so long as we take on with engagement, and without too much distraction, the implications of the role offered, we may have fun. Partly, of course, games share with the theatre and novels the fact that if what is going on becomes tedious or too much for us, we can stop. We can exit again through the membrane, back into the outer world.

There are many important implications of Goffman's analysis—for instance that emotions are not simply positive and negative. Within the membrane of a game or the theatre we may feel frightened, sad or angry. All of these are conventionally taken as negative. But we take part in games and the theatre partly to be able to experience such emotions. We experience them by becoming engaged in a role that is offered. As compared with real life, in a game or theatre we can control our transitions through the semi-permeable membrane. We can say we feel tired and leave. Or at the end of a theatrical performance we put on our overcoat and go out into the street. For a few moments the world on the stage and the world of the street mingle, but then we can leave behind what we were involved in. Scheff (1979) presents this matter as one of being able to control the emotional distance between ourselves and an experience. If the distance is too small, as when crushing events happen directly to us, then fear, sadness or anxiety can overwhelm us. If the distance is too great, as in a play or game where we are not involved, we become disengaged, and we experience no emotions at all. But at a certain distance we not only experience the emotions, but can reflect on them. We can be both actor and observer. At that distance, according to Scheff, our emotions can be cathartic.

To exit through the outermost membrane of our world is to die—and, as we all know, this is a step that occasionally people take voluntarily. Perhaps they take it when they no longer feel able to maintain the performance expected of them, or when, as with Anna Karenina, the effects of the roles available to them no longer afford a sense of that self who they believe themselves to be. In the case of Primo Levi's death in 1987, perhaps the evil of the camps had still been gnawing away in this most gentle of men.

EMOTIONS AT THE JUNCTURES OF PLANS

Oatley and Johnson-Laird (1987) and Oatley (1988) have argued that emotions are signals that accompany transitions between one kind of action and another.

Emotions are like alarm bells, indicating that something important has happened, and what kind of thing it is, but not exactly what it is or exactly what to do about it. They mark potential transitions between plans. With an emotion we become ready to continue what we were doing or to do something else. Mandler (in this volume) elaborates the argument based on the idea that emotions occur where there are interruptions. An interruption is something unexpected. At that moment a disturbance occurs, as a punctuation marking a transition between one sequence of action and another.

Roles are plans of a social kind. A role is one part in a habitual joint plan, which we enact with one or more other people. Within the membrane of any particular kind of role structure it is likely that a certain mood will predominate. In a game it is fun, at a funeral grief, and so on. Moods are maintained states, which resist, to a certain extent, any new transitions that might be triggered by extraneous events.

But when there is a transition between roles an emotion often occurs, just as it does with an interruption or transition between plans of someone acting alone or with respect to the physical world.

We can thus build a description in which each role has some characteristic mood or moods associated with it. When a role transition occurs an emotion often accompanies it, either prompting the transition or resulting from it.

DIFFICULTIES IN SUSTAINING A ROLE

Goffman's (1961) essay 'Fun in games' is in part a reworking of Freud's *The Psychopathology of Everyday Life.* Again we have the contrast between a Victorian and a modern view. Freud proposed that the mistakes and slips of everyday life occur because of inner conflict, the result of multiple goals jostling for expression. Goffman treats these same phenomena as social.

So, in one of his illustrations, a patient in a mental hospital 'asks for the salt in a voice that covers the whole table with misery and gloom' (Goffman, 1961,

p. 24). This can be seen to occur not necessarily as Freud might say because of the patient's conflict between punishing others as he feels punished himself and the more socialized imperatives of polite society. It occurs because there has been an inadvertent role slippage. The other participants at the table feel the emotional shock of the transition. The patient has slipped out from the membrane and conventions of eating-a-meal-together into the wider sphere of his life in which something has gone terribly wrong, and the whole mood of the occasion changes. Psychiatrists, as Goffman points out, are liable to describe such slippages as showing 'inappropriate affect', and to regard them as symptoms of affective disorder.

More straightforwardly they are members of a whole family of occurrences in which a person, rather than sustaining the self and other in the engagement of face-to-face interaction within a particular membrane and with particular rules, 'floods out' as Goffman calls it. By doing this the person questions the social definition of what is going on, and can even, as at the meal in the mental hospital, succeed in redefining what is occurring.

To take part in a role is to attend to some matters and to disattend others which are defined as irrelevant, perhaps such as details of one's own personal history, one's abilities or disabilities, one's social status. So in a game of chess or a social gathering such as a wedding, the income, sex, race, age, health and social status of the participants is officially irrelevant. But at the same time, the ability to import personal characteristics through the membrane of the encounter is what allows these very characteristics to be transformed in order for their bearer to experience herself of himself in particular ways in that setting. One may have fun when the outcome of the encounter is both somewhat uncertain, and when one's self is engrossed in it. The enjoyment occurs when interactions are called forth from the encounter itself, and are not purely for show, and not purely going through the motions.

But now comes the difficult part. Much of the pleasure of a role comes with the transformations that more enduring characteristics undergo within the membrane of a particular kind of encounter. Here a tension must exist, but must not be too great. Football between teams from different towns has about the right degree of rivalry and allows spectators to become engaged in the game as such. Football between teams of different religious backgrounds, say, would already be straying very near the edge of transformations that could be successfully accomplished by spectators or players. A wedding celebration in which the family of one of the new spouses was very rich and the other poor would make it difficult for members of the two families to sustain the interactions required by the occasion in a pleasurable way.

So what happens when an interaction becomes difficult to sustain is that tensions develop, jokes, and byplays in which collusive nods and winks between pairs of participants may take place. Leaky words or symbolic incidents may occur, which suddenly bring to mind an officially unattended focus, as when,

say, a white person talking politely to an Indian says 'Things are looking pretty black for the government at the moment.' Alternatively, a participant in a serious meeting may burst into laughter, tears or embarrassment, in a way that threatens to redefine the whole of what is going on.

In general, the participants at a gathering work together to sustain the definition of the interaction, and its predominant mood. But if the tension grows too great between whatever attributes are imported by the participants from outside the membrane and the officially attended matters within it, then the definition breaks down. The encounter fails, and transition occurs to some other kind of role structure.

In another of the classic texts on this subject Hochschild (1983) has shown how, again in our century, there has grown up a kind of work, performed mostly by women, which has the specific purpose of maintaining a particular kind of mood in certain role encounters. Again, perhaps the theme is not altogether new, in that prostitutes accomplish this kind of commercial function. The profession is, we are told, an old one. What seems to be new, as Hochschild describes, is work with the purpose of deliberately maintaining the mood of large quantities of people, bosses in offices, travellers in airlines, customers in stores. It is work done usually by women who must respond to these people in ways that maintain the role relationship in a designed emotional tone. They must support this tone despite events and actions that could threaten to cause transitions to quite other kinds of role and quite other kinds of mood.

Hochschild studied the training of stewardesses in Delta Airlines, which had as a house style the idea of cabin staff as gracious Southern Belles. Here, as she points out, not only do we find the importation of techniques of theatrical acting into an apparently quite different job, but the efforts that the women make to avoid slipping out of role are often considerable. One preferred technique is the Stanislavski method. As one Delta flight attendant put it: 'You think the new person resembles someone you know. *You see your sister's eyes in someone sitting at that seat.* That makes you want to put out for them. I like to think of the cabin as the living room of my own home' (p. 105; emphasis in original).

Face-to-face interaction with another is potent in sustaining a role. As Goffman says: 'there seems to be no agent more effective than another person in bringing a world for oneself alive or, by a glance, a gesture, or a remark, shriveling up the reality in which one is lodged' (p. 41). Our attention to the rules of relevance and irrelevance, and our playing of the parts afforded in our roles, is partly convention and adherence to rules, but it is not 'mere' convention. It is the stuff of which our reality is constructed and sustained.

EMOTIONS AS TRANSITIONAL ROLES

Although emotions can effect role transitions, and emotions can result from role transitions, they can also themselves be transitional roles. So to state this

hypothesis at its most forceful, emotions may be understood as complex states which can act as temporary roles, managing a transition from one relatively stable role to that of another.

Let me take just one example, which also happens to be one in which we in modern society are very interested: anger. In another classical text on the subject of roles and role transitions, Averill (1982) has argued that anger typically functions to readjust roles that have become unsatisfactory for one participant. Averill draws his evidence from a variety of sources. I will mention just two. The first is the law on homicide in Anglo-Saxon cultures such as Britain and North America. In essence homicide can be of two kinds: intentional and unintentional. Murder involves killing someone 'with malice aforethought' or 'in cold blood', in the course of a deliberate plan. Killing someone in the heat of passion is quite different. It is regarded as manslaughter. Partly at least it is regarded as unintentional. Though not blameless it carries much lower penalties. The legal argument, mounted on a cultural theory about the nature of anger codified as law, is as follows.

When one is angry there is an involuntary component. When one acts in anger to kill someone, this is not as blameworthy as to kill someone as part of a deliberate plan. So to mount a defence of this kind the counsel must argue that anger was provoked by an event, that the killing took place while the perpetrator was angry, without undue delay, and that it conformed to certain rules. So, if between the event arousing the anger and the killing, the perpetrator makes a phone call—then this kind of defence collapses. The rules that define killing in anger disallow intrusion of such side-issues. To make a phone call is part of a deliberate plan, and therefore is not consistent with the idea of anger being caused involuntarily by the event and then motivating the killing.

Anger, in other words, is both an involuntary state, and it is a temporary role with its own rules. It suspends for a brief period some of the most binding obligations of our culture. If a particular kind of event occurs, typically involving a role relationship concerning love, or a stranger breaking into one's home, these usual rules may be suspended.

Averill also describes an important study of more everyday episodes of anger that did not reach the law courts, as experienced by a sample of 80 students and a similar-sized community sample. He also had diaries kept by a sample of people at whom anger had been directed. Episodes of anger in this study were quite common, with the majority of subjects experiencing an episode once or twice a week. For the majority it occurred with someone they knew well. Both angry people and the targets of anger rated the experience as unpleasant, but a majority of both experiencers and targets regarded the angry incident as important in readjusting some aspect of a relationship.

In other words, a role such as occurs between friends, relations, lovers, neighbours, people at work and so on, has a kind of inertia. It tends to continue as it is, even when one participant experiences it as unsatisfactory in some way,

and in particular if that person regards the other as failing to fulfil the obligations and expectations of the role. Anger typically occurs when the other's failing to sustain their part of the obligations of the role becomes too much to tolerate. It is, then, a partly involuntary reaction to this failing of the other with some physiological accompaniments. But more importantly it is a temporary role with its own rules, that the participants of the more lasting role relationship can enter, to allow them to redefine the rules of their more permanent relationship.

An alternative to readjustment is that a role is not adjusted but discontinued. Though termination may also be accompanied by angry encounters. Averill found that this is less common than readjustment.

ROLE LOSS

In the ordinary course of things a human life can run smoothly, even contentedly, along the rails of habit and familiar roles. Habits and roles enable us to be effective in controlling a limited aspect of our world, and to sustain a self in relation to the other people with whom we interact. But if habits and the familiar are denied us, or if we are cast suddenly into an unfamiliar role, then it can be as if the world crumbles. Practised actions and stored knowledge become useless. We become clumsy, unable to act in a coordinated way, ineffective. Through the gap between familiar patterns of action, and new patterns that we have yet to construct, a new vision of the world as alarming and unpredictable can appear. Prosaically, in social science this vision and the implications of this gap are called 'stress'.

From the earliest research on human stress the challenges to physical skills and habits have been seen as less important than challenges to established roles. Thus in Holmes and Rahe's (1967) original inventory of 43 items involving adaptive challenges predicting psychosomatic illness, 24 items, including the large majority of those with high scores, can straightforwardly be understood as role transitions. In research based on the more sophisticated and exacting techinque of semi-structured interviewing, Brown and Harris (1978, 1989) explicitly characterize the majority of potentially severe life events and difficulties as those which terminate or challenge an important role.

Brown and Harris's book of 1978 is the fourth classic social scientific work I will discuss. It contains the proposal that when events occur in which a familiar role is completely lost, or undermined, or when a new role has to be constructed from uncertain foundations, the experience is profoundly threatening to the person's sense of self. It can provoke clinical depression.

Brown and Harris showed that a depressive breakdown, of the severity at which psychiatrists would normally see people in outpatient clinics, is not usually a matter of something going wrong in people's brains, or even their personalities. It is a matter of something going wrong in their lives.

Brown and Harris constructed a semi-structured interview, based on a Schedule of Life Events and Difficulties. Using it, the interviewer asks the subject about a range of potentially threatening sudden events, such as bereavements, separations, deleterious changes in relationships at work and at home, as well as longer-term difficulties such as those brought about by poor housing or living with a husband who drinks. The great majority of the events and difficulties that are capable of provoking depression are serious losses, typically losses of a valued role, though sometimes of a valued idea of the self. Among women, between 80 and 90 per cent of depressive breakdowns discovered in samples randomly selected from voters' lists in London, and more than 60 per cent of depressive episodes occurring to people who were psychiatric patients, were preceded by a severely threatening event or difficulty of this kind. Moreover, Brown and Harris went on to show that whether a seriously threatening event or difficulty succeeded in provoking a breakdown depended on the presence of what they called 'vulnerability factors'. Of these the most important is social support.

Oatley and Bolton (1985) reviewed cross-sectional studies published up to that date with the hypothesis that depression is most often associated with role loss in the presence of a low social support. Brown and Harris's findings have been replicated widely. Oatley and Bolton (1985) proposed that a person who suffers a serious role loss will not become depressed if there is social support that provides an alternative role within which the person may feel valued. But without social support the loss of role can leave the person without any means of experiencing herself or himself in a positive way. The symptoms of depression, with its tumultuous emotions, its hopeless despair, self-denigration and lack of positive plans may result.

Following these cross-sectional studies there have been longitudinal studies, including one of our own (Bolton and Oatley, 1987) and one by Brown and his collaborators (1986). These two have confirmed and extended the general hypothesis: clinical depression is most often caused not biologically but socially, and is the result of loss of a valued role, when alternatives to it are difficult or impossible to construct.

CONCLUSIONS

Roles are collaborative joint plans, that involve expectations that there will be further episodes of interaction on a similar pattern. The idea of role has the same relation to joint plan as habit does to the plan of a single actor. That is to say it carries implications of practice, of skilled performance, and finally of enactment with minimal conscious attention.

Transitions between roles are of great importance, and involve many potential vicissitudes. Emotions occur at these junctions as they do at transitions between

the plans of single actors. Indeed, many of the issues of accomplishing transitions between roles, or conversely of maintaining a role interaction in the face of events which might make for transitions, can be called emotional. Emotions function to manage the transitions between plans and roles.

Emotions not only occur at transitions, but they can themselves have role-like properties. They can act as temporary transitional roles, allowing readjustment of longer-lasting roles which, because of their habitual inertia, would otherwise be difficult to change.

Among the most serious kinds of transitions are losses of roles. When such losses occur, and alternative roles are not available to allow people a sense of worthwhile self, such events can have the most serious consequences. A whole structure of practised interaction can become obsolete, while new roles have not been constructed, or perhaps even conceived. In this interregnum not only do symptoms of depression occur, in addition to already tumultuous emotions, but at these moments we can have a sudden sense of how fragile is the floor of reality upon which at other times our sense of self is supported without concern.

REFERENCES

Apuleius, L. (1950) *The Golden Ass: The transformations of Lucius*. Harmondsworth: Penguin (translated by R. Graves from the Latin original published in the 2nd century AD).

Averill, J. R. (1982) *Anger and Aggression. an essay on emotion*. New York: Springer.

Bolton, W. and Oatley, K. (1987) A longitudinal study of social support and depression in unemployed men. *Psychological Medicine*, **17**, 453-460.

Brown, G. W., Andrews, B., Harris, T. O., Adler, Z. and Bridge, L. (1986) Social support, self esteem and depression. *Psychological Medicine*, **16**, 813-831.

Brown, G. W. and Harris, T. O. (1978) *The Social Origins of Depression*. London: Tavistock.

Brown, G. W. and Harris, T. O. (1989) *Life Events and Illness*. London: Unwin Hyman.

Freud, S. (1960) *The Psychopathology of Everyday Life*. In J. Strachey (ed.), *The Standard Edition of the Complete Psychological Works of Sigmund Freud*, Vol. 6. London: Hogarth Press (translated by A. Tyson from the German original published in 1901).

Goffman, E. (1961) Fun in games. In *Encounters: two studies in the sociology of interaction*. Indianapolis, IN: Bobbs-Merrill.

Hochschild, A. R. (1983) *The Managed Heart: the commercialization of human feeling*. Berkeley, CA: University of California Press.

Holmes, T. H. and Rahe, R. H. (1967) The social readjustment rating scale. *Journal of Psychosomatic Research*, **11**, 213-218.

Levi, P. (1966) *If This is a Man*. London: Bodley Head (translated by S. Woolf, from the Italian original published in 1958).

Linton, R. (1936) *The Study of Man*. New York: Appleton-Century-Crofts.

Oatley, K. (1988) Plans and the communicative function of emotions: cognitive theory. In V. Hamilton, G. H. Bower and N. H. Frijda (eds), *Cognitive Perspectives on Emotion and Motivation*. NATO ASI, Series D, No. 44. Dordrecht: Kluwer.

Oatley, K. and Bolton, W. (1985) A social-cognitive theory of depression in reaction to life events. *Psychological Review*, **92**, 372-388.
Oatley, K. and Johnson-Laird, P. N. (1987) Towards a cognitive theory of emotions. *Cognition and Emotion*, **1**, 29-50.
Scheff, T. J. (1979) *Catharsis in Healing, Ritual and Drama*. Berkeley, CA: University of California Press.
Stevenson, R. L. (1886) *The Strange Case of Dr Jekyll and Mr Hyde*. London: Longmans.
Tolstoy, L. N. (1901) *Anna Karenina*. London: Heinemann (translated by C. Garnett from the Russian original work published in 1878).

6 The Transition Cycle: Causes, Outcomes, Processes and Forms*

NIGEL NICHOLSON
Centre for Organizational Research, London Business School

This chapter draws together ideas and research findings from nearly 10 years of studying work role transitions at the University of Sheffield Social and Applied Psychology Unit. Research from other sources will also be reviewed, but the main purpose of the chapter is to outline the framework of ideas that has been emerging from our programme.

First we shall briefly consider the causes of transitions and the current social trends governing their occurrence. Second, the challenge of adjustment will be reviewed by looking at three approaches to theory and research: predictive—seeking to explain differing outcomes to transition; process—modelling transition as an experience through time; and taxonomic—identifying the characteristics of types of transition. The chapter concludes by briefly considering future directions for the study of transitions.

CAUSES AND TRENDS

In a recent collaborative project for the EEC with Danish psychologist Gert Graversen (Graversen and Nicholson, 1988), one objective we set ourselves was to evaluate trends in labour mobility over the next 15 years. To do this we consulted with experts from many fields: sociologists, labour economists, technical scientists and others, asking them to identify significant macroscopic sources of social change; consider which areas of workers' and citizens' lives these will impact upon; and predict probable future trends. We then extrapolated,

*The middle sections of this chapter are an updated and revised version of an article which first appeared in Research in Personnel and Human Resources Management, edited by K. M. Rowland and G. R. Ferris, published by JAI Press, Inc., 1987.

On the Move: the Psychology of Change and Transition. Edited by S. Fisher and C. L. Cooper.

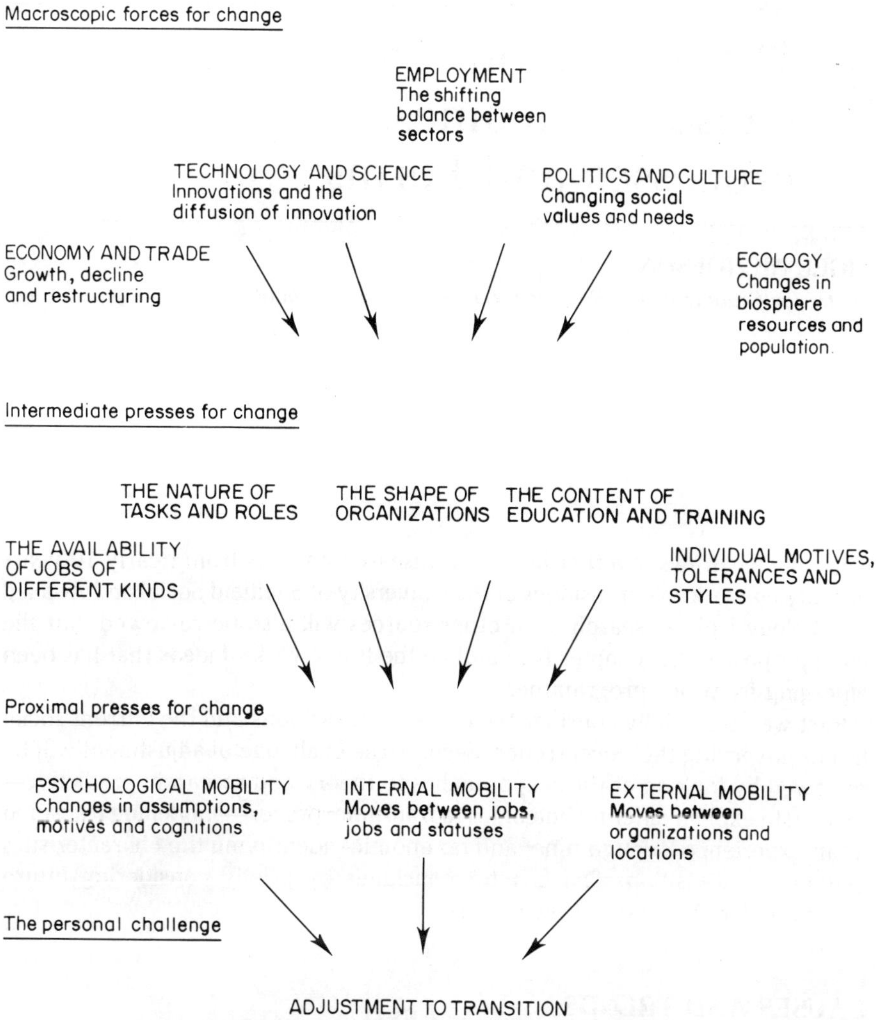

Figure 6.1. The causal chain of change

with their help, to the likely impact on job mobility. It is not my purpose here to review the many complex themes this process uncovered, but to summarize our conclusions, as shown in Figure 6.1.

Among our panel of experts there was unanimity in several specific areas—e.g. the reconfiguration of employment into a skilled core and casualized periphery; as well as consensus about where lay the principal areas of unresolvable uncertainty; e.g. all-important cultural developments. There was also general agreement about the cascading influence from the most macroscopic forces, shown in the top line of the figure, through the more proximal 'presses'

(to borrow Henry Murray's term) that bear upon individuals and groups, to the immediate impact on job change, and the challenge of adjustment. This analysis bore witness to how much we live in times of great instability in almost all of the most macroscopic forces, which can be expected to find more intermediate expression in changes in the work and life systems that engage us more directly. These stimulate or inhibit mobility of three kinds: moves between jobs within institutions, migrations between employers or organizations and, more minimally, altered expectations and perspectives.

From our review we concluded that most of these forces, for the foreseeable future, will be acting to increase rather than decrease rates of all three forms of mobility. Increasingly, people can expect to change jobs regularly, or confront demands that they adapt to changes going on around them in administrative systems or technology. It is thus not surprising that, across the range of our research projects in this area, we have consistently found there to be a great thirst for practical and theoretical understanding into the nature of these challenges. The topic of work role transitions is one that immediately engages the most central life interests of individual respondents. It is also a source of great perplexity to organizations, who are aware of the challenge it presents but are profoundly uncertain about what could or should be done to meet the challenge. The management of transitions remains currently an underdeveloped area of human resources management policy, beyond the traditional concerns of recruitment, training and assessment. Answers are needed to such questions as: What kinds of job moves yield positive and negative outcomes? What kinds of people adapt best to radically new demands? What practices should organizations undertake to maximize the benefits and minimize the costs of the rising tide of transitions? The conceptual frameworks and research findings reviewed in this chapter aim to begin answering such questions.

THE CHALLENGE OF ADJUSTMENT—THEORY AND RESEARCH

Transitions are such commonplace events that it is probably true to say that stabilized living and working conditions are the exception rather than the rule. Yet theories and methods in psychology often continue to depend upon ahistorical conceptions, and embody assumptions of static social conditions. There is still relatively little attention in theory and research to adjustment to change. In my own work I have been trying to develop theoretical frameworks of three kinds to help us understand what happens to people who experience job mobility and transitions.

PREDICTIVE THEORY

First, from available knowledge about individual behaviour and organizations, it has been possible to propose predictive theory about how the outcomes of

transitions depend upon certain prior influences (Nicholson, 1984). The theory of work role transitions focuses on two principal outcome dimensions: personal change—alterations in identity to accommodate the demands of new roles; and role development—behaviours enacted to reshape role and context to make them better fit personal qualities (also termed 'role innovation' by scholars; Schein, 1971; Van Maanen and Schein, 1979). The theory identifies three main sets of independent variables governing these outcomes: organizational socialization-induction practices, individual characteristics, and role requirements. The theory was mainly concerned with the last two of these: the motives and needs of people entering transitions, and how the characteristics of the roles into which people move differ from roles previously occupied.

Without attempting to describe the theory in detail, or studies bearing upon it, some general conclusions can be drawn on the basis of available evidence. Our study of 2300 managers' role transitions (Nicholson and West, 1988) showed that individuals with high growth needs have a propensity towards role development, as predicted, and those who are more anxious prior to a transition are more likely to experience personal change. Movement into high discretion roles also favours role development, but not exclusive of personal change: the two modes of adjustment often go hand in hand. Indeed, it may be concluded that job changes, especially those that are radical—involving simultaneous shifts of context, function and status—generally yield psychologically beneficial outcomes (see also Roborgh and Stacey, 1987). Contrary to the expectation of stress theory, moving enhances psychological adjustment, while immobility, even over a short period, leads to reductions in well-being (West and Nicholson, 1989). This is consistent with a growing body of evidence that most of the stresses accompanying job change are outweighed by positive outcomes (Keller and Holland, 1981; Brett, 1982; Werbel, 1983; Kirjonen and Hanninen, 1986). Indeed, one can go so far as to say that stress is often embraced as an integral feature of beneficial change (Latack, 1984).

However, this needs to be qualified by attention to differences in the impact of job change on work and non-work domains. Where transition is between different environments and involves job movers and their families, i.e. many geographical relocations, difficulties are likely to be concentrated in the non-work sphere. Problems over housing, children's schooling, spouse's employment and community involvements are the major sources of hassles, worries and stress (Brett and Werbel, 1978; Munton and Forster, 1990).

A PROCESS MODEL—THE TRANSITION CYCLE

Several writers have recognized the importance of viewing transitions as experiences through time, noting that the nature of the experience alters as one moves from the initial point of impact into more strategic adjustments (Graen, 1976; Feldman, 1976; Hopson and Adams, 1976; Van Maanen, 1976; Bridges,

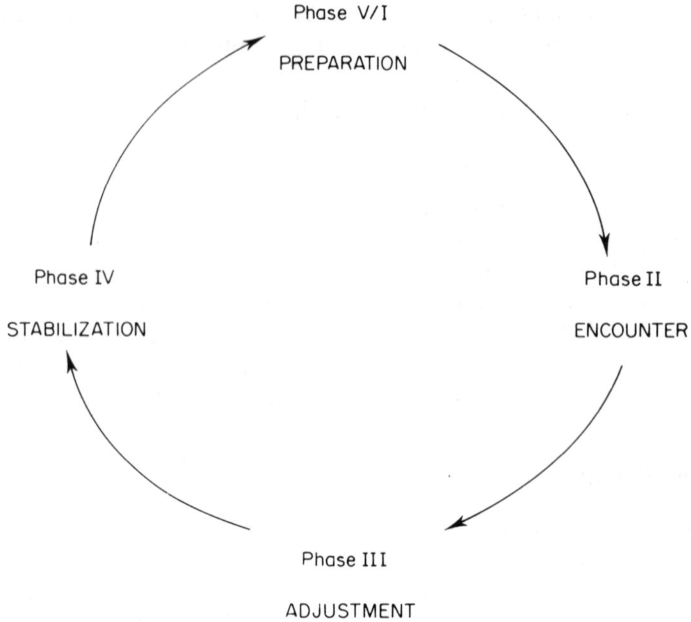

Figure 6.2. The transition cycle

1980; Katz, 1980). The present writer has synthesized and extended these insights into a general model of the transition cycle (Nicholson, 1987a).

This model differs from its antecedents by aiming to be non-normative—it does not prescribe that certain experiences will or will not occur. It aims to be a systematic general framework, allowing for the full range of extremely different experiences we know people encounter in transition to be interpolated and interpreted. It does so with the aid of three guiding principles: recursion, disjunction and interdependence. Figure 6.2 shows the basic model.

Recursion

Each one of us is at some point on one or more transition cycles. Movement is continuous. Even the most stabilized conditions contain the possibility of future change, and therefore embody varying states of readiness for the onset of a new cycle. For this reason, in Figure 6.2, Stage I is also Stage V. Each experience of transitions, in some way, affect one's future experience of transitions.

Disjunction

Experiences and events are divided into stages because of their distinctive qualities. Different psychological processes can be seen to hold sway at each

stage. Expectations and motives rule the *Preparation* stage (the period leading up to the point of change); emotions and perceptions are pre-eminent in the *Encounter* stage (the first days and weeks of familiarization with a new job); assimilation and accommodation govern the *Adjustment* stage (the period of developing performance and psychological change); and relating and performing dominate the *Stabilization* stage (the steady state achieved after Adjustment). Following the logic of this division it is apparent that different areas of theory could be applied to each stage: Expectancy-valence and occupational choice theories to Preparation, stress-coping and information-processing to Encounter, theories of personal development and organization change to Adjustment, and leadership and role theory to Stabilization. This reasoning is consistent with the argument that we need more than one middle range, rather than a single 'grand', theory to explain complex organizational behaviours (Pinder and Moore, 1984).

Interdependence

What happens at one stage exerts a powerful influence over what happens at the next. One's state of preparation (i.e. readiness for change) can soften or sharpen the immediate impact of Encounter. Equally, how acute, benign, or demanding is one's first Encounter with changed circumstances can set the direction for the Adjustment strategies one will be predisposed to enact in the longer term. Whether adjustment modes are reactive or proactive (personal change vs. role development) establishes the kind of Stabilized connection that will be achieved between self and situation. The Stabilized patterns arrived at in work and relationships are a form of Preparation and springboard for future change.

These three assumptions can be illustrated by looking at the tasks and challenges people face as they travel around the transition cycle, at the problems and pitfalls that await them, and at the solutions they and their managers may seek. First, Figure 6.3 shows tasks and goals. Achieving a state of readiness is the core task of the Preparation stage. If one knows a change is imminent it is helpful to have clear and realistic expectations about what is to come, to be positively motivated toward the change, and to be aware of one's feelings about it. If change comes without warning, psychological readiness can still be attained in the form of positive self-appraisal, low risk-aversion, and a sense of self-direction. However well prepared for change one thinks one is, Encounter will always bring new and unexpected experiences (Louis, 1980a). The ideal orientation to novelty is a sense of one's own competence to cope, and enjoyment in the challenge of sense-making and exploration. The central task of the Adjustment stage is to achieve a consonant relationship between self and environment through self-development (personal change) and effective innovations (role development) which improve the quality of one's work, relationships and organizational culture. The goals of the Stabilization stage are personal and

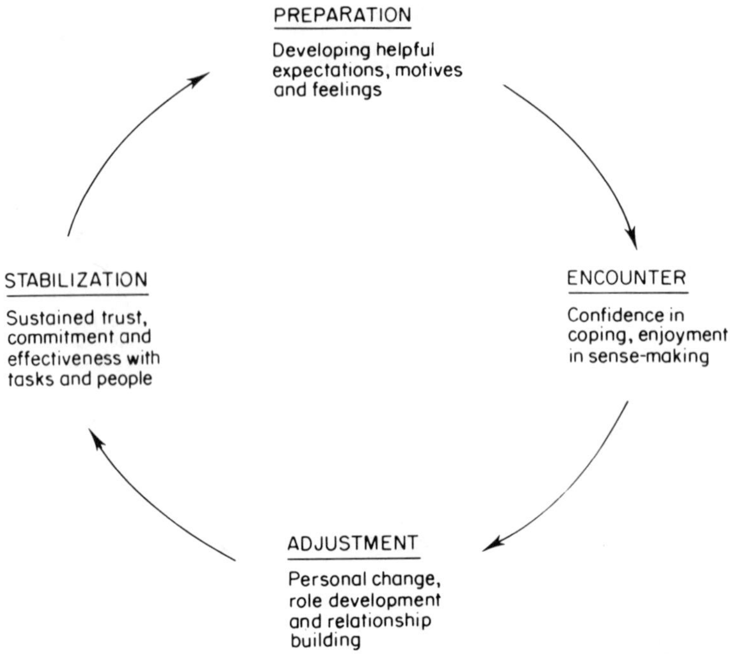

Figure 6.3. Tasks and goals through the transition cycle

organizational effectiveness, ideally in a climate of high mutual trust and commitment that will enable individuals to realize their potential in their roles.

The principle of interdependence can be clearly seen through these tasks and goals. Success at one stage facilitates success at the next. But, in like manner, failure can beget failure through the transition cycle, as suggested in Figure 6.4. Even when confronting expected changes in the Preparation stage, people may feel fearful, unready and reluctant to change, sometimes disablingly so. One is equally ill-equipped in the opposite condition: when change is anticipated with exaggerated optimism and starry-eyed idealism. In either event, the 'reality shock' (Hughes, 1958) of Encounter may be hard to handle (Weissman and Furnham, 1987). The stress of early experience can occasion bitter regret and a variety of defensive-coping strategies, such as seeking group refuge, defensive hostility and withdrawal behaviours (Hopson and Adams, 1976; Fisher and Hood, 1987). Indeed, when transitions are excessively painful in their early stages, quitting is a rational response (Raelin, 1984), but there may be many constraints foreclosing this option, especially in the 'golden handcuffs' of large paternalist organizations or unfavourable labour markets (Hirschman, 1970).

Unsatisfactory adjustment occurs where the only adaptation the individual is willing or able to make results in person-environment misfitting (French, Caplan and Van Harrison, 1982). Grieving for one's lost past or forgone

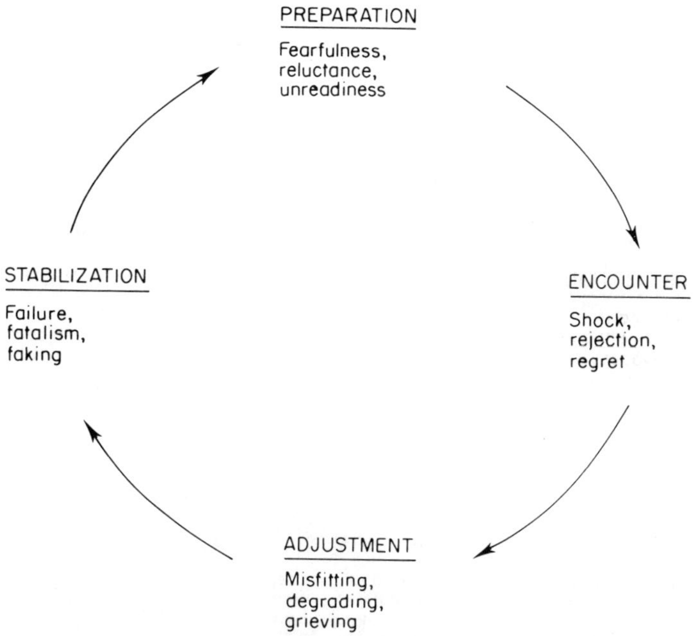

Figure 6.4. Pitfalls and problems in the transition cycle

opportunities, or the sense that one's skills are degrading and atrophying with disuse, are observable when people are locked into their new situations (Bridges, 1980). The counterpart in Stabilization of these miseries are various dysfunctional relationships with work and colleagues. Underachievement and failure are probably the most visible of these, but less perceptible performance problems such as 'faking' are to be found where people have the opportunity to conceal their own shortcomings, or find it easier to comply with the letter rather than the spirit of control systems (Lawler and Rhode, 1976). Feelings of fatalism may operate as a self-fulfilling prophesy in states of unsatisfactory Stabilization, notably where people feel trapped by their advanced age, minority status, professional obsolescence or some past unfavourable evaluation of their abilities in 'tournament' promotion systems (Legge, 1973; Rosenbaum, 1984).

In cases of both successful and unsuccessful traverse around the transition cycle, it is easy to see how the onset of a new cycle can be affected. Hall's 'success syndrome' (1976) is functionally equivalent to those cases where effectiveness in the Stabilization stage encourages good Preparation for future change in the form of self-directed and confident targeting. Equally, a 'failure syndrome' can be derived from our transitions model. Unsuccessful adaptation can be corrosive to self-belief and weaken the motivational underpinning necessary for future proactive coping (Raelin, 1980). Indeed, one corollary of the notion of the

transition cycle that merits further investigation is the effect of different sequences of positive and negative cycles. What, for example, happens when a career-long sequence of 'good' cycles is followed by a 'bad' one? Wide individual differences in response are to be expected. For some the psychic damage of sudden disconfirming experience may be unrecoverable; others will try to fight back by enacting radical and innovative shifts in their lifestyle and career goals. Both reactions have been observed in cases of late-career redundancy among executives (Fineman, 1983; Latack and Dozier, 1986). The perspective on careers afforded by the idea of the transition cycle can be illustrated by considering the phenomenon of being plateaued. This is functionally equivalent to sequences of transition cycles where positive outcomes progressively diminish over the career span (Feldman, 1988).

The main research implication of the transition cycle is that it may be a useful building block for analysing career patterns, or a tool for taking meteorological readings of the climate of change within organizations. The notion of the transition cycle also has practical implications, supplying an analytical framework for individual career accounting, either through biographical self-appraisal or in careers counselling. It suggests employees could be usefully asked, or ask themselves, the following kinds of questions:

1. Where am I now on the transition cycle?
2. How did I get here?
3. Has there been a pattern to my experience of previous cycles?
4. Does this contain any warnings about what is going to happen to me next?
5. Can I foresee my next cycle, and if not, why not?
6. Is there something I should do to determine what happens next or what the next cycle will be like?
7. What might management systems do to help me through my current stage, the next stage and future cycles?

From the foregoing analysis, strategies can be proposed for achieving personal and organizational goals, and for finding remedies to the problems that arise through transition. It can also be envisaged which management or other support systems could play a role in delivering these remedies. Figure 6.5 summarizes strategies and remedies, and Figure 6.6 shows the relevant management systems.

In the Preparation stage, to maximize readiness, a guiding principle should be 'forewarned is forearmed'. This proves to be particularly problematic when people are about to cross the boundary between two organizations. Recruitment systems are clearly implicated, for they commonly suffer from two general maladies which lead to mystification, misinformation and mismatch. The first malady is the delusion of scientism—the belief that people and jobs can be precisely measured and matched—where the use of psychometric assessments is allowed to deflect the responsibility for selection decisions from company

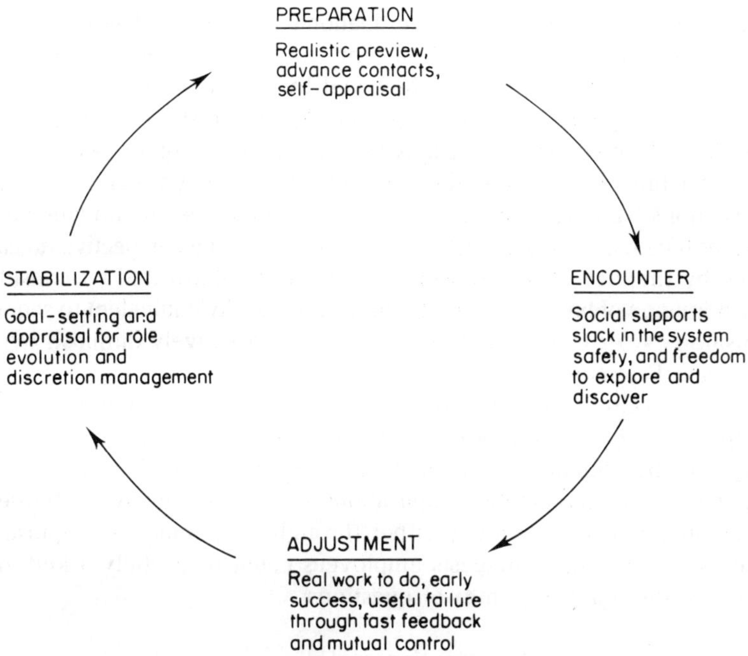

Figure 6.5. Strategies and remedies for the transition cycle

agents to impersonal and mechanistic criteria. 'Scientific' selection is usually based upon static rather than dynamic assumptions, and one dangerous outcome of this is that job applicants are assessed on criteria which are trainable, i.e. chosen or rejected on factors which are subject to change after entry. It also ignores the cultural dimension to recruitment and in no way ensures that a good fit between individual value systems and organizational cultures will be achieved. The second malady is the opposite case of 'impressionism', where sole reliance is on subjective judgements without any attempt to clarify objectives and job requirements. Here recruitment can degenerate into a bilateral sales pitch between candidate and organization—each trying to project to the other an attractive image to secure a favourable contract, while concealing their shortcomings, misgivings and genuine requirements.

To some degree, both the scientific and impressionistic strategies do have a role to play in recruitment, so long as they can be complementary. Unambiguous criteria for selection *are* needed, but at the same time the recruitment interview should give both parties the opportunity to explore each other's less definable qualities. Yet, however sophisticated organizations and individuals are in their approach to selection, it is unwise and unhealthy to allow the central episodes of selection procedure to bear sole responsibility for achieving a good match. Prior or ancillary activities are needed by both parties. Organizations should

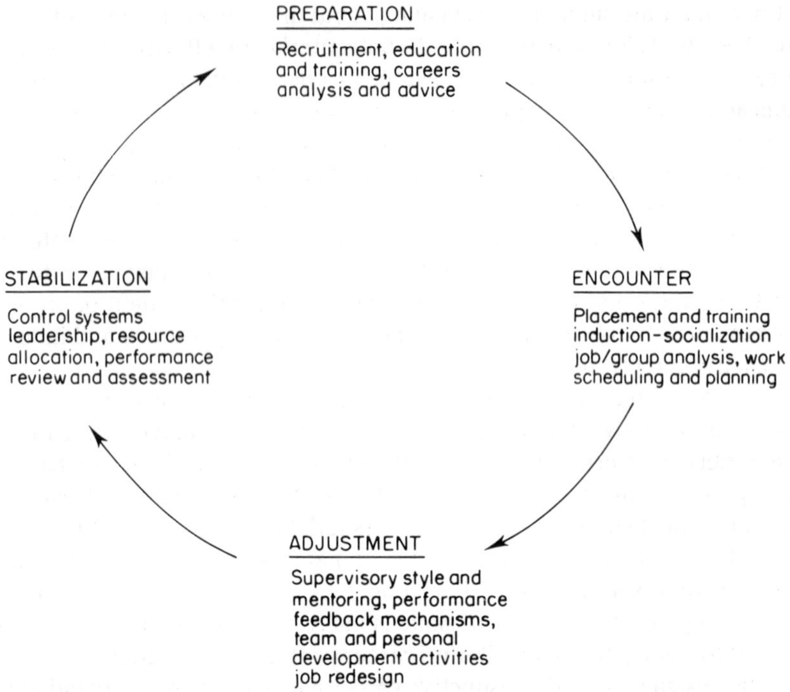

Figure 6.6. The role of management systems round the transition cycle

aim to provide realistic job previewing opportunities for the candidate, independent of selection procedures (Wanous, 1980), and the applicants should engage in systematic self-appraisals to be clear about their own goals, needs and self-images (Herriot, 1984). Advance contacts with people who are members of the new organization can help greatly in these endeavours.

Many of these observations apply equally to intraorganizational transitions, although typically these suffer from even greater neglect by companies than interorganizational moves. There is important work to be done in the design of education, training and careers counselling to help people target future change and achieve a state of readiness for both internal and external moves (Schlossberg, 1984).

At the Encounter stage, to minimize the impact of negative emotions and to avoid defensive coping, the individual needs a map, a bicycle and good weather. The good weather is a climate of psychological safety and supports, and the bicycle is psychological freedom to explore and pathfind in the new environment; but the maps which organizations are usually able to give people are totally inadequate. Organigrams are at best opaque, and at worst downright misleading, about the 'real' design of the organization—its informal networks of communication, power and decision-making. In all but a very few exceptions,

job descriptions are similarly unrevealing about the 'contextual rules' of conduct (Van Maanen, 1980) and the operational criteria for effective performance. Where circumstances decree that reliable or uncontroversial maps of jobs and organizations cannot be supplied, the newcomer should be encouraged to draw his or her own. This means that the new boss needs to signal clearly the legitimacy of exploratory activities, such as talking to colleagues to find out what they do and investigating how one's own job fits into the work of the organization. Indeed, this can be usefully formalized as an induction strategy by setting the newcomer the task of generating some such map as a first job project. The information yielded by this task also has the benefit of providing management with useful feedback on how company operations and induction systems are perceived.

In too many cases it is apparent that organizations are as unready for the transition as are newcomers, especially for lower-level management entry jobs and a variety of internal transfers. Little or no thought is given to what kinds of prior preparations should be made for the incoming person. Indeed, placement itself is often made on the basis of the vicissitudes of company openings, rather than strategic awareness of longer-term company needs. A consequence of this is that newcomers may be placed in 'good' jobs that are actually unsuitable for early learning, or the converse mistake is made of placing experienced people into good training jobs which offer no career prospects. Placement and training should be designed to fit the distinctive career and learning needs of individuals at varying stages of professional development. This means that, minimally, there is a need for some systematic prior job analysis and consideration of work-group demography (Wagner, Pfeffer and O'Reilly, 1984). The latter is particularly important to demography (Wagner, Pfeffer and O'Reilly, 1984). The latter is particularly important to ensure a convivial and productive integration of individuals into their new work group (Moreland and Levine, 1983). Induction-socialization practices (as discussed by Van Maanen and Schein, 1979) and the scheduling of first work assignments and subsequent tasks should be planned with desired outcomes in mind.

In the Adjustment stage, active consideration needs to be given to how to help prevent the individual from declining in morale, self-esteem and performance, and to avoid the emergency of deviant adaptations. Having a 'real' job to do, as opposed to 'makework', is an essential prerequisite for healthy adjustment. Hall's (1976) injunction about the importance of early success is of prime relevance—nothing succeeds like success. This means that feedback mechanisms need to be swift and reliable, and organizational agents need to be vigilant about how accessible is feedback from direct job indicators: work outputs, client groups, superiors, colleagues and subordinates. The experience of failure should not be avoided, but constructively managed. The complete absence of errors or negative feedback is unhealthy. As Peters and Waterman (1982) have noted, it is a warning symptom of risk-aversive and ineffective

climates. It is also important for the act, not the person, to be the focus of negative feedback and for it to be administered in a supportive climate (Hamner and Organ, 1978). With these provisos, useful failure becomes a necessary element in personal and organizational development.

Supervisory style, and hence supervisory training, lies at the heart of the processes and outcomes of success and failure. The immediate boss has a primary role in generating feedback and mediating its effects, but an important shift in style of supervision needs to take place from the Encounter to the Adjustment stage. In the Encounter stage, warmth, encouragement, and a fairly low profile of visibility are helpful, so that the boss is not an intrusive or inhibiting presence, but can be called upon for help if needed. This benign posture begins to look like neglect if carried over into the Adjustment stage. Indeed, it can pose an apparently insoluble problem for subordinates who feel positive about the supervisor as a friend and co-worker, but know that in some way they are not getting the guidance they need, with the result that they feel unable to confront the boss with these negative feelings. The subordinates may be then more likely to attribute doubts and frustrations to their own inexperience and inadequacy, rather than to the shortcomings of a powerful and expert boss.

In the Adjustment stage the boss's style thus needs to become vigilant without being oppressive, actively incorporating feedback and developmental strategies that will help harmonize personal change and role development (Davies and Easterby-Smith, 1984). If the person's relationship with the job seems to be heading toward some deadlocked misfit or dysfunctional adaptation, then more radical job redesign may be needed. Since in many non-technical jobs the boss *is* the job design—by virtue of the decisions the boss takes to delegate or allocate responsibilities—the help of some third party may be necessary. Mentoring systems and personnel functions can be especially valuable if they are able to exercise real influence and do so with expertise and tact (Hunt and Michael, 1983).

In the Stabilization stage the goal is dynamic equilibrium, which means monitoring changes in the internal and external environments and making continual adjustments that will sustain effective performance. In accordance with our earlier analysis this means that leaders need to watch over and steer a balance between control and discretion to ensure that organizational goals and individual needs are met (Fulk and Cummings, 1984). It is their responsibility to oversee how roles evolve over time.

Control systems, such as reward and punishment contingencies and bureaucratic mechanisms for the standardization of performance, are well known to decay over time in the absence of active attempts to service and update them (Crozier, 1964). Resource allocation occupies a central role in all stabilized work performance, but it is not only of functional importance; it also carries great political significance (Pfeffer, 1981). Attention needs to be paid to the meanings that will be attributed to any shifts in resource allocation so that high trust and commitment can be sustained.

Performance appraisal is widely used to monitor stabilized work patterns, but often it is narrowly conceived, inexpertly conducted and unintegrated with other management systems (Fletcher and Williams, 1985). Undue emphasis is given to the literal meaning of 'appraisal'—the weighing and accounting of individual qualities—giving it a predominantly retrospective focus and conveying exclusive connotations of punishment and control. These are not illegitimate management functions, but they do need to be allied to developmental and future-oriented review methods. The extensive literature on management by objectives and goal-setting (Locke, Shaw, Saari and Latham, 1981) provides convincing evidence of the motivational and performance benefits of such methods. Effectively handled, they set the agenda for future change, bringing the person smoothly on to the stage of Preparation for the next transition cycle. This is an idealized sequence, for Stabilization will flow naturally into Preparation and the onset of a new transition cycle only in environments where change opportunities can be reliably targeted and executed. But the reality in many settings may be a good deal more uncertain than one might wish (Nicholson, West and Cawsey, 1985). The forces that give rise to transitions may not easily be comprehended and controlled by employees or management systems. Employee's life circumstances outside work may change unexpectedly, the external labour market may throw up unanticipated opportunities and demands, and intra-organizational moves may be compelled by events outside the sphere of the person's immediate role set.

In career planning and development systems these potential sources of uncertainty need to be confronted realistically. Many organizations persist in the fiction of orderly planning, when a dispassionate appraisal of past history would argue its futility. The best way to manage preparation for change under these conditions is to cultivate a sense of competence, flexible strategies for action and a regularly updated review of the opportunities and constraints in the internal and external environments.

The transition cycle is therefore a process model for management practice and employee awareness. Yet it is apparent that the forces and events we have considered are of great complexity and variety, and they impinge on the change process to produce many forms of transition. No two transition cycles are identical; this suggests the need for futher analysis. One way of proceeding is to attempt to construct typologies of transitions.

TAXONOMIC MODELS

Three kinds of typologies have been suggested by writers. First, transitions have been classified according to which boundaries the person crosses: functional, status, 'inclusionary' (between centre and periphery of organizational space), geographical, interorganizational and combinations of these (Schein, 1971; Louis, 1980b; Watts, 1981). Second, transitions have been classified according to

their temporal location in the life/career span (Miller and Form, 1951). Third, the people making transitions have been grouped into types according to their career patterns and motivational orientations (Rapoport, 1970).

These different approaches can be unified by a fourth analytical method, growing out of the transition cycle model. This is a nine-dimensional system, through which it is proposed any single instance of transition can be comprehensively and precisely profiled. The system can also be used to summarize the patterns exhibited by individuals over time (i.e. careers and work histories), or the characteristic forms observed within a given social system (i.e. occupational or organizational mobility cultures). The account of the nine dimensions that follows is, of necessity, abbreviated. Readers are referred to the original source (Nicholson, 1987a) for a more complete account of their origins, outcomes and relation to management systems.

The notion of a cycle is a metaphor, and to understand the nine dimensions of transitions, summarized in Table 6.1, it may be helpful to hold in mind the image of a turning wheel. The motion of a wheel may be characterized by how fast it is turning (speed), its size and shape (amplitude and symmetry), how smooth is its action (continuity and complexity), how it is set in motion (propulsion), what helps or hinders its movement (discretion and facilitation) and where it is going (significance). Let us briefly summarize the meaning of each of these in the light of available evidence.

I. Speed

There are enormous individual differences in the rate at which transitions occur. Amongst our 2300 British management sample we found the rate of change to have a highly skewed distribution (Nicholson and West, 1988): the peak of the bell-curve is at the short time end of the horizontal axis—i.e. most are changing jobs around once every two years—but with a long-drawn-out tail towards the long tenure end of the axis—i.e. a sizeable minority are relatively immobile. There are also wide differences across types of organizations and occupations. Movement is slow and steady in some (often large institutions, or highly specialist occupations), and bewilderingly fast in others.

Which is more psychologically beneficial? This depends upon other dimensional characteristics of the cycle. Rapid moves are generally welcome where they are not too complex (VI) or significant (IX), but speed can be dysfunctional when it short-circuits the cycle. The more complex and significant the change, the longer required for Encounter and Adjustment, and people may find themselves moving on before they have had a chance to reap the benefits of adjustment, achieve stabilized performance, or prepare adequately for the next transition (Beehr and Newman, 1978; Stokols, Shumaker and Martinez, 1983; McEnrue, 1988). The opposite danger of too low a speed of movement is feelings of frustration of 'stuckness' (Kaye, 1982; Stout, Slocum and Cron, 1988).

Table 6.1. Nine dimensions of transition cycles

I	Speed	How often do they occur?	Fast	vs. Slow
II	Amplitude	How radical is the change?	High amplitude	vs. Low amplitude
III	Symmetry	How much time adjusting vs. time performing?	Long adjustment time	vs. Short adjustment time
IV	Continuity	Any meaningful connection between transitions?	High continuity	vs. Low continuity
V	Discretion	How much autonomy in controlling the process?	High discretion	vs. Low discretion
VI	Complexity	Are multiple adaptations and adjustments required?	High complexity	vs. Low complexity
VII	Propulsion	Who started the cycle and why?	Self-propelled	vs. System-propelled
VIII	Facilitation	Who/what helps progress through the cycle?	High facilitation	vs. Low facilitation
IX	Significance	Does adjustment change the individual or organization?	High significance	vs. Low significance

II. Amplitude

This dimension connotes how novel or radical are the demands of any transition cycle. Its objective determinants are the differences and contrasts between new and old role, and its subjective determinants the degree of preparation and foreknowledge the individual has about the change to come. For most managerial and professional roles amplitude is generally high. Managers characteristically shift between quite radically differing functional role demands (Nicholson and West, 1988) and graduates entering industry are generally ill-prepared for what they find (Mabey, 1986; Nicholson and Arnold, 1989a).

However, the shocks and surprises of high amplitude are not always stressful to any profound degree. This depends very much upon the individuals' non-specific personal qualities of confidence and purpose—i.e. their self-efficacy (Lent and Hackett, 1987), and the kinds of social support they call upon during the transition (Pinder and Schroeder, 1987). In other words, the effects of amplitude are mediated by propulsion (VII) and facilitation (VIII).

III. Symmetry

The 'shape' of the cycle means the relative length of time spent on each stage. Some transitions are characterized by short Encounter and long Adjustment stages—for example, an intraorganizational move involving the adoption of major new responsibilities. Others show quite different forms of asymmetry, such as the relatively long Encounter and short Adjustment experienced by recruits to the armed services, the police, nursing and other highly institutionalized occupations (Becker, Geer, Hughes and Strauss, 1961).

Thus symmetry is strongly associated with the movers' career stage, and with their occupational function. It generates its effects via complexity (III) and amplitude (II)—the more complex the change the longer the Adjustment time needed; the higher the amplitude, the longer the Encounter phase (Pinder and Schroeder, 1987). Whether these yield positive or negative outcomes depends how the process is managed (facilitation, VIII), and how much the person is able to schedule the pace of his/her own experiences (discretion, V).

IV. Continuity

Continuity denotes how transition cycles succeed one another—whether they follow a logical, orderly or cumulative sequence, vs. an arbitrary or incoherent pattern. In general, it may be said that continuity is paradoxical; it is lower than people commonly believe, but at the same time it is greater than appears on the surface.

It is lower than most of us imagine in the sense that careers in reality involve less of the continuous vocational development than is portrayed by the imagery of fiction, educational curricula, careers guidance services and organizational recruitment propaganda. In this sense careers *are* a fiction (Nicholson and West, 1989). Our research has shown that not only are managers' moves typically between functional areas and organizational types of markedly different types (Nicholson and West, 1988), but they are also highly unexpected to the movers themselves (Nicholson, West and Cawsey, 1985).

On the other hand, this surface appearance of incoherence in careers is also misleading, since it masks deeper and more subtle interconnections and themes in personal experience and life histories. People are supremely skilled at blending unpredictable and ill-assorted experiences via the crucible of personal identity into harmonious portfolios of interests (Osherson, 1980; Sheehy, 1982). In this they are aided by the qualities of adaptability and self-efficacy, referred to earlier, which allow continual purposeful pathfinding in the face of uncertainty. In short, continuity is mediated by amplitude (II)—i.e. it is undermined by excessive novelty; and by propulsion (VII)—it is enhanced by purposeful striving.

V. Discretion

We have already identified discretion as a key attribute of role requirements in relation to the outcomes of transition. Here we extend the concept to denote the scope the person has to determine the content and scheduling of experiences through each stage of the cycle.

This is determined chiefly by status—it is almost universal that discretion increases with seniority of position in social systems (Jaques, 1976). It is also a product of interdependence—how tightly coupled is the focal role with others, and how institutionalized are methods of induction and training. In other words,

discretion is high when the role is highly independent and when induction-socialization is highly individualized (Van Maanen and Schein, 1979; Jones, 1986).

Generally speaking, discretion aids adjustment, though this will vary according to the needs of individuals and to circumstances. Scheduled and circumscribed experience may be more welcomed by novices, and by people in highly specified technical roles (Zahrly and Tosi, 1989). The effects of discretion are also mediated principally by amplitude (II) and complexity (VI), in what may be expected to be a curvilinear relationship. The more novel and complex the transition, the more discretion will aid adjustment, except at extremely high levels of amplitude and complexity, where more structured experience is likely to be welcomed as a guard against role ambiguity, or at extremely low levels where too much discretion becomes inefficient (Warr, 1987).

VI. Complexity

Complexity means not just the sophistication of task requirements but, more broadly, the range of demands made upon the life-space and psyche of the individual. Complex transitions are those where demands to adapt occur simultaneously across a spectrum of experiential domains—typically: functional role, relationships, status requirements, culture, and material circumstances. Complex transitions are wheels within wheels—transition cycles embedded within one another, each with different time horizons. Thus we often find it takes longer to get to know a new locality than a new boss, or longer to get to know new co-workers than task demands, and so on (Moreland and Levine, 1983; Colarelli, Dean and Konstans, 1987).

Complexity also has a curvilinear relationship with stress (Warr, 1987)—transitions are most manageable when neither excessively mundane and uncomplicated, nor overwhelmingly multifaceted. The one is routinized and unstimulating, the other produces conflicts of time and energy. We have seen that complexity and speed (I) have a critical interaction. Symmetry (III), amplitude (II), discretion (V) and facilitation (VIII) are also implicated—to cope with complex transitions one needs long enough to be allowed for Adjustment, for Encounter shock to be minimal, for discretion to be moderate (too much creates the stress of role ambiguity, too little the stress of role conflict), and for supports or resources to aid the Adjustment process.

VII. Propulsion

Propulsion refers to who or what determines the onset of a transition cycle. Extremes of self and situational propulsion are easy to identify—cases where people actively choose to submit themselves to a transition, versus those where they are compelled by circumstantial forces. The latter are relatively rare, and especially associated with experiences of loss—downward status moves,

redundancy and dismissal being the most commonly observed examples. Complete freedom of choice over moves is also rare—we mostly have to concede the limitations of opportunity, or compromise with the pressures pushing us in one direction more than another. Research indicates that a sense of self-propulsion is critical to well-being. Even if we are heavily constrained, still to have had the possibility of saying no is crucial; and even a slight measure of self-determination, say over the timing or scheduling of a change, helps to engender commitment, effort and positive developmental outcomes (Graversen and Nicholson, 1988).

Propulsion is clearly related to one's labour market position. People with a profile of skills that are unique, generalizable across situations and highly valued in the community will be more able to choose their moves than those with particular situation-specific skills, or with low-level general abilities which are widely shared by others in the labour market. Propulsion also rests upon psychological orientation—individuals differ in their propensity determinedly to wring opportunities out of uncertainty, or to wrest choices out of constraint (Langer, 1983; Winchie and Carment, 1988). The research record indicates that self-propulsion begets self-propulsion. People who experience success from self-determination have strengthened impulses to exercise it in the future (Brousseau, 1983; Kohn and Schooler, 1983). From this it can be deduced that propulsion is mediated by continuity (II) and discretion (V).

VIII. Facilitation

Help in dealing with the tasks of transition may come from many sources, both formal and informal. Our review of the transition cycle, in the previous section, was largely concerned with how these can come into play at different phases of the cycle. It is generally the case that supports and resources are offered by socializing agencies, and sought out by movers, in quite different ways according to type of move and type of mover. Novices and newcomers are more likely to depend upon informal social sources of peer support, while more familiar intraorganizational movers make more use of impersonal systems and resources (Feldman and Brett, 1983; Louis, Posner and Powell, 1983).

Training and mentoring systems are some of the chief methods used by organizations to facilitate transition (Schlossberg, 1984), but it is evident that organizations differ widely in the sophistication and adequacy of their provision for the needs of job changers. Generally, it is large organizations which devote resources most systematically to this (albeit, ineffectually in many cases) while in small organizations facilitation is a more organic process of flexible learning and support. It is in middle-sized organizations (100-3000 employees) where neglect is felt most (Nicholson and West, 1988). Facilitation is also determined by organizational climate, for even organizations of similar size and type can differ greatly in their emphasis upon the management of mobility (Hall, 1976; Derr, 1986; Gunz, 1989).

Whether the absence of facilitation is critical to the well-being and effectiveness of the mover depends, therefore, upon the individual's scope for self-determination (discretion, V and propulsion, VII), and how radical are the demands of the change (amplitude, II; symmetry, III and complexity, VI).

IX. Significance

This dimension embodies the main reason why transitions should be of interest to researchers and practitioners—because of their long-term consequences. The theory of work role transitions (Nicholson, 1984), briefly summarized above, has considered two key outcome dimensions: personal change and role development. The former implicates the importance of transitions for the growing identity of the individual (Kohn and Schooler, 1983; Mortimer, Lorence and Kumka, 1986); the latter points to how the transition of people into new roles can be the stimulus for far-reaching organizational innovations (Cox and Cooper, 1988; West and Farr, 1989).

The likelihood of these outcomes depends on four sets of factors. First is the characteristics of the mover. The significance of transitions differs according to career/life stage (Isabella, 1988), and to personality variables, i.e. propulsion (VII). Second is how the transition is managed. Different tactics of socialization can act to limit or enhance the impact of change (Van Maanen and Schein, 1979; Jones, 1986); i.e. discretion (V), facilitation (VIII) and symmetry (III). Third are the characteristics of the new and old role, as described earlier in relation to the theory of transitions. Broadly speaking, we can say that the more radical the change the more significant its outcomes (Latack, 1984; Nicholson and West, 1988); i.e. amplitude (II) and complexity (VI). Fourth are contextual factors; principally the characteristics of the organizations and occupations in which transitions occur. The concept of 'mobility culture' summarizes these factors, denoting how organizations and occupations differ in the frequency and form of transitions they characteristically exhibit, and in what consequences flow from this, i.e. speed (I) and continuity (IV). For example, in risk-aversive cultures moves are incremental and rapid, allowing little scope for personal change or role development, whereas in developmental cultures one finds a paced fluidity of job mobility that encourages the continual transformation of people and jobs (Nicholson and Arnold, 1989b).

In summary, it can be seen that the nine dimensions intersect in complex ways and that the last of them, significance, depends upon all the others. From this dimensional modelling we can begin to construct profiles of common types of transitions. The first task is to identify their observable characteristics. These involve four main facets of transitions: whether they involve changes of context (i.e. migrations), altered status (i.e. promotions and demotions), different relationships (i.e. loss and gain) and new functions (i.e. lateral shifts). The author is currently developing specific analyses of these facets in relation to the transition

Table 6.2. Types of transition: applying the 9 dimensions

	Illustrative transitions			
	Simple promotion	Lateral relocation	Career change	Retirement
Facets of change				
Context	None	Major	Major	Minor
Relationships	Minor	Major	Major	Moderate
Status	Moderate	Minor	Minor	Major
Function	Minor	Minor	Major	Major
Nine dimensions				
Speed	Varies	Infrequent	Infrequent	Infrequent
Amplitude	Low	Low	High	Moderate
Symmetry	Short phases	Long Encounter	Long phases	Long Adjustment
Continuity	High	High	Low	Low
Discretion	Moderate	Low	Varies	High
Complexity	Low	High	High	Low
Propulsion	Situation	Situation	Self	Situation
Significance	Low	Moderate	High	High

cycle (Nicholson, in preparation). Table 6.2 summarizes how these facets differ for some typical examples of transition, and how the nine dimensions of the cycle can be used to profile their unique properties more precisely.

Any specific instance of transition will have its own profile. These illustrations are not intended to be definitive; their aim is to show how dimensional analysis of transitions can help to clarify our understanding of their demands, and help agents and movers to think strategically about choices and actions. This schema can also be used in counselling settings to identify which critical features of transitions have typified an individual's past experience, and what might be needed to aid their future psychological development. Similarly, organizational and occupational settings could be profiled by these means to display what pathologies or patterns typify their operation (Glowinkowsi and Nicholson, 1986).

FUTURE DIRECTIONS

Now let us conclude by considering the implications of this review for the future of the field of transitions. These can be found in three areas: research, theory and intervention.

One of the most immediate tasks of *research* is to enlarge upon the as yet small data base that currently exists about transitions. The literature is growing, but via small-scale piecemeal studies, rather than concerted attack on the main unresolved questions. In particular we need to know how different influences

on the outcomes of transitions interact; for example, the interdependence of individual differences and mobility cultures. We also need improved measures of many of the conceptually rich constructs in the area, and to use them to generate reliable comparative data across settings. Time-based processes deserve more attention; we need more qualitative research that tells us about the onset of different factors in the transition process, and the latency period of causal influences. Group dynamic processes in adjustment and socialization have also been neglected, and there is scope for more research on the relationship between work and non-work factors.

In the area of *theory*, more systematic testing of propositions is needed, as well as the development of models which incorporate additional variables. The relationship between emotion and cognition in the adjustment process has not been adequately analysed, and stress-coping models should be revised to take better account of the positive outcomes of much change experience. Attribution theory may have a significant role to play here. There is also a need for integration with careers theory, which to date has lacked a clear recognition of the role of transitions as building blocks in work histories (Mihal, Sorce and Comte, 1984; Nicholson and West, 1989). The question of personal control is also important, with scope for theory-building to explain how individuals differ in their strategies for dealing with elements of change. Last, we need to develop theory which locates these processes in their social context, by relating knowledge about group dynamics and mobility cultures to established theory of organizational functioning.

Finally, there is considerable scope for useful *intervention* strategies on this topic. Even from what we know so far, some unequivocal advice can be offered to practitioners about how a wide range of human resource management techniques can be deployed more systematically to aid adjustment, well-being and effectiveness. Taking a 'transitions perspective' can recast thinking and practice in many areas, such as recruitment and placement methods, induction-socialization tactics, supervision and appraisal, career counselling and guidance, job design, team building, manpower planning, promotion and transfer policies, organizational design and the operation of information-control systems (Nicholson, 1987b).

SUMMARY

The chapter reviewed theory and research on work role transitions by considering their causes, forms, process and outcomes. Problems of adjustment and remedies were analysed through the transition cycle model, which shows how the tasks of preparation, encounter, adjustment and stabilization are (a) recursive, (b) distinctive and (c) interdependent. A nine-dimensional analytical system was proposed which can be used to portray the characteristics of

individual transition cycles, and summarize the features exhibited by common types, sequences and aggregates of transitions, i.e. single job changes, move types, work histories and mobility cultures. The implications for future work in the field were discussed.

REFERENCES

Becker, H. S., Geer, B., Hughes, E. C. and Strauss, A. L. (1961) *The Boys in White.* Chicago, IL: University of Chicago Press.

Beehr, T. A. and Newman, J. E. (1978) Job stress, employee health and organizational effectiveness: a facet analysis, model and literature review. *Personnel psychology*, **31**, 665-699.

Brett, J. M. (1982) Job transfer and well-being. *Journal of Applied Psychology*, **67**, 450-463.

Brett, J. M. and Werbel, J. D. (1978) *The Effect of Job Transfers on Employees and their Families.* Washington, DC: Employee Relocation Council.

Bridges, W. (1980) *Transitions: Making Sense of Life's Changes.* Reading, MA: Addison-Wesley.

Brousseau, K. R. (1983) Toward a dynamic model of job-person relationships: findings, research questions, and implications for work system design. *Academy of Management Review*, **8**, 33-45.

Colarelli, S. M., Dean, R. A. and Konstans, C. (1987) Comparative effects of personal and situational influences on job outcomes of new professionals. *Journal of Applied Psychology*, **72**, 558-566.

Cox, C. J. and Cooper, C. L. (1988) *High Flyers: An Anatomy of Managerial Success.* Oxford: Blackwell.

Crozier, M. (1964) *The Bureaucratic Phenomenon.* Chicago, IL: University of Chicago Press.

Davies, J. and Easterby-Smith, M. (1984) Learning and developing from managerial work experience. *Journal of Management Studies*, **21**, 169-183.

Derr, C. B. (1986) *Managing the New Careerists.* San Francisco, CA: Jossey-Bass.

Feldman, D. C. (1976) A contingency theory of socialization. *Administrative Science Quarterly.* **21**, 433-452.

Feldman, D. C. (1988) Career plateaus reconsidered. *Journal of Management*, **14**, 69-90.

Feldman, D. C. and Brett, J. M. (1983) Coping with new jobs: a comparative study of new hires and job changers. *Academy of Management Journal*, **26**, 258-272.

Fineman, S. (1983) *White Collar Unemployment: Impact and Stress.* Chichester: John Wiley & Sons.

Fisher, S. and Hood, B. (1987) The stress of transition to university: a longitudinal study of psychological disturbance, absent-mindedness and vulnerability to homesickness. *British Journal of psychology*, **78**, 425-441.

Fletcher, C. and Williams, R. (1985) *Performance Appraisal and Career Development.* London: Hutchinson.

French, J. R. P., Caplan, R. D. and Van Harrison, R. (1982) *The Mechanisms of Job Stress and Strain.* Chichester: John Wiley & Sons.

Fulk, J. and Cummings, T. G. (1984) Refocusing leadership: a modest proposal. In J. G. Hunt, D. M. Hosking, C. A. Schriesheim and R. Stewart (eds), *Leaders and Managers: International Perspectives on Managerial Behavior and Leadership.* Oxford: Pergamon.

Glowinkowski, S. and Nicholson, N. (1986) The promotion pathology: a study of British police inspectors. *Personnel Review*, **15**, 12-21.

Graen, G. (1976) Role-making processes within complex organisations. In M. D. Dunnette (ed.), *Handbook of Industrial and Organizational Psychology*. New York: John Wiley & Sons.

Graversen, G. and Nicholson, N. (1988) *Measures to Facilitate the Adaptation to Technological and Social Change*. Report to the European Commission, Brussels.

Gunz, H. (1989) *Careers and Corporate Cultures*. Oxford: Blackwell.

Hall, D. T. (1976) *Careers in Organizations*. Pacific Palisades, CA: Goodyear.

Hamner, W. C. and Organ, D. W. (1978). *Organizational Behavior*. Dallas, TX: Business Publications.

Herriot, P. (1984) *Down from the Ivory Tower: Graduates and their Jobs*. Chichester: John Wiley & Sons.

Hirschman, A. O. (1970) *Exit, Voice and Loyalty*. Cambridge, MA: Harvard University Press.

Hopson, B. and Adams, J. (1976) Towards an understanding of transition: defining some boundaries of transition dynamics. In J. Adams, J. Hayes and B. Hopson (eds), *Transition*. London: Martin Robertson.

Hughes, E. C. (1958) *Men and their Work*. Glencoe, IL: Free Press.

Hunt, D. M. and Michael, C. (1983) Mentorship: a career training and development tool. *Academy of Management Review*, **8**, 475-485.

Isabella, L. A. (1988) The effect of career stage on the meaning of key organizational events. *Journal of Organizational Behavior*, **9**, 345-358.

Jaques, E. (1976) *A General Theory of Bureaucracy*. London: Heinemann.

Jones, G. R. (1986) Socialization tactics, self-efficacy, and newcomers' adjustments to organizations. *Academy of Management Review*, **8**, 262-379.

Katz, R. (1980) Time and work: toward an integrative perspective. In B. M. Staw and L. L. Cummings (eds), *Research in Organizational Behavior*, Vol. 2. Greenwich, CT: JAI Press.

Kaye, B. L. (1982) *Up is Not the Only Way*. Englewood-Cliffs, NJ: Prentice-Hall.

Keller, R. T. and Holland, W. E. (1981) Job change: a naturally occurring field experiment. *Human Relations*, **34**, 1053-1067.

Kirjonen, J. and Hanninen, V. (1986) Getting a better job: antecedents and effects. *Human Relations*, **39**, 503-516.

Kohn, M. L. and Schooler, C. (1983) *Work and Personality*. Norwood, NJ: Ablex.

Langer, E. J. (1983) *The Psychology of Control*. Beverly Hills, CA: Sage.

Latack, J. C. (1984) Career transitions within organizations: An exploratory study of work, nonwork and coping strategies. *Organizational Behavior and Human Performance*, **34**, 296-322.

Latack, J. C. and Dozier, J. B. (1986) After the axe falls: job loss as a career transition. *Academy of Management Review*, **11**, 375-392.

Lawler, E. E. and Rhode, J. G. (1976) *Information and Control in Organizations*. Santa Monica, CA: Goodyear.

Legge, K. (1973) Obsolescence of people—in context. *Management Decision*, **11**, 27-49.

Lent, R. W. and Hackett, G. (1987) Career self-efficacy: empirical status and future directions. *Journal of Vocational Behavior*, **30**, 347-382.

Locke, E. A., Shaw, K. N., Saari, L. M. and Latham, G. O. (1981) Goal-setting and task performance. *Psychological Bulletin*, **90**, 125-152.

Louis, M. R. (1980a) Surprise and sense-making: what newcomers experience in entering unfamiliar organizational settings. *Administrative Science Quarterly*, **25**, 226-251.

Louis, M. R. (1980b) Career transitions: varieties and commonalities. *Academy of Management Review*, **5**, 329-340.

Louis, M. R., Posner, B. Z. and Powell, G. N. (1983) The availability and helpfulness of socialization practices. *Personnel Psychology*, **36**, 857-866.

Mabey, C. (1986) *Graduates into Industry*. Aldershot: Gower.
McEnrue, M. P. (1988) Length of experience and the performance of managers in the establishment phase of their careers. *Academy of Management Journal*, **31**, 175-185.
Mihal, W. L., Sorce, P. A. and Comte, T. E. (1984) A process model of individual career decision making. *Academy of Management Review*. **9**, 95-103.
Miller, D. C. and Form, W. H. (1951) *Industrial Sociology*. New York: Harper & Row.
Moreland, R. L. and Levine, J. M. (1983) Socialization in small groups: temporal change in individual group relations. *Advances in Experimental Social Psychology*, **15**, 137-192.
Mortimer, J. T., Lorence, J. and Kumka, D. S. (1986) *Work, Family and Personality*. New York: Ablex.
Munton, A. G. and Forster, N. (1990) Job relocation: stress and the role of the family. *Work and Stress* (in press).
Nicholson, N. (1984) A theory of work role transitions. *Administrative Science Quarterly*, **29**, 172-191.
Nicholson, N. (1987a) The transition cycle: a conceptual framework for the analysis of change and human resources management. In J. Ferris and K. M. Rowland (eds), *Personnel and Human Resources Management*, Vol. 5. Greenwich, CT: JAI Press.
Nicholson, N. (1987b) Good and bad practices in graduate development. *Personnel Management*, February, pp. 34-38.
Nicholson, N. (in preparation). *The Transition Cycle*.
Nicholson, N. and Arnold, J. (1989a) Graduate entry and adjustment to corporate life. *Personnel Review*, **18**(3), 23-35.
Nicholson, N. and Arnold, J. (1989b) Graduate early experience in a multinational corporation. *Personnel Review* (In press).
Nicholson, N. and West, M. (1988) *Managerial Job Change*. Cambridge: Cambridge University Press.
Nicholson, N. and West, M. (1989) Transitions, work histories and careers. In M. B. Arthur, D. T. Hall and B. S. Lawrence (eds), *Handbook of Career Theory*. Cambridge: Cambridge University Press.
Nicholson, N., West, M. A. and Cawsey, T. F. (1985) Future Uncertain: Expected versus attained job mobility among managers. *Journal of Occupational Psychology*, **58**, 313-320.
Osherson, S. (1980) *Holding on or Letting Go: men and career change at midlife*. New York: Free Press.
Peters, T. J. and Waterman, R. H. (1982) *In Search of Excellence*. London: Harper & Row.
Pfeffer, J. (1981) *Power in Organizations*. Marshfield, PA: Pitman.
Pinder, C. C. and Moore, L. F. (eds) (1984) *Middle Range Theory and the Study of Organizations*. London: Martinus Nijhoff.
Pinder, C. C. and Schroeder, K. G. (1987) Time to proficiency following job transfers. *Academy of Management Journal*, **30**, 336-353.
Raelin, J. A. (1980) *Building a Career*. Kalamazoo, MI: Institute for Employment Rsearch.
Raelin, J. A. (1984) An examination of deviant/adaptive behaviors in the organizational careers of professionals. *Academy of Management Review*, **9**, 413-427.
Rapoport, R. (1970) *Mid-career Development*. London: Tavistock.
Roborgh, P. and Stacey, B. G. (1987) Happiness and radical career change among New Zealanders. *Journal of Psychology*, **121**, 501-514.
Rosenbaum, J. E. (1984) *Career Mobility in a Corporate Hierarchy*. London: Academic Press.
Schein, E. H. (1971) Occupational socialization and the professions: the case of the role innovator. *Journal of Psychiatric Research*, **8**, 521-530.

Schlossberg, N. K. (1984) *Counselling Adults in Transitions: linking practice with theory*. New York: Springer.
Sheehy, G. (1982) *Pathfinders*. New York: Bantam.
Stokols, D., Shumaker, S. A. and Martinez, J. (1983) Residential mobility and personal well being. *Journal of Environmental Psychology*, **3**, 5-19.
Stout, S. K., Slocum, J. W. and Cron, W. L. (1988) Dynamics of the career plateauing process. *Journal of Vocational Behavior*, **32**, 74-91.
Van Maanen, J. (1976) Breaking-in: socialization to work. In R. Dubin (ed.), *Handbook of Work, Organization and Society*. Chicago, IL: Rand McNally.
Van Maanen, J. (1980) Career games: organizational rules of play. In C. B. Derr (ed.), *Work, Family and Career*. New York: Praeger.
Van Maanen, J. and Schein, E. H. (1979) Toward a theory of organizational socialization. In B. M. Staw (ed.), *Research in Organizational Behavior*, Vol. 1. Greenwich, CT: JAI Press.
Wagner, W. G., Pfeffer, J. and O'Reilly, C. (1984) Organizational demography and turnover in top-management groups. *Administrative Science Quarterly*, **29**, 74-92.
Wanous, J. P. (1980) *Organizational Entry*. Reading, MA: Addison-Wesley.
Warr, P. B. (1987) *Work, Unemployment and Mental Health*. Oxford: Oxford University Press.
Watts, A. G. (1981) Career patterns. In A. G. Watts, D. E. Super and J. M. Kidd (eds), *Career Development in Britain*. Cambridge: Hobsons Press.
Weissman, D. and Furnham, A. (1987) The expectations and experience of a sojourning temporary resident abroad: a preliminary study. *Human Relations*, **40**, 313-326.
Werbel, J. D. (1983) Job change: a study of an acute job stressor. *Journal of Vocational Behavior*. **23**, 242-250.
West, M. A. and Farr, J. L. (1989) Innovation at work: Psychological perspectives. *Social behaviour*, **4**, 15-30.
West, M. A. and Nicholson, N. (1989) The outcomes of job change. *Journal of Vocational Behavior*, **34**, 335-349.
Winchie, D. B. and Carment, D. W. (1988) Intention to migrate: a psychological analysis. *Journal of Applied Social Psychology*, **18**, 727-736.
Zahrly, J. and Tosi, H. (1989) The differential effect of organizational induction process on early work role adjustment. *Journal of Organizational Behavior*, **10**, 59-74.

Section II: Specific Contexts and Characteristics of Transition

In this section concern focuses on the specific experiences of change and transition in the real world. Although obviously it is impossible to include all forms of change, we have asked leading researchers concerned with some of the most important or frequently experienced form of change to provide accounts of specified events.

The accounts begin with the transition to parenthood and progress through studies of transition in adolescence, moving to new schools, new job and office environments, leaving home and country, living abroad, the transition to the unemployed state and the stress of moving to an institution in the elderly.

Some workers focus on the immediate experiences these transitions create, and some emphasize aspects of coping and adjustment. The section thus provides a set of collated material on change and transition in different life contexts as well as providing hints as to the nature of vulnerability, resilience and adjustments.

7 The Transition to Parenthood and the Importance of Social Support

CAROLYN E. CUTRONA and **JULIE A. SUHR**
Department of Psychology, University of Iowa

On the second day that I was home alone with my newborn son and my 19-month-old daughter, I vividly remember sinking to the floor of the children's room in total exhaustion, and shouting, 'HELP!' at the top of my lungs. The moment passed quickly, but I believe that it exemplified the experiences of many new parents. Most new parents feel the need for some kind of tangible or emotional assistance during the early months of parenthood. Various aspects of assistance from others, or 'social support' in easing the transition to parenthood will be the focus of this chapter.

OVERVIEW

For some people the transition to parenthood is a major crisis, whereas for others it is not (Dyer, 1963; LeMasters, 1957; Hobbs, 1965; Hobbs and Cole, 1976; Russell, 1974). Findings regarding variables that determine the severity of stress imposed by the birth of a child will be reviewed, with an emphasis on interpersonal variables. The quality of the marital relationship, and the extent to which the spouse is perceived as providing social support, emerge as particularly potent determinants of adjustment to parenthood. However, one of the most consistent findings in the marital literature is a significant decline in marital satisfaction following the birth of the first child. Thus, women are confronted with the dilemma of needing support from an individual with whom they are feeling increasingly dissatisfied. This issue will be considered, followed by a summary of research literature that documents the beneficial effects of adequate social support on the psychological health, physical health and parenting behaviors of new mothers, as well as on the developmental outcomes of their infants. Although our understanding of the mechanisms through which social support affects adjustment is limited, research relevant to the psychological

On the Move: the Psychology of Change and Transition. Edited by S. Fisher and C. L. Cooper.

processes that are facilitated by support from others will be discussed. Finally, an integration of findings from the marital interaction literature and the social support literature regarding the transition to parenthood will be attempted, and suggestions for future research directions will be offered.

WHAT IS SOCIAL SUPPORT?

Social support refers to the psychological and tangible resources available to individuals through their relationships with family, friends, neighbors, work associates and other nonprofessionals with whom the individual has contact. Although social support is often viewed as primarily beneficial during times of stress, research shows that those with rich support resources have better mental and physical health than those low in support, even in the absence of significant life stress (Cohen and Wills, 1985).

Although a number of different types of social support have been proposed, researchers appear to have converged on a set of five specific interpersonal qualities and behaviors that constitute support. These five support types can be classified into those that directly promote problem-solving (instrumental support) and those that primarily promote emotional adjustment (emotional support). Included among instrumental support components are tangible aid and informational support. *Tangible aid* refers to concrete assistance, wherein goods or services are provided (e.g. financial assistance, transportation). *Informational support* involves information, advice or guidance concerning possible solutions to a problem. Included among emotional support components are expressions of caring or attachment, network support and esteem support. *Attachment* represents love and comfort that provide security in times of stress. Social integration or *network support* refers to feeling part of a group where members share common interests and concerns. *Esteem support* consists of bolstering the person's sense of competence or self-esteem. Providing the individual with positive feedback on skills and abilities, or indicating a belief that the person is capable of coping with a stressful event, are examples of this type of support.

THE TRANSITION TO PARENTHOOD AS A CRISIS

A lively debate ensued during the 1960s and 1970s regarding whether or not the transition to parenthood constitutes a 'crisis' in the lives of married couples (e.g. LeMasters, 1957; Dyer, 1963; Hobbs, 1965; Hobbs and Cole, 1976; Russell, 1974). Although readjustments are always required following the birth of the first child, research suggests that there are marked individual differences in the extent to which the transition to parenthood is experienced as overwhelming. A number of variables have been identified that predict the ease with which

this transition is accomplished. Both personal and interpersonal predictors of adjustment will be summarized below.

In general, women rate the transition to parenthood as more stressful than do men (Hobbs and Cole, 1976; Russell, 1974). This is not surprising, since women still assume much greater responsibility for childcare than do men (Kotelchuck, 1976; Russell and Radin, 1983; Ruble, Fleming, Hackel and Stangor, 1988). Personal predictors of lower perceived crisis include greater number of years married, higher income, a planned pregnancy, prior training or experience with infants, realistic expectations concerning parenting, assigning high priority to one's role as a parent, good health of mother and infant, a temperamentally 'easy-going' infant, and finally, a match between the mother's preferred and actual situation, i.e. returning to work versus staying home (Cutrona and Troutman, 1986; Dyer, 1963; Hobbs, 1965; Hobbs and Cole, 1976; Levitt, Weber and Clark, 1986; Ross, Mirowsky and Huber, 1983; Russell, 1974).

Interpersonal factors are also important determinants of adjustment in the transition to parenthood. A positive relationship with one's mother and a low level of interference from family members are associated with positive outcomes (Hobbs, 1965; Levitt, *et al.*, 1986). As will be reviewed in detail in a later section, the availability of both emotional and instrumental social support from a variety of sources is important for adjustment (Cutrona, 1984). However, among married women, the relationship with the husband appears to be the most potent determinant of adjustment to parenthood. The quality of the marital relationship (including supportiveness) has consistently been found to predict level of adjustment among new parents of both genders (Dyer, 1963; Hobbs and Cole, 1976; Levitt *et al.*, 1986; O'Hara, 1985; Paykel, Emms, Fletcher and Rassaby, 1980; Russell, 1974; Stemp, Turner and Noh, 1986; Wandersman, Wandersman and Kahn, 1980).

THE DILEMMA OF DECLINING MARITAL SATISFACTION

The importance of the marital relationship in adjustment to parenthood gives rise to a troublesome dilemma. For women in particular, the birth of the first child is associated with a significant decline in marital satisfaction (Brown, Bhrolchain and Harris, 1975; Miller and Sollie, 1980; Ruble, *et al.*, 1988; Ryder, 1973; Waldron and Routh, 1981). Ninety-three percent of married couples reported more conflict and disagreement postpartum than during pregnancy, in a study by Cowan and Cowan (1987). In this study, marital satisfaction dropped dramatically from the time of birth to six months postpartum, but dropped even more sharply from six to 18 months after delivery. Division of labor appears to be the most frequent topic of disagreement between new parents (Cowan and Cowan, 1987; Ruble *et al.*, 1988). Women whose burden of household chores increases the most from prepartum to postpartum experience the greatest decline in marital satisfaction (Belsky, Lang and Huston, 1986). However, the rewards

of shared household responsibility appear to fall only to the wives. One study found that wives are less depressed if their husbands help with the housework, but that husbands are *not* less depressed as a result of helping (Ross *et al.*, 1983).

IMPLICATIONS FOR SOCIAL SUPPORT

Thus, the exchange of social support between spouses following the birth of the first child involves a number of interesting dynamics. As described above, tangible social support (task assistance) is itself a focus of controversy among new parents. This distinguishes the transition to parenthood from many other stresses which do not involve a long-term increase in shared task responsibilities (e.g. divorce, job loss, death of a friend). Second, the birth of the first child is associated with a decline in emotional closeness or intimacy between spouses (Brown *et al.*, 1975; Ruble *et al.*, 1988). This may interfere with the provision of emotional support to one another in the months following childbirth.

In sum, it appears that social support between spouses in the months following the birth of the first child is complicated by marital dynamics that may render the provision of support somewhat more difficult, especially in the later months of the first year, when the novelty of parenthood and assistance from extended family has diminished. Nevertheless, social support from the spouse appears to be highly effective in buffering new mothers from the stress of the transition to parenthood. Studies are needed that explore changes in the nature of supportive interactions between spouses that occur after the birth of the first child. In particular, it would be informative to gain insight into factors that allow some couples to overcome the difficulties described above and to provide effective social support to one another. In general, the social support field has suffered from a lack of process-oriented research. Studies are needed that consider the effects of relationship conflict, intimacy, quality of communication and other relevant variables that may affect the extent to which individuals are able to provide effective social support to each other.

SOCIAL SUPPORT AND THE TRANSITION TO PARENTHOOD

Adequate social support during the transition to parenthood has been linked to four important outcome variables: maternal psychological health, quality of parenting behavior, maternal physical health and infant developmental outcomes. Findings relevant to the role of social support for each will be summarized below.

MATERNAL PSYCHOLOGICAL HEALTH

Depression is the most frequent psychological problem experienced by childbearing women. In the first week after delivery a high proportion

(33–70 percent) experience transitory postpartum 'blues', which typically resolve within a week or two (Handley, Dunn, Waldon and Baker, 1980; Yalom, Lunde, Moose and Hamburg, 1968). More serious and persistent depressions are experienced by 5–15 percent of women in the first six months after delivery (Cutrona, 1983; Kumar and Robson, 1984; O'Hara and Zekoski, 1988). A very small proportion (one or two per 1000 deliveries) experience a psychotic episode after the birth of a child (Kendell, Chalmers and Platz, 1987).

Studies have rarely tested the association between social support and diagnosable clinical depression. Instead, they have tested for correlations between social support and self-reported symptoms of number and severity of depressive symptoms or other related measures of adjustment (e.g. anxiety, emotional distress, life satisfaction). This is an important distinction, because the role of social support in the etiology of diagnosable depression remains speculative, although a consistent relation has been found between high levels of social support and low levels of subjective distress.

Studies differ considerably in the rigor of their methods. Some studies employ cross-sectional designs, in which both social support and depressive symptoms are assessed at the same point in time. These should be interpreted with caution, because women who are suffering from depressive symptoms at the time of the assessment are likely to evaluate their social networks more negatively than those who are not depressed, in part because of the negative cognitive bias that is inherent in depression (Beck, Rush, Shaw and Emery, 1979). Even longitudinal studies are subject to the effects of depressive bias. If a woman is depressed at the initial assessment she is likely to evaluate her social network in a negative manner. If her depression continues through the follow-up assessment an apparent relation between low initial social support and subsequent depression will be found. This association may reflect nothing more than continuing depression. A more rigorous test of the etiological contribution of social support to depression is to measure social support and depression at the initial assessment, and to statistically control for initial depression in analyses that test initial social support as a predictor of subsequent depression (e.g. using multiple regression or partial correlation techniques).

Two studies were located that tested for a possible link between deficient social support and diagnosable postpartum depression. Nine weeks after delivery, women suffering from a diagnosable depression reported lower levels of instrumental support (assistance with household tasks and childcare) and emotional support from their spouses than did nondepressed women (O'Hara, 1986). Depressed women said that they did not feel able to talk freely to their husbands, and that they could not rely on their husbands for help with childcare. Dissatisfaction with support from parents and in-laws, but not with that from friends, was also expressed more frequently by the depressed women. Although these concurrent associations between spouse support and diagnosable depression were significant, no prospective relation between pregnancy spouse support and postpartum depression was found.

Among childbearing adolescents (80 percent unmarried), those who reported during pregnancy that they could rely on their parents and the baby's father for help (reliable alliance) were less likely to suffer a significant clinical depression following delivery (Cutrona, 1988). This association was significant when appropriate statistical controls for initial diagnostic status were employed. No other types of social support (e.g. attachment, esteem support, guidance) were predictive of depression, nor was support of any type from friends.

Turning next to studies of depressive symptomatology, in almost every study that assessed specific sources of social support (e.g. husband, parents, friends), social support from the spouse was found to predict lower levels of depressive symptoms and/or higher life satisfaction. This pattern was found for all cross-sectional analyses (Crnic *et al.*, 1983; Crnic, Greenberg, Robinson and Ragozin 1984; Levitt *et al.*, 1986; O'Hara, 1986; Paykel *et al.*, 1980; Tietjen and Bradley, 1983) and most longitudinal analyses (Crnic *et al.*, 1984; Cutrona, 1988; Stemp *et al*, 1986; Wandersman *et al.*, 1980), although two longitudinal studies failed to find a significant association between spousal support, assessed during pregnancy, and postpartum adjustment (O'Hara, 1986; Tietjen and Bradley, 1983). In four studies that assessed support from multiple sources, spousal support was the only significant predictor of the new mother's emotional well-being (Crnic *et al.*, 1984; Levitt *et al.*, 1986; Stemp *et al.*, 1986; Tietjen and Bradley, 1983). Thus, the bulk of evidence supports the importance of a supportive relationship with the spouse in the transition to parenthood, although longitudinal studies provide less consistent results.

A few studies also found social support from sources other than the spouse to predict mental health following delivery. Findings regarding the effects of friendship support are mixed. Women who reported that they had a confiding relationship with someone other than their spouse were less likely to report depressive symptoms, in a study by Paykel *et al.* (1980). However, two studies found that women who received high levels of support from their friends during the transition to parenthood were *more* depressed (O'Hara, 1986; Tietjen and Bradley, 1983). The latter studies were interpreted as reflecting deficient spousal support, which necessitated reliance on friends.

Studies of adolescent mothers, many of whom are not married, are of particular interest in understanding how mothers cope when they do not have a designated 'helpmate' such as a spouse. Social support during pregnancy from both family and friends (but not from the baby's father) were associated with greater life satisfaction and lower anxiety one month after delivery in a sample of rural low-income teenaged mothers (Unger and Wandersman, 1986). As reported above, Cutrona (1988) also found that social support from parents was a significant deterrent against postpartum depression among adolescent mothers, along with social support from the baby's father. Thus, it appears that among very young mothers, social support from the girl's own parents is a valuable resource, as well as support from friends. Although the absence or unreliability

of the baby's father may account for the greater importance of family and friends to the adjustment of adolescent mothers, the developmental level of these individuals must also be borne in mind. It may be that, even among married adolescent mothers, a greater degree of reliance on family and friends would be found.

It is not enough to know the most effective *source* of social support for individuals undergoing the transition to parenthood. It is also necessary to determine what *kinds* of support are most helpful in enhancing women's mental health in the context of childbearing. Not all studies include separate assessments of specific support components, but it is hoped that more investigators will employ multi-dimensional models of social support in the future, so that interventions can be designed that are tailored to the specific support needs of individuals facing specific kinds of stress.

In a longitudinal study of 85 adult, married, first-time mothers, Cutrona (1984) assessed six components of social support during pregnancy as predictors of postpartum depressive symptoms (guidance, reliable alliance, social integration, reassurance of worth, attachment and opportunity to provide nurturance). Statistical controls for initial level of depression were employed in all analyses. Results showed that guidance was important in the first two weeks after delivery, but that social integration became the strongest deterrent of depressive symptoms by eight weeks postpartum. When women were first coping with the unfamiliar tasks of infant care, the availability of advice and information was crucial; however, by the time they had been in the parenting role for two months, a sense of belonging and integration was key.

Several other studies have found a similar pattern of results, in that both instrumental support (advice and tangible assistance) and emotional support (reassurance of caring, esteem and belonging) appeared to protect women against depressive symptoms (Giblin, Poland and Sachs, 1987; Glaser, 1987; O'Hara, 1986; Paykel *et al.*, 1980). However, some studies have found only one or the other category of social support to protect against emotional distress. Emotional support was the only significant correlate of adjustment in two studies (Norbeck and Tilden, 1983; Wandersman *et al.*, 1980); whereas instrumental support was the only significant correlate of adjustment in two other studies, both of which dealt with childbearing adolescents (Boyce, Schaeffer and Uitti, 1985; Cutrona, 1988), whose skills, knowledge and tangible resources are typically deficient, thus necessitating instrumental assistance from others. For older mothers, many of whom are well supplied with the basic necessities of life, emotional support and the sense that their partner is doing his 'fair share' may suffice.

PARENTING AND INFANT OUTCOMES

In a seminal work, developmental psychologist Uri Bronfenbrenner (1979) contends that child development occurs in a social context that can dramatically

influence the quality of the child's experience and subsequent outcomes. He emphasizes that this context is broader than the mother–child dyad, and includes the nuclear family, extended family, friendship network, institutional network and societal framework in which the child lives. Cochran and Brassard (1979) have argued that the mother's social support resources can have both direct and indirect effects on the child's development, indirectly through enhancing the mother's adjustment and parenting skill, and directly through the child's contact with individuals in the mother's social network. Citing work on antecedents of altruism, Cochran and Brossard reason that when the mother's own psychological needs are met by her support system, she is then more likely to recognize and meet the needs of her child.

In this section, research linking social support to parenting attitudes and behaviors, and to the developmental outcomes of infants, will be reviewed. This is an area that is attracting considerable attention, with social support a key variable in many developmental studies.

Among low-income, rural, adolescent mothers, anxiety in the parenting role was lower among those with adequate social support from both family and friends during pregnancy, and from the baby's father one month after delivery (Unger and Wandersman, 1986). More competent parenting behavior was observed among adolescents who received childcare assistance from the baby's father and who had relatives living nearby. Better infant developmental outcomes were associated with overall level of perceived social support and childcare assistance from the baby's father, and from the baby's grandmother.

In a longitudinal study of preterm and full-term mother–infant pairs, a number of parenting and infant variables were related to the adequacy of the mother's social support resources, especially support from the spouse (Crnic *et al.*, 1983, 1984; Crnic and Greenberg, 1987). Significant concurrent correlations were found between intimate (spousal) and community supportiveness and satisfaction with parenting at one, eight and 18 months after delivery. Maternal enjoyment and responsiveness while interacting with her infant were correlated with intimate support at four months, community support at eight months, and both intimate and community support at 12 months (Crnic *et al.*, 1984). Maternal intimate support was also associated with greater infant responsiveness and positive emotional tone at four months of age. However, neither community nor intimate support was significantly associated with measures of infant cognitive and language development at any time point.

In a study of infant–mother attachment, Crockenberg (1981) found that infants, especially those rated high on irritability, showed more secure attachment to mothers who reported high levels of social support. Results were interpreted as evidence that social support has its greatest impact when families are under stress; in this case the stress of a temperamentally difficult infant. However, Levitt *et al* (1986) found no relation between social support from any source and security of infant attachment.

Cutrona and Troutman (1986) found that women with temperamentally difficult infants tended to have less confidence in their ability as parents and reported more depression three months after delivery, but that those with high levels of social support were protected from both of these negative effects.

To summarize, evidence is compelling for a relation between social support and positive attitudes towards parenting, such as self-confidence, enjoyment and satisfaction with the parenting role. Regarding the most important sources of support, positive parenting outcomes seem to be less specific to the spouse than maternal mental health outcomes. Women whose spouses, families and friends are available to them feel more comfortable and capable as mothers, perhaps benefiting from the knowledge and advice of more experienced parents. Not only parenting attitudes, but actual behaviors, such as responsivity of mother and child to one another, have been linked to maternal social support. This suggests that the caring which is communicated to the mother by her supportive providers finds expression in her relationship with her infant. The data are inconsistent regarding the role of social support in the security of mother–infant attachment. There is some evidence that social support can protect against the deterioration of attachment that may occur when the family is under stress, but further research is needed to confirm this association. Finally, evidence is particularly weak regarding a link between maternal social support and the cognitive and motor development of the infant, with a single study finding a significant association. It may be that the dimensions of parental behavior that are influenced by social support have a specific effect on the child's social development rather than on the child's cognitive or motor development. Research is needed on the effects of maternal social support on the child's social development to test this hypothesis.

PHYSICAL HEALTH

One of the most widely cited studies in the social support literature documented a dramatic difference between women high and low on psychosocial assets in complications of pregnancy (Nuckolls, Cassel and Kaplan, 1972). In this study an interaction between number of stressful life events and psychosocial assets was found, such that among women who had experienced many stressful events, those with low psychosocial assets were found to have a 91 percent rate of pregnancy complications; whereas those high in psychosocial assets had only a 33 percent rate of complications. It should be noted, however, that social support was only one component of 'psychosocial assets', which also encompassed measures of personality and attitudes towards the pregnancy.

In a replication of the Nuckolls *et al.* (1972) study, Norbeck and Tilden (1983) attempted to determine whether social support alone had the same effect on complications of pregnancy and delivery. Although the effect was not as strong as that found by Nuckolls *et al.* (1972), a significant interaction was found between

tangible social support and life stress during pregnancy for three types of pregnancy complications. In an experimental intervention, low-income Guatemalan women who were assigned a supportive companion who stayed with them throughout labor had significantly shorter labors (among those without complications) and fewer perinatal complications, including fewer Cesarean sections and fewer infants admitted to intensive care (Klaus, Kennell, Robertson and Sosa, 1986). Among childbearing adolescents, Cutrona, Troutman, and Engeldinger (1989) found that degree of emotional closeness to the labor partner was correlated with number of perinatal complications. Regardless of whether the baby's father, the girl's mother or another relative was present during labor, a high degree of closeness to that individual (rated during pregnancy) was associated with fewer complications. In another study, more anesthesia during labor and delivery was required by women who were highly anxious and had low social support (Barnett and Parker, 1986). However, Boyce *et al.* (1985) found no relation between emotional or tangible support and perinatal complications. Finally, fewer postpartum illnesses were reported among women with high levels of instrumental support in the first six months following delivery (Lenz, Parks, Jenkins and Jarrett, 1986).

These studies provide mounting evidence that social support can positively influence physical well-being among childbearing women. A number of processes may account for this relationship. First, women who have high levels of support during pregnancy may seek prenatal care earlier and more regularly. In support of this hypothesis, emotional support from the baby's father was positively correlated with number of prenatal clinic visits in a study of urban pregnant adolescents (Giblin *et al.*, 1987). When the social network is caring and responsive, women may be more likely to follow through on medical regimens, and may eat more nutritious meals, both because of reminders from others, and because of an enhanced sense of self-worth (Cohen, 1988). During labor and delivery the woman may reap the benefits of better prenatal care and nutrition. She may also experience less fear and be better able to relax and cooperate with the physician's instructions during labor and delivery if she is accompanied by someone she trusts. After the child is born, women who have others they can count on for assistance may avoid exhaustion and feelings of demoralization, which may in turn allow their immune systems to function with maximum effectiveness (Cohen, 1988).

IMPLICATIONS FOR FUTURE RESEARCH

MARITAL INTERACTION AND SOCIAL SUPPORT

The most consistent finding in the social support literature on the transition to parenthood is the importance of social support from the spouse, especially in promoting positive mental health among new mothers. Women who can rely

upon their husbands for both emotional support (encouragement, comfort, affection) and assistance with childcare and household responsibilities are much less likely to become depressed following childbirth than those who lack these resources. However, achieving this kind of partnership is not easy. The marital interaction literature documents a marked decline in marital satisfaction, especially for women, following the birth of the first child. Arguments often center around the division of labor (Cowan and Cowan, 1987; Ruble *et al.*, 1988). Thus one of the most important components of social support, instrumental assistance, is itself a topic of controversy.

The birth of a child brings a dramatic increase in responsibility to the household. Managing this added responsibility appears to pose a major test of the marital relationship. It is of interest that virtually all *concurrent* analyses find that higher support from the spouse is associated with more positive outcomes for the new mother, but that spousal support assessed during pregnancy less consistently predicts maternal well-being after the birth of the child (e.g. O'Hara, 1986; Tietjen and Bradley, 1985). One interpretation of this pattern is that husbands who are perceived as supportive and helpful during pregnancy may not continue to provide adequate levels of support when faced with the increased stress of the new infant. In fact, Ruble *et al.* (1988) found that spousal support during pregnancy was significantly higher than that provided following delivery.

Cultural tradition reinforces the primary role of the mother in childcare. In the United States, only women are guaranteed paid leaves of absence following the birth or adoption of a child. Thus, men are often not permitted to spend a significant amount of time involved in infant care, except evenings and weekends. A gratifying trend away from this pattern is just beginning in the United States, in that some employers are beginning to offer guaranteed paid paternity leaves.

More research is needed on the process of negotiation that occurs following the birth of the first child, regarding both instrumental (childcare and housework) and emotional (providing comfort and encouragement) task allocation between spouses. Systematic investigation of the factors that predict successful readjustment following the addition of a child to the family should include personality variables, characteristics of the marital relationship (e.g. frequency of conflict, similarity of attitudes, communication skill), family resources, nonfamilial childcare options (e.g. childcare centers, babysitters), and employment parameters (e.g. whether both spouses work outside the home, parental leave policies, flexibility of work hours).

CHILDREARING AND PHYSICAL HEALTH

Although a relatively direct link between deficient social support and maternal depression is easy to envision, links between social support and other outcomes

are probably less direct. For example, a correlation between the adequacy of the mother's social support and the behavior of her infant may be mediated by the mood state of the mother and the responsivity of her caretaking behaviors. Similarly, an association between maternal social support and number of obstetric complications may be mediated by health-maintenance behaviors during pregnancy and heightened self-confidence during labor. There is a need to conceptualize and test more complete causal models that incorporate emotional, cognitive, interactional and environmental variables.

The beneficial contribution of supportive relationships with others in the transition to parenthood has been amply documented. However, questions remain regarding the processes through which social support has its effects. It is important to consider multiple factors in trying to understand the process of adjustment to parenthood. It is also important to remember that parenting occurs within many different family contexts (e.g. single-parent, inaccessible extended family), and that different kinds of support sources and resources may be needed as a function of the specific context.

SUMMARY AND CONCLUSIONS

For new mothers, both emotional and instrumental support from the spouse are needed to enhance adjustment and prevent postpartum depression. However, the birth of the first child is frequently associated with increased marital conflict and decreased marital happiness, thus making it difficult for spouses to provide support to one another. Social support is associated with positive attitudes toward parenting, better parenting skills and maternal health, including fewer complications of pregnancy and delivery. Research is needed to further our understanding of factors that facilitate the provision of social support to new parents, and of the mechanisms that link social support to positive outcomes.

REFERENCES

Barnett, B. and Parker, G. (1986) Possible determinants, correlates and consequences of high levels of anxiety in primiparous mothers. *Psychological Medicine*, **16**, 177–185.

Beck, A. T., Rush, A. J., Shaw, B. F. and Emery, G. (1979) *Cognitive Therapy of Depression*. New York: Guilford Press.

Belsky, J., Lang, M. and Huston, T. L. (1986) Sex-typing and division of labor as determinants of marital change across the transition to parenthood. *Journal of Personality and Social Psychology*, **50**, 517–522.

Boyce, W. T., Schaefer, C. and Uitti, C. (1985) Permanence and change: psychosocial factors in the outcome of adolescent pregnancy. *Social Science and Medicine*, **21**, 1279–1287.

Brofenbrenner, U. (1979) Contexts of childrearing: problems and prospects. *American Psychologist*, **10**, 844–850.

Brown, G. W., Bhrolchain, M. N. and Harris, T. (1975) Social class and psychiatric disturbance among women in an urban population. *Sociology*, **9**, 225–254.

Cochran, M. M. and Brassard, J. A. (1979) Child development and personal social networks. *Child Development*, **50**, 601–616.

Cohen, S. (1988) Psychosocial models of the role of social support in the etiology of physical disease. *Health Psychology*, **7**, 269–297.

Cohen, S. and Wills, T. A. (1985) Stress, social support, and the buffering hypothesis. *Psychological Bulletin*, **98**, 310–357.

Cowan, C. P. and Cowan, P. A. (1987) A preventive intervention for couples becoming parents. In C. F. Z. Boukydis (ed.), *Research on Support for Parents and Infants in the Postnatal Period.* Norwood, NJ: Ablex, pp. 225–251.

Crnic, K. A. and Greenberg, M. T. (1987) Transactional relationships between perceived family style, risk status, and mother–child interactions in two-year-olds. *Journal of Pediatric Psychology*, **12**, 343–362.

Crnic, K. A., Greenberg, M. T., Ragozin, A. S., Robinson, N. M. & Basham, R. B. (1983) Effects of stress and social support on mothers and premature and full-term infants. *Child Development*, **54**, 209–217.

Crnic, K. A., Greenberg, M. T., Robinson, N. M. and Ragozin, A. S. (1984) Maternal stress and social support: effects on the mother–infant relationship from birth to eighteen months. *American Journal of Orthopsychiatry*, **52**, 224–235.

Crockenberg, S. B. (1981) Infant irritability, mother responsiveness and social support influences on security of mother–infant attachment. *Child Development*, **52**, 857–865.

Cutrona, C. E. (1983) Causal attributions and perinatal depression. *Journal of Abnormal Psychology*, **93**, 378–390.

Cutrona, C. E. (1984) Social support and stress in the transition to parenthood. *Journal of Abnormal Psychology*, **93**, 378–390.

Cutrona, C. E. (1988) Social support and the incidence of major and minor depression among childbearing adolescents. Paper presented at the annual meeting of the Midwestern Psychological Association, Chicago, IL. (May).

Cutrona, C. E. and Troutman, B. R. (1986) Psychosocial outcomes of adolescent pregnancy: maternal and child effects. *Seminars in Adolescent Medicine*, **2**, 235–242.

Cutrona, C. E., Troutman, B. R. and Engeldinger, J. (1989) Social support in pregnancy and effects on outcomes among primiparous adolescent mothers. Paper presented at the meetings of the International Society for Psychsomatic Obstetrics and Gynecology, Amsterdam (May).

Dyer, E. D. (1963) Parenthood as crisis: a re-study. *Journal of Marriage and Family Living*, **25**, 196–201.

Giblin, P. T., Poland, M. L. and Sachs, B. A. (1987) Effects of social supports on attitudes and health behaviors of pregnant adolescents. *Journal of Adolescent Health Care*, **8**, 273–279.

Glaser, K. (1987) A comparative study of social support for new mothers of twins. In C. F. Z. Boukydis (ed.), *Research on Support for Parents and Infants in the Postnatal Period.* Norwood, NJ: Ablex, pp. 41–60.

Handley, S. L., Dunn, T. L., Waldon, G. and Baker, J. M. (1980) Tryptophan, cortisol and puerperal mood. *British Journal of Psychiatry*, **136**, 498–508.

Hobbs, D. F. (1965) Parenthood as crisis: a third study. *Journal of Marriage and the Family*, **27**, 367–372.

Hobbs, D. F. and Cole, S. P. (1976) Transition to parenthood: a decade replication. *Journal of Marriage and the Family*, **38**, 723–731.

Kendell, R. E., Chalmers, J. C. and Platz, C. (1987) Epidemiology of puerperal psychoses. *British Journal of Psychiatry*, **150**, 662–673.

Klaus, M. H., Kennell, J. H., Robertson, S. S. and Sosa, R. (1986) Effects of social support during parturition on maternal and infant morbidity. *British Medical Journal*, **293**, 585–587.

Kotelchuck, M. (1976) The infant's relationship to the father: experimental evidence. In M. E. Lamb (ed.), *The Role of the Father in Child Development*. New York: John Wiley & Sons, pp. 58–81.

Kumar, R. and Robson, K. M. (1984) A prospective study of emotional disorders in childbearing women. *British Journal of Psychiatry*, **115**, 797–805.

LeMasters, E. E. (1957) Parenthood as crisis. *Marriage and Family Living*, **19**, 352–355.

Lenz, E. R., Parks, P. L., Jenkins, L. S. and Jarrett, G. E. (1986) Life change and instrumental support as predictors of illness in mothers of 6-month-olds. *Research in Nursing Health*, **9**, 17–24.

Levitt, M. J., Weber, R. A. and Clark, M. C. (1986) Social network relationships as sources of maternal support and well-being. *Developmental Psychology*, **22**, 310–316.

Miller, B. C. and Sollie, D. L. (1980) Normal stresses during transition to parenthood. *Family Relations*, **29**, 459–465.

Norbeck, J. S. and Tilden, V. P. (1983) Life stress, social support, and emotional disequilibrium in complications of pregnancy: a prospective, multivariate study. *Journal of Health and Social Behavior*, **24**, 30–46.

Nuckolls, K. B., Cassell, J. and Kaplan, B. H. (1972) Psychosocial assets, life crisis, and the prognosis of pregnancy. *American Journal of Epidemiology*, **95**, 431–441.

O'Hara, M. W. (1986) Social support, life events, and depression during pregnancy and the puerperium. *Archives of General Psychiatry*, **43**, 569–573.

O'Hara, M. W. (1985) Depression and marital adjustment during pregnancy and after delivery. *American Journal of Family Therapy*, **13**, 49–55.

O'Hara, M. W. and Zekoski, E. M. (1988) Postpartum depression: a comprehensive review. In R. Kumar and I. F. Brockington (eds), *Motherhood and Mental Illness: causes and consequences* Guildford: Butterworths, pp. 17–63.

Paykel, E. S., Emms, E. M., Fletcher, E. J. and Rassaby, E. S. (1980) Life events and social support in puerperal depression. *British Journal of Psychology*, **136**, 339–346.

Ross, C. E., Mirowsky, J. and Huber, J. (1983) Dividing work, sharing work, and in-between: Marriage patterns and depression. *American Sociology Review*, **48**, 809–823.

Ruble, D. N., Fleming, A. S., Hackel, L. S. and Stangor, C. (1988) Changes in the marital relationship during the transition to first time motherhood: effects of violated expectations concerning division of household labor. *Journal of Personal and Social Psychology*, **55**, 78–87.

Russell, C. S. (1974) Transition to parenthood: problems and gratifications. *Journal of Marriage and the Family*, **36**, 294–302.

Russell, G. and Radin, N. (1983) Increased paternal participation: The father's perspective. In M. E. Lamb and A. Sagi (eds), *Fatherhood and Family Policy*. Hillsdale, NJ: Lawrence Erlbaum, pp. 149–165.

Ryder, R. G. (1973) Longitudinal data relating marriage satisfaction and having a child. *Journal of Marriage and the Family*, **35**, 604–606.

Stemp, P. S., Turner, R. J. and Noh, S. (1986) Psychological distress in the postpartum period: the significance of social support. *Journal of Marriage and the Family*, **48**, 271–277.

Tietjen, A. M. and Bradley, C. F. (1985) Social support and maternal psychosocial adjustment during the transition to parenthood. *Canadian Journal of Behavioral Science*, **17**, 109–121.

Unger, D. G. and Wandersman, L. P. (1985) Relationship of social support and social networks to the adjustment of adolescent mothers. *Journal of Social Issues*, **41**, 29–45.

Waldron, H. and Routh, D. K. (1981) The effect of the first child on the marital relationship. *Journal of Marriage and the Family*, **43**, 785–788.

Wandersman, L., Wandersman, L. and Kahn, S. (1980) Social support in the transition to parenthood. *Journal of Community Psychology*, **8**, 332–342.

Yalom, I. D., Lunde, D. T., Moos, R. H. and Hamburg, D. A. (1968) 'Postpartum blues' syndrome: a description and related variables. *Archives of General Psychiatry*, **18**, 16–27.

8 Transitional Stress in Children and Young Adolescents Moving to New Environments

ERIC M. VERNBERG
University of Miami

and

TIFFANY FIELD
Mailman Center for Child Development, University of Miami

INTRODUCTION

Transitions are an integral part of the life experience of children and adolescents. Normative transitions, such as starting school and moving from elementary school to middle school or junior high, serve as important markers of change in roles, expectations and privilege. These transitions are, for the most part, predictable in timing and sequence, and occur almost universally in western cultures. Nonnormative transitions, such as residential relocation, reassignment to new schools, and changes in the family due to divorce or illness, also serve as markers of change in important aspects of a child's life. Although most children and adolescents experience at least some transitions of this type, the timing and sequence of these transitions are more idiosyncratic and the meaning more ambiguous. These differences notwithstanding, both types of transitions place adaptational demands on children and adolescents, and thus are likely to produce a certain amount of stress.

The purpose of this chapter is to provide a framework for understanding children's responses to life transitions and to apply this framework to the relatively understudied transitions of changing schools and residential relocation. These two transitions are notable for requiring major changes in the child's extrafamilial relationships (e.g. friends, teachers) and day-to-day settings. Both have received far less attention from researchers than have transitions involving separation from primary attachment figures, such as hospitalizations (e.g. Bowlby,

On the Move: the Psychology of Change and Transition. Edited by S. Fisher and C. L. Cooper.

Robertson and Rosenbluth, 1952; Field and Reite, 1984, Rutter, 1981), divorce (Hetherington, 1981; Wallerstein, 1983; Emery, 1988), and bereavement (Bowlby, 1980; Furman, 1974; Rutter, 1966), perhaps because they are less dramatic in comparison. None the less, these transitions do indeed pose a variety of adaptational challenges for children and their families, and are worthy of greater scrutiny.

CONCEPTUALIZING CHILDHOOD TRANSITIONS

As described elsewhere in this volume, several conceptual models can be applied to the understanding of transition and change (e.g. attachment theory, control theory). A common element emerging from these various models is the idea that the individual involved in the transition is faced with a number of tasks which make demands on his or her adaptive resources. Some of these tasks are psychological, such as accepting the loss of an important person, activity, or object (cf. Wallerstein, 1983). Others are social or interpersonal, such as establishing new friendships and relationships with teachers. Still others are physical, such as performing new behaviors required in a new role or setting. The particular model used to conceptualize a given transition directs one's attention to the tasks most likely to be crucial to the successful negotiation of the transition, although certain tasks may emerge across models. The delineation of major tasks or challenges posed by a transition is a necessary step in understanding how children may be affected by a move, a change of school and so forth. Once major tasks accompanying a transition are identified, attention can be turned to identifying the multiple factors that influence how successfully these tasks will be accomplished. Informed by a clear understanding of these two steps, guidelines can be established for knowing how and, most importantly, when to intervene to facilitate the successful negotiation of a transition or event. Complicating this three-part process is the recognition that developmental differences exert influences at each step.

This three-component process for organizing information (identifying major adaptational tasks, specifying factors influencing successful negotiation, deciding when and how to intervene) is more complete for some transitions than for others. Separations due to hospitalizations, for example, have been viewed profitably as potentially disruptive to the attachment process (Rutter, 1981). One task facing the hospitalized child, from this perspective, is to maintain the security provided in a primary attachment relationship during the hospitalization. Access to an attachment figure may be particularly important as the child faces a variety of novel experiences, many of which are uncomfortable or painful. Data pertaining to the second step come from studies suggesting that longer hospital stays (over one week) and repeated admissions are associated with subsequent increases in behavioral distress, especially if the hospitalizations occurred

between the ages of six months and four years (Rutter, 1981). Using this information the sensible solution of providing more continuous access to a primary attachment figure during hospitalizations of children during this age range has been widely adopted.

In contrast to the case of hospitalization, empirical evidence pertaining to the three components suggested above is less well developed when applied to the issues of school change and relocation. In the subsequent sections the knowns and unknowns regarding transition stress associated with changing schools and residences will be described.

TASKS OF THE CHILD

As with many transitions, relocating and changing schools place the dual demands of leaving familiar settings and entering new ones. A major, two-part challenge for children undergoing these transitions is to separate from familiar peers and to form new peer relationships in the new setting. Despite the frequent reference to strong peer attachments in children, separations between peers and the subsequent establishment of new relationships are rarely studied.

For younger children, studies on monkey infant peer separations (Reite, Harbeck and Hoffman, 1981; Suomi, Collins and Harlow, 1976) and peer separations in preschool children (Field, 1984) and infants (Field, Vega-Lahr and Jagadish, 1984) suggest that the disorganizing effects of separations are not limited to mother-infant dyads. In a study by Reite and his colleagues, two pigtail infant monkeys who had been reared together showed behavioral and physiological disorganization following their separation (Reite *et al.*, 1981). Just as in other studies on infants separated from their mothers, agitated behavior followed separation, with increases in activity and vocalizations. Subsequently, both infants showed a decrease in play behavior and an altered cellular immune response. The impaired cellular immune function and agitated behaviors noted in these infant monkeys suggest that significant behavioral and psychological changes accompanied the separations of young primate peers.

Infants and toddlers as young as 15 months old also appear to experience distress when separated from their peers (Field *et al.*, 1984). In this study, 15-month-old infants, following 14 months in an infant nursery, were transferred to a toddler nursery, and 24-month-old infants were graduated from a toddler nursery to a preschool nursery. During the week immediately preceding the transfer and the week following the transfer (as opposed to baseline data collected one month prior to the transfer), infants and toddlers showed increases in activity level, wandering about aimlessly and fantasy play. Increases were also noted in fussiness, physical aggression and physical affection. Naptime sleep became more irregular, with longer latencies to sleep, more crying during sleep and less time spent sleeping. The parents and teachers noted changes in eating and

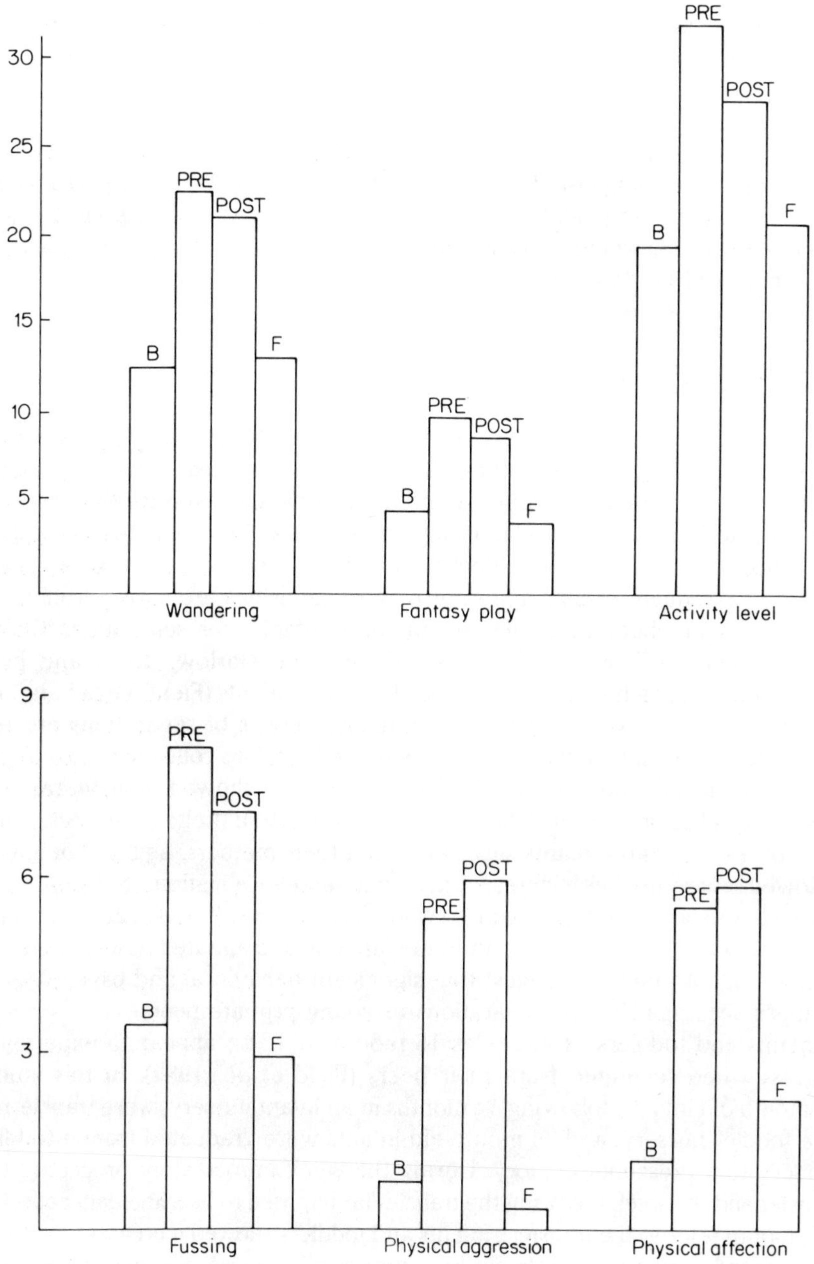

Figure 8.1. Proportion of infant/toddler play time that wandering and fantasy play occurred, activity level (actometer measure), and proportion of time that fussing, physical aggression and physical affection occurred during baseine (B), pre-separation (Pre), post-

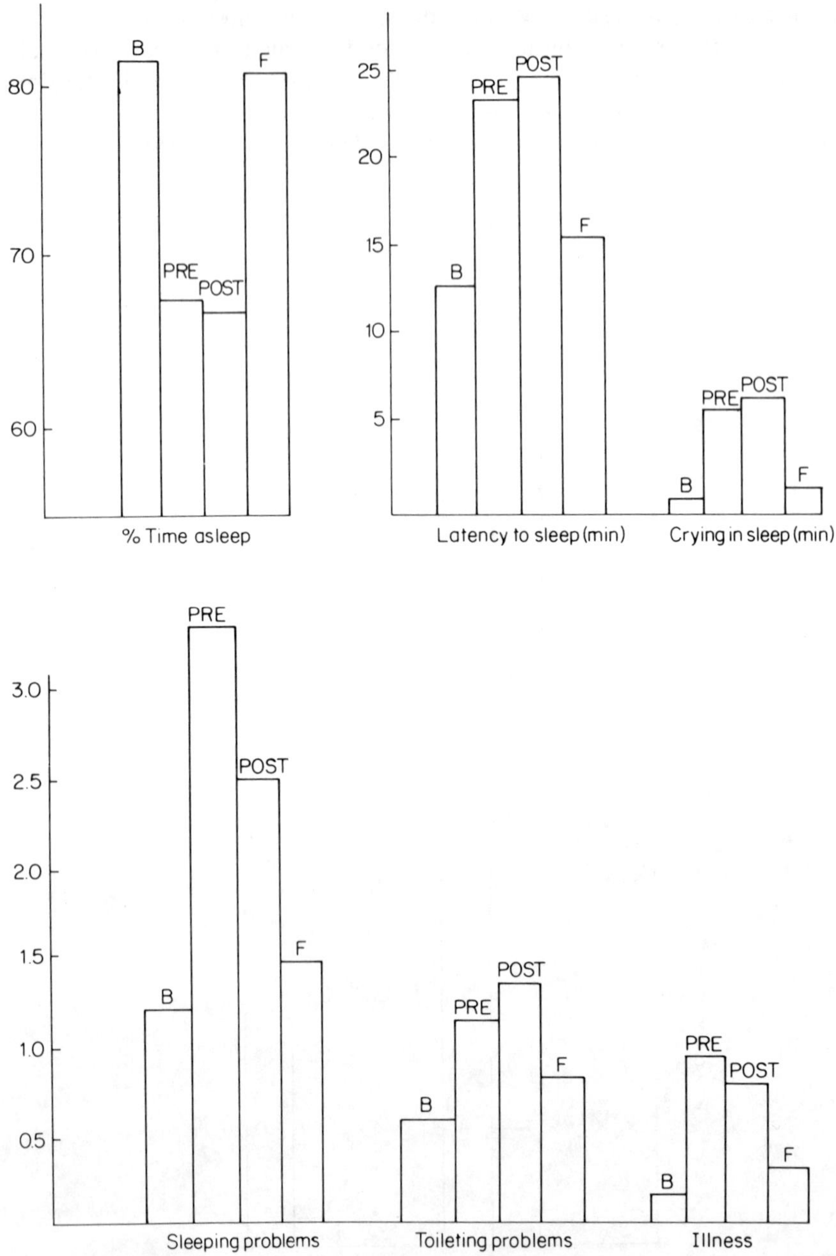

separation (Post) and follow-up (F) play observation periods. Percentage of naptime spent asleep, latency to sleep (minutes) and mean number of sleeping problems, toileting problems and illnesses during these periods.

sleeping patterns as well as a greater incidence of absenteeism (see Figure 8.1). A comparison between the infants and toddlers suggested that the toddlers experienced greater changes in their behaviors during the period just prior to the transfer to the new nursery, suggesting that the toddlers were experiencing more anticipatory distress than the infants. This is not surprising inasmuch as

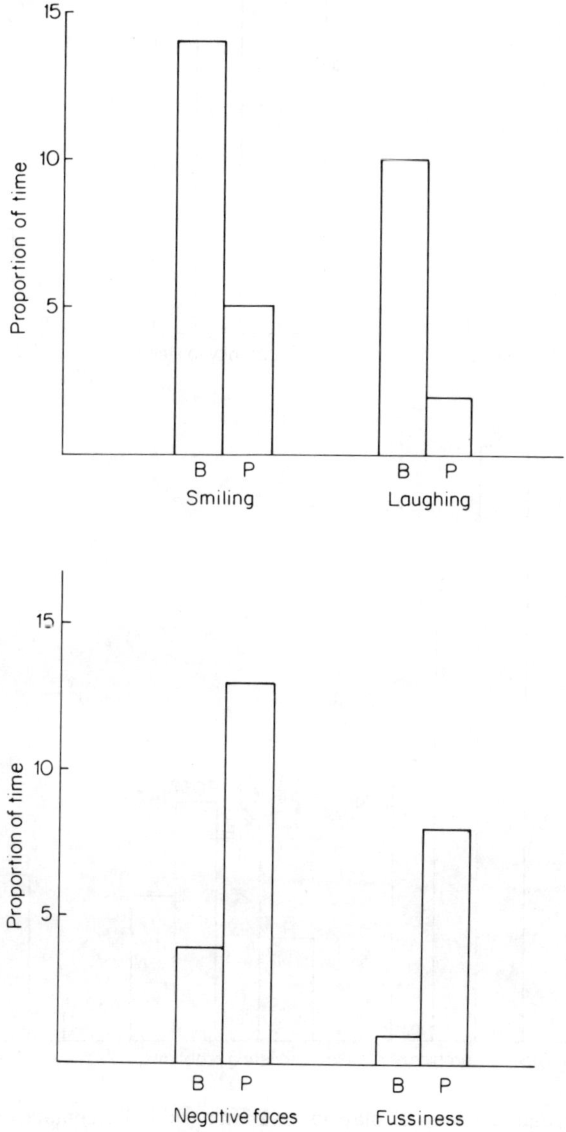

Figure 8.2.

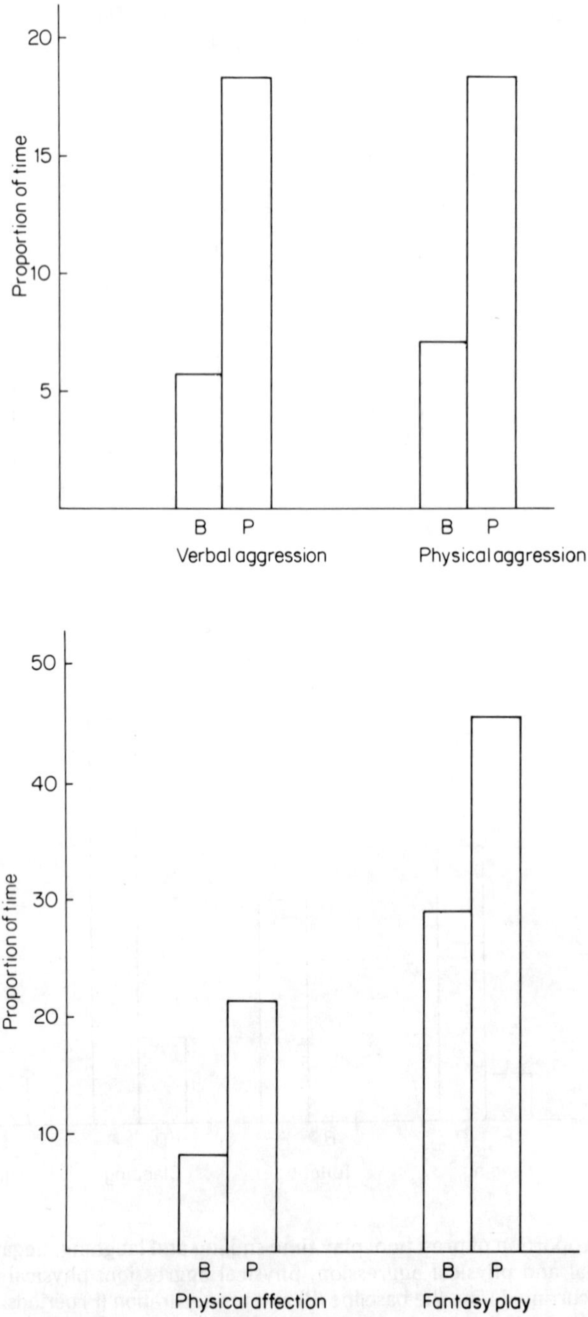

Figure 8.2. (*continued*)

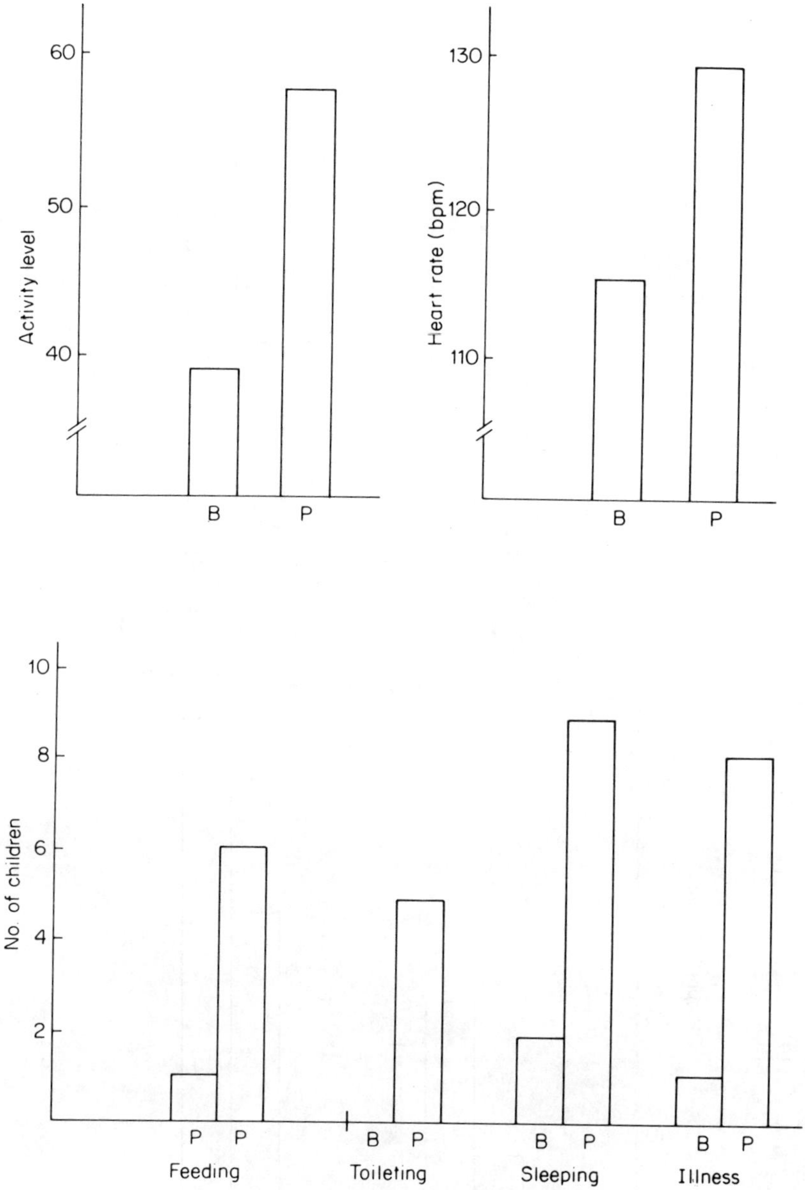

Figure 8.2. Proportion of preschool play time smiling and laughing, negative faces and fussiness, verbal and physical aggression, physical aggression, physical affection and fantasy play occurring during the baseline (B) and pre-separation (P) periods. Mean activity level and heart rate in beats per minute (BPM) and number of children experiencing feeding, toileting, sleeping and illness problems during these periods.

the toddlers had experienced a transfer of this kind nine months earlier, when they moved from the infant to the toddler nursery, a transfer which they may have remembered.

Similar findings have been reported for older preschool children. In one study, preschool children who were transfering to new schools after having been classmates for three to four years were observed during a two-week period prior to separation from their classmates (Field, 1984). The children who were leaving the school showed increases (compared to baseline observations three months earlier) in fantasy play, physical contact, negative statements and affect, fussiness, activity level, tonic heart rate and illness, as well as changes in eating and sleeping patterns (see Figure 8.2). In addition to the changes in play behaviors and in vegetative functions, the children's drawings of themselves manifested agitation and disorganization (see Figure 8.3). The drawings included distorted facial and body parts and sad faces. Shortly after the children's departure, this agitated behavior appeared to diminish in the children who were leaving the school.

The anticipatory reactions to separations by these children appeared to mimic the immediate responses to peer separations in young monkeys (Reite *et al.*, 1981). They were also very similar to those behaviors noted in young children immediately following the hospitalization of their mothers for the birth of another child (Field and Reite, 1984). In these studies the increase in fussiness, negative affect, aggressive behavior, physical activity level and tonic heart rate are suggestive of agitation. Other similarities across studies include changes in eating, as well as sleep disturbances and more frequent illness. Although changes in eating patterns were variable, with some children eating more and others eating less, as has also been noted following mother–child separations (Field and Reite, 1984), sleep disturbances were uniformly similar across these studies, with more frequent night-wakings, crying and delayed onsets of sleep. Increased illness, in this study and in the study on mother–child separation, is consistent with reports of changes in the immune system of young primates during mother and peer separations (Reite *et al.*, 1981; Reite and Snyder, 1982).

Although elevated tonic heart rate may be mediated by increases in activity (Obrist, 1981), both activity level and heart rate increases, as well as sleep disturbances, have been attributed to activation of the sympathetic andrenergic system (Breese *et al.*, 1973). Because these behavioral changes have been noted in active coping situations, in contrast to passive coping situations, the data were interpreted as active coping on the part of the child. That the children leaving the school appeared to experience an anticipatory reaction to the impending separation whereas young primates show these behavioral changes only subsequent to the separation can, of course, be attributed to the children's cognitive abilities. Their cognitive awareness of the impending separation may have been enhanced by preparatory remarks and discussion by their parents and teachers. Although these data are confounded by the potential anxiety

(a)

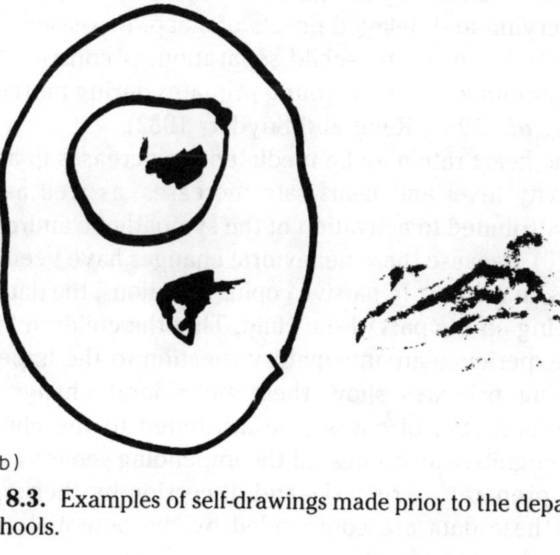

(b)

Figure 8.3. Examples of self-drawings made prior to the departure of children attending new schools.

associated with attending a new school, this confound may be instructive. The children who were leaving the school did not appear to experience the biphasic process of agitation followed by depression, as had occurred in the mother-child separation study. Of course there were no reunions and altered relationships to contend with, which seemed to contribute to the children's depression in the mother-child separation study. But in addition, the anxiety related to attending a new school and making new friends may have counteracted the expected decrease in beta-adrenergic activity and associated depression. Perhaps the stressfulness of the situation presented active coping opportunities.

The studies by Field and her colleagues present a picture of behavioral and physiological disruption around the period of transfer to a new school. Far less is known about these reactions to transitions involving peer separations during the elementary and junior high school years. Data pertaining to anticipatory anxiety are almost completely lacking, although there are some data to suggest that the process of leaving old friends and entering new peer settings is the most salient aspect of residential relocation during the elementary school years. In one study asking 10–12-year old Swedish children to report their greatest concerns about moving, 80 per cent worried about making new friends or leaving old friends, whereas fewer than 35 percent reported concerns about school work, and fewer than 25 percent worried about teachers or other problems (Schaller, 1974). Rakieten (1961) obtained similar results in her study of third- through sixth-graders in the New Haven, Connecticut, area. In this study almost all children reported concerns about how peers would accept them, whereas relatively few worried about the schoolwork or other aspects of moving.

School-aged children's emotional adjustment following a move or change of schools has also received relatively little empirical attention. Although a number of authors have suggested that these changes sometimes trigger increases in psychiatric symptomatology (Schaller, 1972; Tooley, 1970), a large-scale study of the adjustment of children and adolescents following a long-distance move found no evidence, based on mothers' responses to a set of questionnaires, of increased behavioral distress for this group compared to the general population on which the Louisville Behavior Checklist (Miller, Barrett, Hampe and Noble, 1971) was normed (Barrett and Noble, 1973). Further investigation of this issue is clearly needed, perhaps including self-report measures from the children and teacher ratings.

There is some evidence to indicate that the task of establishing satisfactory peer relationships following relocation is difficult for a number of older children and young adolescents. Over 30 percent of the mothers of older children and adolescents (11–18 years old) in the Barrett and Noble (1973) study reported that their child found it difficult to make friends after moving, compared to only 10 percent of mothers of younger children (6–10 years old).

A more recent study utilized self-report, parent-report, and observational measures of seventh- and eighth-graders who began the academic year in a new

school due to change of residence versus classmates who had lived in the same residence for at least the previous two years (Vernberg, 1990a). Measures were taken three months after the beginning of school, and again at the end of the year. The recently mobile adolescents, compared to their residentially stable counterparts, had less contact with peers (see Figure 8.4) and less intimacy and sharing in their relationship with their best friend throughout the year (see Figure 8.5). Boys who had moved, but not girls, also reported more frequent incidents of rejection (operationalized by self-reports of having been teased or 'picked on' in a mean way and having been hit or threatened in a mean way) by peers compared to the comparison groups of nonmobile adolescents (see Figure 8.6). This study suggested that relocation during this age range might expose adolescents to a more difficult array of experiences than does residential stability. These experiences may not be entirely positive, in that a number of the relocating adolescents went through an extended period of diminished contact with peers and, in the case of boys, increased rejection.

FACTORS INFLUENCING SUCCESSFUL NEGOTIATION OF TASKS

Children, just as adults, vary in the manner that they respond to stressful situations. Variations in response occur on a number of dimensions, ranging from differences in physiological reactions to differences in purposeful attempts to cope with stress (see Compas, 1987, for a recent review). Some of the differences

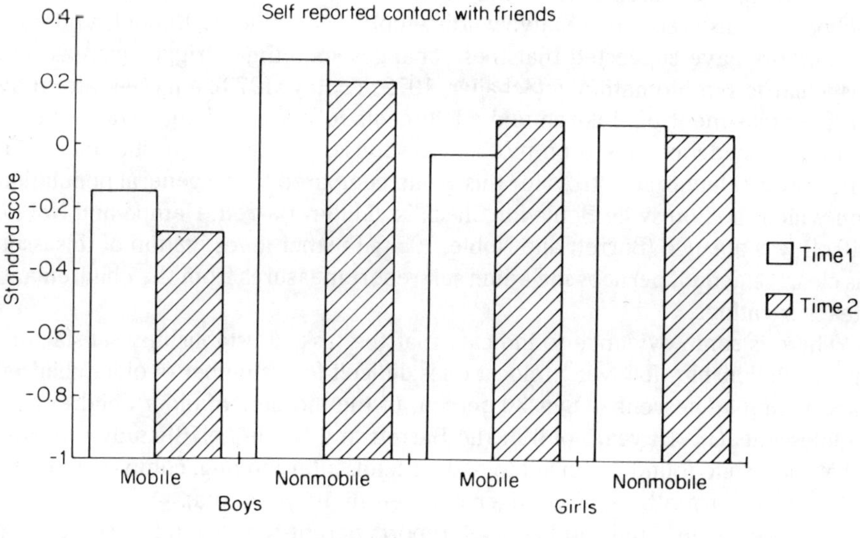

Figure 8.4.

in response to stressors have to do with dispositional characteristics of the child, and others with various aspects of their environment (Lazarus and Folkman, 1984). In the current context it is helpful to consider factors that seem likely to make transitions go smoothly for some children but less smoothly for others.

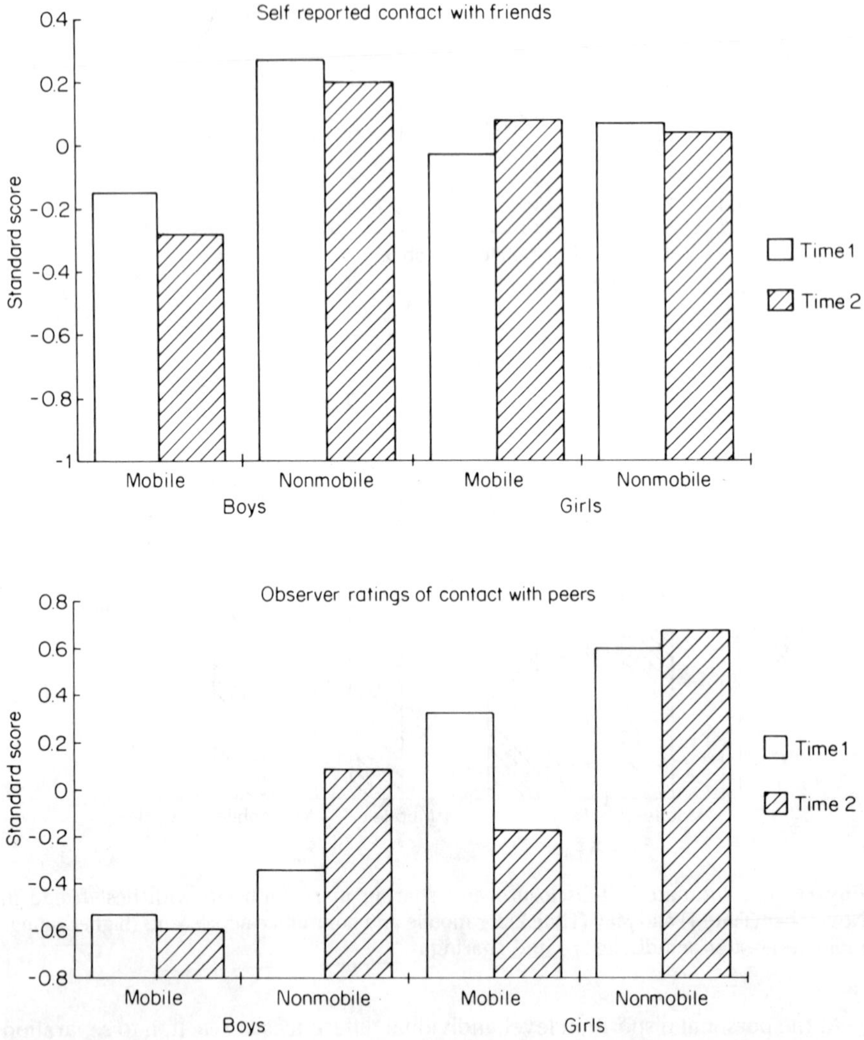

Figure 8.4. Self-report, parent-report, and observer ratings of contact with friends in November (Time 1) and May (Time 2) for seventh- and eighth-graders who began the year in a new school (Mobile) or were residentially stable for at least the prior two years (Nonmobile).

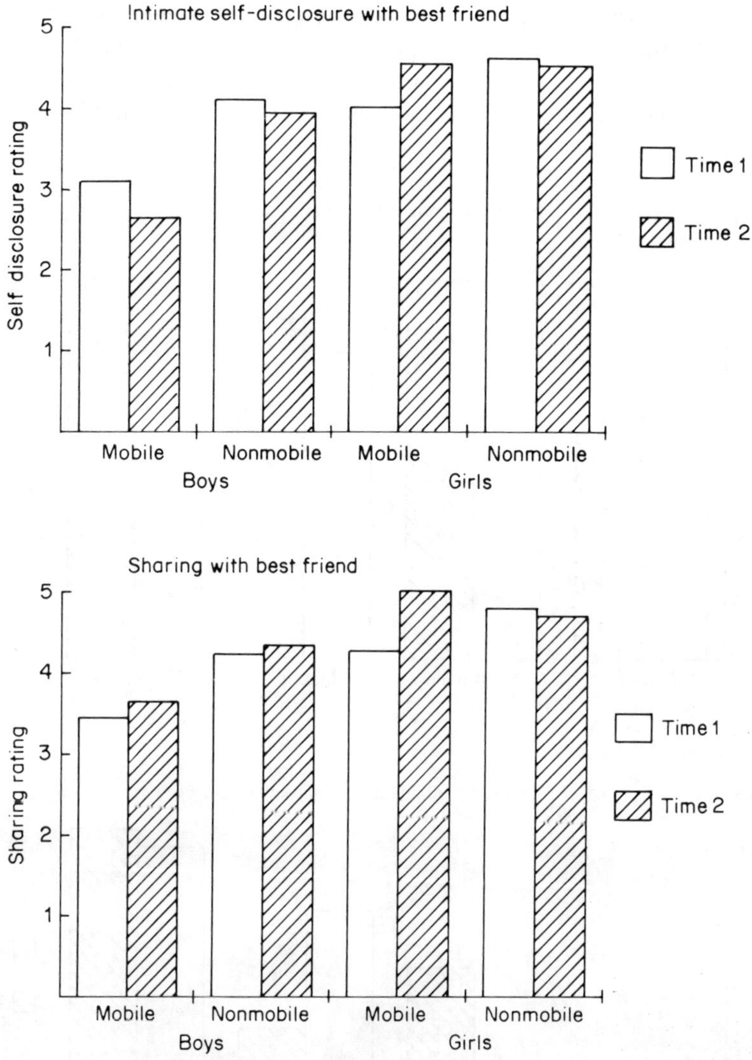

Figure 8.5. Intimate self-disclosure and sharing in relationship with best friend in November (Time 1) and May (Time 2) for mobile and nonmobile adolescents (higher ratings indicate greater self-disclosure and sharing).

At the personal disposition level, individual differences in reaction to separation from peers during early childhood have been found on the dimension of internalizing (physiologically reactive) versus externalizing (behaviorally reactive) response styles (Field *et al.*, 1984). As can be seen in Figure 8.7, the externalizers in that study spent more time engaging in fantasy play and showed a higher

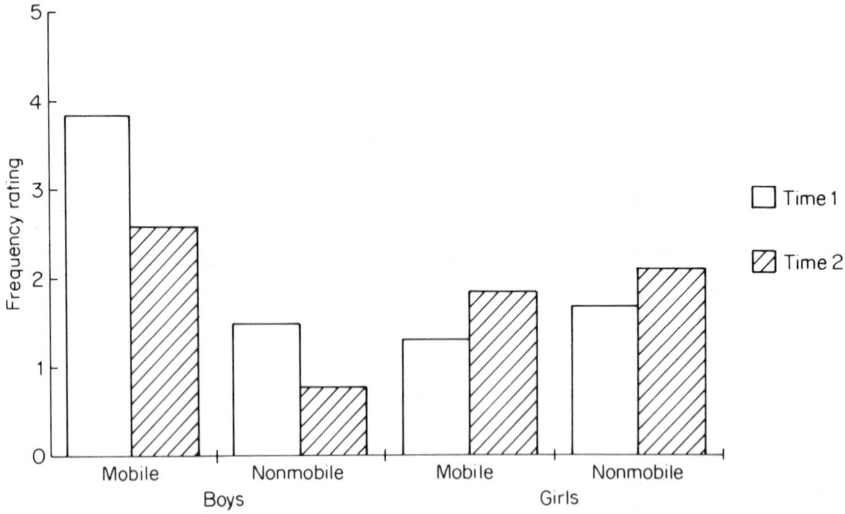

Figure 8.6. Rejection experiences for mobile and nonmobile adolescents from the beginning of school year through November (Time 1) and from January through May (Time 2). Rejection experience scores based on sum of six-point frequency estimates (none, once, two or three times, four or five times, once a week, a few times a week, every day) for being teased/picked on and hit/threatened.

level of activity, as well as a higher level of physical aggression and physical affection, while the internalizers showed a greater number of awakenings during naptime, and experienced more eating problems and illness than the externalizing children.

This difference in response style, which has been described in older children in the context of divorce (Hetherington, 1981), has potentially important ramifications for the child as he or she goes through the biphasic process of leaving old friends and establishing new peer relationships. More extreme manifestations of stress-induced externalizing behavior may make entry into new groups more problematic, as difficulties inhibiting socially undesirable behaviors such as aggression appear to contribute to rejection by peers, particularly in early and middle childhood (Parker and Asher, 1987). Externalizing symptoms also place the child at risk for conflict with adults, thus compounding problems by leading to increases in the use of aversive behavior management techniques and sanctions against the child (Hetherington, 1981). More extreme internalizing responses also pose some risks for the child in transition. Obviously, eating and sleeping problems and illnesses are unpleasant symptoms in and of themselves, and compound the task of maintaining physiological and psychological equilibrium. There is also evidence to suggest that depressive symptoms, at least by middle childhood and early adolescence, make children appear less desirable as friends and more likely to

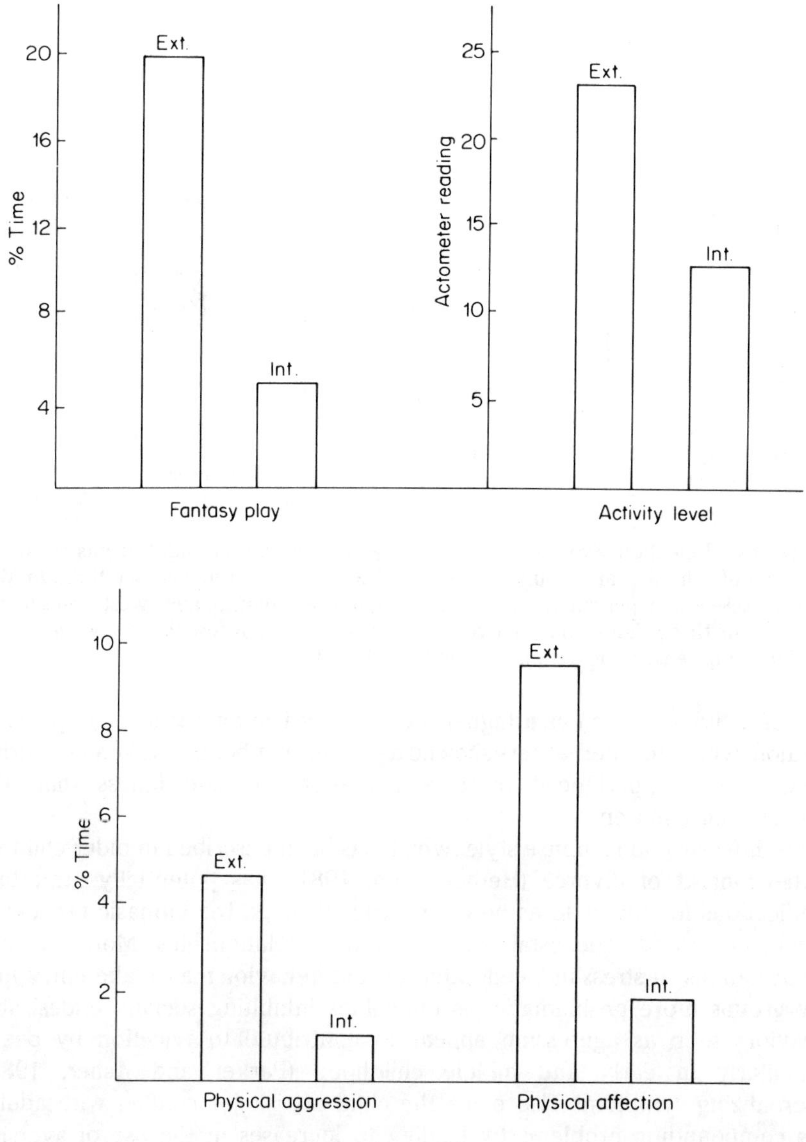

Figure 8.7.

be rejected by peers (Peterson, Mullins and Ridley-Johnson, 1985). In a prospective analysis using the sample of seventh and eighth-graders described earlier (Vernberg, 1990a), for example, depressive symptoms during the first measurement period were predictive of increases over time in rejection experiences, even after controlling for initial level of rejection (Vernberg, 1990b).

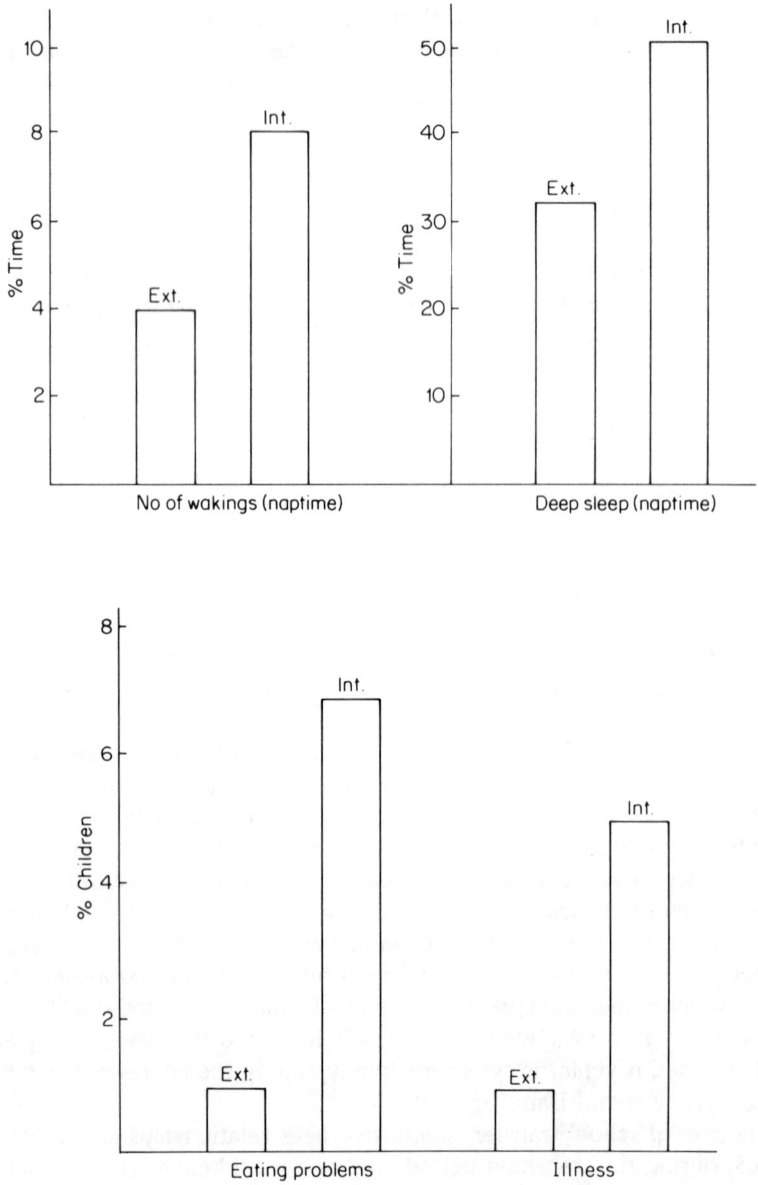

Figure 8.7. Proportion of post-separation play time infants and toddlers who were externalizers (Ext.) or internalizers (Int.) spent engaged in fantasy play, mean activity level (actometer reading), proportion of play time spent engaging in physical aggression and physical affection, number of wakings and deep sleep during naptime, and percentage of infants/toddlers who experienced eating problems and illness.

At the same time, less contact with friends, less intimacy with a best friend, and greater rejection experiences during the first measurement period contributed to increases in depressive affect over time, even after taking into account initial levels of depressive affect. Taken together, these results support a pattern of reciprocal causation in which internalizing symptoms contribute to rejection by peers, and rejection by peers and poorer-quality friendships contribute to increases in depressive symptoms.

In addition to individual variations in reactions to separations and stressors associated with entering new settings, the availability of supportive relationships during transitions is likely to influence a child's adaptation. Supportive relationships potentially serve at least three broad functions for the child in transition: enhancing decision-making and problem-solving, providing an opportunity for shared pleasurable activity and intimacy and regulating deviant behavior (Rook, 1985). Families are likely to provide a major source of many types of social provisions (Furman and Buhrmester, 1985), and a child's reliance on family members seems likely to increase during transition periods, particularly if the transition involves a loss of extrafamilial social networks. From this reasoning one would expect transitions to be more difficult for children who lack access to strongly supportive relationships within the family, either due to chronically poor intrafamilial relationships or temporary circumstances which diminish access to important sources of support. In the divorce literature, for example, a close, stable relationship with the custodial parent appears to afford some protection from extreme distress to children following marital separation, and factors that contribute to diminished support from parents (e.g. parental depression, time constraints) are also linked to poorer post-divorce adaptation (Emery, 1988). Empirical evidence pertaining to these expected effects is less available, although not entirely nonexistent, in the literature on relocation and school transfer. In Vernberg's sample of early adolescents who relocated, greater adolescent-reported social support within the family was associated with less self-reported depression over the nine months following a move (Vernberg and Daugherty, 1988). Factors thought to contribute to diminished availability of parental support, including greater numbers of concomitant stressful life events and living in one- versus two-parent households, were associated with greater parent-reported psychiatric symptomatology among the adolescents who had moved (Vernberg and Daugherty, 1988).

In the case of school transfer, supportive peer relationships are sometimes available during the transition period, and one would expect this availability to make adjustment to the new school less problematic. Evidence to support this expectation for young children is found in a comparison between infants and toddlers who were transferred to new nurseries without close friends versus those who were transferred with close friends (Field *et al.*, 1984). As can be seen in Figure 8.8, those infants and toddlers who were transferred with close friends showed less fussiness and less physical aggression, but more physical affection

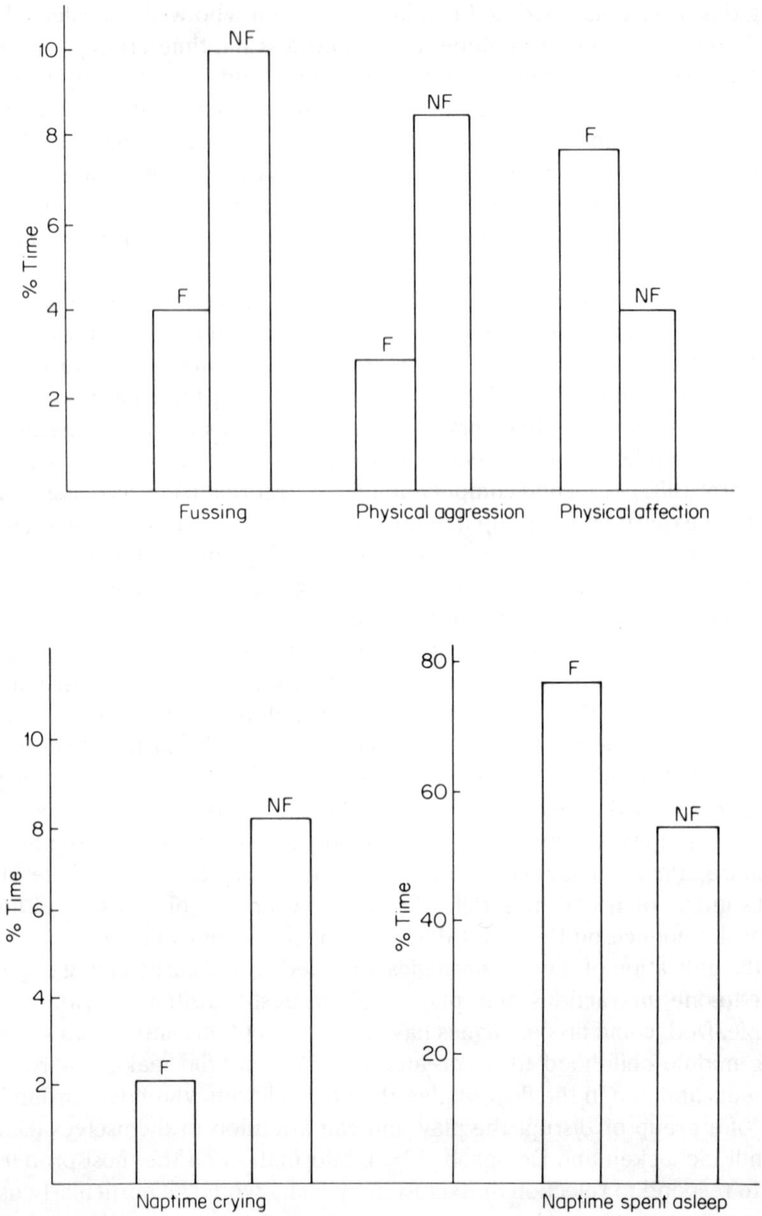

Figure 8.8. Proportion of post-separation play time infants and toddlers transferred with close friends (F) or without close friends (NF) spent fussing and showing physical aggression and physical affection, crying during naptime and sleeping during naptime.

during this transitional period. In addition, children who were transferred with close friends spent more naptime asleep and less naptime crying.

Less detailed information is available for older children regarding the effects of having a close friend present after a school transfer, although there are ample reasons to believe that making a transfer with old friends would be helpful. For example, seventh-graders who saw themselves as having made a 'good start' following the normative transition from elementary school to junior high attributed their success most frequently to the presence of old friends (Mittman and Packer, 1982).

Support from within a new setting is also likely to play a role in the manner in which a transition is experienced. In an experimental study addressing this factor directly, Felner and his colleagues carried out an intervention to ease the transition from junior to senior high by restructuring the role of homeroom teachers to make these teachers the primary administrative-counseling link between the students, their parents and the rest of the school (Felner, Ginter and Primavera, 1982). A second component included reorganizing class assignments so that the experimental group members stayed with homeroom classmates in each of four primary academic subjects. At the end of the ninth grade, experimental participants compared to control group students had better grades and attendance records, more positive self-concepts, and perceived the school environment as more clearly organized and the teachers as more supportive.

Specific skills or attributes may also contribute to the ease with which a transition is made. Greater attractiveness (Langlois and Stephan, 1977) and athletic ability (Krebs and Adinolfi, 1975) have been found to be modest correlates of popularity by middle childhood, although neither was predictive of peer experiences following relocation in Vernberg's sample of relocating adolescents (Vernberg and Daugherty, 1988). Skills in social problem-solving (see Spivack and Shure, 1985, for a review) might also be expected to play a role in the establishment of friendships following a move or school transfer, although empirical evidence on this point does not appear to be available. In a similar vein, the utilization of specific strategies for entering and participating in groups or one-to-one interactions may play a role in post-transition adjustment. For example, Dodge and his colleagues have found acceptance into group activities during middle childhood to be greater for children who make task-relevant comments and join in the flow of play than for children who hover around the edges of a group or disrupt the play and call attention to themselves (Dodge, Schlundt, Schocken and Delugach, 1983). Information on the most productive ways to respond to rejection or exclusion by peers would be particularly useful in the context of school change and relocation in light of the evidence that the incidence of these experiences may be increased for older boys who have moved (Vernberg, 1990a).

The degree of change between new and old settings also seems likely to affect the ease of a transition. Dramatic changes in rules, norms or values make mastery

of a new setting more difficult, especially if the new norms, rules and values are not explicit. Following divorce, for example, failure to enforce familiar rules and major differences in rules between paternal and maternal households are associated with decrements in child adjustment (Hetherington, Cox and Cox, 1982). In changing schools it is reasonable to expect the degree of change in rules, norms and values to be greater for longer-distance as opposed to shorter moves. Consistent with this expectation, poorer experiences with peers during the nine months following a move increased as the distance moved increased in Vernberg and Daugherty's (1988) sample of early adolescents. In one telling example from this study, a 13-year-old boy who reported great difficulty establishing friendships after moving related ruefully how playing ice hockey had provided a major source of companionship, pleasurable experience and peer approval in his rural Vermont home. His knowledge and skills in this sport won him no friends in his new home in a southeastern city with neither an ice rink nor widespread interest in ice hockey!

Finally, inner resources, such as positive self-esteem, a sense of self-efficacy (Bandura, 1981), and internal locus of control (e.g. Connell, 1985), seem likely to contribute to the manner in which a transition unfolds. The beneficial effects of these qualities may be seen in at least two important ways. First, higher levels of these resources may make a child more resistant to distress in the face of adverse circumstances (Garmezy, 1983). Second, persistence in the face of failure (e.g. rejection by peers) may be more likely for children with higher levels of these resources (cf. Dweck and Wortman, 1982).

HOW AND WHEN TO INTERVENE

The question of how and when to intervene to prevent or relieve distress during life transitions is sure to arise in any discussion of transition stress. Studies of young children undergoing a school transfer demonstrate the disorganizing effects of separation from peers at both a behavioral and physiological level. A sizeable proportion of older children seem to struggle with the task of forming new friendships after relocating, with many lagging behind more residentially stable peers on measures of peer relationships for at least nine months following a move (Vernberg, 1990a). Should parents and professionals try to ease transitions? How should this occur?

The answers to these questions, as suggested in the introduction, lie in developing a clear understanding of the nature of the adaptive tasks facing children during specific transitions and of factors influencing the successful negotiation of these tasks. Young children undergoing a school transfer, for example, must cope with anticipatory anxiety, much of which seems related to the impending separation from familiar peers and teachers. During the pre-transfer period some disruption in the children's behavioral and physiological

functioning is likely to occur and it may be helpful for parents and teachers to recognize the impending transfer as a cause of this change. Awareness of this phenomenon may allow caretakers to maintain greater patience when confronted with disruptive behavior by a normally compliant child or withdrawal by a typically engaging child. It may also prove helpful to provide some means of expressing thoughts and feelings (e.g. drawings, directed discussions) on topics made salient by the transfers, such as leaving old friends or entering a new school. With older children who relocate or transfer schools, some difficulties in establishing new friendships may be anticipated, and in the case of boys, increases in active rejection may occur. Normalizing these experiences by providing information that these are frequently occurring consequences of relocating may help an older child maintain positive self-perceptions by attributing these potential difficulties to situational rather than personal factors. At the same time it may be possible to help the older child establish new friendships by helping to develop strategies for solving interpersonal problems or by setting the stage for friendships to develop (e.g. enabling participation in group activities with peers, providing an opportunity for one-to-one interaction with peers).

More intensive interventions seem best reserved for children who are likely to encounter particular difficulty over the course of a given transition, and interventions are most likely to be helpful when targeted specifically towards those aspects of the child or environment that lead to distress or dysfunction. The importance of these points can be seen in the history of social skills intervention programs for socially neglected or rejected children, as there has been increasing movement away from globally applied interventions in favor of interventions targeted to the specific difficulties facing a given child (Furman and Robbins, 1985; Ladd, 1985). This trend in intervention is in part the result of careful evaluation studies showing less generalization and maintenance of treatment effects than expected to aspects of functioning and other settings not specifically targeted.

In the case of school transfer and relocation, transition stress may be exacerbated by a number of factors, including temperamental characteristics such as a tendency towards extreme physiological or behavioral reactivity when stressed; a chronic or temporary absence of warm and supportive relationships; high levels of concurrent stressful life events; deficits in social, cognitive or physical skills; extreme changes in norms, values and rules; and a paucity of inner resources such as positive self-esteem or self-efficacy. Further empirical efforts are clearly needed to develop efficient and effective methods of targeting for intervention children who are likely to experience significant difficulties during these transitions. Although it is possible, based on currently available information, to make relatively well-informed predictions as to what constitutes a picture of risk, systematic investigation of children and adolescents undergoing school change and residential relocation is needed to develop a solid empirical

base for knowing how and when to intervene at the level of primary prevention (i.e. before significant distress or dysfunction occurs).

Finally, controlled evaluations of efforts to facilitate the successful negotiation of a change of schools or residences are sorely needed. Although a number of intuitively appealing intervention programs have been suggested or carried out (Cornille, Bayer and Smyth, 1983), only a few have utilized randomly assigned experimental and control groups (Jason *et al.*, 1990; Felner *et al.*, 1982). Among these, greater attention has been paid to academic rather than social goals, even though the process of separating from old friends and establishing new peer networks seems to be one of the most salient and pressing concerns for children and adolescents during these transitions.

SUMMARY AND CONCLUSIONS

The process of leaving familiar settings and entering new ones poses a variety of adaptational challenges for children and young adolescents, and the available evidence suggests that measurable changes in adjustment occur both before and after this type of transition occurs. Separation from familiar peers and adults and the establishment of interpersonal relationships in new settings are prominent features of these transitions. A number of factors seem likely to influence the intensity, duration, and direction of these changes in adjustment, including the developmental level and personal characteristics of the child, the circumstances surrounding the transition period, and various features of the old and new settings.

In organizing the relevant literature along a three component model (identifying major adaptational tasks, specifying factors influencing successful negotiation, deciding when and how to intervene), gaps in our knowledge base become quite apparent. Although some empirical information is available pertaining to each of these three components, the coverage varies greatly for different ages and specific types of transitions. For most ages and most transitions of this type, further research is needed before truly informed decisions regarding preventive interventions can be made.

REFERENCES

Bandura, A. (1981) Self-referent thought: a developmental analysis of self-efficacy. In J. H. Flavell and L. Ross (eds), *Social Cognitive Development: frontiers and possible futures*. Cambridge: Cambridge University Press, pp. 200–239.

Barrett, C. L. and Noble, H. (1973) Mothers' anxieties versus the effect of long distance move on children. *Journal of Marriage and the Family*, **35**, 181–188.

Bowlby, J. (1980) *Attachment and Loss: III: Loss, Sadness, and Depression*. New York: Basic Books.

Bowlby, J., Robertson, J. and Rosenbluth, D. (1952) A two-year-old goes to the hospital. In R. S. Eisler, A. Freud, H. Hartmann and E. Kris (eds), *Psychoanalytic study of the child*, Vol. 7. New York: International Universities Press, pp. 82-94.

Breese, G. R., Smith, R. D., Mueller, R. A., Howard, J. L., Prange, A. J., Lipton, M. A., Young, L. D., McKinney, W. T. and Lewis, J. K. (1973) Induction of adrenal catecholamine synthesizing enzymes following mother-infant separation. *Nature*, **246**, 94-96.

Compas, B. E. (1987) Coping with stress during childhood and adolescence. *Psychological Bulletin*, **101**, 393-403.

Connell, J. P. (1985) A new multidimensional measure of children's perceptions of control. *Child Development*, **56**, 1018-1041.

Cornille, T. A., Bayer, A. E. and Smyth, C. K. (1983) Schools and newcomers: a national survey of innovative programs. *Personnel and Guidance Journal*, **62**, 229-236.

Dodge, K. A., Schlundt, D. C., Schocken, I. and Delugach, J. D. (1983) Social competence and children's sociometric status: the role of peer group entry strategies. *Merrill-Palmer Quarterly*, **29**, 309-336.

Dweck, C. S. and Wortman, C. B. (1982) Learned helplessness, anxiety, and achievement motivation: neglected parallels in cognitive, affective, and coping responses. In H. W. Krohne and L. Laux (eds), *Achievement, Stress, and Anxiety*. Washington, DC: Hemisphere, pp. 93-125.

Emery, R. E. (1988) *Marriage, Divorce, and Children's Adjustment*. Newbury Park, CA: Sage.

Felner, R. D., Ginter, M. and Primavera, J. (1982) Primary prevention during school transitions: social support and environmental structure. *American Journal of Community Psychology*, **10**, 277-290.

Field, T. (1984) Separation stress of young children transferring to new schools. *Developmental Psychology*, **20**, 786-792.

Field, T. and Reite, M. (1984) Children's responses to separation from mother during the birth of another child. *Child Development*, **55**, 1308-1316.

Field, T., Vega-Lahr, N. and Jagadish, S. (1984). Separation stress of nursery school infants and toddlers graduating to new classes. *Infant Behavior and Development*, **7**, 277-284.

Furman, E. (1974) *A Child's Parent Dies: studies in childhood bereavement*. New Haven, NJ: Yale University Press.

Furman, W. and Buhrmester, D. (1985) Children's perceptions of the personal relationships in their social networks. *Developmental Psychology*, **21**, 1016-1024.

Furman, W. and Robbins, P. (1985) What's the point? Issues in the selection of treatment objectives. In B. H. Schneider, K. H. Rubin and J. E. Ledingham (eds), *Children's Peer Relations: issues in assessment and intervention*. New York: Springer, pp. 41-54.

Garmezy, N. (1983) Stressors of childhood. In N. Garmezy and M. Rutter (eds), *Stress, Coping, and Development in Children*. New York: McGraw-Hill, pp. 43-84.

Hetherington, E. M. (1981) Children and divorce. In R. Henderson (ed.), *Parent-Child Interaction: theory, research, and action*. Academic Press, pp. 33–58.

Hetherington, E. M., Cox, M. and Cox, R. (1982) Effects of divorce on parents and children. In M. Lamb (ed.), *Nontraditional Families*. Hillsdale, NJ: Lawrence Erlbaum, pp. 233-288.

Jason, L. A., Betts, D., Johnson, J., Smith, S., Krueckeberg, S. and Cradock, M. (1990). An evaluation of an orientation plus tutoring school based prevention program. *Professional School Psychology* (In press).

Krebs, D. and Adinolfi, A. A. (1975) Physical attractiveness, social relations, and personality. *Journal of Personality and Social Psychology*, **31**, 245-253.

Ladd, G. W. (1985) Documenting the effects of social skill training with children: process and outcome assessment. In B. H. Schneider, K. H. Rubin and J. E. Ledingham (eds), *Children's Peer Relations: issues in assessment and intervention*. New York: Springer, pp. 243-269.

Langlois, J. H. and Stephan, C. F. (1977) The effects of physical attractiveness on children's behavioral attributions and peer preferences. *Child Development*, **48**, 1694-1698.
Lazarus, R. S. and Folkman, S. (1984) *Stress, Appraisal, and Coping*. New York: Springer.
Miller, L. C., Barrett, L. C., Hampe, E. and Noble, H. (1971) Revised anxiety scales for the Louisville Behavior Checklist. *Psychological Reports*, **29**, 503-511.
Mittman, A. and Packer, M. (1982) Concerns of seventh graders about their transition to junior high school. *Journal of Early Adolescence*, **2**, 319-338.
Obrist, P. A. (1981) *Cardiovascular Psychophysiology*. New York: Plenum.
Parker, J. G. and Asher, S. R. (1987) Peer relations and later personal adjustment: Are low-accepted children at risk? *Psychological Bulletin*, **102**, 357-389.
Peterson, L., Mullins, L. and Ridley-Johnson, R. (1985) Childhood depression: Peer reactions to depression and life stress. *Journal of Abnormal Child Psychology*, **13**, 597-609.
Rakieten, H. (1961) The reactions of mobile elementary school children to various elementary school induction and orientation procedures. Unpublished doctoral dissertation, Teacher's College, Columbia University.
Reite, M., Harbeck, R. and Hoffman, A. (1981) Altered cellular immune response following peer separation. *Life Sciences*, **29**, 1133-1136.
Reite, M. and Synder, D. S. (1982) Physiology of maternal separation in a bonnet macque infant. *American Journal of Primatology*, **2**, 115-120.
Rook, K. S. (1985). The functions of social bonds: Perspectives from research on social support, loneliness, and social isolation. In I. G. Sarason and B. R. Sarason (eds), *Social Support: theory, research, and applications*. Dordrecht: Martinus Nijhoff, pp. 243-268.
Rutter, M. (1966) Children of sick parents: an environmental and psychiatric study. *Institute of Psychiatry Maudsley Monographs* (Whole No. 16).
Rutter, M. (1981) Stress, coping, and development: some issues and some questions. *Journal of Child Psychology and Psychiatry*, **22**, 323-356.
Schaller, J. (1972) Residential change and emotional maladjustment in childhood and adolescence: a review of research. *Goteborg Psychological Reports*, **2**, 1-11.
Schaller, J. (1974) Experienced and expected problems reported by children after a family move. *Goteborg Psychological Reports*, **4**(16), 1-12.
Spivack, G. and Shure, M. B. (1985) ICPS and beyond: Centripetal and centrifugal forces. *American Journal of Community Psychology*, **13**, 226-243.
Suomi, S. J., Collins, M. L. and Harlow, H. F. (1976) Effects of maternal and peer separations on young monkeys. *Journal of Child Psychology and Psychiatry*, **17**, 101-112.
Tooley, K. (1970) The role of geographic mobility in some adjustment problems of children and families. *American Academy of Child Psychiatry Journal*, **9**, 366-378.
Vernberg, E. M. (1990a). Experiences with peers following relocation during early adolescence. *American Journal of Orthopsychiatry*, **60**, 466–472.
Vernberg, E. M. (1990b) Psychological adjustment and experiences with peers during early adolescence: reciprocal, incidental or unidirectional relationships? *Journal of Abnormal Child Psychology*, **18**, 187–198.
Vernberg, E. M. and Daugherty, T. K. (1988) Predictors of social experiences and adjustment following relocation during adolescence. Paper presented at the Annual Convention of the American Psychological Association, Atlanta (August).
Wallerstein, J. S. (1983) Children of divorce: the psychological tasks of the child. *American Journal of Orthopsychiatry*, **53**, 230-243.

[illegible] and Hall, [illegible] (19[illegible]) [illegible] physical [illegible] and [illegible] [illegible]

[illegible] Harrell [illegible]

[illegible] (198[illegible]) [illegible] adolescents [illegible]

Oerter, [illegible] [illegible] Developmental Psychology. New York: [illegible]

Parker, J. G. and Asher, S. R. (1987) Peer relations and later personal adjustment: Are low-accepted children at risk? *Psychological Bulletin*, **102**, 357–389.

Peterson, L., Mullins, L. and Ridley-Johnson, R. (1985) Childhood depression: Peer reactions to depression and life stress. *Journal of Abnormal Child Psychology*, **13**, 597–609.

Roskens, R. (1961) The relationships between [illegible] elementary school children [illegible] Unpublished doctoral dissertation, [illegible]

[illegible] H. [illegible] (19[illegible]) [illegible] New York: [illegible]

[illegible] and [illegible] (19[illegible]) [illegible] maternal [illegible] *Journal of* [illegible] *Psychology*, [illegible]

Rook, K. S. (1985) The functions of social bonds: Perspectives from research on social support, loneliness, and social isolation. In I. G. Sarason and B. R. Sarason (eds), *Social Support: Theory, Research, and Applications*. Dordrecht: Martinus Nijhoff, pp. 243–268.

Rutter, M. (1970) Children of sick parents: an environmental and psychiatric study. *Institute of Psychiatry Maudsley Monographs* (Whole No. 16).

Rutter, M. (1981) Stress, coping, and development: some issues and some questions. *Journal of Child Psychology and Psychiatry*, **22**, 323–356.

S[illegible], [illegible] (1972) Residential change and emotional adjustment in childhood and adolescence: A review of research. *Catholic Psychological Record*, **2**, 1–11.

Schaller, J. (1975) The experienced and expected problems reported by children after a family move. *Goteborg Psychological Reports*, [illegible]

Spivack, G. and Shure, M. B. (1985) ICPS and beyond: centripetal and centrifugal forces. *American Journal of Community Psychology*, **13**, 226–243.

Suomi, S. J., Collins, M. L. and Harlow, H. F. (1976) Effects of maternal and peer separations on young monkeys. *Journal of Child Psychology and Psychiatry*, **17**, 101–112.

Tooley, K. (1970) The role of geographic mobility in some adjustment problems of children and families. *Journal of the American Academy of Child Psychiatry*, **9**, 366–378.

Vernberg, E. M. (1990a) Experiences with peers following relocation during early adolescence. *American Journal of Orthopsychiatry*, **60**, 466–472.

Vernberg, E. M. (1990b) Psychological adjustment and experiences with peers during early adolescence: Reciprocal, incidental, or unidirectional relationships? *Journal of Abnormal Child Psychology*, **18**, 187–198.

Vernberg, E. M. and Dougherty, [illegible] K. (1989) Predictors of social experiences and adjustment following relocation during adolescence. Paper presented at the Annual Convention of the American Psychological Association, Atlanta (August).

Wallerstein, J. S. (1983) Children of divorce: the psychological tasks of the child. *American Journal of Orthopsychiatry*, **53**, 230–243.

9 The Psychological Effects of Leaving Home: Homesickness, Health and Obsessional Thoughts

SHIRLEY FISHER
Centre for Occupational & Health Psychology, University of Strathclyde

'I cannot stop thinking about home' (student nurse, f. 19 yrs); 'I am so lonely and lost, I imagine myself to be at home—and then it hurts more' (student, m. 19); 'I stand on the wards and in my head I am at home' (student nurse, f. 21); 'I want to go home so badly that I imagine it all the time and I sometimes believe I am there. It is like living a dream' (mature student, m. 33); 'I was alright until I had a bath and then I thought I was in the bath at home but the towel was in the wrong place, then I found myself crying and shaking and all I could think about was home' (student, f. 20).

INTRODUCTION

Whilst many people leave home for short or long periods, and for different reasons, the majority of those who leave home are youngsters—children, adolescents and young adults. In the British private-sector educational system children as young as seven years old are sent to boarding school, usually in preparation for boarding later in secondary schools. The effects of these early forms of distancing from parents are largely unresearched. Most primary and secondary boarding schools report considerable distress at the initial separation from home at the end of the holidays. For some children the experience is relatively short-lived; for others it is a protracted experience involving considerable distress. The experience recurs across the school years, always following visits home or associated with being ill or punishments at school. Generally less of the school population experiences homesickness as time at the school passes. This has been found to be roughly true for university students (see Fisher, Murray and Frazer, 1985).

Very little is known about the effects of leaving home for short or long periods in the general adult population. This may occur for vocational training, because of commitments to organizations such as the armed services where leaving home

On the Move: the Psychology of Change and Transition. Edited by S. Fisher and C. L. Cooper.

may be part of military training or experience; sabbatical leave from academic, medical or commercial institutions; holidays which are protracted. In all these cases a mature adult may be separated from home and family whether it be parental or marital background. There is also homelessness; people who seek jobs in big cities, who are without financial resources or who have drifted down the social system, may live rough devoid of home contacts or may even have no home. Finally, being institutionalized for crimes committed may create conditions of homesickness compounded by the distress of punishing living conditions and restricted contact with family and friends.

In the above cases very little is known about the experiences which ensue. Many adults have confessed informally that they often experience considerable homesickness and distress but could not admit it to anyone. There may be a large reservoir of unknown distress in the general population, which will increase as job mobility increases. The advent of the single European market will inevitably lead to a greater need to leave home for meetings, conferences or job commitments in Europe. Job mobility may be an increasing aspect of the modern workplace.

If the label 'homesickness' is provided as a label on a scale about 50–70 per cent of most populations endorse it. If the label is not available for endorsement, just under 20 per cent will spontaneously think to use the term to describe their early experiences when newly resident in an institution. This is in spite of the fact that they will describe distress and unhappiness from time to time (see Fisher, Frazer and Murray, 1984). This implies that people do not think to use the term, or that it is not socially acceptable to use it.

In fact evidence (to be published) suggests that homesickness is not socially desirable. It will bias judges against a person if he or she is described as having suffered from it. This is true when intelligence, ability to mix with others, etc., are judged. An important implication of this is that people may be ashamed of adverse experiences when leaving home to become residential elsewhere. There may be grief-like responses which are associated with shame because homesickness is not socially acceptable in the way that bereavement is. This may in part account for the tendency of the homesick to hide themselves away, not making contacts or finding out about the new institution. An apparently counterproductive piece of behaviour may be functional in some respects.

Across a large number of studies there have been no age or sex differences in incidence or level of homesickness reporting. The only exception was in a study of homesickness in an isolated boarding school in the Australian Bush. The students had a year out from normal education to learn to cope with an outward-bound existence. The life was physically demanding. Under these rather special circumstances of 60-mile treks, hard physical labour on the campus and long hours of academic and physical activity, females were more homesick than males. This does suggest that the nature of the current environment may be influential in determining the homesick experience. This argument will be developed further later.

THEORIES WHICH ACCOUNT FOR DISTRESS FOLLOWING TRANSITION

SEPARATION-ANXIETY AND LOSS

Bowlby (1969, 1973) showed that maintenance of a close bond between child and parent creates a sense of security and is particularly sought at times of stress. Threat to the immediate availability of the attachment figure will result in protest and searching, accompanied by distress. Weiss (1975, 1978, 1982) has identified evidence of similar attachment behaviour in adults, within marriages, between close friends or between parent and offspring in adult life. However, although attachment in adults has some characteristics in common with infant attachment, it differs in that the bond involves peer relationships rather than a caretaker relationship. The peer may be fostering the individual's capacity for mastering challenge. Attachment in adults does not appear to overwhelm other activities in the same way that it does in infants, and the focus of attachment, together with the capacity to represent attachment and loss symbolically, are age-related. Weiss (1982) argues that as adolescents move on in their development, there are increasing intervals during which the accessibility of parents is not necessary for feelings of security, although they may require evidence of parental support. However, Weiss notes the similarity of the response to loss across all age levels, and this suggests the operation of a single perceptual emotional system which changes only in the object of focus.

INTERRUPTION OF LIFESTYE

Change is also inextricably linked with interruption. Laboratory studies of interruption have indicated the profound effects that it can have on cognitive systems. Zeigarnic and Lewin (1927) reported enhanced recall of interrupted tasks. Although not all experimental evidence has shown this effect (see Van Bergen, 1968), there is some support for the notion of persistence in cognition of interrupted material.

Laboratory studies by Mandler (1975) have suggested that interrupted tasks create the conditions for raised tension, and when no response is available the consequence is anxiety, distress or fear. Mandler and Watson (1966) state that there is, in addition: (1) persistence toward completion of the interrupted sequence, (2) increased vigour with which the sequence is pursued, (3) substitution of alternative elements or sequences.

There is little direct evidence concerning how the interruption enforced by change and transition in life affects the individual. A possibility is that interruption has a powerful effect because plans which supervise daily routine behaviour remain active, dominating cognition and driving inappropriate activity for the new environment. This might provide a basis for understanding the effects of moves.

The domination of inappropriate plans reduces the resources available for coping with the new environment. It is also conceivable that the sense of separation and loss is triggered and maintained by the dominance of old plans. Thus, perhaps, the separation and interruption mechanisms have mutually reinforcing properties.

REDUCED CONTROL

Transition and change have been argued by Fisher (1986) to result in a period of reduced control, defined as power or mastery of the psychosocial environment. A person must learn about new places, people, routines and procedures. Separation from support offered by family and friends may additionally increase loss of control over a number of immediate problems. Because the post-transition environment is high in novelty, there may also be high demands on the individual. Karasek (1979) reported that, in groups of Swedish and American workers, job strain is reported when demand (workload) is high and discretion (control) is low. The person who experiences loss, including separation from home, could be argued to encounter just this sort of job strain environment.

Fisher (1984) developed a cognitive model of the perception of control in terms of the resolution of the discrepancy between a desired goal and perceived reality. Failure for selected action to be successful implies an unmodified discrepancy in memory. After a series of unsuccessful trials, the unmodified discrepancy will be interpreted as evidence of 'no control' and would trigger the arousal system. In terms of this model the effects of separation might be to create reduced perceived control and an activated arousal system.

ROLE CHANGE AND SELF-CONSCIOUSNESS

A different conceptualization is that transition produces a change in perceived role: one set of commitments ends and a new set is initiated. The necessity of taking on new roles has implications for self-concept. The focus of attention shifts from the environment to the self. The amount of perceived self-focus increases with the strangeness of a new environment (Wickland, 1982). Hormuth (1984) argues that lack of discrepancy between achieved and desired state of self will have a stabilizing function, but if the transition involves the end of a commitment, then the self-concept is not stable. Following a relocation, a person is assumed to be motivated to avoid this adverse state by becoming familiar with the new environment. On this analysis, self-consciousness and striving would be expected psychological effects. Raised anxiety would be concomitant.

HOMESICKNESS, PSYCHOLOGICAL DISTURBANCE AND HEALTH

Studies of university students reporting homesickness (Fisher, Murray and Frazer, 1985; Fisher and Hood, 1987) have indicated that they are distinguished from their

non-homesick counterparts by raised levels of psychoneurotic scores on non-clinical scales such as the Middlesex Hospital Questionnaire (MHQ; Crown and Crisp, 1966) and raised absent-mindedness scores on the Cognitive Failure Questionnaire (CFQ; Broadbent, Cooper, Fitzgerald and Parkes, 1982). Taken collectively, the practical implication is that the homesick person is distressed and likely to behave non-effectively in the new environment. Perhaps not surprisingly, the evidence from both the above studies also indicates poorer adaptation to university life as assessed by the College Adaptation Questionnaire (CAQ; Crombag, 1968).

PSYCHONEUROTIC SYMPTOMS

The Middlesex Hospital Questionnaire was used for the assessment of psychological state because it does not prejudge the types of symptoms which will occur in a particular condition. A range of short subscales include depression, anxiety, phobias, hysteria, obsessionality and somatic symptoms.

As illustrated by Table 9.1, a longitudinal study by Fisher and Hood (1987) showed that, following the transition to university, the symptoms which are elevated in the homesick are depression, obsessional symptoms, somatic symptoms and anxiety. Overall, the level of psychoneurotic symptoms (MHQ) is raised following transition.

Table 9.1. Cognitive failure, mental health, and adjustment profiles before and after the transition in homesick and non-homesick residents[a]

	Not homesick (n=42)		Homesick (n=22)	
	$\bar{x}$	SD	$\bar{x}$	SD
At home				
MHQ1	22.81	(8.6)	29.2[c]	(12.5)
Obsessional (personality)	2.61	(2.2)	3.72[b]	(2.7)
Somatic	3.21	(2.5)	4.54[b]	(2.7)
Depression	1.89	(1.6)	3.82[c]	(2.8)
CFQ1	32.64	(10.66)	36.9 (NS)	(12.3)
Sixth week at university				
MHQ2	23.0	(11.54)	33.04[c]	(14.1)
Anxiety	3.78	(3.1)	6.48[c]	(3.7)
Somatic	2.63	(2.1)	5.17[d]	(2.9)
Depression	2.56	(2.3)	4.48[c]	(3.2)
Obsessional (symptoms)	2.54	(1.6)	3.35[b]	(2.1)
CFQ2	38.21	(11.88)	42.78 (NS)	(13.5)
CAQ	100.69	(17.7)	84.31[d]	(18.2)
DRI	4.0	(3.2)	8.50[d]	(4.2)

[a]As designed by 'not homesick' versus three other categories of 'homesick' on self-rating scale (from Fisher and Hood, 1987).
[b]$P<0.05$.
[c]$P<0.01$.
[d]$P<0.001$.
NS = not significant.
SD = Standard deviation

PHYSICAL HEALTH

As reported above, there are signs that homesickness is associated with ill-health. There are elevated somatic symptoms on both the Middlesex Hospital Questionnaire and the General Health Questionnaire (Fisher and Hood, 1987; Kane, 1987). The latter research indicates an association with somatic symptoms. Table 9.2 shows the results of a study conducted retrospectively, at the end of the first school year on 117 boarding school pupils (all female, ages 11-14 years). The results indicate that there were more days off school for non-traumatic illness for the homesick group as compared with the non-homesick group. Equally, the homesick group had seen a doctor more times. There was no similar difference for the reporting of traumatic ailments such as sprains, breakages, cuts and grazes. This latter finding argues against an explanation in terms of reporting bias.

ABSENT-MINDEDNESS

Studies by Fisher *et al.* (1985) and by Fisher and Hood (1987) showed that cognitive failure levels were significantly raised in those who reported homesickness. Moreover, Fisher and Hood (1987) reported raised cognitive failure scores in all students, following the transition to university (in the context of the longitudinal study referred to in the previous section). However, in this case the raised absent-mindedness score was not significant for the homesick group. Collectively the results support the hypothesis that the transition to university is a stressful experience which creates increased absent-mindedness, and that in general the level of absent-mindedness is likely to be greater in the homesick students. Reports from homesick university students (Fisher *et al.*, 1985)

Table 9.2. Variables associated with homesickness reports for boarding-school pupils (from Fisher *et al.*, 1986)

Variable	Homesick ($n=83$) $\bar{x}$	Homesick ($n=83$) SD	Non-homesick ($n=34$) $\bar{x}$	Non-homesick ($n=34$) SD
Non-traumatic ailments	2.95	1.62	2.38[a]	1.28
Days affected	27.28	45.72	14.53[a]	12.71
Activities affected	3.94	11.59	6.09 (NS)	10.16
Number of times doctor seen	1.88	1.49	1.32[a]	1.17
Traumatic ailments	0.06	0.24	0.09 (NS)	0.29
Days affected	1.95	10.99	1.53 (NS)	5.23
Activities affected	1.95	11.11	0.73 (NS)	3.68
Number of times doctor seen	0.06	0.24	0.09 (NS)	0.29

[a]$p<0.05$.
Note: Larger means indicated higher scores on the attributes listed.
NS=not significant.

indicate that about one-third of the group experienced loss of concentration, had poor attendance at lectures, or handed in work late.

There were also significant positive correlations between the *frequency* measure of homesickness (how frequently homesickness episodes are experienced, as reported on a five-category rating scale) and the degree to which work was reported as affected (0.46), the degree to which there was lack of concentration (0.47), work handed in late (0.42). (All correlations were significant at at least $p<0.05$.)

The explanation of the effect of the transition on level of absent-mindedness is difficult. Since *all* students show a rise in score level following the transition relative to levels at home (Fisher and Hood, 1987) any explanation must take account of this. One possibility is that the transition to university is stressful for all students who undertake it, irrespective of whether they leave home or remain home-based, and that absent-mindedness reflects the increased stress. The second possibility is that leaving home *creates a step-function change in demand*—new faces and locations have to be learned, new procedures and rules have to be mastered because university environments are very different from school environments. Analysis of problems reported by students has indicated that difficulties associated with academic pressures, organizational factors and financial problems are paramount. Maybe cognitive efficiency levels do not change but demand on cognitive systems increases.

SEX DIFFERENCES

With the exception of homesickness reports in an Australian boarding school (Fisher, Elder and Peacock, 1990) homesickness reporting does not generally differentiate the sexes. However, as illustrated in Table 9.3, studies have revealed

Table 9.3. Sex differences in psychoneurotic scores and absent-mindedness in first year students following the transition to university. From Hood, MacLachlan and Fisher (1987)

	Males ($n=189$)		Females ($n=153$)	
	$\bar{x}$	SD	$\bar{x}$	SD
MHQ total	24.1	(10.5)	29.2	(10.9)[b]
Anxiety	3.9	(3.1)	5.9	(3.5)[b]
Obsessional (persons)	2.9	(2.3)	3.1	(2.3) NS
Obsessional (symptoms)	2.6	(1.7)	2.7	(1.6) NS
Somatic	3.2	(2.5)	3.6	(2.5) NS
Depression	6.1	(3.2)	6.1	(3.4) NS
Phobia	2.7	(2.1)	4.3	(2.7)[b]
Hysteria	2.7	(2.5)	3.5	(2.5)[b]
CFQ	38.9	(12.7)	42.3	(13.3)[a]

[a] $p<0.05$.
[b] $p<0.001$.
NOTE: All probabilities are two-tailed.

sex differences in both level of psychoneurotic symptoms and level of cognitive failure; females have raised scores on both sets of measures (Fisher and Hood, 1988; Hood, MacLachlan and Fisher, 1987).

There is substantial research literature in the area of mental disorder which has established that there are sex differences in incidences and magnitude of effect. Department of Health and Social Security figures indicate that about 40 per cent more females than males are psychiatric cases, although there are diagnostic differences. More females than males are likely to be depressed, or to be treated for psychoneurotic symptoms. The difference is greater than 100 per cent (e.g. see details provided by Cochrane, 1983).

Explanations of such well-established differences are varied. The suggestion that there are biological reasons would indicate that there should be more consistency in different social groups, and over time, than is apparent. Moreover, mood changes which may be associated with, for example, postnatal states or pre-menstrual tension, could not account for a large effect on random sampling. There are also sex and marital status interactions in that, as noted by Cochrane, in terms of mental disorder females are less protected by marital status than males. This again makes it difficult to assume that there is a basic vulnerability factor which is biologically based.

The possibility remains that the sex role has a direct influence on mood state. In traditional roles the dominant male has more power and mastery than the female, and this may mean that females are more readily helpless in society. If females depend for their rewards on being able to please other people, this is unpredictable and therefore is a low control experience. Against this are the data which suggest that the increased female propensity to mental disorder is a relatively recent phenomenon. It would be expected that since, overall, women's roles have changed substantially in the direction of equality in the past 30 years, if anything their control over the environment should have increased. To counter this, it might be argued that the recent emergence of women into potentially important positions in western culture creates direct competition in which women fare less well in general; thus the contrasts may be exacerbated for all but the successful few.

One interesting set of contradictions from the work on homesickness is that females report more signs of psychoneurotic disorder but do not generally report more homesickness, and adapt better to university (on the College Adaptation Questionnaire designed by Crombag, 1968). Taken collectively, these results suggest the females to be stressed at the new challenges they face but reacting positively. The source of their increased distress may be the challenge, the extra effort required and the fear of failure, rather than the loss of contact with home.

A less comprehensive explanation is that females express emotional symptoms more readily than males, and that the distress levels reported appear consequently higher. However, we found no evidence of the interaction of sex and homesickness factors in psychoneurotic symptoms.

Overall, the results do suggest that females are more stressed by the transition to university. They even report moves as more stressful than their male counterparts. Yet the reasons for the stress might be different; perhaps there is a greater 'job strain' element which creates anxiety. However, females do show greater adaptation to university, suggesting that the strain may reflect the operation of coping strategies.

VULNERABILITY FACTORS IN HOMESICKNESS REPORTING

DECISIONAL CONTROL OVER THE MOVE

Little information is available on how the decision to go to university is made. The decision to leave home for school is different in that, for the schools studied, the pupil is enlisted early, sometimes even at birth, and he or she may have very little direct influence on his fate because of the authority of parents at this age. We found very few school pupils who felt that there was much personal control over the decision to go away to boarding school.

Work on the perception of control as a moderating variable in stress (Fisher, 1984) suggests that having control over an event frequently lessens the threatening nature of that event. This is perhaps best illustrated by laboratory studies in animal and human populations where having control over unpleasant experiences, such as shock, generally ameliorates the stressful effects. For animals this is manifest in terms of physical symptoms, whereas for human beings tolerance is the most affected variable (see Fisher, 1986, Chapter 2).

The difficulties of defining control in a variety of different life situations make extrapolation from laboratory to real-life settings problematic; nevertheless it might be argued that a person would be less threatened by a move from home to attend an institution if there was control over the decision to go, if the university had been personally selected in the first place, or if there were positive reasons for wanting to go (as compared with being forced by family).

One reason would be that if there is high decisional involvement then there is self-selection in favour of those who want to go to university. If there is low decisional involvement there may be either willingness or unwillingness to make the transition. A second reason is that the act of taking the initiative may be a positive sign of willingness to become committed. There is, of course, the problem that the homesick might 'rewrite history' and perceive the decisions of the past differently when viewing them from the perspective of a distressed state. The possibility of such state-dependent distortions must be borne in mind.

Results from studies in which those reporting homesickness were asked to indicate on a category-rating scale the perceived level of responsibility for the decision to go to university, indicated that it was less for homesick as compared with non-homesick students (Fisher, Murray and Frazer, 1985). However, there

was no such effect for boarding-school pupils. One interpretation is that schoolchildren generally do not expect to have much control over decisions affecting their lives because they are used to parental authority. Absence of decisional control might be more stressful at later stages in developmental history when the expectancy and need for operating control is greater.

PERSONAL SATISFACTION

Data from homesick university students (Fisher, 1985) showed that satisfaction with residence was lower for the homesick than for the non-homesick group. A similar effect has been reported by Kane (1987) in studies conducted in Manchester. The homesick group also were more pessimistic in their ratings of current friendships relative to previous friendships than non-homesick students, and indicated that they had expected better friendships. Overall, the data did not suggest dissatisfaction but rather a lack of the same level of satisfaction as indicated by the non-homesick.

Informally, one or two wardens of the university residences indicated that very often those who are homesick appear to have the less desirable rooms and more often than not are randomly allocated shared rooms. Perhaps some kind of cognitive evaluation of assets obtained and assets lost may create the preconditions for missing home.

PERSONAL DESIRE FOR VISITS HOME

Homesick students were found to indicate greater intensity of desire to make visits home than were non-homesick students. There was also a positive correlation between the desire to go home and the frequency of homesickness reporting for those who reported homesickness ($r=0.22$; $p<0.05$). However, the reported desire in the homesickness group to go home more frequently was not actualized because the number of visits home in the first six weeks of term did not distinguish the homesick and non-homesick groups (data reported in Fisher *et al.*, 1985). Perhaps the existence of the desire, but the lack of attempt to consummate it, represent important features of the homesick state. The homesick person may be locked into a conflict whereby he or she is forced to stay in the new environment because of the realization that opportunities for the future are offered.

PERSONALITY CHARACTERISTICS

Of those features examined, extraversion showed an association with homesickness reporting but this was a low correlation (-0.19, $p<0.05$). 'Hysteria', on the Middlesex Hospital Questionnaire, also correlated negatively with homesickness reporting (-0.31, $p<0.05$) and the non-homesick had consistently

higher scores ($p<0.03$). However, 'hysteria' has some special properties on the MHQ (see Crown and Crisp, 1966), and this makes interpretation difficult.

The hypothesis that low and high self-esteem do not distinguish reactions prior to a life event, but do so after a life event, was examined in the context of a transition from home. No difference was found between self-esteem levels in homesick and non-homesick groups. However, there was one interesting finding which may have confounded this effect; the Scottish students were found to have lower self-esteem than the students from England. We have no explanation as to why this should be the case. If anything, the English who come up to Scottish universities often do so through the clearing-house system because they have not qualified for their first choice; it might have been predicted that they would have had lower self-esteem. This issue clearly needs looking at again in greater detail, and may be of interest to counsellors.

GEOGRAPHICAL DISTANCE

A situational factor of importance is geographical distance. There are two reasons for predicting that it might be influential. First, the greater the distance incurred the greater the likelihood of change in culture—hence the greater the likelihood of culture shock. Secondly, the greater the distance incurred the greater the possibility that the individual will feel cut off from home and unable to visit it. The financial cost of long-distance telephone calls, or journeys home, could prove daunting for a student on a low financial budget. There is also cost in terms of time for long journeys, especially if this is to be done on a limited financial budget and involves, for example, hitch-hiking.

Fisher *et al.* (1985) reported the results of a study in which the frequency of homesickness was indicated on a category-rating scale from 'never' through to 'extremely frequent'. The scale therefore afforded a dichotic measure of incidence ('never' as compared with the other frequency categories) and also afforded a measure of level of frequency. The results for incidence showed that, for university students, distance from home distinguished homesick and non-homesick groups. The average distance from home for the homesick was 364 miles, whereas the average distance for the non-homesick group was 203 miles. This was significantly different ($p<0.05$); although the absolute difference in distance appeared not large, it is large within the UK context. However, the frequency measure of homesickness reporting in the homesick groups was not differentiated by geographical distance. This suggested that geographical distance could be assumed to operate as an initiating rather than an augmenting factor.

Research in Scottish boarding schools showed that geographical distance was not a factor influencing homesickness reporting. This provides an interesting contrast with the result for students, and may suggest that a more protective and restrictive context which limits visits home may be beneficial. Thus, the importance of contextual factors in determining the conditions of homesickness is emphasized.

PERSONAL VULNERABILITY

Research has established that early loss of parents by death, divorce or separation, predisposes an individual for depression later in life (see Brown and Harris, 1978) and in females loss of a parent before the age of 13 increases the vulnerability to a premarital pregnancy. No clear evidence of a comparable vulnerability factor in the case of homesickness has been found.

However, Fisher and Hood (1987) reported, in the context of a longitudinal study, that mild depression two months prior to leaving home is predictive of homesickness six weeks after arrival in university residence for the first time. There may be a number of explanations for this. The first is that it might be a hangover from examinations and the stress of leaving school. It may arise from anticipation of the move. Finally, it may be a manifestation of vulnerability. Interestingly, it was found that, whilst mild depression predicted the distress response to the move, it was anxiety which interacted with it. The mildly depressed manifest the effect of the move by increase in alarm.

The prevalence of passivity and lack of new commitment in the mildly depressed may be responsible for the effect in that lack of enthusiasm and involvement in the new environment would be predicted. Stokols *et al.* (1983) reported that low exploratory tendency was a factor in the failure to adjust to a move to a new job. Those who do not explore the new environment, or create friends, may not be developing the possibilities for adjustment. Mildly depressed or passive people may well be likely to behave like this, perhaps because they cope with the alarm created by the move by protective withdrawal.

Fisher (1989) argued that depression may arise from the operation of a protective strategy and is a form of social defeat. When asked to type a word and, without seeing the result, judge whether or not there had been a typing error, the depressed were no more likely than their non-depressed counterparts to make word typing errors or to judge correctly typed words as errors. After 100 word-typing trials, however, the depressed overestimated their error levels relative to the non-depressed, when asked to provide a percentage estimate. One interpretation is that trial-by-trial assessments remain accurate because they are not seen as statements of competence, merely aspects of a detection task. The depressed respond badly to public statements of competence or effectiveness.

However, this behaviour could logically lead to passivity and to lack of personal involvement, especially if there are self-confirming features encouraged by the attitude of other people. The person who constantly implies that he or she is no good is encouraging that opinion in others. In turn this may feed back because of the attitude of others. He or she is perceived by others as no good because of personally stated attitudes to self-performance on tasks and in many situations.

VULNERABILITY AND THE DISTRACTION MODEL OF HOMESICKNESS

In turn passivity and lack of public response create the conditions which lead to adverse effects being perpetrated following change. A person is most vulnerable following exposure to a new environment where there is relatively low control.

The first part of Figure 9.1 illustrates the possibility that different degrees of intensity or frequency of homesickness experience may directly reflect the level of threat imposed by separation from home. Thus the mental resource of a person is assumed to be differentially determined by separation.

However, Fisher *et al.* (1985) established that homesickness is generally reported as episodic in nature, and that the day's events have the capacity to keep it attenuated, leaving early morning and late night as particularly vulnerable times. This suggests that, for the majority of those suffering distress, distraction created by the new environment is effective. It was also found that 'mental' activity and passivity are more likely to be associated with homesickness.

The second part of Figure 9.1 therefore illustrates the possibility that the new environment (following transition) may provide sources of distracting material which compete with the demands made by distressing thoughts of home. On this model the episodic reporters are able to make use of the new environment effectively in controlling homesickness. Those who are non-episodic reporters (continuously homesick) may either be in an environment which does not provide competing demand or may be less able to take advantage of it. Mild depression prior to leaving home may identify those least able to cope with change, precisely because passivity is a feature which reduces the ability to create sources of distracting activity in the new environment.

If this explanation is valid then training people to be active rather than passive, and to explore new opportunities, might be a very useful strategy. In school or military environments where there is more discipline and control by staff, enforced activity and stimulating conditions (rather than punishing marches or runs) might help to create the beneficial distractions which aid adaptation. Selecting the active and gregarious for prolonged stays abroad might prove financially expedient for commercial organizations.

THE JOB STRAIN MODEL

More recent research has indicated that the new environment may play a more powerful role than was previously envisaged. It was found that over a third of the students who self-reported homesickness six weeks into the first university term had not arrived homesick, but had developed the experience with increasing time. In other words it seemed that the break with home was not the critical factor; it was prolonged experience of the new environment that was influential (See Fisher, 1989).

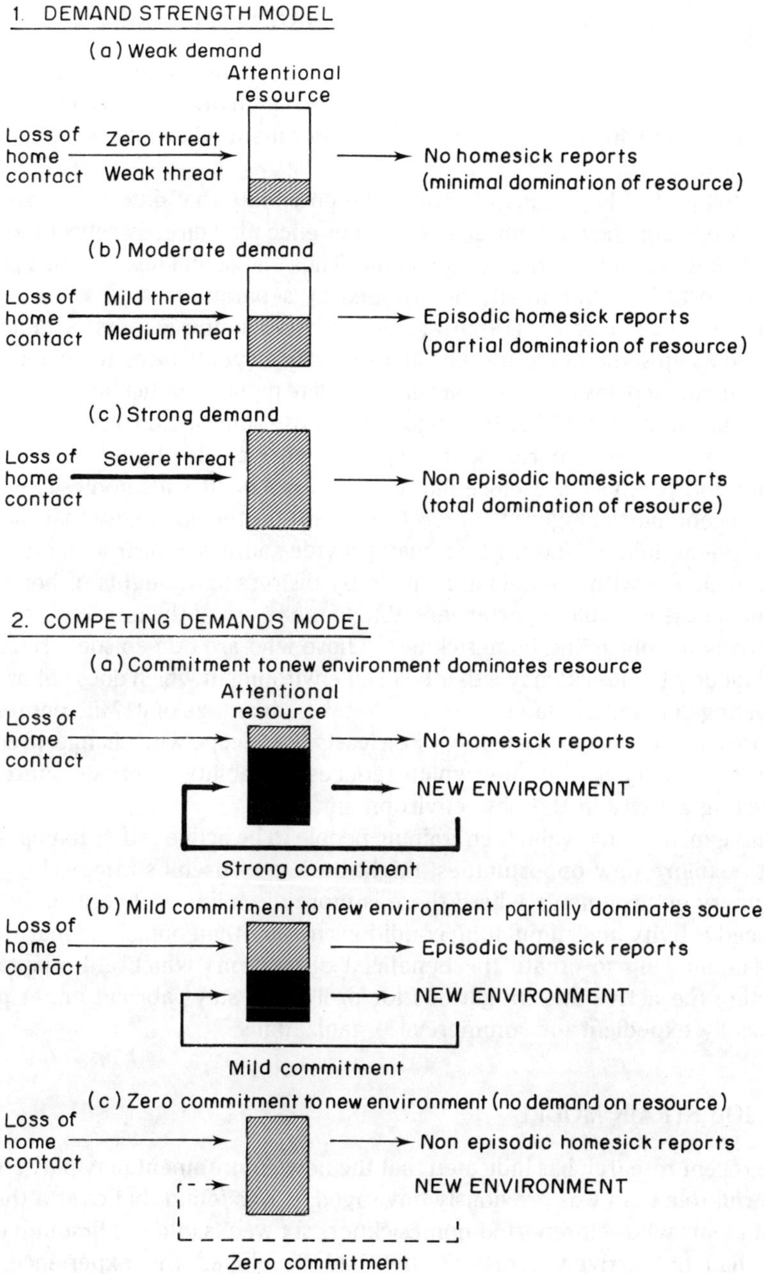

Figure 9.1. Attentional demand models of homesickness reporting. Reproduced by permission of Lawrence Erlbaum Associates from Fisher, 1989

Karasek (1969) showed, from results obtained from self-assessments of Swedish and American workers, that when demand is high and control is low the prevailing experience is that of job strain. Figure 9.2 illustrates that when students are provided with five-category rating scales and asked to indicate in general terms how much control they have over their lives, there is no difference between homesick and non-homesick groups in terms of average rating score. This makes intuitive sense since students could generally be expected to have high control over their lives. When a more specific question about control over academic demands is made instead, homesick students distinguished from their non-homesick counterparts in terms of reduced levels of perceived control. Thus whether by cause or consequence, the high demand imposed on university students is perceived as less controllable by the homesick group.

One possible explanation is that the homesick group are experiencing job strain. This makes sense of the findings that a third of the students who self-reported homesickness after experience of university rather than when first leaving home to become residential.

Figure 9.3 illustrates the possibility that the post-transition environment not only has a moderating influence on the experience of homesickness by providing distraction, but may also have a more complex role to play in creating or augmenting homesickness. This implies that people who move to congenial, user-friendly, pleasant environments may be expected to be less distressed by the

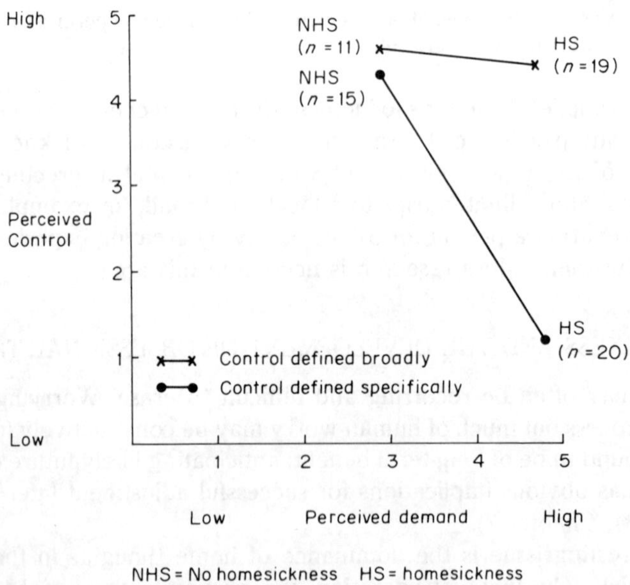

Figure 9.2. Perceived demand models of homesickness reporting. Reproduced by permission of Lawrence Erlbaum Associates from Fisher, 1989

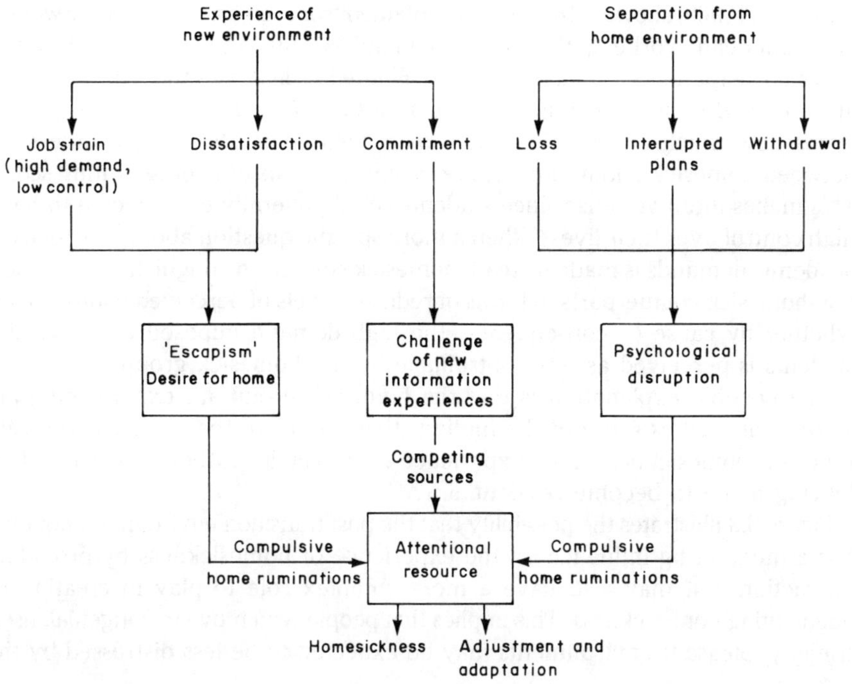

Figure 9.3. A composite model of homesickness. Reproduced by permission of Lawrence Erlbaum Associates from Fisher, 1989

move. It also implies that efforts to increase the attractiveness of the environment in physical and psychosocial terms might prove useful. Prior knowledge and experience of the new environment would be helpful in erecting the right expectancies. Short, limited trips to a location abroad, for example, might be a way of preparing a person for a longer stay by creating experiences which can aid adjustment. More research is needed in this area.

HOMESICKNESS AND THE DEVELOPMENT OF OBSESSIONAL THINKING

Thoughts may often be recurring and difficult to erase. Worrying implies a negative process but much of human worry may be constructively focused and has been found to be of long-term benefit; anticipating likely future events and outcomes has obvious implications for successful adjustment later in life (see Fisher, 1984, Chapter 2).

One interesting issue is the dominance of home thoughts in the minds of the homesick. On first consideration the preponderance of home-related thoughts when a person is in a new environment seems essentially non-adaptive. Preoccupation with the old environment not only slows adjustment to

the new but should create mental states not conducive to survival in a challenging environment. We should have evolved minds which adapt to change and are not prepossessed by past experience.

On the other hand, the plans of the past may have a useful role to play in the development of the plans for the future. Effective use of previous experience may mean a carry-over across change of old habits and routines, until they are incorporated into new habits.

On this analysis homesickness may be an epiphenomenon associated with the gradual incorporation of previous resources into new plans for the future. This would be compatible with the finding that selective moves away from home, particularly to reside in an institution, are associated with reduced incidence of homesickness reporting.

Attempts to control intrusive thoughts of home may have the power to increase obsessionality (Wegner, 1989), because distractors inevitably become linked to the thought that a person is trying to prevent. Also, as Wegner points out, self-distraction may be used to escape unwanted thoughts in the short term, but may not be the ultimate solution in the long term.

In the case of moves to a new environment, home continues to exist. There remain friends, family, routines and customs to contemplate. In this sense the home-bereaved is less fortunate than the traditionally bereaved, who can never restore the dead person—because home continues to exist. The good news is that enhanced familiarity with the new environment should gradually begin to input more and more into new routines. Students who return home for Christmas after two or three years at university often report that they miss their friends and university pursuits, find their home boring and look forward to the new environment. Perhaps, following adaptation, they are beginning to become 'university-sick'.

SUMMARY AND CONCLUSIONS

Leaving home for temporary or permanent reasons can have a profound effect on some people. Those who are mildly depressed and likely to be passive appear more at risk to alarm and distress following the move. A number of contextual factors surrounding the move may be influential. Adaptation to the new environment can be encouraged by pretraining, prior experience and by increasing a person's sense of personal control. Obsessional thinking about home may decrease a person's involvement and capacity to cope with the new environment.

REFERENCES

Bowlby, J. (1969) *Attachment and Loss*. Vol. 1: *Attachment*. New York: Basic Books.

Bowlby, J. (1973) *Attachment and Loss*. Vol. 2: *Separation, Anxiety and Anger*. New York: Basic Books.

Broadbent, D. E., Cooper, P. F., Fitzgerald, P. and Parkes, K. R. (1982) The Cognitive Failures Questionnaire (CFQ) and its correlates. *British Journal of Clinical Psychology*, **21**, 1-16.

Brown, G. W. and Harris, T. H. (1978) *The Social Origins of Depression: a Study of Psychiatric Disorders in Women*. London: Tavistock.

Cochrane, R. (1983) *The Social Creation of Mental Illness*. London: Longman.

Crombag, H. F. M. (1968) *Studie Motivatie en Studie Attitude*. Croningen: Walters.

Crown, S. and Crisp, A. H. (1966) A short clinical diagnostic self-rating for psycho-neurotic patients. *British Journal of Psychiatry*, **112**, 917-923.

Fisher, S. (1984) *Stress and the Perception of Control*. London: Lawrence Erlbaum.

Fisher, S. (1986) *Stress and Strategy*. London: Lawrence Erlbaum.

Fisher, S. (1989) *Homesickness, Cognition and Health*. Hove, Sussex: Lawrence Erlbaum.

Fisher, S. and Hood, B. (1987) The stress of the transition to university: a longitudinal study of vulnerability to psychological disturbance and homesickness. *British Journal of Psychology*, **78**, 425-441.

Fisher, S. and Hood, B. (1988) Vulnerability factors in the transition to university: self-reported mobility history and sex differences as factors in psychological disturbance. *British Journal of Psychology*, **79**, 1-13.

Fisher, S., Frazer, N. and Murray, K. (1984) The transition from home to boarding school: a diary-style analysis of the problems and worries of boarding school pupils. *Journal of Environmental Psychology*, **4**, 211-221.

Fisher, S., Murray, K. and Frazer, N. (1985) Homesickness and health in first year students. *Journal of Environmental Psychology*, **5**, 181-195.

Fisher, S., Elder, L. and Peacock, G. (1990) Contextual determinants and homesickness reporting. *Children's Environment Quarterly* (in press).

Hood B., MacLachlan, M. and Fisher, S. (1987) The relationship between cognitive failures, psychoneurotic symptoms and sex. *Acta Psychiatrica Scandinavica*, **76**, 33-35.

Hormuth, S. (1984) Transitions in commitments to roles and self-concept change: relocation as a paradigm. In V. L. Allen and E. Van de Vlert (eds), *Role Transitions: explorations and explanations*. New York: Plenum.

Kane, G. (1987) Studies of coping in stressed populations. Dissertation for the degree of Doctor of Philosophy at the University of Manchester, UK.

Karasek, R. A. (1979) Job demands, job decision latitude and mental strain; implication for job redesign. *Administrative Science Quarterly*, **24**, 285-309.

Mandler, G. (1975) *Mind and Emotion*. New York: John Wiley & Sons.

Mandler, G. and Watson, D. L. (1966) Anxiety and the interruption of behaviour. In C. D. Spielberger (ed.), *Anxiety and Behaviour*. New York: Academic Press.

Stokols, D., Schumaker, S. A. and Martinez, J. (1983) Residential mobility and personal well-being. *Journal of Environmental Psychology*, **3**, 5-19.

Van Bergen, A. (1968) *Task Interruption*. Amsterdam: North Holland.

Wegner, D. M. (1989) *White Bears and Other Unwanted Thoughts*. New York: Penguin.

Weiss, R. (1975) *Marital Separation*. New York: Basic Books.

Weiss, R. (1978) Couples' relationships. In M. Corbin (ed.), *The Couple*. New York: Penguin.

Weiss, R. (1982) Attachment in adult life. In C. M. Parkes and J. Stevenson-Hinde (eds), *The Place of Attachment and Loss in Human Behaviour*. London: Tavistock.

Wickland, R. A. (1982) Self-focused attention and the validity of self-reports. In M. P. Zanna, E. T. Higgins and C. P. Herman (eds), *Consistency in Social Behaviour: the Ontario Symposium*, Vol. 2. Hillsdale, N. J.: Lawrence Erlbaum.

Zeigarnik, B. (1927) Das Behalten erledigter und unerledigter Handlungen. *Psychologische Forschung*, **9**, 1-85.

10 Moving House and Home

TERENCE LEE
University of St Andrews

No-one who has experienced the hectic uprooting and laborious replanting process of moving to a new house in a new location would question the effort involved. It represents a physical, social and psychological upheaval that in rare cases may proceed smoothly, but in others, where circumstances are less conducive, will exact a heavy toll. This applies even when the end appears to justify the means.

Major change in residence is one of the experiences assessed on the scale devised by Holmes and Rahe (1965) to compare life events for their potentially stressful qualities. It is ranked 24th on the basis of judgements by normally healthy people in the USA. This may not seem too serious, but for an elderly person whose capacity for physical mobility (let alone for seeking new friends) is severely restricted, whose relocation is enforced to an inferior setting and preceded by a long period of anticipatory anxiety, the rank order would be substantially higher. Indeed, for those who are not 'normally healthy' but prone to anxiety, depression or self-doubts, relocation could strike where they are most vulnerable (Leff, Roatch and Bunney, 1970).

At the opposite end of the scale, of course, the highly mobile, well-educated executive, for whom every geographical relocation is associated with career advancement and upward social mobility, will take such transitions in his stride, devoting his organizational skills and multiple networks of influence to smoothing the passage. Robinson Crusoe is the classic example of mastery over unanticipated and not altogether desirable relocation. Defoe allowed him only rare moments of despair and his articulate and ingenious control over, indeed mastery of, the alien environment rarely faltered. 'Crocodile Dundee' is a well-known contemporary example of the same phenomenon.

Reverting to the real executive, sometimes the wives of such paragons, seeing themselves and their own occupational or other interests being traded off for their husband's career, are the unregarded victims of the transition and become depressed, physically ill or have recourse to pharmacological antidotes. Not uncommonly, they turn to the short-lived palliative comforts of alcohol.

On the Move: the Psychology of Change and Transition. Edited by S. Fisher and C. L. Cooper.

It can be seen from these examples, however, that there are many obstacles to the systematic study of relocation stress. One is that there is no clear dividing line between the normal demands and challenges that 'build character'—and the excessive impositions that deplete reserves and weaken the capacity to cope in the future (Selye, 1974).

A second problem is that people are often unwilling to admit to a loss of control; successful coping is a social value, so respondents are inclined to deny to themselves and others that they are under strain. This is familiar to researchers as the phenomenon of 'faking good'.

Yet another difficulty is the much more commonplace one of correlation and causality. Relocation is frequently associated with or precipitated by other stressful life events such as retirement, ageing, divorce or bereavement. Unpacking these factors to lay bare the geographical move itself is not easy. It is even questionable whether this is the right way to go, when the major adversities in life are interactions.

URBAN RENEWAL AND RELOCATION

During the postwar decades in particular, renewal or redevelopment of the urban environment quite often entailed the forcible rehousing of large numbers of people. Hartman (1975) describes the process in the USA as follows: 'Urban renewal . . . might more properly be labelled a dehousing program'. This programme was introduced in the 1949 Housing Act as 'slum clearance', but was taken over at the local level by those who wished to reclaim urban land occupied by the poor for commercial, industrial, civic and upper-income residential uses. Over half a million households, two-thirds of them non-white and virtually all in the lower-income categories, have been forcibly uprooted. A substantial percentage of these persons were moved to substandard and overcrowded conditions and into areas scheduled for future clearance, at a cost of considerable personal and social disruption (p. 107).

In the UK there was a massive housebuilding programme in the postwar years, but this was strongly controlled by central and local government, through detailed legislation and by making subsidy contingent on strict building and planning legislation. Hence relocation generally meant a move to superior physical conditions. But since the allocation of housing was based on a points system, which governed position on the 'housing list', established communities were almost invariably split asunder and families were normally reassembled with strangers as neighbours in homogeneous 'estates' (often in unpopular tower blocks) well away from the familiar bustle of down town.

Duhl (1963) drew attention to the dangers in removing natural supports from people who have established themselves in a community. But the classic study of forced relocation is that of Fried (1963), whose article had the evocative title

'Grieving for a lost home'. A group of over 500 low-income residents were forcibly moved from Boston's West End. This was an old-established neighbourhood and quite a high proportion of the residents were elderly and retired. In intensive follow-up, 50 per cent of them reported feelings of 'grief' up to one year after the event, and 25 per cent up to two years. The figure was even higher among those who reported that they had 'liked the [previous] area very much'. Of these, 75 per cent were still experiencing 'severe grief' two years after the move. Particularly baleful effects were felt by those who claimed to have had five or more of their closest friends in the West End.

The loss of close neighbourly support and the disruption of stable networks occurred at the same time as the need to re-adjust their behaviour patterns and roles to a completely new environment. On the face of things their new environment was an improvement; better houses in a superior district, offering the opportunity for upward social mobility. None the less, many spoke of the experience as if they had been bereaved, had lost a loved one. They reported feeling depressed and helpless. Some relief was gained from 'transitional objects', treasured possessions that seemed to form a bridge to the old environment. Some residents admitted to making nostalgic visits back to the old haunts.

Anticipating later findings on the variability in coping responses, Fried reported that 72 per cent of the higher-income group had made a reasonable adjustment, compared with only 22 per cent of their lower-income counterparts. Again, he showed that 'preparedness for transition' was a critical predictor of good adjustment. Unfortunately, the well-educated officials who organize mass relocations are prone to assume that everyone shares their own sense of control over the environment. This is not so.

Kasteler, Gray and Carruth (1968) studied the effect of the involuntary relocation of a sample of 500 elderly people living in a medium-sized city in the western United States. A new interstate highway precipitated the move. They reported behavioural changes for the worse on dimensions such as general health, friendship patterns, churchgoing and 'total personal adjustments'. Attitudes such as concern for economic security, family happiness and other aspects of their lives, were also adversely affected. The authors concluded that 'Involuntary relocation was an especially stressful experience for older persons whose ties are generally more firmly established and who, by the process of ageing, may be more resistant to change than are younger persons.'

Although this seems self-evident when stated in such emphatic terms, and when considered with the research data on institutional relocations to be quoted later, we should perhaps pause to ask whether it is necessarily so; that is, is relocation stress an inevitable consequence of the ageing process *per se*, or does it arise only because of the frequent combination of ageing with circumstances arising from the moving process itself; with the nature of the new environment or the degree and mode of preparation for the move?

After all, although the elderly may be more 'set in their ways', and less economically and physically mobile, they also have certain advantages over the young. In particular they have more time, less occupational stress and fewer family responsibilities.

This is why the well-known Victoria Plaza Study is important. Carp (1966) measured the effects of *voluntary* relocation into a local authority high-rise complex in San Antonio, Texas, specially designed for the elderly. A comparison between those who moved and those who had applied unsuccessfully (the basis of selection is, unfortunately, not reported) showed a 'dramatic effect of improved life setting' for the former. The highest satisfaction was far from transitory; it was confirmed up to eight years later (Carp, 1974).

The effects on health were the most clearly documented, but a range of evaluative and attitudinal factors were also positive. However, Carp (1974) adds a list of variables that are predictive of a good prognosis, and these give some insight into the areas of social and psychological functioning that are put under strain by relocation. Conversely, although these factors may not be directly controllable in advance, they indicate where education on coping strategies and tactics might help in relieving stress. The factors referred to are intelligence, good health, living with spouse, self-esteem, sociability and a degree of optimism that one's standard of living can be maintained.

However, although the Victoria Plaza study provides some encouragement, it has to be pointed out that two major factors (inevitably confounded) characterized this particular situation that are often absent in others. The moves were made voluntarily and the tenants perceived the quality of the new housing to be vastly superior to the old.

Lawton and Cohen (1974) studied the adaptation of tenants moving into five different new housing schemes, some private low-income, some public and some sponsored by charitable organizations. Non-moving community residents were used as controls and a regression model was applied to remove the effect of demographic variables and pre-move scores.

The results broadly confirmed the Victoria Plaza findings, although they were less emphatic overall. There was also an important exception. It appears that 'functional health' declined. This seems rather a surprising result if cognitive and attitudinal factors improved; it suggests that either the physical exertion or psychological trauma of the moving process itself may have taken its toll, despite a new environment and lifestyle that proved stimulating and satisfying.

Another possible explanation would rely on the close association between moderate physical activity and good health in the elderly; it is possible that the new environments made fewer demands on walking and working activities.

Most research on relocation has made only broad distinctions (e.g. institutional versus private or public housing) between different types of new environment, and very little has been reported on the particular qualities that characterize these environments. An exception is a paper by Lawton, Nahemow and

Teaff (1975). They found the greater well-being was associated with smaller community size, non-profit sponsorship and low-rise buildings.

On this latter point it should be mentioned that in some of the postwar rehousing in the USA, and most in the UK, including what was earlier indelicately referred to as 'slum clearance', the new housing was seen as physically superior in every way by those responsible for providing it. This view was not always shared by the tenants. High-rise was particularly unpopular, as was the geographical inconvenience of outer suburb locations, the sharply increased running costs and the lack of shops and pubs. However, there is little doubt that people's evaluation of the physical quality of the housing itself was and still is negatively influenced by the social rootlessness and depersonalization that is often associated with relocation. Hopes and expectations were not confirmed and this, according to Stokols (1979), predisposes to stress.

Young and Wilmott (1957), in their study of Bethnal Green, encouraged planners to move one housing block at a time in order to avoid this kind of disruption, and there have been some similar attempts by social scientists since this time. Fried argued that communities should be redeveloped by demolishing and reconstructing small parcels of land in sequence and rehousing existing tenants. This would enable the neighbourhood to keep its identity. Hartman (1975) urged planners to rehabilitate existing buildings instead of disrupting them, and this is a message that is at last being heard, in the UK at least. As usual, it seems to be driven by aesthetics more than by social concerns.

In the USA Swanson, Swanson and Dukes (1980) have encouraged not only the development but the systematic evaluation of publicly supported programmes for improving and conserving neighbourhoods with the aim of avoiding or reducing the human costs of relocation. Similarly, Holahan (1976) has offered a large number of practical design suggestions that would improve the quality of life for residents of high-rise housing projects in New York City's Lower East Side. Following a study of street life and social networks, he makes design suggestions that would encourage, in ways compatible with the local culture, the use of a variety of outdoor shopping, leisure and other functional activities. Then, by the provision of innovative design features such as nooks, benches, games tables and recreational equipment, he aims to capture the informal encounters that have been promoted and strengthen them into more enduring relationships. It seems likely that architects could make a useful contribution to the minimization of relocation stress in these and other ways.

Forced relocation sometimes arises from environmental threats. A good example is the Love Canal incident (Levine, 1982; Gibbs, 1983) where relocation was imposed by the government, consigning people to 'the death of a town' and 'a future among strangers'. The scale of resettlement following the Chernobyl nuclear accident in 1986 is probably without precedent, and the reports in media documentation, on which we have to rely at present, suggest widespread loss of morale, deep depression and a variety of physical ills attributed to the disaster

and earning the uncharitable and probably inaccurate diagnosis of 'nuclear phobia' from the medical establishment. Again, however, we have the major life event of forced relocation confounded with the realities or attributions of a physical disaster.

Terreberry (1967) found a similar effect with the forced relocation of an urban population. He concentrated mainly on the residents' own expression of their reactions. Four out of five believed that the event had had a negative effect on their lives. Forty per cent who were interviewed between one and three years later still reported a 'sense of loss'.

Needless to say, there is much confounding among the complex set of variables that bear on the issue. The gravity of social problems often appears to be inversely related to their research amenability.

Schooler, in a series of studies, has attempted to unravel at least some of the confounding (Schooler, 1973, 1976). One of the most important sources is that the trauma of the move itself is generally inseparable from the effects over subsequent months or years of adjusting to the replacement environment. The original sample for his study was drawn from a cross-sectional survey of 4000 people, representative of the whole of the USA. These data were used to extract, by factorial analysis, four dimensions, yielding factor scores for the domains of health, morale, social relations and environmental circumstances. To these were added demographic characteristics.

The author, in referring to the analysis of this first cross-sectional phase of the study, claims: 'in a nutshell that it had demonstrated that some variation in health and morale may be associated with or attributed to variation in environmental characteristics' (Schooler, 1976, p. 282).

Three years later a group of 571, drawn to over-represent those who had moved in the intervening period, were interviewed. It is this 'before–after' analysis that is of particular interest.

First, the anticipation of moving: those who had *expected* to move were compared after three years with those who had not. There was a significant decline in morale on three of the four measures for the 'anticipation' group. However, the health measures were more equivocal. The index of 'general health' showed a small decline, but the two other measures, each of disability, showed an improvement that was contrary to prediction. It seems possible that, following Stokol's (1979) congruence theory of stress (see below), those in the anticipation group had come to expect that things would take a serious turn for the worse, so far as their disability was concerned, in the new environment; and in the event it was not so.

What, then, about the process of moving itself? Changing homes was found to have a detrimental effect in two of the four morale factors and in two of the three health factors.

So, Schooler's evidence thus far is that the main effects of 'anticipation' and 'moving' may each lead to a decline, though not, of course, invariably. This is

clearly an area where interactions are important. Indeed, the most obvious one is the combination of expecting to move with actually moving and this, sure enough, produced a large, unequivocal reduction in both health and morale. Another obviously relevant factor is the relative quality of the new environment compared with the previous one, and in this case Schooler was able to compare the quality of the dwelling, convenience of service and the availability of social services. This highlights a critical variable in all moves and, indeed, in changes of all kinds—that is their *direction*; are they for better or worse? In the present study the group characterized by negative anticipation, by an actual move and by a move to an environment that compared unfavourably with their present one, showed the most extreme effects on both the health and morale measures.

As a methodological postscript it seems likely that in many relocation projects the negative trauma of the move itself is accompanied by an improvement in the physical quality of the new home, and this produces spuriously low correlations, unless the various influences are teased out. The fact that some *elderly* people, in particular, feel that the move has 'turned out quite well on balance' may deflect attention from the fact that it could have been made much more positively beneficial overall by the provision of support during the anticipatory phase, with the move itself or with improvements to the physical and social characteristics of the replacement environment.

FREQUENT MOVERS

Stokols, Shumaker and Martinez (1983) approached their study, entitled 'Residential mobility and personal wellbeing', with a wide-ranging *contextual* analysis; that is, instead of regarding the moving experience as a single, acute life event, they analysed the incidence of residential mobility retrospectively through the entire lifetime of their respondents, together with the moderating variables of attitude to the current home, aspirations for the future and general taste for mobility.

They argue convincingly that stress effects ('disruptive potential') are likely to arise from a mismatch between the person's hopes and expectations and his current situation. This potential incongruence applies not only to the home itself but also to work, commuting and recreational facilities. These will be familiar to most people as the 'disappointing aspects' that sometimes characterize a new home.

In the temporal, as distinct from the spatial, dimension, the degree of attachment to a past home or homes is clearly important as Fried (1963) so clearly demonstrated. However, Stokols *et al.* commendably consider also the *future* time perspective of movers. It makes a good deal of difference whether people perceive their new home as a place where they expect to be able to 'settle' for a reasonably prolonged period (in the case of retired people, as the ultimate

or as a convenient or necessary transition. The energetic, socially upwardly mobile family may even welcome moving as a reaffirmation of their progress, a very public indication of their rising status.

Stokol *et al.*'s initial sample consisted of 242 non-faculty university employees, predominantly women. They were asked to list every home they had lived in, and mobility rate was then computed by adjusting for age. Each of their previous environments was evaluated for the degree to which it was 'missed'; its perceived desirability was rated on another scale and the comparison level computed between the current situation and the recent past. A further scale assessed the degree to which attractive alternative options were realistically available to the respondents. Satisfaction with the present home was rated, using a five-point scale, on no fewer than 19 dimensions of its physical qualities and the characteristics of its neighbourhood setting.

Finally, an index of 'environmental exploratory tendency' was derived from further items about preference for familiar or unfamiliar places, the degree of enjoyment in meeting new people and of making residential moves; basically, a 'taste for mobility' scale. The dependent variable was, of course, health, but initially only two very general self-assessment questions about perceived health and level of energy were included.

Three months after this initial stage there was a follow-up. One purpose of this was to establish re-test reliability, but very much more detailed information about health and morale during the intervening three months was elicited, including an extensive symptom checklist.

About 10 per cent of the initial sample had left their employment but, more seriously (though perhaps understandably in view of the demands made), a high percentage were unwilling to repeat the exercise and the sample was reduced overall to half, i.e. 121. Although demographic composition remained about the same, there was no way of guarding against the probable biased loss of people who had been unwell. On the other hand, any selective loss, if it occurred, would have been conservative for the outcome.

A particular virtue of this study was that the design allowed for an assessment of the reliability of the questionnaire data and this turned out to be satisfactory, with the possible exception of the 'congruence scales', i.e. those describing the degree of satisfaction with the current home and neighbourhood by comparison with aspirations. Another virtue of the study was the separation in time of the independent and main dependent measures, although the authors acknowledge that the assumption of a causal link from mobility to well-being could be challenged; for example, it could be argued that poor health promotes mobility.

The results broadly conform to the main hypothesis. A high rate of mobility was associated with having more illness-related symptoms and a lower sense of community in relation to the new environment. Health and energy status was also correlated with housing quality; with the feeling of satisfaction towards the current housing and neighbourhood by comparison with expectation (the

'congruence measure'), and with a negative verdict on the comparison between the actual current and previous homes and with the same sort of comparison over the work situation. It seems that frequent movers pay a price.

The study confirmed that the main relationship between mobility and health is not invariably negative, but depends on a number of mediating factors. Some results were contrary to the initial prediction. For example, low-mobility persons with restricted residential choice or control and those with low congruence had marginally poorer health than high-mobility persons. This, however, is intuitively plausible if it arises because the low level of mobility is enforced, and its result is also to confine its victims within an environment that they rate as inferior in quality.

Among high-mobility residents there was poorer general health and energy among those who clearly found the frequent moves to be necessary but unwelcome; that is, the non-exploratory persons. These are described as those who are reluctant to explore the various possibilities of the psychosocial environment.

Despite the wealth of data thrown up by this study, the authors point out that it still remains an open question whether it is the severance of old, social networks or the difficulty of establishing new ones that is the most stressful. We would add that the conflict between the process of consolidating social and work-related goals in the new environment on the one hand, and the physical and economic demands made by the process of putting the new home into shape, adjusting its hooks and shelves, its decoration, floor covering and, in some cases, its unkempt garden space, may also be a source of stress. Knocking the new place into a congenial shape to fit the lifestyle and standards of its changed occupant is often a demanding task. Apart from the work itself, it involves choice between conflicting alternatives, which is stressful.

MOVING FROM HOME INTO AN INSTITUTION

The first of many studies of the potential trauma for elderly people of being involuntarily assigned to an institution was undertaken by Lieberman (1961). In this and other early studies the rather crude but unequivocal index of mortality was used. Lieberman demonstrated that the mortality rate for his sample was three times higher during the first year in the institution than during the four to six months waiting period. He compared retrospectively those who had died with the survivors, and concluded that health factors could not explain the difference.

As mentioned earlier, one rather obvious variable in all relocations is whether they are enforced or voluntary, and this applies equally to institutional moves. Farrari (1963) made a comparison, again of mortality, after as short a period as 10 weeks. His sample of enforced movers was small, but the death toll of

94 per cent (16 or 17) was dramatic, while only 3 per cent (1 of 38) of the voluntary group had died. However, there was obviously scope for confounding in this comparison if the more severely health-disabled persons were also the ones unable to choose. Attitudinal measures were used by Sherwood, Glassman, Sherwood and Morris (1974), who graded the degree of control that people felt that they had exercised over the decision to move. Those who admitted to least control were subsequently least satisfied with life, whereas the more autonomous group reported greater life satisfaction in their new environment.

INTER-INSTITUTIONAL TRANSFER

There is some evidence that transfers from one institution to another are less disturbing than the major transition from home into an institution. Schulz and Alderman (1973) found that the former patients lived for an average of one month longer. It seems likely that the major disruption occurs when the freedom and autonomy of home life has to be relinquished, but it must also be noted that those making inter-institutional moves are already preselected for robustness, having previously made and survived the move from home.

There are conflicting findings for elderly mental patients relocated within and between institutions. Aleksandrowicz (1961) reported a 20 per cent death rate among mental patients during a 12-week period after transfer, compared to 7.5 per cent during the three preceding months. Killian (1970) found mortality rates were up to nine times greater for transferred compared to non-transferred patients with a similar prognosis. Aldrich and Mendkoff (1963) traced the history of a sample of nursing-home residents following transfer and found during the first three months that the mortality rate for those moved was three times higher than expected, and for people aged over 70 it was as much as three and a half times higher. The comparison in this study was based on a natural experiment arising from the closure of the Chicago Home for Incurables. A population of 233 disabled elderly people (162 of whom were over 70) were relocated.

These studies, if confirmed, would seem to have profound implications for current policies in the National Health Service and elsewhere, which are based on the premise that re-absorption into the community is the best way to combat the depersonalization of institutional living.

RELATIVE CHANGE IN INSTITUTIONAL ENVIRONMENT

Bourestom and Tars (1974) studied *forced* relocation in two Michigan hospitals and compared these with a control hospital in a neighbouring state where no relocations took place. One of the samples forced to move showed significantly higher mortality rates, but not the other. This was clearly attributable to the

degree of disturbance. In one case there was only a moderate change to a new building a few hundred yards away, within the same general setting. In the other a much more radical change of scene was involved, from a local government facility to a much larger private institution with new staff, a new programme, completely different physical environment and a different set of patients.

This does not definitively identify the effort of adaptation to a drastically changed environment as the true cause of the stress; patients would undoubtedly be aware in advance of the adjustment demanded of them, so that anticipatory attitudes and associated anxieties may have played a part.

Pastalan (1973) also referred specifically to the important difference between the social milieu of one institution and another. He used the concept of 'home range' used by environmental psychologists in urban research. This refers to the number of social contacts or social settings that are used by a subject, together with their geographical range. He reported from a secondary analysis of the Bourestom and Tars study (1974) that patients with connections to more than 10 behaviour settings in a day all survived, whereas those with fewer than seven settings were 'highly vulnerable'. Following the conceptual approach of the ecological psychologists a social setting could be any formal or informal situation such as a coffee group, sewing bee, whist four or gossip circle. Bourestom and Pastalan (1975) also referred to an institution transfer involving a completely new staff programme and physical plant where 43 per cent of the patients died within six months of the change.

THE ATTITUDE OF THE RELOCATEES

Although the social quality of the new environment is clearly an important variable, it must interact with the personality style of the residents. Turner, Tobin and Lieberman (1972) found that in institutions that stressed high levels of interaction, activity and aggressiveness, a 'vigorous if not combative' style was conducive to adjustment.

Many studies in other areas have demonstrated that the way in which the stressor is perceived may profoundly affect the reaction. Some interesting findings on the attitudes towards relocation of the patients were reported in the study by Aldrich and Mendkoff described earlier. Those who expressed anger, or who adopted a philosophical attitude towards the anticipated move, made a reasonable adjustment, whereas those who retreated into regression or denial fared less well. On the other hand, Miller and Lieberman (1965) and Markson and Cumming (1974) did not find an excess over the expected mortality rate. The former, however, did report a higher incidence of 'maladaptive responses' in the relocated patients and in both studies the periods of follow-up were short, i.e. 18 weeks and 11 weeks, respectively.

Similarly, Pastalan (1976) reported a mortality rate as high as 41 per cent among those who adopted an internalized rejecting attitude (resentment?) to the proposed move, while only 14 per cent of those who were accepting subsequently died within the same period.

Markus, Blenkner, Bloom and Downs (1972) predicted post-relocation mortality on the basis of perceptual field dependency/independency, mental status and seven indices of physical status. However, this regression equation, which predicted satisfactorily in one institution did not work for another, probably because the quality of the new environment, the degree of change from one environment to the other or the anticipation period were not taken into consideration.

THERAPEUTIC SUPPORT FOR RELOCATION

There is a fair amount of evidence in the literature that the degree of preparation given to the transferee, together with the appropriate design of the transitional environment, will relieve stress. This gives further emphasis to the importance of the anticipatory period and echoes findings in other problem areas, such as preparation for major surgery.

Jasnau (1967) compared a mass enforced move with a more participatory approach involving individual preparation and consent. Those subjected to the mass move had a mortality rate 35 per cent higher than during the preceding year, whereas those more appropriately prepared had a rate lower than expected.

Zweig and Csank (1975) studied male ex-servicemen of 64 years and over, suffering from chronic incapacity. They were given a preparation programme to relieve pressure, to allay anxiety and to build realistic expectations of the move. Again, there were favourable implications for survival.

Gutman and Herbert (1976) also studied extended-care male patients and found that careful planning and allocation to rooms that were based on mutual compatibility and friendship helped a good deal, as did also careful attention to continuity in and lack of disturbance to their personal belongings. The mortality rate did not show the increase sometimes associated with this kind of relocation.

Pastalan (1976) provided 'extensive preparation'. He concentrated on physical adaptive measures to moving, such as health and well-being. Others have de-emphasized these factors in favour of more cognitive, psychological factors. In his study Pastalan found that the post-move rate of mortality was lower than both the state and the national average but, as reported earlier, there were substantial differences between those patients who had a rejecting attitude and those who had an accepting attitude. The aims of any programme to ease the stress of relocation would include an attempt to modify these anticipatory

attitudes, but much tact and skill must be needed for success. In his later review of the field, Pastalan (1983) concludes that the main factors involved in effective relocation are: (1) degree of choice; (2) degree of environmental change; (3) degree of prior health; (4) degree of anticipatory preparation and (5) methodology of study.

SOME THEORETICAL UNDERPINNING

Despite the recurrent methodological difficulties, the weight of evidence suggests that relocation frequently imposes strain on individuals, and this sometimes results in quite serious stress symptoms. Regretfully, no researchers appear to have addressed the family as a unit of study, but it seems inevitable that problems are sometimes magnified at this level, when responses are discordant; on the other hand, they may sometimes be mitigated by mutual support.

Predisposing factors, which are closely interrelated, are the degree of attachment to the home base; prior physical and mental health; the existence of a period of ruminative, anticipatory anxiety; a voluntary or involuntary decision to move; the relative quality of the new environment; the personality and social skills relevant to establishing a new life and, finally, the availability of therapeutic preparation.

The model of loss, with consequential grief, seems particularly relevant. It was Bowlby's (1951) seminal study of maternal deprivation, prompted by the devastating wartime incidence of child relocation and parental loss, that originally highlighted this source of explanation. Loss is not only particularly poignant when it afflicts children, but their responses are more readily observable. The model has also been extensively applied in studies of bereavement. It was therefore an imaginative step for Fried (1963) to apply it to the loss of a much-loved home. Subsequent research on maternal deprivation has attempted to establish whether the relationship with the loved one is an indispensable, innate characteristic of the species or a wholly functional, acquired dependency.

There is no space here to debate this issue; sufficient to say that Harlow's (1971) research on contact comfort in young monkeys, as well as Bowlby's subsequent studies, have tended to confirm the primary nature of attachment and loss (Bowlby, 1969, 1973, 1980). Weiss (1975, 1978, 1982) has shown that its powerful effects are by no means limited to childhood relationships.

What, then, can we deduce about the loss of a home? It can be and often is a cherished object. Moreover, some kind of home base or environmental niche is essential to human existence, though if necessary it can shift frequently in the nomadic style. In such cases the qualities of the home are invested in the movable objects, plus whatever is common to each new site. It is significant that, even if home is a cardboard box, a regular location is preferred.

Moving house is not a temporary parting of the kind that might induce homesickness (Fisher, 1989)—it is closer to bereavement in its finality. The nostalgic revisiting referred to by Fried (1963) is more analogous to cemetery mourning than to a return to base; the base has gone. The importance of transitional objects has already been emphasized, but it has a converse. For elderly people in particular, the house itself may have come to symbolize the much-loved spouse, now deceased, or the children, now departed, who had become an integral part of it. Loss of the home in such circumstances could compound the bereavement grief.

Although territorial appropriation must lie deep in the evolutionary history of the species, there is no way of determining whether the reaction to loss of a home is partly reflexive or wholly due to a learning process. As with any loss, there would obviously be evolutionary advantage. Fisher (1989) refers to the possible existence of 'loss detectors' in the CNS that trigger arousal via the autonomic nervous system; this drives the distress signals that mobilize help and the searching behaviour that could solve the problem.

This model fits the child deprivation or adult bereavement situation more closely than relocation; however, it could be argued that the same mechanism is invoked by relocation simply because it is perceived as similar by the victim. If such 'loss detectors' exist, it is unlikely that they are capable of fine discriminations.

It may be helpful to look more closely at the nature of specifically environmental attachment. Lee (1967) argued that spatial cognition is profoundly important to normal functioning, and its efficiency is correlated with personal effectiveness. Control over the environment, essential to the minimization of stress, requires extensive knowledge of local geography and some competence at navigation. Without this control there is the devastating emotional experience of being lost, leading to panic followed perhaps by helplessness. A child that is lost is a pitiful sight. Adults may only rarely experience 'lostness' because they are careful to restrict themselves to known territory. Sometimes, as in relocation, they are forced into the unknown.

The model developed over a number of years by Lee (1963, 1967, 1968, 1969, 1976) is that social space is isomorphic with physical space, and hence that social disorientation is congruent with geographical disorientation. The process that underlies spatial cognition is the construction, from repeated experiences, of mental representations of the environment. These spatial schemas reflect the particular needs of the individual, who has to consult them ('turn round on his own schemata'; Bartlett, 1932) when constructing plans to satisfy his/her needs. Without structured knowledge of the 'whereness' of objects in the environment, knowledge of their 'whatness' is of little value. Moreover, many of the most critical objects are social, because it is through other people that many of our most important needs are met. Hence, in the organization of cognition, it is efficient, not to say essential, to represent both social and physical object

knowledge in the same sociospatial schema. There is a particular advantage to social relationships in this arrangement because they tend to be mobile—so we organize them on the more static framework of the physical world. (Studies of very early perception suggest that this is optional and that babies begin by stabilizing on the mother while perceiving the world of physical objects in movement.) Hence, a sociospatial schema is a continuously constructed package of knowledge about the environment, a map of those parts of the world that have most functional significance for the individual. Their possession enables us to coordinate physical movement with social interaction. Their construction is not atomistic, but dynamic; each new piece of information is assimilated if it 'fits', but sometimes the schema must be 'accommodated' to make this possible. Once the schema is constructed it governs the active search for new knowledge and controls the ways in which it is perceived.

The model of sociospatial schema was first invoked to explain detailed findings on the urban neighbourhood (Lee, 1963, 1968). This is a cognitive representation of the geographical and social environment surrounding the home. It incorporates the place and the people, inextricably merged into a single schema. It is, of course, possible to think abstractly of the physical and social as separate entities, but they remain isomorphic—the people having a corresponding position in the place and the places each having corresponding people who inhabit them. Most people construct such a sociospatial schema, beginning on the first day they move into a new home. It was found to be unique but to show consistent variations with age, length of residence, stage in the life cycle, social class, location of work and similar variables.

A home is also a sociospatial schema and it is nested within the neighbourhood, as the neighbourhood is nested within the schema of the city itself. At the heart of this hierarchy is the schema of self. Moving outwards from here, the schemata are each invested with their own set of feelings and emotions, together with a considerable range of associated activities; certain things are done in the home and other actions are relevant to the neighbourhood. The possession of such sociospatial schemata is essential to adaptation; without them it would be impossible to formulate and execute the many plans of action, e.g. sleeping, cooking, shopping, schooling, working and making friends—on which basic living depends.

Moving house renders these laboriously constructed schemata null and void. Bearing in mind that for some, but especially the elderly, they comprise a high proportion of the entire life space, the reaction is one of being lost, with all that this entails in terms of panic, anxiety and feelings of loss of control, possibly leading on to helplessness and depression.

Although drawn from a different area of research, a study concerned with the effects of the relocation of young children from home to school provides a good illustration of this phenomenon (Lee, 1957). The problem setting arose from the policy of closing small rural primary schools and substituting what may

have been a short walk to school with extended journeys by bus. A sample of 883 children from 57 schools were assessed by their teachers on systematic scales of social–emotional adjustment and the results were compared with the type and length of journey to school. It was initially predicted that long journeys would have negative results because of the associated fatigue. However, the least fatiguing form of transport, the school bus, was associated at all journey lengths with consistently higher incidence of general anxiety, inability to concentrate, depression, withdrawn behaviour, eating difficulties, poor response to affection and other symptoms. The findings were interpreted within a schema model. The young child has a well-formed schema of home by the time he/she goes to school, but the new and unfamiliar location is an unknown world at first, in which it is easy to feel lost. Control, which reduces stress in such contexts, means acquiring a sociospatial schema, not only of the school but of the space intervening between home and school. The bus offers the child nothing of this; not only is there no possibility of control and little spatial learning, but the bus is removed as soon as delivery has been effected. Walking, on the other hand, gives full control. The intervening space is fully articulated by action and a schema is constructed that can be consulted at any time that a plan is imagined to return to the safety and comforts of home.

There is no conflict between the model of sociospatial schema and that of loss and bereavement. When applied to relocation the latter is applied to the object itself, i.e. the home. It evokes an analogy between home and loved one in order to explain the affective reactions to loss of a home, which resemble grieving. The schema model applies to the mental representation of the home and the neighbourhood, not to the objects themselves. It asserts that the symptoms of grief are in fact symptoms of being lost and disoriented in social and physical space. The reactions are likely to resemble those occurring in bereavement because this is the loss of a landmark figure in the sociospatial schema of the home.

Relocation makes redundant most of the physical components of the home schema and most of the social and physical components of the neighbourhood schema. Control in this situation refers to the ability, possessed by some, to adapt old plans, to construct new schemata and to invest them with positive feelings. This will lead to a growing feeling of familiarity and environmental congeniality. Its absence will be manifested as stress.

SUMMARY

Since Fried compared relocation with loss and bereavement, invoking the compelling image of 'grieving for a lost home', it has been widely recognized that moving house is a potentially stressful experience.

Subsequent research has extended to several areas, i.e. housing renewal projects, moves from home to institutions, inter-institutional transfers and the

history of frequent movers. Results confirm that deterioration in physical health, depression, anxiety, low morale and (among the elderly) disturbingly accelerated mortality rates, are common. Strong attachment and prolonged anticipation of enforced relocation exacerbate these effects. However, where moves are voluntary, prior health is good and the quality of the new environment is perceived as significantly higher, favourable outcomes have been reported.

Certain robust or flexible qualities of personality (e.g. sociability) or the adoption of effective coping attitudes, give a positive prognosis. There is also some evidence that therapeutic programmes of preparation are effective.

The theory of attachment and loss appears to be mainly an analogy. An alternative explanation is proposed in terms of the sociospatial schemata of home and neighbourhood that are rendered suddenly obsolete by the move. This causes disorientation and a loss of control over the physical and social environment until new schemata can be constructed.

REFERENCES

Aldrich, C. and Mendkoff, E. (1963) Relocation of the aged and disabled. *Journal of the American Geriatric Society*, **11**, 185–194.

Aleksandrowicz, D. (1961) Fire and its aftermath on a geriatric ward. *Bulletin of the Menninger Clinic*, **25**, 23–32.

Bartlett, F. C. (1932) *Remembering*. Cambridge: Cambridge University Press.

Bourestom, N. and Pastalan, L. (1975) *Forced Relocation*. Ann Arbor, MI: University of Michigan, Institute of Gerontology.

Bourestom, N. and Tars, S. (1974) Alterations in life patterns following nursing home relocation. *Gerontologist*, **14**, 506–510.

Bowlby, J. (1951) *Maternal Care and Mental Health*. Geneva: World Health Organization.

Bowlby, J. (1969) *Attachment and Loss*, Vol. 1: *Attachment*. New York: Basic Books.

Bowlby, J. (1973) *Attachment and Loss*, Vol. 2: *Separation, Anxiety and Anger*. New York: Basic Books.

Bowlby, J. (1980) *Attachment and Loss*, Vol. 3: *Loss, Sadness and Depression*. New York: Basic Books.

Carp, F. M. (1966) *A Future for the Aged: Victoria Plaza and its Residents*. Austin, TX: Hogg Foundation.

Carp, F. M. (1974) Short-term and long-term prediction of adjustment to a new environment. *Journal of Gerontology*, **29**, 444–453.

Duhl, L. H. (1963) *The Urban Condition*. New York: Basic Books.

Farrari, N. (1963) Freedom of choice. *Social Work*, **8**, 105–106.

Fisher, S. (1986) *Stress and Strategy*. London: Lawrence Erlbaum.

Fisher, S. (1989) *Homesickness, Cognition and Health*. London: Lawrence Erlbaum.

Fried, M. (1963) Grieving for a lost home: psychological costs of relocation. In L. Duhl (ed.), *The Urban condition*. New York: Basic Books, pp. 151–171.

Gibbs, R. (1983) Community response to an emergency situation: psychological destruction and the Love Canal. *American Journal of Community Psychology*, **11**, 116–125.

Gutman, G. M. and Herbert, C. P. (1976) Mortality rates among relocated extended care patients. *Journal of Gerontology*, **31**, 352–357.

Harlow, H. (1971) *Learning to Love*. San Francisco: Albion Publishing.

Hartman, C. (1975) *Housing and Social Policy*. Englewood Cliffs, NJ: Prentice-Hall.

Holahan, C. J. (1976) Environmental effects on outdoor social behaviour in a low-income urban neighbourhood: a naturalistic investigation. *Journal of Applied Social Psychology*, **6**, 48–63.

Holmes, T. H. and Rahe, R. H. (1965) The social readjustment rating scale. *Journal of Psychomatic Research*, **11**, 293–311.

Jasnau, K. (1967) Individualized versus mass transfer of nonpsychotic geriatric patients from mental hospitals to nursing homes with special reference to death rate. *Journal of the American Geriatric Society*, **15**, 280–284.

Kasteler, J. M., Gray, R. M. and Caruth, M. L. (1968) Involuntary relocation of the elderly. *Gerontologist*, **8**, 276–279.

Killian, E. (1970) Effects of geriatric transfers on mortality rates. *Social Work*, **15**, 19–26.

Lawton, M. P. and Cohen, J. (1974) The generality of housing impact on the well-being of older people. *Journal of Gerontology*, **29**, 194–204.

Lawton, M. P. Nahemow, L. and Teaff, J. (1975) Housing characteristics and the well-being of elderly tenants in federally assisted housing. *Journal of Gerontology*, **30**, 601–607.

Lee, T. R. (1957) On the relation between the school journey and social and emotional adjustment in rural infant children. *British Journal of Educational Psychology*, **27**, 101–114.

Lee, T. R. (1963) Psychology and living space. *Transactions of the Bartlett Society*, Vol. 2. Bartlett School of Architecture, University College London. London: Bartlett School of Architecture.

Lee, T. R. (1967) The conception of space and control of environment. *Architectural Association Journal*, **82**, 172–175.

Lee, T. R. (1968) Urban neighbourhood as a socio-spatial schema. *Human Relations*, **21**, 241.

Lee, T. R. (1969) The psychology of spatial orientation. Architectural Association Quarterly, **1**, 11–15.

Lee, T. R. (1976) Cities in the mind. In D. T. Herbert and R. J. Johnston (eds), *Social Areas in Cities* Vol. 2. *Spatial Perspectives on Problems and Policies.* Chichester: John Wiley & Sons, pp. 159–187.

Leff, M. J., Roatch, J. F. and Bunney, W. E. (1970) Environmental factors preceding the onset of severe depressions. *British Journal of Psychiatry*, **33**, 293–311.

Levine, A. (1982) *Love Canal: Science, Politics and People.* Lexington, MA: Lexington Books.

Levine, A. (1983) Community response to an emergency situation: psychological destruction and the Love Canal. *American Journal of Community Psychology*, **11**, 116–125.

Lieberman, M. A. (1961) Relationship of mortality rates to entrance to a home for the aged. *Geriatrics*, **16**, 515.

Markson, E. and Cumming, J. (1974) A strategy of necessary mass transfer and its impact on patient mortality. *Journal of Gerontology*, **29**, 315–321.

Markus, E., Blenkner, M., Bloom, J. and Downs, T. (1972) Some factors and their association with post-relocation mortality among institutionalized aged persons. *Journal of Gerontology*, **27**, 376–382.

Miller, D. and Lieberman, M. (1965) The relationship of affect state and adaptive capacity to reactions to stress. *Journal of Gerontology*, **20**, 492–497.

Pastalan, L. A. (1973) Involuntary environmental relocation: death and survival. In W. E. F. Preiser (ed.), *Environmental Design Research*. Proceedings of the 4th Environmental Design Research Associates Conference, Vol. 2. Stroudsburg, PA: Dowden, Hutchinson & Ross, p. 410.

Pastalan, L. A. (1976) *Report on Pennsylvania Nursing Home Relocation Program*. Ann Arbor: University of Michigan, Institute of Gerontology.

Pastalan, L. A. (1983) Environmental displacement. In G. D. Rowles and R. J. Ohta (eds), *Aging and Milieu*. New York: Academic Press.

Schooler, K. K. (1973) Some consequences of environmental change in an elderly sample. Paper presented at the American Psychological Association, Montreal, Quebec, 27 August.

Schooler, K. K. (1976) Environmental change and the elderly. In I. Altman, and J. F. Wohlwill (eds), *Human Behaviour and Environment: Advances in Theory and Research*. London: Plenum, chap. 7.

Schulz, R. and Alderman, D. (1973) Effect of residential change on the temporal distance to death of terminal cancer. *Omega*, **4**, 157–162.

Selye, H. (1974) Stress Without Distress. New York: Lippincott.

Sherwood, S., Glassman, J., Sherwood, C. and Morris, J. N. (1974) Preinstitutional factors as predictors of adjustment to a long term care unit. *Aging and Human Development*, **5**, 95–105.

Stokols, D. (1979) A congruence analysis of human stress. In I. G. Sarason and C. D. Spielberger (eds), *Stress and Anxiety*, Vol. 6. Washington, DC: Hemisphere Press, pp. 27–53.

Stokols, D., Shumaker, S. A. and Martinez, J. (1983) Residential mobility and personal well-being. *Journal of Environmental Psychology*, **3**, 5–19.

Swanson, D., Swanson, L. A. and Dukes, M. J. (1980) The evaluation and design of neighbourhood preservation strategies to minimise the negative aspects of displacement. Paper presented at the Annual Conference, Environmental Design Research Association, Charleston, SC.

Terreberry, S. (1967) Household relocation: resident's views. In E. Wolf and C. Lebeaux (eds), *Change and Renewal in an Urban Community: Five Case Studies in Detroit*. New York: Plenum Press.

Turner, B., Tobin, S. and Lieberman, M. (1972) Personality traits as predictors of institutional adaptation among the aged. *Journal of Gerontology*, **27**, 61–68.

Weiss, R. (1975) *Marital Separation*. New York: Basic Books.

Weiss, R. (1978) Couples' relationships. In M. Corbin (ed.), *The Couple*. New York: Penguin.

Weiss, R. (1982) Attachment in adult life. In C. M. Parkes and J. Stevenson-Hinde (eds), *The Place of Attachment and Loss in Human Behaviour*. London: Tavistock Press, pp. 171–184.

Young, M. and Wilmott, P. (1957) *Family and Kinship in East London*. New York: Free Press.

Zweig, J. and Csank, J. Z. (1975) Effects of relocation on chronically ill geriatric patients of a medical unit. *Journal of the American Geriatric Society*, **23**, 132–136.

11 Cultural Bereavement and Homesickness

MAURICE EISENBRUCH
Royal Children's Hospital Research Foundation, Victoria, Australia

INTRODUCTION

There has been a growing recognition of the relationship between culture and health. Social scientists suspect that rapid social change as a result of immigration can have adverse effects on health (Eisenbruch, 1988; Erikson, 1976; Fisher, 1988; Marris, 1986). This process is called health transition, and mental health forms a part of it.

Anthropologists such as S. Ryan Johansson have suggested that social violence or an upsurge in unwanted pregnancies may indicate difficulties in this transition. Eisenbruch argues that, in a multicultural society, cultural bereavement is another manifestation of the transition that is closer to the source: that cultural bereavement explains a connection between disruptions at several levels—'health', 'interpersonal', 'social', and 'community relations'.

This study of health transition aims to promote awareness of the diverse cultures in Australian society, to education mainstream health workers about the many methods of healing used in ethnic communities, to eliminate prejudices of health workers to 'foreign' concepts of health and to enable Australians from all ethnic backgrounds to participate in mainstream health services by bringing their cultural traditions of health to them.

Part of this study concerns traditional medicine, both its importance to immigrants and its potential for enriching the health system. Australians have always looked outside the mainstream health systems to alternative methods of healing, which immigrants regard as standard practices. Acupuncture, for example, a traditional Chinese method of treatment, is used in many areas of medicine in Australia.

Members of ethnic communities often have more confidence in their healers than in western practitioners (World Health Organization, 1983), and should not be discouraged from maintaining their traditional beliefs and practices. Other Australians (including those in the mainstream health-care system) should be

On the Move: the Psychology of Change and Transition. Edited by S. Fisher and C. L. Cooper.

encouraged to take greater interest in learning what is healthy and unhealthy about the former patterns of living and beliefs of immigrants.

MAKING SENSE OF DISTRESS AND SICKNESS

Immigrants bring to their new country belief systems that are shaped by culture, and it is not unusual for a gap to develop between patients and professionals in explaining the causes of sickness. Studies in clinically applied medical anthropology use the concept of explanatory models of illness (Blumhagen, 1981; Helman, 1986; Hielscher and Sommerfield, 1985; Katon and Kleinman, 1981; Stein, 1986), and the cultural basis of help-seeking behaviour (Blakemore, 1983; Keefe, 1982); western diagnostic systems and treatments that ignore a patient understanding of his or her illness are associated with lack of compliance and high costs (Kleinman, 1980).

Even when immigrants are settling in well, they may be affected by subtle forms of cultural bereavement that can have an effect long after they arrive. A central question is how stress and distress are culturally shaped, how immigrants make sense of their emotional reactions to resettlement and to illness. There are already well-documented differences in physical disease profiles among immigrants in Australia (Armstrong and McMichael, 1984; Dunt, 1982; Hopkins, Margetts, Cohen and Armstrong, 1980; McMichael, 1985), but there are few local studies on the cultural basis of maladjustment. While those in the health-care system know so little about the cultural construction of stress, distress and illness, they will be limited in their ability to diagnose and treat illness.

Clinical work with immigrants is often based on ethnocentric interpretations of difficulties in adjustment, but poor mental health may be shaped by cultural constructs which give meaning to the patient's post-immigration experiences and which in turn shape any resultant clinical problems. Psychological disorders, for example, can be present with somatic symptoms. In many societies health disorders are put down to natural and supernatural causes (Landy, 1983). Health professionals in a multicultural society need anthropologically informed yardsticks if they are to care effectively for their ethnic patients.

REACTIONS TO LOSS OF SOCIETY AND CULTURE

In 1983 the author was called upon by an Indo-Chinese mental health service in Boston to help Cambodian refugee children in crisis. The Cambodians proved to be appropriate for a study of the mental health impact of uprooting because, like all refugee children, they had suffered a traumatic loss of society and culture and were obliged to adapt rapidly to a new country; they could also be seen as representing other displaced people. The author's fieldwork and community

health research with Southeast Asian refugee youths in England, the United States and Australia suggested that adjustment is worsened by lack of access to culturally familiar practices. Beliefs about the causes of misfortune and illness were often based on Buddhist and folk systems seldom recognized by westerners involved with refugees. The well-being of refugees was improved when they were allowed to validate their beliefs through culturally appropriate rituals and behaviour (Eisenbruch, 1988a).

METHOD

After a year of clinical work with Cambodian refugees and several months of participant observation, a theory of 'cultural bereavement' and a tool to measure

Table 11.1. Structural basis of cultural bereavement interview

Constructs from bereavement theory	Areas explored in Cultural Bereavement schedule	Summary of items within Cultural Bereavement Schedule
Perceptions of past	1. Memories of family	Who? What? Trigger? Response?
	2. Continuing experiences	Presence? Communication? Exhort? Feeling?
Communication with past	3. Ghosts/spirits from past	Exhort? Response? Contact? Trigger? Feeling?
	4. Dreams	Trigger? Dream scene? Exhort? Outcome? Response?
Survivor guilt	5. Guilt	Guilt? Reason for flight? Wrong to flee? Rationale for flight?
	6. Clarity of recall of past	Difficulty recognizing family? Difficulty being recognized? Response? Available souvenirs? Response?
Violence of separation and death	7. The structuring of the past in the homeland	Memories before vs. after revolution? Structure of memories? Transfer to host country?
No leave-taking	8. Experiences of death	Who died? Cause? Certainty? Participation? Whose fault? Leave-taking ritual? Expectation of return? Yearning?
Anger and ambivalence	9. Response to separation from homeland	Understanding of flight? Instigator? Past anger? Anger now? Fear of violence/war? Political context?
Antidote to C.B.	10. Comfort from religious belief	Beliefs? Permission to express? Impact of revolution?
	11. Comfort from religious practice	Which practices helpful? Motive? Response?

it were developed. A semi-structured schedule, which combines descriptive and self-rating measures, was composed for clinical and fieldwork. Themes are organized in an appropriate sequence and examine memories of family in homeland, continuing experiences from the past, including ghosts or spirits, dreams, guilt, clarity of recall structuring of the past experience of death, anxieties, morbid thoughts, anger in response to separation and comfort from religion and religious practices. There are 50 items (Eisenbruch, 1988b). The structural basis is shown in Table 11.1.

Two groups of unaccompanied refugee adolescents were studied, 47 fostered in Cambodian group care in Australia and 32 placed in foster families (some Americans, some Cambodians) in the USA. It was postulated that those living with American families would experience greater cultural bereavement than their counterparts with Cambodian families (in the USA) or in Cambodian group care (in Australia). In some cases those fostered with American families saw little of their fellow-Cambodians and had little or no access to Cambodian culture.

The youths in Australia had been resettled for an average of 28.21 (SD = 11.22) months, whereas those in the USA had been resettled for an average of 15.94 (SD = 8.27) months. The effects can be explored by comparing groups of youths determined according to the country and period of settlement. Three periods were used: up to 16 months, 17–32 months, and greater than 32 months. For each of the cultural bereavement items three specific hypotheses were tested. These analyses were carried out using a generalized approach to non-parametric statistics with an experiment-wise error rate of 0.05 (Meddis, 1984).

A comparison of country of settlement was made, a test for decreasing bereavement (for each item) with length of settlement was set up, and the effect of length of stay on country of settlement was examined. This third comparison of the interaction of country and period of residence was carried out for the first two time groupings (<33 months). This analysis was intended to indicate whether country of settlement and length of residence factors were interdependent, at least in the initial stages.

RESULTS

ITEM ANALYSIS

Mean scores on the cultural bereavement items ranged from a high of 8.0 for memories during Pol Pot times to a low of 1.0 for ghosts and spirits (Table 11.2). Anger at the time of separation and regret about unfinished business in Cambodia scored highly, as did comfort derived from religious beliefs and rituals.

DIFFERENCES BETWEEN USA AND AUSTRALIA

There was a significant difference according to country of settlement for six of the 15 items. These were: thinking more often about the family than before,

Table 11.2. Summary of statistics for cultural bereavement items

	Mean	Standard deviation	Mode	Percentage with positive scores
Bad memories during Pol Pot times	8.0	2.1	9 (69.1%)	93.8
Comfort derived from traditional cultural ritual	7.0	2.1	9 (29.9%)	86.2
Regret unfinished business in country of origin	6.8	3.0	9 (49.4%)	81.6
Anger experienced at the time of separation	6.4	3.3	9 (42.5%)	77.0
Comfort derived from traditional religious belief	6.2	2.8	9 (28.7%)	75.9
Thinking often about family and homeland	5.8	2.8	9 (20.7%)	66.7
Thinking more about family/ homeland than previously	5.3	3.0	9 (23.0%)	62.1
Regret leaving Cambodia	5.2	3.3	9 (25.3%)	60.9
Want to go back to Cambodia	4.9	3.1	9 (19.5%)	59.8
Angry now	4.7	3.2	9 (18.4%)	54.0
Difficulty recalling appearance of parents	4.2	4.0	0 (39.1%)	47.1
Dreams	3.2	2.7	0,1 (17.4%)	31.4
Increased fear of danger and death	2.5	2.9	0 (27.9%)	22.1
Bad memories before Pol Pot times	1.4	2.3	0 (56.4%)	10.3
Ghosts and spirits	1.0	2.3	0 (71.3%)	10.3

Table 11.3. Average rank by country for cultural bereavement items

	USA	Australia
Bad memories during Pol Pot times*	40.41	31.08
Comfort derived from traditional cultural ritual	42.35	35.26
Regret unfinished business in country of origin	41.85	35.58
Anger experienced at the time of separation*	47.35	32.11
Comfort derived from traditional religious belief*	44.91	33.64
Thinking often about family and homeland*	44.86	33.67
Thinking more about family/homeland than previously	32.90	41.22
Regret leaving Cambodia	39.91	36.79
Want to go back to Cambodia	42.48	35.17
Angry now*	49.88	30.51
Difficulty recalling appearance of parents	40.38	36.50
Dreams	44.98	33.60
Increased fear of danger and death	33.02	40.39
Bad memories before Pol Pot times*	26.71	40.30
Ghosts and spirits	35.50	39.58

*5 per cent significance.

memories of life before Pol Pot times, memories of life during Pol Pot times, anger at the time of separation and anger now, and comfort derived from religion. Table 11.3 illustrates that the youths placed in the USA scored higher average ranks than those placed in Australia for all but one of these items.

TIME DIFFERENCES

For most of the items the length of stay in the country of settlement had no influence, which suggests that it might not account for the country differences. There was a decreasing trend of strength of comfort from religion with length of stay in the new country. Mean ranks for the three time groupings, from shortest stay to longest stay, were 42.3, 41.86 and 27.7 respectively. It thus appears that for longer term refugees religion provides less comfort.

THE EFFECTS OF TIME AND COUNTRY OF SETTLEMENT

For most of the items on cultural bereavement there was no interaction of period of settlement and country of settlement. Interesting differences between Australian and US youths appear on thinking often about the family and regret about leaving Cambodia. The mean ranks for the four groups are shown in Table 11.4. For the youths placed in Australia there tends to be an increase in thinking often about the family; for youths in the USA there appears to be a decrease with time. Conversely, the youths in Australia tend to experience a decrease in regret about leaving Cambodia; those in the USA tend to experience a progressive increase in regret.

The interaction between time and country of resettlement for the two items (thinking about the family and regret leaving Cambodia) shown in Table 11.4 is intriguing. It seems that youths in the USA start out by being more immersed in the past than are the youths in Australia, and by all accounts this immersion has a painful and nostalgic quality. With the passage of time it appears that the nostalgia *decreases* for youths in the USA while it *increases* for those in Australia, and the mean ranks show a crossover. How are these changes in nostalgic reminiscences associated with regret over leaving the homeland? The youths in the USA started out by feeling relatively less regret than their counterparts in Australia, but with time their regret grew, while the youths in Australia seemed

Table 11.4. Effects of time and country of settlement

	USA		Australia	
	Time 1	Time 2	Time 1	Time 2
Thinking often about family/homeland	50.1	40.0	26.3	45.5
Regret leaving homeland	34.1	45.5	45.2	20.7

to come to terms with their lives in the new country and their regret fell. Again these relative changes were pronounced as shown by the crossover in the mean ranks.

DISCUSSION

The results show that the youths continue to be immersed in the past, thinking often about their families, indeed more preoccupied than they had been when they arrived. Certainly there appears to be a sustained feeling of regret over leaving the homeland coupled with a wish to go back, and it is consistent with the wish, commonly expressed in the fieldwork, that youths wished to participate in the rebuilding of their country once the political situation allowed. Very powerful bad memories of atrocities during the Pol Pot times lingered, with a recollection of anger and regret at the time of leaving the homeland.

The youths seemed to feel that these painful feelings could be combated by traditional religious beliefs and access to ritual. Sometimes the importance of these feelings is ignored by policy-makers and care-givers who feel that rapid integration into western thought, behavior and religion is better for the refugee children, especially as they are young. The fieldwork indicated that much good could be done by promoting access of the refugee youths to Buddhist monks and to Cambodian traditional healers, including *kru Khmer*.

Participation in traditional ceremonies does more than simply 'treat' the individual's grief. Any treatment of the individual patient (even if the treatment seems culturally appropriate) can be frustrating because the patient returns to a community which is itself in a state of collective grief. Group participation promotes a restoration of the patient's old culture and acts as an antidote not only to his or her cultural bereavement but also to that of the entire community. Successful treatment will ultimately depend upon community intervention to arrest and reverse the group's cultural bereavement. If, for example, the community is encouraged to re-establish traditional religious institutions (such as the Buddhist *wat*), refugee children will have a place to gather and worship. The enhanced sense of community and the availability of acceptable social supports both help with resolution of grief.

The trend for both groups of Cambodian youths towards the decreasing comfort derived from religion could reflect a reduction in need, or greater difficulty in access, to Buddhist *wat* (pagoda), or that alternative solutions are available.

Policy-makers should be wary of jumping to conclusions on the basis of reports from recently arrived refugees. Nostalgic reminiscences may be a positive sign that refugees are responding to a permissive and safe environment that encourages the expression of painful latent feelings, or they may reflect an acute estrangement from self-identity and past culture that demands an opportunity

for restitution. Similarly, the expression of regret over fleeing the homeland can express a healthy working-through of feelings of loss and guilt over surviving, or the development of unresolved guilt, which can lead to psychological problems, such as depression, or potentially disruptive social problems, such as involvement in revanchist political or paramilitary movements.

EXTRAPOLATIONS

The findings on this group of unaccompanied youths seem consistent with the impressions gained about a range of immigrants. Health workers who rely solely on western formulations in multicultural settings may fail to recognize the full extent of a patient's loss and grief, and cultural bereavement may be overlooked. Patients' beliefs and actions may suggest to a western clinician that they are psychotic. It is not unusual to see, for example, Cambodian patients possessed by spirits, troubled by visitations of ghosts, hearing voices commanding them to make merit to ancestors, and feeling that they are being punished for surviving. All these can occur as culturally normal signs of bereavement, and patients often respond quickly to social and culturally appropriate intervention (Eisenbruch, 1987). But the uninformed health worker can be misled. It can be difficult to distinguish those patients who may truly be suffering a psychotic condition. It is essential not to diagnose a psychotic disorder wrongly and to initiate an inappropriate treatment regime.

An understanding of cultural bereavement could help to identify cases where intervention might need to be extended by active intercession from traditional sources within the patient's community. The health worker could collaborate with religious functionaries or with traditional healers to negotiate a healthier 'separation' from the past.

An understanding of cultural bereavement could help in the clinical care of uprooted people in several ways by: providing a clinical framework for exploring the patient's personal and cultural bereavement; clarifying the 'structure' of the patient's reactions to loss; complementing the currently used diagnostic categories and thus avoiding misdiagnosis; acknowledging the cultural system of meaning held by the patient; and providing information that can be used in planning social supports or interventions.

Cultural bereavement interviews are now being used in further studies of the adjustment of refugees in Australia, Canada and Israel, and in other community health research, for example, in a study of Ethiopian refugees. As modifications of the cultural bereavement interview are used with various uprooted cultural groups, more will be learned about their salient experiences, and it will be possible to identify crucial areas of need. The probe questions cannot be universally suitable and may need to be tailored to the circumstances and culture of a particular group. Ultimately, community health workers should be able to

use the cultural bereavement interview as a diagnostic and therapeutic aid with a range of affected groups: refugees, victims of disaster, those subjected to rapid modernization, and others profoundly affected by a rapid loss of their past.

POLICY AND HEALTH TRANSITION

In their review of cultural determinants of health in different countries, Caldwell *et al.* (1988) emphasize the need for anthropological research that takes as its starting point the findings of international comparisons and then explains the situation in a single society. The research in this chapter has argued that the 'mental health' of immigrants is not merely a question of the individual's state of mind but can be influenced by interplay with the host country. The Cambodian youths studied were subject to different policies, and the results were evident in fieldwork and the cultural bereavement study.

There are various policies in several countries for dealing with uprooted youths who have no families to care for them. Policy-makers around the world continue to debate the relative merits of group care, fostering and independent living (Jockenhövel-Schiecke, 1984; Leer, 1979, 1983; Refugee Documentation Project, 1984; United States Catholic Conference, 1983; Walter, 1979). One policy, followed by countries such as Australia, is to allow the refugees to live together in group care while having every opportunity to integrate into the host society at their own rate. Thus refugees are able to maintain their cultural identity. A second policy is followed in European countries, such as Denmark, West Germany and France, where unaccompanied minors are structurally separated from the host society. Another policy of placing the refugee with a foster family has been followed primarily in the USA, but has been adopted for other countries for other ethnic groups.

There are important differences in intensity and quality of cultural bereavement among the Cambodian minors resettled in the USA and Australia. Why should it be that, in comparison with their counterparts in Australia, the youths placed in the USA are more afflicted by bad memories of Pol Pot times, should recollect greater anger at the time of leaving their homeland, should have stronger persistence of anger, should continue to be immersed in thinking about their parents and their country, and at the same time should make stronger claims for traditional religious practice? One possible explanation is that the youths in the USA are placed with Cambodian or American foster families. When placed with the latter they are usually expected to adjust rapidly and to adopt the behavior and sometimes the attitudes of American youth. Their counterparts in Australia were placed in group care, where they have been encouraged to maintain a Cambodian ethos and practice, and have had no overt pressure to acculturate. It is suggested that the prevailing ideology in the USA and Australia

of 'doing good' for the health of others has a distinct influence on the health status of the young Cambodian refugees.

REFUGEE CHILDREN AND HEALTH TRANSITION

Earlier papers have suggested that resettled refugees may need a moratorium during which they are under less pressure to acculturate. But the cultural bereavement of many refugees (especially the more traditional or those who were older when they arrived) will not be alleviated simply by a slowed rate of westernization. Here one can see how classical grief theory is inadequate when considering cultural bereavement. Classical grief theory suggests that refugees will 'work through' their loss when they accept it and acquire new attachments and relationships, but many exiles clearly do not want to abandon their attachments to homeland, and nurture a hope of return.

Policy-makers, program providers and health workers are in need of proper criteria by which they can judge the impact of their interventions upon the refugees. But when they begin with the belief that refugee health lies in rapid acculturation, and that 'living in the past' is a signal of illness, the result can be self-fulfilling. By systematic measurement of that which is 'good' about current policy for refugee resettlement (for example, acquisition of acculturation skills), and by systematically failing to measure that which is 'not good' (for example, the suppression of traditional social structures and cultural meanings), the prevailing policy is confirmed as successful. The absence of recognizable sadness is regarded as a sign of good adaptation; too much nostalgic 'living in the past' is regarded as an illness (perhaps depressive disorder) that impedes adaptation. The cluster of nostalgia and sadness may be managed with western treatments (such as anti-depressants), so that the refugee can get on with acculturation. The use of exclusively western psychiatric instruments scales as criteria of 'wellness' might then confirm the 'success' of intervention. But the failure to measure the refugee's cultural construction of reality allows the continuation of therapies, policies and programs that are potentially iatrogenic.

According to the conventional models, alienation results from the failure by the refugee to acculturate to the host society; helping professionals and others intervene to 'improve' acculturation by providing opportunities to learn the host society's language, social customs and values. Personal and cultural bereavement are ignored. The alternative model shows why attempts to acculturate refugees rapidly do not always 'succeed'. Indeed, difficulties in acculturation are the end-result of alienation. This loop results from accelerated and forced acculturation. The new model suggests that bereavement should be encouraged and the refugee allowed time to mourn the loss of country and culture.

The alternative model, which recognizes cultural bereavement, suggests that intervention should take place at three levels: to allow for and encourage the

natural expression of bereavement within the refugee's cultural idiom; to provide refugees with a moratorium on acculturation; and to teach the refugees survival skills. The model suggests that, in comparison with American foster families, placement with Cambodian foster families is less likely to disrupt the young refugee's grief; will allow respite during which they feel less alienated; and will enable them to feel under less overt pressure to acculturate. Placement with a culturally familiar foster family is a positive intervention, and placement in a small group with Cambodian house parents would be likely to lead to a similar outcome.

The findings of this study throw into doubt some commonly held assumptions about uprooted youths. Refugee youths, for example, live in the past a lot more than is generally acknowledged. This is not to say that they should be encouraged to do so, or that they should be encouraged to plan their repatriation (Douki *et al.*, 1982). 'Living in the past' is a crucial phase in their experiences, not only because it is a key to the process of bereavement, but also because without it the youths cannot reconstitute their sense of identity so brutally fractured by war. Uprooted youths must be enabled to carry out their grief without compounding their problems of alienation from their host society by also inducing alienation from their own culture.

Cultural bereavement does not take place in a vacuum. The attitudes of refugee care-givers will allow or disallow the youths to grieve. Some foster parents and even agency workers feel threatened by any revivalist sentiment on the part of the youths and need to resist their tendency to prohibit the expression of the wish to return to Cambodia. If care-givers cannot tolerate these challenges to their esteem, their foster children will pick up the message that they are not supposed to talk about their yearnings. These interactions between foster parents and young refugees need to be recognized and worked with.

Young refugees also need to continue familiar religious practices that can aid in the grieving process. Foster parents may need to learn the principles of Buddhism and to be advised against explicit attempts at evangelism. Some refugees living with American families or in refugee camps, for example, are under severe pressure to convert to Christianity and be 'saved'.

It is possible that the unaccompanied Cambodian minors can be a guide to the experiences of other uprooted children. Before generalizing from unaccompanied minors to other uprooted youths with parents, some qualifications are needed. There are fundamental differences between young refugees with and without their parents. Future research should compare these groups, and should be carried out with a range of ethnic groups because there are culture-specific responses to loss that are based on differences both in the culture's theodicy (the charter for explaining human suffering) and its eschatology (the cultural explanation of death). Figure 11.1 shows a proposed model of the impact of immigration on core culture and the effects of cultural bereavement on clinical outcome and on the 'success' of multiculturalism.

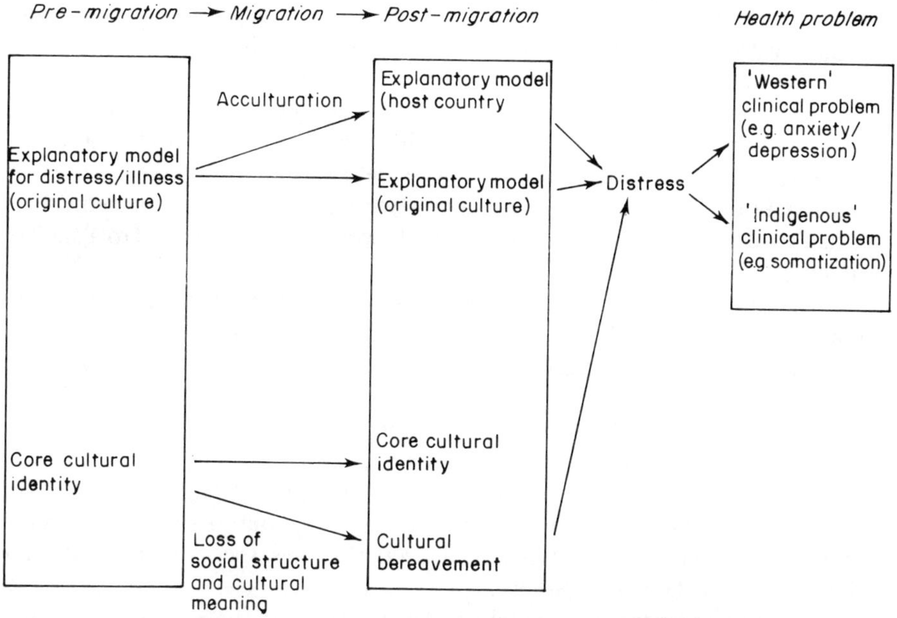

Figure 11.1. The impact of immigration on core culture and the effects of cultural bereavement on clinical outcome.

It is postulated that there is a causal relationship between health beliefs, clinical presentation and cultural bereavement. It works as follows: immigration and the associated losses of familiar social structures and cultural meaning might be associated with cultural bereavement, with an effect on the person's core cultural identity. Cultural bereavement might be associated with the development of mental distress, which will be shaped by the culture of origin. The uprooted person might draw upon culturally determined explanations of mental distress. The development of symptoms might reflect the way that the patient understands loss of culture and the post-immigration experience. This understanding will be based on ideas both from the original culture (such as somatization) and from the host culture (such as anxiety or depression). The clinical effects of loss are proportional to the cultural gap between the immigrant's culture of origin and the culture of the host society. Culturally inappropriate health care may intensify cultural bereavement, leading to a vicious cycle in which cultural bereavement causes ill-health and leads to inappropriate treatment.

The research reported leads to the proposition that immigrants in multicultural Australia must be experiencing health transition as a result of their shifting cultural identity and attitudes to health and illness. It seems possible that cultural bereavement could intensify with an increasing cultural difference of the immigrant group from the mainstream Australian culture. Immigrants whose

cultural background is very different from that of Australian-born patients will use terms to explain their mental distress that are less familiar to Australians, while Australian patients will more often use western explanations; and patients experiencing more cultural bereavement will use more non-western explanations and fewer western explanations for distress.

It is essential to avoid overgeneralizing when drawing inferences from one group of refugees to groups of nations and peoples. Kunitz has warned of this danger, which arises from indiscriminate aggregation of data (Kunitz, 1989). It is necessary now to develop national community-based research programs that can explore these issues by anthropologically informed studies of selected communities. Samples of patients who represent the whole society could be examined in detail in a multidisciplinary strategy embracing medical anthropology, community medicine and transcultural psychiatry. The research agenda outlined in this chapter can help to identify why immigrants sometimes are 'doing better and feeling worse' and how they make sense of their immigrant experience and any associated stress and social misfortune. The two latter factors tend to worsen the structural barriers no matter what the mainstream health system might try to do to overcome them.

Government departments in Australia are seeking to improve ethnic health, and human services have emphasized the need for access and equity programs. At the federal level the Office of Multicultural Affairs has encouraged portfolios including Community Services and Health to develop access and equity. State Ethnic Affairs Commissions are also active in implementing access and equity strategies. In the area of health promotion for ethnic communities the problem is worsened by the lack of a measure of outcome, whereas in areas such as language the success of teaching and learning provides more obvious indicators. WHO has proposed the development of a public health index and of health impact statements, but to the best of my knowledge the algorithms do not include a factor for ethnic health. As Caldwell *et al.* (1988) have pointed out, it is hard to know how to measure care that does not result in sickness, and to measure sickness that does not result in death. This chapter suggests that cultural bereavement could be a significant marker of health transition. There could be a case for including appropriately scaled measures of cultural bereavement, with other applicable psychosocial indicators, as a part of the public health index or health impact statements.

CONCLUSION

There are important ethical issues for multiculturalism and health transition. In considering 'health maintenance behavior', Caldwell *et al.* (1988) have noted that an interaction between individuals and healers tends to reduce mortality and probably morbidity. Examples from Kerala and Sri Lanka, with the most

highly developed traditional health systems in South Asia, confirm the value of traditional beliefs and practices as contributing to health. Health beliefs are a cornerstone of people's identities, and these must be maintained if cultural identity is to be sustained. If the host society is sensitive to the need for cultural maintenance then immigrants are more likely to do well.

There is nothing radical in suggesting the importance of culture maintenance for people undergoing transition in developing countries, yet somehow this principle has not always filtered through to immigration authorities and health policy-makers in developed countries. Sometimes host countries try to 'sanitize' people by 'educating' them to be emancipated from their outmoded and 'unhealthy' beliefs. Cultural maintenance is more than an optional extra, for if traditional social structures and cultural meanings are not augmented in the new country, some immigrants may become prone to ill-health and be unable to retrieve a key piece of their identity. Indeed, when some immigrant groups learning new habits in host countries become more prone to worse physical or mental health than they were in their country of origin, 'multiculturalism' has failed in its promise to enrich their lives.

SUMMARY

This chapter aims to demonstrate that the reactions of refugees to their new country can be defined in terms of cultural bereavement, the traumatic loss of society and culture; that these reactions are strongly coloured by the policies of the host country; and that cultural bereavement is important in the health transition of immigrants. The chapter reports a study that developed a means of measuring cultural bereavement.

Cambodian refugees living in Australia and the USA were studied to assess the impact on them of cultural bereavement, difficulty in adapting to a new and different society, and associated poor mental health. Significant differences were found between unaccompanied minors placed in American or Cambodian care. Those placed in a culturally alien environment adapted somewhat better but suffered more cultural bereavement; their counterparts in Khmer cultural settings were less acculturated but suffered less cultural bereavement. The well-being of the refugees was improved when they were allowed to validate their cultural beliefs through appropriate rituals and behavior.

REFERENCES

Armstrong, B. K. and McMichael, A. J. (1984) Cancer in migrants. *Medical Journal of Australia*, **140**, 3-4.

Blakemore, K. (1983) Ethnicity, self-reported illness and use of medical services by the elderly. *Postgraduate Medical Journal*, **59**(696), 668-70.

Blumhagen, D. W. (1981) On the nature of explanatory models. *Culture, Medicine and Psychiatry*, **5**(4), 337-40.

Caldwell, J., Caldwell, P., Gajanayake, I., Orubuloye, I. O., Pieris, I, and Reddy, P. H. (1988) Cultural, social and behavioral determinants of health and their mechanisms: A report of related research programs. Paper at Health Transition Workshop. Cultural, Social and Behavioral Determinants of Health. Canberra, 15-19 May.

Dunt, D. R. (1982) Recent mortality trends in the adult Australian population and its principal ethnic groupings. *Community Health Studies*, **6**, 217-22.

Eisenbruch, M. (1987) The impact of cultural bereavement on identity among Cambodian refugees in the United States and Australia. 86th Congress, American Anthropological Association, Chicago, 17-21 November.

Eisenbruch, M. (1988a) The mental health and cultural development of refugee children. *International Migration Review*, **22**, 282-300.

Eisenbruch, M. (1988b) The mental health of refugees: A suitable case for treatment. Invited keynote paper at Refugee Mental Health Conference, Wellington, 12-15.

Eisenbruch, M. (1990) The cultural bereavement interview: a new clinical research approach for refugees. *Psychiatric Clinics of North America* (In press).

Erikson, K. (1976) *Everything in its Path*. New York: Simon & Schuster.

Fisher, S. (1988) Homesickness and health. *Psychologist*, **9**, 351-2.

Helman, C. G. (1986) Communication in primary care: the role of patient and practitioner explanatory model. *Social Science and Medicine*, **20**(9), 923-31.

Hielscher, S., and Sommerfield, J. (1985) Concepts of illness and the utilization of health care services in a rural Malain village. *Social Science and Medicine*, **21**(4), 469-81.

Hopkins, S., Margetts, B. M., Cohen, J., and Armstrong, B. K. (1980) Dietary change among Italians and Australians in Perth. *Community Health Studies*, **4**, 67-75.

Jockenhövel-Schiecke (1984) Unaccompanied minors in European resettlement countries. Documentation of Seminar. Frankfurt: International Social Service.

Katon, W. and Kleinman A. (1981) Doctor-patient negotiation and other social science strategies in patient care. In Leon Eisenberg and Arthur Kleinman (eds), *The Relevance of Social Science for Medicine*. Dordrecht: D. Reidel.

Keefe, S. E. (1982) Help-seeking behavior among foreign-born and native-born Mexican Americans. *Social Science and Medicine* **16**(16), 1467-72.

Kleinman, A. (1980) *Patients and Healers in the Context of Culture*. Berkeley, CA: University of California Press.

Kunitz, S. J. (1989) The quest for anomalies: the value of particularism in the study of mortality. Paper at Health Transition Workshop. Cultural, Social and Behavioral Determinants of Health. Canberra, 15-19 May.

Landy, D. (1983) Medical anthropology: a critical appraisal. In J. L. Ruffini (ed.) *Advances in Medical Social Science*, Vol. 1. New York: Gordon & Breach.

12 From Education to Job Markets

JOHN ARNOLD
Manchester School of Management

INTRODUCTION

This chapter will examine the transition which occurs when people complete their full-time education for at least the foreseeable future. It will do so chiefly in terms of the person's entry into the labour market. Clearly there are other significant dimensions to the transition, particularly perhaps the parental or marital family context. However, full-time education occurs during 'working hours', so the work setting is the most appropriate post-transition environment to examine.

Even with this focus, it is not easy to generalize about the transition, since people leave education at different ages with varying educational accomplishments and prior experiences. They then experience different post-transition environments. Nevertheless, this chapter will first look for general features of the transition, since these help to provide a framework for understanding its nature and significance. They also supply some suggestions about how the transition is likely to be experienced, and what its consequences are likely to be.

Then I will examine research on the transition for two distinct groups separately: school-leavers and graduates. Together these groups include a high proportion, though not all, of the young people who leave education. The groups vary considerably in many ways, the most obvious being age and educational achievement. These in turn have implications for the transitioner's concerns, the labour market conditions they encounter and their transitional experiences. Partly for these reasons, many research and intervention efforts have focused on one group or the other, not both. The kind of research conducted with each group has also varied quite substantially, as we shall see later. Nevertheless, the distinction does not fit well with all the relevant research. Where this is the case, it will be pointed out. Where the institutional context is important, conditions prevailing in the United Kingdom will form the basis of discussion.

On the Move: the Psychology of Change and Transition. Edited by S. Fisher and C. L. Cooper.

The chapter will end with a look at what existing knowledge and theory on the transition from education to labour market adds up to. Conclusions will be drawn concerning what is and is not known about the transition from education to labour market.

THE NATURE OF THE TRANSITION

Writers on transitions have made numerous attempts to classify them and to identify their key features (e.g. Reese and Smyer, 1983). The result has been a profusion of potential factors to consider, the choice of which has usually been based on the particular interests of the writer concerned, as Sugarman (1986, chapter 6) has pointed out. It is nevertheless possible to discern certain common themes. Most researchers and practitioners are interested in the extent to which a transition is likely to produce positive or negative affective outcomes, and in the extent to which a person's adaptive capacities are taxed by the transition (Brim and Ryff, 1980; Danish, Smyer and Nowak, 1980). Especially within the occupational field, there has also been considerable recent interest in the extent to which transitions (in the form of starting work and subsequent job changes) lead to personal change and/or to innovation on the part of the person (Nicholson, 1984; Jones, 1986; Nicholson and West, 1988). Overlaid on all this have been attempts to map out processes of personal adjustment which could be applicable across a range of transitions (Schlossberg, 1981; Hopson, 1982; Nicholson, 1987). Writers with a sociological orientation have tried to identify the institutional socialization and other tactics employed to facilitate transition processes (Van Maanen, 1976; Van Maanen and Schein, 1979).

A key feature of this transition is that its occurrence is on the whole easily anticipatable. Not only is it virtually certain that one will experience it at some time in one's life, but it is usually fairly clear when it will happen. Barring unexpectedly good or poor educational performance, or perhaps an unforeseen opportunity, it is possible to predict accurately the month and year in which one's full-time education will end. This anticipatability can have several effects, some of which are likely to make the transition smoother and more pleasant for the person experiencing it. In some respects anticipatability increases the young person's opportunity to exert control over the precise form the transition takes. In particular it enables planning ahead regarding job or other applications, and also exploration of possibilities of this kind (Stumpf, Colarelli and Hartman, 1983; Grotevant and Cooper, 1988). Anticipatability also allows the opportunity to 'think oneself' into future roles so that appropriate attitudes and behaviour patterns can be rehearsed before the transition occurs. This 'anticipatory socialization' (Merton, 1957) is often discussed, but, it must be noted, less often demonstrated (e.g. Korte and Sylvester, 1982). Secondly, and linked to anticipatability, is the fact that leaving education is experienced by many

people, including those with whom one lives day-to-day. One's contemporaries are likely to be good sounding boards for discussing plans, hopes and fears. Older relatives and friends are likely to offer their own perspectives on an event which has already happened to them. There is, then, nothing taboo or covert about the transition from education to labour market. Glaser and Strauss (1971) emphasize this point in their work on transitions of this kind, which they refer to as status passages:

> One of the hallmarks of status passages, especially ones deemed important by pasagees or other interested parties, is the astonishingly frequent and free discussion of status passages, for these are open rather than tabooed subjects (p. 4).

This open discussion may heighten control, anticipatory socialization, and exploration. It may also perhaps decrease anxiety through familiarizing the young people with possible post-transition environments, and by reminding them that they have plenty of company in facing it (see Schachter, 1959, and Morris *et al.*, 1976, for experimental analogues).

Anticipatable though it usually is, the transition from education to labour market can be abrupt when it comes. Examinations taken in the summer demand increasing commitment and effort in the old role (of student/pupil) even as the time when that role will end draws nearer. This is likely to have two effects. Firstly, some young people suspend exploration and planning for their future while they cope with these short-term demands. Secondly, it is that much harder to let go of a role if you have recently been putting a lot into it (Becker, 1960). On the other hand, examinations themselves can constitute powerful 'rites of passage' (Van Gennep, 1960) which signal that the role of student or pupil is ending (Hall, 1968). This may help the young person to let go.

The relatively inflexible timing of the transition makes the young person vulnerable to events such as economic and/or technological change which can crucially affect his or her experience of the transition, but which are completely outside his or her control. Such events can be regional as well as national or international. They can have dramatically different effects on different individuals, and these may be long-term as well as short-term, though perhaps not life-long (Elder, 1979). Thus the anticipatability of timing of leaving education may in some circumstances work against anticipatability of the post-transition environment awaiting the young person.

It is perhaps particularly difficult to generalize about the amount of novelty (Nicholson, 1984) experienced by a young person in their first post-education work setting. It depends by definition on the person's prior experiences as well as their post-transition environment. Whilst there may be substantial change in day-to-day work requirements, young people may already have had extracurricular experience of activities which are typical of their post-transition environment. The same is true of interpersonal relationships, change in which

is seen by many theorists (e.g. Wells and Stryker, 1988) as an important predictor of the adjustment demands made of a person, and of personal change. In any case, some young people keep substantially the same network of friends for a considerable time after the transition, and some are already accustomed to regular and substantial change due to parental family moves. In summary, then, the transition may not bring highly novel role requirements, and even if it does the young person may be practised at adjusting to novelty. It is therefore tempting to agree with Ashton and Field (1976), that problems faced by young people when they leave education: 'do not differ significantly from problems of adjustment young people have already faced and will continue to face in both work and non-work situations' (p. 15).

The transition from education to work is often equated with that between adolescence and adulthood (Honess, 1989). That transition is seen as crucial to societal stability in many cultures and is consequently managed with care. It is not surprising then that young people are offered substantial institutional mechanisms to smooth the path of transition. Some of these are formal; some informal. In some cases it is not clear whether they aim to smooth the path for the young adult or for the institutions themselves. Thus, in educational institutions, substantial resources and critical attention are devoted to careers services (see, for example, Watts, 1986; Ross, 1988; Watts and Sampson, 1989), and also increasingly to curricular changes designed to increase 'vocationalism' of courses. In the post-transition environment (most frequently employment) formal induction procedures and also more *ad-hoc* attempts are made to socialize newcomers into the 'right' ways of thinking, though often much of the socialization is done by newcomers to each other (Becker, Geer, Hughes and Strauss, 1961; Schein, 1971a; Van Maanen and Schein, 1979).

Placing the transition in a life-span perspective helps us appreciate its personal as well as societal significance. According to many theorists, (e.g. Erikson, 1963; Super, 1957, 1980) the mid/late teens and early twenties are times of exploration and identity formation. The young person is exploring possible selves and possible futures, and in doing so will be developing his or her own sense of self as an independent and grown-up person (Haan, 1981). This is likely to predispose the young person to view leaving education as a welcome symbol of attainment of adulthood, especially if it also involves attainment of an adult role such as employment. We have here, then, another reason why a young person is likely to tackle the transition with purpose and welcome its arrival. On the other hand, this, together with the non-reversibility of the transition for many young people, is predicted to heighten its salience (Gurin and Brim, 1984), and make the consequences of self-perceived failure all the more negative.

We can now briefly summarize some general and important points about the transition from education to labour market. These points are not precise enough to be called hypotheses, nor are they the only phenomena of interest. Rather,

they are general propositions which can be derived from considering the nature of the transition.

1. The transition is likely to be welcomed by the transitioner.
2. It is likely to be seen as personally significant by those who experience it.
3. People who experience the transition are likely to have had considerable opportunity to influence its course and adjust in advance.
4. Those who take that opportunity are more likely to find the transition a positive experience than those who do not.
5. The relatively inflexible timing of the transition can work against individual influence at times of rapid social, economic or technological change.
6. At such times, young people who are in some sense 'flexible' will navigate the transition more successfully than others.
7. There are likely to be many institutional interventions aimed at managing the transition.
8. Finally, the design and nature of these interventions will have a substantial impact on transition outcomes.

With this context in mind, let us now turn to an examination of existing empirical research on the transition from education to labour market.

FROM SCHOOL TO LABOUR MARKET

OLDER RESEARCH

A number of substantial studies were conducted in the UK over a period of 20 years or so starting in the late 1950s (e.g. Carter, 1962; Veness, 1962; Maizels, 1970; Ashton and Field, 1976; Keil, 1976; Willis, 1977). These and others have been well summarized by Clarke (1980), and a few more of the same kind appeared after Clarke's review (e.g. Ryrie, 1983; West and Newton, 1983).

Most of this earlier work described youngsters' experiences in the months before and after leaving school. Particular emphasis was placed upon preparing for jobs, obtaining them, and adjusting to them. Unemployment was less prevalent then than in more recent years, and government-sponsored training schemes were virtually unknown, at least for school-leavers. There was a predisposition amongst researchers to construe the transition as somehow 'difficult' for young people, especially regarding adjustment demands, though we have already seen that Ashton and Field (1976) did not subscribe to that view. This predisposition did not on the whole distort conclusions drawn from the research, but it did of course influence the questions asked and approaches adopted.

It seems that most youngsters were perfectly happy about the prospect of leaving school, and were excited about entering more independent and adult

roles. There was little sign that school-leavers had inflated expectations of work, or indeed well-defined expectations of any kind. Many did not obtain the type of work they most wanted, but they seemed to adjust fairly readily to this reality (see also Dowling and O'Brien, 1981). On the whole they seemed reasonably satisfied with their employment, although it was clear that the initial excitement quickly wore off. Strong feelings of all kinds tended to turn into indifference, and self-consciousness soon gave way to more automatic and routinized behaviour.

In the absence of widespread easily discernible adjustment problems amongst school-leavers entering employment, researchers and policy-makers looked for other possible symptoms of problems in making the transition. They hit upon rapid job-changing, but on further examination this seemed neither necessarily to be a problem for the young person concerned, nor was it easily predictable on the basis of prior indicators (Cherry, 1976; West and Newton, 1983). Studies of particular occupations did reveal one exception to the picture of relatively smooth, if resigned, adjustment to work: nursing. In the UK this was, and is, mainly a non-graduate profession with many school-leavers, nearly all female, entering it. Menzies (1960), Birch (1979) and West and Rushton (1986) have highlighted the stresses of entering this profession which if anything seem to worsen in years 2 and 3. Surviving the pressure does, however, lead to an enhanced sense of competence.

Pupils were usually only moderately impressed by the input of youth employment officers (nowadays called careers officers), and where they were seen as useful it was for providing job placements rather than ideas about suitable occupations. On the other hand, pupils did seem to monitor their own level of achievement at school, and to develop occupational aspirations consistent with it (Ryrie, 1983). Some of the lower-achieving pupils, especially boys, developed an identity around their low interest in academic work, and the positive value of manual labour (Willis, 1977). Institutional procedures in the work setting also came in for some criticism by school-leavers. They often reported a lack of induction, training and information in their early weeks and months. On the other hand, the work environment was generally seen as being more congenial than school, with more stable workgroups and less heavy-handed supervision (Bazalgette, 1975). Many youngsters seemed to carry over attitudes toward authority from school to the workplace. Girls generally experienced the transition less positively than boys, probably partly because they were on the wrong end of employment discrimination (West and Newton, 1983). Over time, however, the sexes converged somewhat in their views.

A quote from Ryrie (1983, p. 150) perhaps best illustrates the dominant impression from this research with school-leavers:

> While the employment situation with which they were confronted clearly spelled difficulty and frustration for many, the socialising processes in which they had

> been involved had led them to accept their places in the world without any sense of wrong turnings, lost opportunities or the need to break out in the future.

Clarke (1980) and others criticized much of the research as being too purely descriptive, and not sufficiently rooted in any theoretical context. Doubts were also raised about the research methods used, and about the tendency to concentrate on boys at the expense of girls. All these complaints had some validity. Regarding the first, however, it should be borne in mind that theory on transition was very thin on the ground when most of these studies were conducted (as opposed to being richer but fragmented as is the case at the time of writing). Description can be constructed as a necessary preliminary to good theory, and in any case many of the writers, especially the earlier ones, would probably have seen their goal as painting a picture for educationalists, employers and policy-makers to interpret. It should also be noted that some of the later studies did make more explicit use of sociological theory (e.g. Ashton and Field, 1976) and psychological theory (e.g. West and Newton, 1983) in presenting and interpreting their results, though at times it did look as if theory had been worked post-hoc into research reports rather than guiding the original research design.

The most serious limitations of much of this work concern its time-bound nature. As noted earlier, the transition from education to labour market is deeply rooted in institutional, employment and economic conditions. Changes in any one of these can render much research obsolete. Parenthetically, we should note that just how much research is rendered obsolete is itself an interesting question, the answer to which would tell us much about which are the most stable sociological and psychological phenomena. If we accept that some unknown but large segment of research results do come unstuck in changing conditions, then the UK recession, beginning in earnest at the end of the 1970s, put the continuing validity of then-existing research in extreme doubt.

LEAVING SCHOOL IN THE 1980s

By 1979 or 1980 it could no longer be assumed that, for the vast majority, leaving the education system directly after school meant entering employment. Unemployment started to increase rapidly and new training schemes were introduced for young people trying to enter the world of work, principally via the Manpower Services Commission (subsequently re-titled the Training Commission and then re-re-titled the Training Agency).

Quite apart from the dramatic impacts of these changing circumstances on young people and their families, there was also a change in the nature of research on the transition from school to labour market. The importance of institutional and structural factors as opposed to personal ones in determining transition process and outcomes became very evident (Atkins, 1985) and sociology and social policy perspectives began to take a correspondingly larger role in research

(see, for example, Watson, 1983; Walker and Barton, 1986). Much of this work has examined the assumptions lying behind social and educational policy, as well as practical initiatives such as the Youth Opportunities Programme (YOP), its successor the Youth Training Scheme (YTS), and associated educational innovations such as the Technical and Vocational Education Initiative (TVEI).

Substantial criticisms of post-school training schemes have been common (e.g. Willis, 1984; Roberts and Kirby, 1985; Dale, 1986; Gleeson, 1986). Gleeson summed up a general opinion amongst researchers and writers on social policy:

> Perhaps the major weakness of contemporary training policy is that it neither specifies specific skills training nor provides an adequate general education . . . the young lose out both ways; on the one hand, they do not gain marketable or recognised skills and, on the other, they do not acquire knowledge and understanding, however broadly defined, that allow them critical insight into the political or economic workings of society (p. 62).

It might perhaps be pointed out that similar criticisms could have been, and occasionally were, levelled at much post-school *employment*. Nevertheless, the image of school-leavers providing often unwilling cheap labour in narrowly based training schemes with no jobs at the end of them seems compelling. It suggests that for many school-leavers, the transition of leaving education became even more constrained than in earlier years, and also more uncertain in terms of longer-term prospects and the adoption of more autonomous adult roles (Wallace, 1986).

Changing UK economic conditions also provoked much self-examination within the school education system, though some of this had in fact already begun earlier in the 1970s through the then government's 'Great Education Debate'. Much of the work arising from this self-examination has provided a thoughtful critique of the actual and potential roles of school education in times of changing employment conditions. Two general issues have emerged. Firstly, whether (and how) schools should be preparing their pupils for any or all of employment, unemployment and leisure (Watts, 1983a,b) and secondly how should work experience and vocational guidance in the school curriculum be designed in order to ease the transition of leaving school for those who experience it (Jamieson, 1983; Roberts, 1983; Watts, 1983b, 1986; Cherry and Gear, 1987a,b; Bell, Howieson, King and Raffe, 1988; see also Ryrie, 1983, chapter 3). The second issue is more specific than the first, and has therefore attracted more empirical analysis. This has produced widely varying results. The safest conclusion (and it is not particularly safe!) is that out-of-school influences, especially family, have a greater impact on pupils' occupational choices and job-getting than school-based ones. The latter do, however, have some beneficial effects (e.g. some work experience components of TVEI) at least as far as pupils' self-reported progress toward occupational choice is concerned.

Other work has looked more specifically at the destinations and experiences of youngsters leaving school in the 1980s. Not surprisingly, increasing attention has been paid to whether they obtained jobs at all compared with earlier decades when, as we have seen, the emphasis was more on what they made of the jobs they did get. Consistent with this change of emphasis, more work has also been conducted on the impact of unemployment upon young people.

Some research (Raffe, 1983; Jones, 1985) has shown that pupils' achievements and behaviour at school can have subsequent consequences for their success in the labour market. This does not solely concern academic qualifications: truancy, attitudes to school and timing of job search whilst still at school are important in their own right, though themselves linked with qualifications. It also seems that although pupils' occupational aspirations are not necessarily responsive to local labour market conditions (Ryrie, 1983), those conditions play a crucial role in their subsequent ability to obtain and retain jobs, including obtaining a permanent post through YOP or YTS (Ashton and Maguire, 1986). This effect can be so pronounced that it even exceeds social class effects, so that middle-class youths in an area of high unemployment do less well than their working-class contemporaries in less hard-hit localities. Honess (1989) found clear differences between coping strategies and self-concepts of young people in areas of Wales with relatively good and relatively poor labour markets, and that social support was an indicator of obtaining employment only in the latter. On the other hand, high self-esteem was a predictor of obtaining employment across both areas.

The 1980s not surprisingly saw a great deal of research on the psychological impact of unemployment. Young people were the central focus of some of this work, and at least included in much of it. Studies reported by Gurney (1980, 1981); Stafford (1982); Warr, Jackson and Banks (1982); Jackson, Stafford, Banks and Warr (1983); Jackson and Warr (1984); Warr, Banks and Ullah (1985); Feather and O'Brien (1986a,b, 1987); and (the most comprehensive and up-to-date coverage) Banks and Ullah (1988) are amongst the best of the substantial literature arising from research with young people.

With the partial exception of Feather and O'Brien (1986b), the evidence is clear that unemployment has a negative impact on the psychological well-being of school-leavers, just as it does on other age groups. It is toughest on those with most employment commitment. There is little sign of an association between well-being and duration of unemployment, though Banks and Ullah (1988, p. 151) suggest that this may be an artifact of the measurement method used. Young people want to be employed, and not just for financial gain. They do not enjoy being unemployed. Their commitment to the idea of being employed does not generally wane with increasing duration of unemployment. Their job-seeking activity does seem to wane, though Feather and O'Brien (1987) found the reverse amongst their sample of young people in Australia. Black youngsters are more likely to be unemployed than their white contemporaries, even controlling for

other variables such as educational attainment (see also House of Lords Select Committee report, 1982). They are also less likely to get on to the better YTS schemes. It seems that in some respects white youths find unemployment harder to bear than blacks (at least for some months), probably because the latter have already developed strategies for coping with a society that discriminates against them. In spite of the negative picture painted above of YOP and YTS, the evidence is clear that these schemes mimic the beneficial psychological effects of employment relative to unemployment, and can therefore in this respect at least be treated as equivalent to employment. On some other variables (principally psychosocial development and locus of control) there is evidence that employment has positive effects on school-leavers and that unemployment either holds these back or has the opposite impact.

LEAVING SCHOOL IN THE 1990s

At the time of writing the economic pendulum is swinging back away from recession. As one publisher's representative said to the author, 'we just can't sell unemployment any more'. Nevertheless, some parts of the United Kingdom, such as the old industrial centres of South Wales, Scotland and northern England, have not benefited as much as many others. School-leavers with few qualifications in these areas especially are likely to experience continuing difficulty in obtaining employment. For those who have already experienced difficulty, improving labour market conditions can never undo what has already happened (Banks and Ullah, 1988).

Even with these caveats it is clear that jobs for young people are becoming more plentiful than they have been during most of the past decade. This is not only due to the changing supply of jobs. The number of young people in the UK is dropping. For every hundred 18- and 19 year-olds in 1984, by 1995 there will be only 65 (Department of Education and Science, 1986). The number is predicted to rise slightly again by the turn of the century. Many employers are already experiencing difficulties in recruiting school-leavers, particularly those with better than average qualifications, and are offering increasingly generous packages in order to attract them.

Many young people are therefore likely to have more choice than has been the case for some few years. This may well change their preparation for, and experience of, leaving education. It may also change the nature of research, with school-leavers treated more like graduates have been over the years.

FROM HIGHER EDUCATION TO LABOUR MARKET

The UK has a lower participation rate in degree-level education than most other developed nations. Currently about 15 per cent of the relevant age group experience it (Department of Education and Science, 1986). Graduates' employment prospects have been far less susceptible to economic recession than school-leavers, but by no means immune. For example, 1982 was a particularly bad year to graduate in the UK, when about 18 per cent of graduates found

themselves unemployed or in short-term employment four months after graduation (CNAA transbinary database). Even so, employers are keen to recruit graduates, and generally perceive them to be in short supply (Dean, 1983). They value the intellectual and technical skills graduates possess, though they are somewhat critical of UK institutions or higher education for not developing better a wider range of skills, especially social skills, relevant to employment (National Advisory Body, 1986). Graduates themselves tend to agree (Brennan and McGeevor, 1988, chapter 10). So does the UK government, which wishes to shift the balance of subjects studied towards applied science and technology (HMSO 1985, 1987).

Graduates' superior labour-market position is probably one important reason why research with them has focused on how employers can win their loyalty and develop their motivation to a much greater extent than with school-leavers. For example, surveys of graduate job mobility (Hutt and Parsons, 1981; Williamson, 1981) typically find that over the first five years of their careers, 10 per cent per year of graduates leave the companies they start with. This is often construed as quite high, and a problem for employers. The reader will recall that job-changing amongst school-leavers has more often been seen as the youngsters' problem! Research with graduates has also been more clearly rooted in theory than that with school-leavers, probably partly because graduates represent the most accessible population for researchers wishing to test hypotheses and theories in work settings.

Some fairly consistent themes emerge from existing research with graduates. The first is that before entering employment they typically have high expectations of working life in general, and of their prospective jobs and organizations in particular (see Mabey, 1986). It seems that these high expectations are inflated by (among other things) having to choose between attractive alternatives (Vroom, 1966; Vroom and Deci, 1971). Apparently in order to eliminate the dissonant thought that they might have made the wrong choice, graduates exaggerate the attractive features of their chosen job at the expense of those they have rejected. There is also evidence that graduate recruitment takes place in a 'climate of mutal selling' (Schein, 1978, chapter 7), where both sides understandably but damagingly highlight what they consider to be their best points and attempt to hide the rest. This might explain the dissatisfaction of some employers with graduates as well as vice-versa.

Exactly how damaging this phenomenon is to graduates' experiences and attitudes after starting work is slightly less clear, but much research implies a substantial impact for the worse on job satisfaction, commitment to the employer, and voluntary turnover (Kotter, 1973; Lawler, Kuleck, Rhode and Sorenson, 1975; Hutt and Parsons, 1981; Mabey, 1984, 1986). We must, however, note that these outcomes may not be truly negative from the graduate's or employer's point of view if it spurs one or both into a creative solution to the problem. Also, there is some reason to believe that unmet expectations have only a relatively

short-term effect on outcomes. Bray, Campbell and Grant (1974) and Nicholson and Arnold (1989c) have noted how graduates adjust their expectations (of how high they would get in their employing organization) in the light of reality over the first two or three years of their careers. Meyer and Allen (1988) found that unmet expectations had an impact on organizational commitment in the first six months of first jobs after graduation, but not in the second six months.

Although it is tempting to refer to graduate expectations as 'unrealistic', it is more appropriate to describe them as 'high' and (if subsequently appropriate) 'unmet'. Most researchers (but perhaps not employers!) do this. This avoids the implication that graduates themselves are necessarily to blame for their high expectations and responsible for dealing with the consequences. Some employers now use realistic job previews (RJPs) to reduce high expectations amongst newcomers. As the name suggests, RJPs aim to present an accurate picture of the job and organization (Wanous, 1980). They are not, of course, used solely for graduates, but tend to be employed most often where potential recruits are young people with relatively good educational qualifications. In a sense, RJPs show that some employers are taking responsibility for high expectations, but of course they also imply that the onus is on applicants to adjust to the employer's reality. Considerable research has been undertaken to evaluate the impact of RJPs (see Premack and Wanous, 1985, for a review). It seems that they do serve the purpose of reducing expectations, and also lead to a modest though significant reduction in subsequent turnover. They increase organizational commitment, job satisfaction, and self-selection (that is, applicants voluntarily dropping out of the selection process). They also in some circumstances improve job performance, contrary to earlier predictions (e.g. Wanous 1977, 1980). On the other hand it should be re-emphasized that these effects are only moderate, and exactly why they occur is still unclear. Some recent work (Meglino, DeNisi, Youngblood and Williams, 1988) also indicates that raising certain expectations as well as reducing others can bring the most positive results.

We can use several research studies in order to identify specifically which aspects of graduates' experiences fail to live up to their expectations (Mabey, 1984; Arnold, 1985; Newell, 1987; Nicholson and Arnold, 1989a,b). One of the main perceived offenders is management of their employing organizations. Graduates see inefficiency, confusion and personality clashes where they expected smooth running, clarity and rationality. They also tend to report experiencing less challenge, responsibility and training than expected, though this trend varies in strength between studies. Mabey's (1984) sample of engineers suffered more than most in this respect. On a more positive note, graduates generally report a friendly and helpful atmosphere at work, though supervisors are not always perceived to be sufficiently available and informative. Graduates seem not to lose self-confidence or experience lower adjustment over the transition to the world of work (Arnold, 1986a), though this may occur temporarily in some organizations (Nicholson and Arnold, in press). If anything

graduates tend to be pleasantly surprised by their own ability to cope with work demands. Frustration at barriers to achievement rather than anxiety about their own progress seems to be the dominant negative emotion (Keenan and Newton, 1982, 1985) in so far as there is one.

So much for salience of various experiences, but what are their consequences? Some long-standing research has shown that job challenge in the first few months of work is an important predictor of later job success (Berlew and Hall, 1966; Kaufman, 1974). Hall (1971) has proposed a 'success cycle' that can be triggered in these early stages. If graduates have some say about which tasks they take on, if those tasks are challenging, and if they achieve them, then this is said to lead to increased self-esteem, stronger career commitment and a greater tendency to tackle and succeed at subsequent challenging tasks. The linkages in this chain have not been tested fully in empirical work. However, it does seem to be widely accepted amongst researchers (if not so often amongst managers of new graduates) that graduates need early tasks they can call their own, which have a real impact on the organization's functioning, and which present the newcomer with a challenge to their abilities (see also Arnold, 1986b; Nicholson and Glynn Jones, 1987). This is based on the premise that newcomers are especially keen to demonstrate their worth to themselves and their employer, since they are inwardly uncertain about these matters.

This does not, however, mean that new graduates should be left to sink or swim (Schein, 1964). Over the years it has been clearly shown that they value intrinsic features of their work above other factors (e.g. Davis, 1965; Arnold, 1986a), but especially in the early stages they also want and rely upon other people for psychological security, support and information (Hall and Nougaim, 1968; Feldman and Brett, 1983; Ashford and Cummings, 1985; Posner and Powell, 1985). Carefully chosen placements can also help them develop a clear sense of identity within their work setting (Mansfield, 1971). The ideal balance between challenge and safety is likely to vary somewhat between individuals (Arnold, 1986b), though the two are in any case likely to be related because a supervisor sufficiently aware of graduates' needs to provide social support may well also realize that they wish to prove their worth. Supervisors who are sensitive to graduates' needs and unresentful of their likely future progress are a key to graduate development in the early months (Schein, 1964; Blau, 1988).

Some other work has also investigated the impact of pre-transition variables on transition process and outcomes amongst graduates. One prominent strand here has come from social psychological approaches to commitment. Kiesler (1971) defined commitment as 'the pledging or binding of the individual to behavioral acts'. The effect of commitment is to make an act and the cognition associated with it less changeable. Kiesler (1971) argued, and produced experimental evidence in support, that commitment to an act depends on the explicitness of the act (e.g. how public or otherwise unambiguous it is); the importance of the act to the person; the degree of irrevocability of the act; and

the degree of freedom perceived by the person in performing the act. In other words, it is argued that people look back on their own behaviour in a detached fashion, as outlined by Bem (1967), and make inferences about the reasons for it from the surrounding circumstances. On this logic the choice process assumed by Vroom and Deci (1971) to produce dissonance, should instead increase the commitment and thereby reduce the changeability of graduate job choices. There is indeed a certain amount of evidence for this 'retrospective rationality' (Pfeffer and Lawler, 1980; O'Reilly and Caldwell, 1981), but it seems to be rather weak, and less powerful than graduates' experiences after starting work.

Pre-transition variables have also been investigated from other psychological perspectives. It is well known that subject studied at college has a substantial effect on employment prospects (e.g. Committee of Directors of Polytechnics, 1988; Universities' Statistical Record, 1989), as does gender, though it is difficult to disentangle subject and gender since the two are quite highly correlated. There is, however, considerable evidence that women are less likely than men to report feelings of self-efficacy regarding a wide range of occupations (Betz and Hackett, 1981). On the other hand this does not necessarily prevent women considering these occupations as a career (Clement, 1987). Grades obtained in college work seem scarcely related to post-graduation work performance (Howard, 1986). This bears out the suspicions of some employers, and may be one reason why many, though not all, value applicants who have undertaken work experience within or outside their curriculum (Kelly, Griffin and Dorsman, 1986). It also seems that work performance on course placements is unrelated to academic work performance (Lee, 1988; Arnold and Garland, 1990), and that such placements are chiefly valuable for developing familiarity with the world of work rather than integrating the academic and the practical (Smithers, 1976).

Turning to matters more directly concerned with job search, Keenan and Scott (1985) found that educational performance and reading about jobs predicted job-hunting success amongst final-year undergraduate students. So did answering interview questions honestly rather than trying to please the interviewer. Taylor (1985) found some moderate relationships between occupational knowledge and self-concept crystallization (i.e. clarity of self-concept) on the one hand and success in job-seeking amongst business graduates on the other. She also identified some activities which enhance occupational knowledge and self-concept crystallization. These included experiential learning about the world of work. Arnold (1989a) showed that sticking with a career decision over the transition of graduation was associated with higher adjustment, life satisfaction and self-assurance than abandoning a decision. He suggested that having already made a career decision provided a stable point of reference during a period of time when much was changing in the young graduate's life. The general conclusion to be drawn from these studies is that interventions in college designed to enhance students' career decision-making via knowledge of self and world of work could indeed have payoffs over the transition. This should be

encouraging news for the many practitioners and researchers engaged in designing and evaluating careers programmes in higher education (see for example Rayman, Bernard, Holland and Barnett, 1983; Ware and Millard, 1987).

Some other work has looked at whether graduates change and/or are changed by their work characteristics soon after graduation. There is some evidence that in spite of the apparent importance of the first year, the occupational self-concepts of graduates are no more influenced by work characteristics in the first year than in the subsequent few (Arnold, 1986a). It may well be that two propositions often implicitly accepted by writers on transitions are in fact incorrect. The first is that transitions heighten self-consciousness and the second is that self-consciousness leads to personal change (see Scheier and Carver, 1980; Carver, Antori and Scheier, 1985 for experimental studies). Arnold (1989b) found that neither proposition held amongst learner nurses, but an explicit test with recent graduates has not yet been performed to this author's knowledge. Regarding changing the work role (i.e. innovation, see West, 1987), Jones (1986) drew upon the work of Van Maanen and Schein (1979) and found that 'institutionalized' socialization tactics produced less innovation amongst graduates in their first year than 'individualized' tactics, especially for those who were low on self-efficacy. Institutionalized tactics are those where newcomers as a group are put through formally organized experiences which build systematically on each other, where their sequencing and timing are known in advance, and where the newcomers' prior attributes are generally valued by their new employer. Individualized tactics were the opposite of these. Jones's study is hopefully the beginning of a trend towards systematic analysis of the impact of socialization in work organizations.

Finally, just a little research has investigated the impact of unemployment on graduates. Feather and Bond (1983) found that unemployed graduates reported many more depressive symptoms, slightly lower self-esteem and less planful use of time than their employed contemporaries. Whilst remembering that this was a cross-sectional study, with only 43 unemployed graduates, the difference in strength of effect between depression and self-esteem is interesting, and is perhaps due to experience taking some time to impact on self-concept. This distinction is also important when considering employed young people: quite intense experiences may have little or no impact on the way they think of themselves, at least in the short term (Schein, 1971b).

OVERVIEW OF RESEARCH ON THE TRANSITION

Some differences between the kind of research done with school-leavers and with graduates have already been noted. We can now also note some differences between the two groups in the results of research where comparison is possible. Probably the most important generalization is that, amongst school-leavers,

expectations of employment do not seem to be particularly high, initial impressions and reactions are reasonably favourable, but when the novelty wears off a feeling of dulled indifference prevails. For graduates the initial expectations are high, initial disillusionment substantial, but revision of expectations leads to a subsequent improvement in opinions and attitudes. Admittedly this picture extrapolates a little from empirical research, especially regarding events after the first few months. It is, however, consistent with that research. We can also observe that although doubts about own capabilities may be salient immediately after the transition, any subsequent adjustment problems focus on coming to terms with what Schein (1978) has termed 'the reality of the human organization' rather than revising the self-concept. It is very clear that unemployment has negative psychological effects on school-leavers. The same appears to be true of graduates, about whom there is less evidence than school-leavers. Hence it is emphatically not the case that 'you don't miss what you've never had'.

Research with both groups has been geared more directly to the practical concerns of employers, government and educational institutions than to those of young people themselves. This is perhaps a consequence of the fact that the transition is often from one institution to another, unlike (for example) marriage, bereavement or moving house. It is nevertheless also a personal transition, frequently from adolescence to adulthood; from dependence to independence. Not very much research has concentrated specifically on this side of the equation. Most work is geared to answer questions like 'if new employees are not being properly utilized, what should I, the employer, do about it?' But one could also pose the question 'if my employer is not utilizing me properly, what should I, the employee, do about it?' Some research does have implications for what individuals could do for themselves, but there are, of course, problems in communicating research results to individuals by any means except institutional practices. In the case of careers services, individuals often choose not to make use of those services in the first place.

Apart from these points it is difficult to generalize, partly because research with school-leavers and graduates has concentrated on rather different things, and partly because their ages, achievements and labour-market positions differ considerably. Hence we know far more about school-leavers' usage of, and opinions about, various forms of careers help than we do about graduates' usage and opinions. This is particularly true of institutional (i.e. school-based) sources of help. More is also known of a descriptive and qualitative nature about school-leavers' accounts of their early experiences of employment than about graduates' experiences. On the other hand there is more quantitative analysis of graduates' expectations and their early work characteristics than for school-leavers. The same is true of attempts to develop and test theoretical models of personal development in the early stages of employment. These could be tested for their generalizability with school-leavers, but on the whole they have not been.

The research findings on unmet expectations are interesting, but to be maximally useful we need to be able to specify which expectations and which aspects of reality seem to matter most. For graduates we might infer that less job challenge, responsibility and significance than expected are the key, but this has not yet been explicitly tested to an adequate extent. For school-leavers the situation is even less clear. A closely related issue also needs further investigation. Given that unmet expectations have negative effects, what are the costs and benefits (personal and organizational) of adjusting or not adjusting those expectations downwards? Can this be most validly construed as healthy adjustment to reality or as capitulation to an oppressor? Schein (1968) and others might suggest that some kind of half-way house is most desirable, as this preserves the newcomers' capacity to challenge their organization whilst permitting them to exist within its 'pivotal' norms.

It is important to pay more attention to individual differences. Studies by Taylor (1985), Jones (1986), Arnold (1989a) and Honess (1989) all suggest that variables such as career decidedness, self-efficacy and self-esteem can have a direct effect on how a person experiences the transition and/or a moderating effect on the impact of institutional practices on the person. Such variables should therefore not be considered solely, or even mainly, outcomes of the transition process: they are also inputs to it (Louis, 1980). This point is emphasized by research in recent years suggesting that some attitudinal and affective variables previously thought to be mainly determined by circumstances are in fact equally plausibly construed as dispositionally based (Staw, Bell and Clausen, 1986; Costa, McRae and Zonderman, 1987). Also, work by Kobasa and colleagues (e.g. Kobasa and Puccetti, 1983) has demonstrated that some personalities are more 'hardy' than others in dealing with transitions.

Finally, let us return to the eight propositions outlined in the introductory section of this chapter. They fit moderately well with the empirical research reviewed here. The first proposition was that the transition is likely to be welcomed by the young person. This seems generally true for school-leavers, but has not really been examined amongst graduates. The second proposition, that the transition is likely to be seen as personally significant, has not been explicitly on the research agenda. The third and fifth propositions (concerning the impact of transition timing) are perhaps statements of logical truth rather than propositions, and the latter has been more fully reflected in research than the former. The fourth has some empirical support, mainly amongst graduates: planning for the transition can have a beneficial effect over the transition itself. The sixth proposition, that young people who are in some sense flexible will fare better than others, is implied by Kobasa and Puccetti's (1983) work referred to above, but has not been explicitly examined over the transition from education to labour market. The seventh and eighth propositions concerned the prevalence and impact of institutional interventions in the transition. The former is clearly borne out by reality, and evidence is

accumulating about the latter, especially concerning the post-transition institution.

SUMMARY AND CONCLUSIONS

The transition from education to labour market has many implications for both institutional and personal development. Some key features of the transition are dependent upon educational achievements and labour market conditions. In general, research with better-qualified young people has focused on how their talents can be effectively utilized, whilst that with less-qualified youngsters has tended to concern how they adjust to a sometimes unpleasant reality. In general the transition from education to employment does not appear particularly traumatic or dramatic, though a number of personal and organizational variables can affect this conclusion. Future work should focus on how young people respond to their transitional experiences, and it should be located in one or more of the emerging theoretical contexts.

REFERENCES

Arnold, J. (1985) Tales of the unexpected: surprises experienced by graduates in the early months of employment. *British Journal of Guidance and Counselling*, **13**, 308–319.

Arnold, J. (1986a) *Change and stability in occupational self-concepts amongst students and recent graduates. A longitudinal study*. Unpublished PhD thesis, University of Sheffield.

Arnold, J. (1986b) Getting started: how graduates adjust to employment. *Personnel Review*, **15**, 16–20.

Arnold, J. (1989a) Career decidedness and psychological well-being: a two-cohort longitudinal study of undergraduate students and recent graduates. *Journal of Occupational Psychology*, **62**, 163–176.

Arnold, J. (1989b) *The experiences and attitudes of learner nurses during their first year of training*. Unpublished manuscript, Manchester School of Management, UMIST.

Arnold, J. and Garland, N. (1990) Using assessments of sandwich year and academic work performance in degree course development: An example. *Management Research News*, **13**(2,) 9–19.

Ashford, S. J. and Cummings, L. L. (1985) Proactive feedback seeking: the instrumental use of the information environment. *Journal of Occupational Psychology*, **58**, 67–79.

Ashton, D. N. and Field, D. (1976) *Young Workers: from school to work*. London: Hutchinson.

Ashton, D. N. and Maguire, M. J. (1986) *Young Adults in the Labour Market*. London: Department of Employment.

Atkins, M. J. (1985) The pre-employment curriculum: a right of passage. *Youth and Policy*, **11**, 37–40.

Banks, M. H. and Ullah, P. (1988) *Youth Unemployment in the 1980s: Its Psychological Effects*. Beckenham: Croom Helm.

Bazalgette, J. L. (1975) The transition from school to work: an organization approach. *British Journal of Guidance of Counselling*, **3**, 15–30.

Becker, H. S. (1960) Notes on the concept of commitment. *American Journal of Sociology*, **66**, 32–40.

Becker, H. E., Geer, B., Hughes, E. C. and Strauss, A. L. (1961) *Boys in White*. Chicago, IL: University of Chicago Press.

Bell, C., Howieson, C., King, K. and Raffe, D. (1988) *Liaisons Dangereuses? Education–Industry Relationships in the First Scottish TVEI Pilot Projects*. Sheffield: Training Agency.

Bem, D. J. (1967) Self perception: an alternative interpretation of cognitive dissonance phenomena. *Psychological Review*, **74**, 183–200.

Berlew, D. E. and Hall, D. T. (1966) The socialization of managers: effects of expectations on performance. *Administrative Science Quarterly*, **11**, 207–223.

Betz, N. E. and Hackett, G. (1981) The relationship of career-related self-efficacy expectations to perceived career options in college women and men. *Journal of Counselling Psychology*, **28**, 399–410.

Birch, J. (1979) The anxious learners. *Nursing Mirror*, 8 Feb.

Blau, G. (1988) An investigation of the apprenticeship organizational socialization strategy. *Journal of Vocational Behavior*, **32**, 176–195.

Bray, D. W., Campbell, R. J. and Grant, D. L. (1974) *Formative Years in Business*. New York: John Wiley & Sons.

Brennan, J. and McGeevor, P. (1988) *Graduates at Work*. London: Jessica Kingsley.

Brim, O. G. and Ryff, C. D. (1980) On the properties of life events. In P. B. Baltes and O. G. Brim (eds), *Life-span Development and Behavior*, Vol. 3. New York: Academic Press.

Carter, M. P. (1962) *Home, School and Work*. Oxford: Pergamon Press.

Carver, C. S., Antori, M. and Scheier, M. F. (1985) Self-consciousness and self-assessment. *Journal of Personality and Social Psychology*, **48**, 117–124.

Cherry, N. (1976) Persistent job-changing—is it a problem? *Occupational Psychology*, **49**, 203–221.

Cherry, N. and Gear, R. (1987a) Young people's perceptions of their vocational guidance needs. I. *British Journal of Guidance and Counselling*, **15**, 59–79.

Cherry, N. and Gear, R. (1987b) Young people's perceptions of their vocational guidance needs. II. *British Journal of Guidance and Counselling*, **15**, 169–181.

Clarke, L. (1980) *The Practice of Vocational Guidance: a critical review of research in the United Kingdom*. Department of Employment, Careers Service Branch.

Clement, S. (1987) The self-efficacy expectations and occupational preferences of females and males. *Journal of Occupational Psychology*, **60**, 257–265.

CNAA. Transbinary database. Kept and regularly updated at Brighton Polytechnic.

Committee of Directors of Polytechnics (1989) *First Destinations of Polytechnic Students Qualifying in 1987*. London: CDP.

Costa, P. T., McRae, R. and Zonderman, A. B. (1987) Environmental and dispositional influences on well-being: a longitudinal follow-up of an American national sample. *British Journal of Psychology*, **78**, 299–306.

Dale, R. (1986) Examining the gift-horse's teeth: a tentative analysis of TVEI. In S. Walker and L. Barton (eds), *Youth, Unemployment and Schooling*. Milton Keynes: Open University Press.

Danish, S. J., Smyer, M. A. and Nowak, C. A. (1980) Developmental intervention: enhancing life-event processes. In P. B. Baltes and O. G. Brim (eds), *Life-span development and Behavior*, Vol. 3. New York: Academic Press.

Davis, J. A. (1965) *Undergraduate Career Decisions: correlates of occupational choice*. Chicago, IL: Aldine.

Dean, T. E. (1983) Degrees of success into the nineties. *Employment Gazette*, January, pp. 24–28.

Department of Education and Science (1986) *Projections of Demand for Higher Education in Great Britain 1986–2000*. London: HMSO.
Dowling, P. and O'Brien, G. (1981) The effects of employment, unemployment and further education on the work values of school leavers. *Australian Journal of Psychology*, **33**, 185–195.
Elder, G. H. (1979) Historical change in life patterns and personality. In P. B. Baltes and O. G. Brim (eds), *Life-span Development and Behavior*, Vol. 2. London: Academic Press.
Erikson, E. (1963) *Childhood and Society*, 2nd edn. New York: W. W. Norton.
Feather, N. T. and Bond, M. J. (1983) Time structure and purposeful activity among employed and unemployed university graduates. *Journal of Occupational Psychology*, **56**, 241–254.
Feather, N. T. and O'Brien, G. E. (1986a) A longitudinal study of the effects of employment and unemployment on school-leavers. *Journal of Occupational Psychology*, **59**, 121–144.
Feather, N. T. and O'Brien, G. E. (1986b) A longitudinal analysis of the effects of different patterns of employment and unemployment on school leavers. *British Journal of Psychology*, **77**, 459–479.
Feather, N. T. and O'Brien, G. E. (1987) Looking for employment: An expectancy-valence analysis of job-seeking behaviour among young people. *British Journal of Psychology*, **78**, 251–272.
Feldman, D. C. and Brett, J. M. (1983) Coping with new jobs: a comparative study of new hires and job changers. *Academy of Management Journal*, **26**, 258–272.
Glaser, B. G. and Strauss, A. L. (1971) *Status Passage*. Chicago, IL: Aldine.
Gleeson, D. (1986) Further education, free enterprise and the curriculum. In S. Walker and L. Barton (eds), *Youth, Unemployment and Schooling*. Milton Keynes: Open University Press.
Grotevant, H. D. and Cooper, C. R. (1988) The role of family experience in career exploration: A life-span perspective. In P. B. Baltes, D. L. Featherman and R. M. Lerner (eds), *Life-span Development and Behavior*, Vol. 8. London: Lawrence Erlbaum.
Gurin, P. and Brim, O. G. (1984) Change in self in adulthood: the example of sense of control. In P. B. Baltes and O. G. Brim (eds), *Life-span Development and Behavior*, Vol. 6. New York: Academic Press.
Gurney, R. M. (1980) The effects of unemployment on the psycho-social development of school-leavers. *Journal of Occupational Psychology*, **53**, 205–213.
Gurney, R. M. (1981) Leaving school, facing unemployment and making attributions about the causes of unemployment. *Journal of Vocational Behavior*, **18**, 79–91.
Haan, N. (1981) Adolescents and young adults as producers of their development. In R. M. Lerner and N. A. Busch-Rossnagel (eds), *Individuals as Producers of their Development*. London: Academic Press.
Hall, D. T. (1968) Identity changes during the transition from student to professor. *School Review*, **76**, 445–469.
Hall, D. T. (1971) A theoretical model of career subidentity development in organizational settings. *Organizational Behavior and Human Performance*, **6**, 50–76.
Hall, D. T. and Nougaim, K. (1968) An examination of Maslow's need hierarchy in an organizational setting. *Organizational Behavior and Human Performance*, **3**, 12–35.
HMSO (1985) *The Development of Higher Education into the 1990s*. London: HMSO.
HMSO (1987) *Higher Education: Meeting the Challenge*. London: HMSO.
Hopson, B. (1982) Transition: understanding and managing personal change. In A. J. Chapman and A. Gale (eds), *Psychology and People: A tutorial text*. London: Macmillan.
Honess, T. M. (1989) A longitudinal study of school-leavers' employment experiences, time structuring and self-attributions as a function of local opportunity structure. *British Journal of Psychology*, **80**, 45–77.

House of Lords (1982) *Report from the Select Committee of the House of Lords on Unemployment*. London: HMSO.
Howard, A. (1986) College experiences and managerial performance. *Journal of Applied Psychology*, **71**, 530–552.
Hutt, R. and Parsons, D. (1981) Getting the drift of graduate mobility. *Personnel Management*, March, pp. 29–31.
Jackson, P. R., Stafford, E. M., Banks, M. H. and Warr, P. B. (1983) Unemployment and psychological distress in young people: the moderating role of employment commitment. *Journal of Applied Psychology*, **68**, 525–535.
Jackson, P. R. and Warr, P. B. (1984) Unemployment and psychological ill-health: the moderating role of duration and age. *Psychological Medicine*, **14**, 605–614.
Jamieson, I. (1983) Miracles or mirages?: some elements of pupil work experience. *British Journal of Guidance and Counselling*, **11**, 145–159.
Jones, G. R. (1986) Socialization tactics, self-efficacy and newcomers' adjustments to organizations. *Academy of Management Journal*, **29**, 262–279.
Jones, P. (1985) Qualifications and labour-market outcomes among 16-year-old school-leavers. *British Journal of Guidance and Counselling*, **13**, 275–291.
Kaufman, H. G. (1974) Relationships of early work challenge to job performance, professional contributions and competence of engineers. *Journal of Applied Psychology*, **59**, 377–379.
Keenan, A. and Newton, T. J. (1982) *Stressful incidents, stressors and psychological strain in young professional engineers*. Unpublished manuscript.
Keenan, A. and Newton, T. J. (1985) Stressful events, stressors and psychological strains in young professional engineers. *Journal of Occupational Behaviour*, **6**, 151–156.
Keenan, A. and Scott, R. S. (1985) Employment success of graduates: relationships to biographical factors and job-seeking behaviours. *Journal of Occupational Behaviour*, **6**, 305–311.
Keil, E. T. (1976) *Becoming a Worker*. Leicester: Leics Committee for Education and Industry, and the Training Services Agency.
Kelly, M., Griffith, J. and Dorsman, M. (1986) *Approaches to Employment: An Investigation of Graduate Destinations*. London: Council for National Academic Awards.
Kiesler, C. A. (1971) *The Psychology of Commitment*. New York: Academic Press.
Kobasa, S. C. and Puccetti, M. C. (1983) Personality and social resources in stress resistance. *Journal of Personality and Social Psychology*, **45**, 839–850.
Korte, C. and Sylvester, A. (1982) Expectations, experience and anticipatory socialization at a Scottish university. *Journal of Social Psychology*, **118**, 187–197.
Kotter, J. P. (1973) The psychological contract: managing the joining-up process. *California Management Review*, **15**, 91–99.
Lawler, E., Kuleck, W. J., Rhode, J. G., and Sorenson, J. E. (1975) Job choice and post-choice dissonance. *Organizational Behavior and Human Performance*, **13**, 133–145.
Lee, D. M. S. (1988) Academic achievement, task characteristics and first job performance of young engineers. In R. Katz (ed.), *Managing Professionals in Innovative Organizations*. London: Harper & Row.
Louis, M. R. (1980) Surprise and sense-making: what newcomers experience in entering unfamiliar organizational settings. *Administrative Science Quarterly*, **25**, 226–251.
Mabey, C. (1984) Managing graduate entry. *Journal of General Management*, **10**, 67–79.
Mabey, C. (1986) *Graduates into Industry*. Aldershot: Gower.
Maizels, J. (1970) *Adolescent Needs and the Transition from School to Work*. London: Athlone Press.
Mansfield, R. (1971) Career development in first year at work. *Occupational Psychology*, **45**, 139–149.

Meglino, B. M., DeNisi, A. S., Youngblood, S. A. and Williams, K. J. (1988) Effects of realistic job previews: a comparison using an enhancement and a reduction preview. *Journal of Applied Psychology*, **73**, 259–266.

Menzies, I. E. P. (1960) A case study in the functioning of social systems as a defence against anxiety. *Human Relations*, **13**, 95–121.

Merton, R. K. (1957) *Social Theory and Social Structure*. New York: Free Press.

Meyer, J. P. and Allen, N. J. (1988) Links between work experiences and organizational commitment during the first year of employment: a longitudinal analysis. *Journal of Occupational Psychology*, **61**, 195–209.

Morris, W. N., Worchel, S., Bois, J. L., Pearson, J. A., Rowntree, C. A., Samaha, G. M., Wachtler, J. and Wright, S. L. (1976) Collective coping with stress: Group reactions to fear, anxiety and ambiguity. *Journal of Personality and Social Psychology*, **33**, 674–679.

National Advisory Body (1986) *Transferable Personal Skills in Employment: The Contribution of Higher Education*. London: NAB.

Newell, S. M. (1987) The graduates' experience of the transition from higher education to the world of work and its relation to 'floundering'. Paper presented at British Psychological Society London conference, December.

Nicholson, N. (1984) A theory of work role transitions. *Administrative Science Quarterly*, **29**, 172–191.

Nicholson, N. (1987) The transition cycle: a conceptual framework for the analysis of change and human resources management. In J. Ferris and K. M. Rowland (eds), *Research in Personnel and Human Resources Management*, Vol. 5. Greenwich, CT: JAI Press, pp. 167–222.

Nicholson, N. and Glynn-Jones (1987) Good and bad practices in graduate development. *Personnel Management*, **19**(2), 34–38.

Nicholson, N. and Arnold, J. (1989a) Graduate entry and adjustment to corporate life. *Personnel Review*, **18**, 3, 23–35.

Nicholson, N. and Arnold, J. (1989b) Graduate early experience in a multinational corporation. *Personnel Review* **18**(4,), 3–14.

Nicholson, N. and Arnold, J. (in press). From expectation to experience: graduates entering a large corporation. *Journal of Organizational Behavior*

Nicholson, N. and West, M. (1988) *Managerial Job Change: Men and Women in Transition*. Cambridge: Cambridge University Press.

O'Reilly, C. A. and Caldwell, D. F. (1981) The commitment and job tenure of new employees: some evidence of post-decisional justification. *Administrative Science Quarterly*, **26**, 597–616.

Pfeffer, J. and Lawler, J. (1980) Effects of job alternatives, extrinsic rewards and behavioral commitment on attitude toward the organization: a field test of the insufficient justification paradigm. *Administrative Science Quarterly*, **25**, 38–56.

Premack, S. L. and Wanous, J. P. (1985) A meta-analysis of realistic job preview experiments. *Journal of Applied Psychology*, **70**, 706–719.

Raffe, D. (1983) Employment instability amongst less-qualified young workers. *British Journal of Guidance and Counselling*, **11**, 21–34.

Rayman, J. R., Bernard, C. B., Holland, J. L. and Barnett, D. C. (1983) The effects of a career course on undecided college students. *Journal of Vocational Behavior*, **23**, 346–355.

Reese, H. W. and Smyer, M. A. (1983) The dimensionalization of life events. In E. J. Callahan and K. A. McCluskey (eds), *Life-span Development Psychology: non-normative Life Events*. New York: Academic Press.

Roberts, H. and Kirby, R. (1985) Y.b. on y.t.s. why not? *Youth and Policy*, **12**, 1–5.

Roberts, R. J. (1983) Conditions for a justifiable careers education. *British Journal of Guidance and Counselling*, **11**, 170–183.
Ross, R. P. (1988) Establishing careers education within a modular degree system. *British Journal of Guidance and Counselling*, **16**, 203–209.
Ryrie, A. C. (1983) *On Leaving School*. Edinburgh: Scottish Council for Research in Education.
Schachter, S. (1959) *The Psychology of Affiliation*. Stanford, CA: Stanford University Press.
Scheier, M. F. and Carver, C. S. (1980) Private and public self-attention, resistance to change and dissonance reduction. *Journal of Personality and Social Psychology*, **39**, 390–405.
Schein, E. H. (1964) How to break in the college graduate. *Harvard Business Review*, **42**, 68–76.
Schein, E. H. (1968) Organizational socialization and the profession of management. *Industrial Management Review*, **9**, 1–16.
Schein, E. (1971a) Occupational socialization in the professions: the case of role innovator. *Journal of Psychiatric Research*, **8**, 521–530.
Schein, E. H. (1971b) The individual, the organization and the career: a conceptual scheme. *Journal of Applied Behavioural Science*, **7**, 401–426.
Schein, E. H. (1978) *Career Dynamics*. Reading, MA: Addison-Wesley.
Schlossberg, N. K. (1981) A model for analyzing human adaptation to transition. *Counseling Psychologist*, **9**, 2–18.
Smithers, A. G. (1976) *Sandwich Courses: An Integrated Education?* Windsor: NFER.
Stafford, E. M. (1982) The impact of the Youth Opportunities Programme on young people's employment prospects and psychological well-being. *British Journal of Guidance and Counselling*, **10**, 12–21.
Staw, B. M., Bell, N. E. and Clausen, J. A. (1986) The dispositional approach to job attitudes: a lifetime longitudinal test. *Administrative Science Quarterly*, **31**, 56–77.
Stumpf, S. A., Colarelli, S. M. and Hartman, K. (1983) Development of the Career Exploration Survey (CES). *Journal of Vocational Behavior*, **22**, 191–226.
Sugarman, L. (1986) *Life-span Development: Concepts, Theories and Interventions*. London: Methuen.
Super, D. E. (1957) *The Psychology of Careers*. New York: Harper & Row.
Super, D. E. (1980) A life-span life-space approach to career development. *Journal of Vocational Behavior*, **16**, 282–298.
Taylor, M. S. (1985) Roles of occupational knowledge and vocational self-concept crystalization in students' school-to-work transition. *Journal of Counseling Psychology*, **32**, 539–550.
Universities' Statistical Record (1989) *Destinations of University Graduates 1986–7*. Cheltenham: Universities' Statistical Record.
Van Gennep, A. (1960) *The Rites of Passage*. London: Routledge & Kegan Paul.
Van Maanen, J. (1976) Breaking in: socialization to work. In R. Dubin (ed.), *Handbook of Work, Organization and Society*. Chicago: Rand-McNally.
Van Maanen, J. and Schein, E. H. (1979) Toward a theory of organizational socialization. In B. M. Staw (ed.), *Research in Organizational Behavior*, Vol. 1. Greenwich, CT: JAI Press.
Veness, T. (1962) *School Leavers—Their Aspirations and Expectations*. London: Methuen.
Vroom, V. H. (1966) Organizational choice: a study of pre- and post-decision processes. *Organizational Behavior and Human Performance*, **1**, 212–225.
Vroom, V. H. and Deci, E. L. (1971) The stability of post-decisional dissonance: a follow-up study on the job attitudes of business school graduates. *Organizational Behavior and Human Performance*, **6**, 36–49.
Walker, S. and Barton, L. (eds) (1986) *Youth, Unemployment and Schooling*. Milton Keynes: Open University Press.

Wallace, C. (1986) From girls and boys to women and men. In S. Walker, and L. Barton (eds), *Youth, Unemployment and Schooling.* Milton Keynes: Open University Press.
Wanous, J. P. (1977) Organizational entry: newcomers moving from outside to inside. *Psychological Bulletin*, **84**, 601–618.
Wanous, J. P. (1980) *Organizational Entry.* Reading, MA: Addison-Wesley.
Ware, M. E. and Millard, R. J. (eds) (1987) *Handbook on Student Development: Advising, Career Development and Field Placement.* London: Lawrence Erlbaum.
Warr, P., Banks, M. and Ullah, P. (1985) The experience of unemployment among black and white urban teenagers. *British Journal of Psychology*, **76**, 75–87.
Warr, P. B., Jackson, P. R. and Banks, M. H. (1982) Duration of unemployment and psychological well-being in young men and women. *Current Psychological Research*, **2**, 207–214.
Watson, K. (ed) (1983) *Youth, Education and Employment—International Perspectives.* London: Croom Helm.
Watts, A. G. (1983a) *Education, Unemployment and the Future of Work.* Milton Keynes: Open University Press.
Watts, A. G. (ed) (1983b) *Work Experience and Schools.* London: Heinemann.
Watts, A. G. (1986) The careers service and schools: a changing relationship. *British Journal of Guidance and Counselling*, **14**, 168–186.
Watts, A. G. and Sampson, J. P. (1989) Strategic planning and performance measurement: Implications for careers services in Higher Education. *British Journal of Guidance and Counselling*, **17**, 34–48.
Wells, L. E. and Stryker, S. (1988) Stability and change in self over the life course. In P. B. Baltes, D. L. Featherman and R. M. Lerner (eds), *Life-span Development and Behavior*, Vol. 8. London: Lawrence Erlbaum.
West, M. (1987) A measure of role innovation at work. *British Journal of Social Psychology*, **26**, 83–85.
West, M. and Newton, P. (1983) *The Transition from School to Work.* London: Croom Helm.
West, M. and Rushton, R. (1986) The dropout factor. *Nursing Times*, 31 Dec., pp. 29–31.
Williamson, P. (1981) *Early Careers of 1971 Graduates*, Unit for Manpower Studies Research Paper 26, Department of Employment.
Willis, P. (1977) *Learning to Labour: How Working Class Kids Get Working Class Jobs.* London: Saxon House.
Willis, P. (1984) Conclusion: theory and practice. In I. Bates *et al.* (eds), *Schooling for the Dole.* London: Macmillan.

13 Workers' Experiences of Environmental Change and Transition at the Office

DANIEL STOKOLS*, ARZA CHURCHMAN†, TED SCHARF*
and **STEVEN WRIGHT***
**University of California, Irvine*
†The Technion, Israel

INTRODUCTION

The present chapter examines workers' reactions to various kinds of environmental changes in their offices. The workplace is a particularly suitable context in which to examine processes of change and transition since adults spend such a large percentage of their waking hours in work environments and because of the frequency with which changes such as relocations and renovations occur in those settings. In the United States, for example, approximately one-third of all office workers experience shifts in the location of their workspace each year (in some industries this percentage can rise as high as 63 percent) and another 36 percent experience renovations or reconfigurations of their existing workspace annually (cf. Brill, Margulis and Konar, 1984; McMillan, 1987). Thus, environmental changes are quite common in the modern workplace and they are being experienced by an increasing proportion of the workforce. While about 55 percent of all US workers are currently employed in office settings (as compared with manufacturing, agricultural, and other industries), this proportion is expected to grow to about 70–80 percent by the year 2000 (Kleeman, 1986).

As part of the University of California, Irvine's Research Program on Work Environments, we have had the opportunity to study several work groups that experienced office renovations within the same facility, others that relocated from one building to another either across the street or across town, and some that experienced neither of these changes during the same period. The relocation groups completed a pre-move survey one to four months prior to relocation and a post-move survey that was administered six to 12 months after the move. The office renovation and non-change groups also were surveyed twice at

On the Move: the Psychology of Change and Transition. Edited by S. Fisher and C. L. Cooper.

intervals approximating those used for the relocation groups. Workers' feelings about the relocation or renovation, their blood pressure levels, subjective assessments of emotional and physical well-being, and job satisfaction were measured at both time points.

GENERAL THEORETICAL ORIENTATION

Our longitudinal study of office relocations and renovations provides an opportunity to address some important theoretical questions concerning people's reactions to environmental change and transition within major life domains. First, how shall we conceptualize or define environmental change? The term 'change' can be used to refer to the situational circumstances and individual agents that promote transitions in one's social and physical milieu (e.g. organizational developments, managerial decisions and economic forces that bring about office relocations and renovations). On the other hand, the concept of change is sometimes equated with the particular events whose occurrence signals a noticeable shift in the structure of one's environment and his or her relationship to that setting (e.g. the move or renovation itself). Additional meanings often associated with the concept of change include the processes by which individuals enact and cope with environmental transitions (e.g. workers' participation in decisions about the location and rearrangement of their work space); and/or the potential health, behavioral and organizational outcomes of change events and coping processes.

Each of the above facets of environmental change can be further differentiated into several subcategories. For example, events such as residential or work relocations can be construed in relatively global terms as broad categories of environmental change, and characterized according to whether they span large or small distances, occur gradually or quickly, and are viewed as desirable or undesirable by the individuals experiencing them. At a more fine-grained level of analysis, relocations can be studied as 'packages' or streams of events composed of several highly specific elements. Moving to a new workspace, for example, might increase or decrease the level of ambient noise impinging on one's work area, opportunities for social interaction with co-workers, the degree of physical enclosure around one's immediate workstation, and the convenience of one's commute between home and work. These global and more detailed characterizations of change events represent two distinctive but complementary analytic perspectives. At the same time the outcomes of change events can be assessed at several different levels, including shifts in the perceived quality of the social and physical environment, levels of personal health and task performance or organizational productivity and effectiveness. The preceding is a rather incomplete list of change dimensions and outcomes, but it does indicate the diversity of meanings typically associated with the term 'environmental

change', and the importance of specifying those aspects of change emphasized within a particular study.

The research literature on environmental change and transition has given predominant attention to the stressful consequences of major life events such as residential relocation, shifts in employment status, marriage, divorce and chronic illness (cf. Dohrenwend and Dohrenwend, 1974; Holmes and Rahe, 1967; Snyder and Ford, 1987). Much of this work reflects an 'episodic' view of environmental change that gives priority to identifying the short-term health and behavioral costs of exposure to potentially disruptive events. The temporal focus of these studies usually ranges from onset of the target event(s) to about three to six months after their occurrence.

There are at least three limitations inherent in the episodic view of life change and stress. First, the consequences of initially disruptive and/or challenging events can be both positive and negative. These mixed-valence outcomes of environmental and life change may be manifested either simultaneously or sequentially at different levels of response (e.g. in terms of behavioral performance, physical health or developmental maturity). Second, the temporal course of change outcomes may extend beyond the three to six month focus of stressful life event studies. The developmental or organizational gains resulting from exposure to environmental demands such as residential or employment relocation may become evident only after the shorter-term negative impacts of such events have subsided (cf. Aldwin and Stokols, 1988; Minami, 1987; Wapner, 1987). Third, global assessments of people's response to the stresses of moving often neglect the situation-specific nature of relocations and give little attention to contextual and personal factors that influence individual and group reactions to environmental transition (cf. Stokols and Shumaker, 1982).

Another complexity inherent in the study of environmental change concerns the ubiquitous nature of change and transition throughout the course of people's transactions with their surroundings. Transactional analyses (cf. Altman and Rogoff, 1987; Wapner, 1987; Winkel, 1987) assume that the relationships between environment and behavior are reciprocal rather than linear, and that a continual process of personal and environmental change is inherent in these dynamic relationships. Given the prevalence of change in everyday people-environment transactions, how shall we decide which change events and outcomes warrant study, and the criteria by which to set the temporal boundaries of research on these phenomena?

In our research on environmental change we have focused on office relocations and renovations for a number of reasons. First, while these events are becoming increasingly common in the workplace, they are still a relatively non-routine aspect of individuals' daily or weekly activities and, as such, they can be expected to stand out amidst the day-to-day flux in people's transactions with their environments. Moreover, these change events have the potential to transform the quality and patterning of people-environment relationships in significant

ways. Stokols' (1987, 1988) discussion of the 'transformational' perspective in environment-behavior research focuses on circumstances and events within a particular situation at time-1 that have the capacity to promote a fundamental restructuring of that situation by time-2. Within the context of work environments, for example, office relocations can be viewed as triggering events that have the potential to alter or 'unfreeze' pre-existing patterns of social interaction among workers and to promote new patterns of social contact and levels of organizational performance. As noted earlier, office relocations can modify other important aspects of one's overall life situation, such as the distance and quality of the commute between home and work.

RESEARCH QUESTIONS AND ANALYTIC APPROACH

The design and hypotheses of our research are based on the preceding assumptions about the transformational potential of office relocations and the possible benefits, as well as costs, of these events for individuals and groups. First, as noted earlier, we implemented a longitudinal panel design in which workers exposed to varying levels of environmental change were surveyed both before and after their offices were reconfigured or moved. The post-change survey was administered between six and 12 months after the environmental changes occurred, to allow sufficient time for workers to accommodate to their new or renovated surroundings. Also, we incorporated multiple measures to assess a variety of relocation and renovation outcomes, including pre- and post-move indices of physiology, illness symptoms, job satisfaction, perceived quality of the social environment at work and employees' retrospective accounts of significant changes that occurred in the organization of their work lives following the relocation or reconfiguration of their offices. Workers' subjective accounts of environmental change experiences were obtained to assess the mixed-valence nature of relocation outcomes and the transformative influence of office modifications on the structure and organization of worklife.

The analyses reported in this chapter are organized around two major research questions. First, is exposure to varying levels of environmental change at work associated with differential health, behavioral and organizational outcomes? To assess this question we arrayed the participating work groups along a four-level continuum ranging from minimal to more extensive experiences of environmental change. The four levels of change experienced by the participants in our study included: (1) no relocation or renovation, (2) on-site renovation only, (3) short-distance relocation (to a facility across the street from the original work site) and (4) longer-distance relocation (to a building located about 10 miles from the original office). We hypothesized that higher levels of environmental change would be associated with greater perceived disruption of work tasks prior to the change event, and more illness symptoms, higher blood pressure levels and

perceptions of greater change in the quality of the social environment and work activities several months after the office moves and renovations had occurred.

Second, we assumed that the health, behavioral and organizational consequences of environmental change would be moderated by certain situational and personal factors. These factors include the perceived desirability of the change prior to its occurrence and individual differences in workers' exploratory tendencies, or their preferences for moving to new places and exploring unfamiliar surroundings. Earlier studies of residential relocation have found that desirable moves are associated with significantly fewer health problems (cf. Krantz and Schulz, 1979; Pastalan, 1980; Schulz and Brenner, 1977). Also, among individuals experiencing a high degree of residential mobility, those who are predisposed to avoid new and unfamiliar places report lower levels of energy and health than those who are highly exploratory by nature (Stokols, Shumaker and Martinez, 1983).

In accord with these earlier findings we predicted interactive effects between the levels of environmental change and the measures of change desirability and exploratory style, respectively. Specifically, we expected that more positive and fewer negative consequences of environmental change would be reported among those participants who looked forward to the change as a desirable event and those inclined to explore new places, particularly within the office relocation groups. The influence of the desirability and exploratory style factors was expected to be less evident among individuals exposed to lower levels of environmental change (i.e. those within the Non-relocation/Non-renovation and Renovation-only groups).

Our analytic approach blends the global and situation-specific perspectives on environmental change mentioned earlier. That is, we are interested in office relocations and renovations both as broad categories of environmental change and as highly specific events whose behavioral and health consequences are moderated by an array of situational and personal factors. An integration of these perspectives would seem to be valuable in that previous research on life transition has focused primarily on residential moves and has given little attention to work environment relocations and renovations, either as broad categories of environmental change or as highly specific events whose impacts on people depend on a variety of contextual factors (see Brett, 1980, 1982; Oldham, 1988, for exceptions).

In this chapter we focus on a small number of situational and personal factors that presumably moderate the behavioral and health consequences of work environment moves and alterations, but we do not delve into the myriad of highly specific environmental changes associated with these events. As part of our research, however, we were able to gather data on several physical features of participants' work environments both before and after they experienced a relocation or reconfiguration of their workspace (e.g. recordings of ambient noise, lighting, temperature and humidity; levels of physical enclosure surrounding

one's workstation; proximity to windows). The effects of changes in these specific environmental dimensions on workers' performance and well-being are discussed elsewhere (cf. Stokols *et al.*, 1989) and will be analyzed more extensively in subsequent reports. See also Brill *et al.*'s (1984) and Oldham's (1988) analyses of workers' reactions to changes in the physical enclosure of their work areas.

RESEARCH METHODS

PARTICIPANTS

A total of 80 workers participated in this study as members of our panel groups. An additional 82 individuals completed surveys at only one of the two major testing periods (i.e. those who completed the pre-change survey but were unable or chose not to complete the post-change survey; and those who joined their department after the first survey had been administered but volunteered to participate during the second testing period). The longitudinal analyses reported in this chapter are based only on the data from our 80 panel group members. Of these individuals, 22 percent were males and 78 percent females, and 84 percent were Caucasian as compared to 16 percent non-Caucasian. The age distribution of respondents was as follows: 8 percent at age 25 or younger, 25 percent at age 26–35, 31 percent at age 36–45, 21 percent at age 46–55 and 15 percent at age 56 or older. Forty-three percent of the respondents were college graduates, 25 percent held graduate degrees, and the remaining 32 percent were high-school graduates, often with some college credits. Employees' job status was measured as a three-level variable distributed as follows: 35 percent, non-supervisory support staff; 34 percent, supervisory support staff and entry-level professional staff; and 31 percent, supervisory professional staff.

To assess possible demographic differences between the 80 panel group members and the additional 82 respondents who participated in only one of the two testing periods, a series of *t*-tests and chi-square analyses were run, comparing the composition of these groups on the dimensions of age, gender, job status, education, ethnicity and number of years worked in one's current department or organization. The panel and non-panel groups differed only with respect to the average number of years employees had worked in their department, $t(160) = -3.30$, $p < 0.001$, with panel group respondents reporting an average of 7.1 years as compared to 4.3 years for the non-panel group. This difference is partly attributable to the fact that several participants in the phase 2 (post-change) survey joined their departments subsequent to our administration of the phase 1 survey. However, the difference remains significant when comparing the panel group with those non-panel respondents who participated during phase 1 only.

PROCEDURE

Data were gathered as part of the UCI Facilities Survey, conducted between October 1986 and December 1987. Employees from five different administrative units at the University of California, Irvine, and from one private firm located near the UCI campus, participated in the panel study. Three of the campus departments relocated from UCI's administration building to an office building across the street during November 1986–February 1987. The private firm, an environmental and transportation planning company, moved its headquarters from an office building in Newport Beach to one located about 10 miles away in Irvine, during late March and early April 1987. Another group at UCI reconfigured their offices without moving during July–September 1987. A fifth group at UCI neither moved nor renovated their offices during the course of this study. All groups were surveyed initially during November and December 1986 and about six to 12 months after the various moves and renovations had been completed. The dates of our pre- and post-change survey administrations varied to accommodate changing relocation and renovation schedules.

The managers of those campus departments scheduled for office moves or renovations (as well as the non-move/non-renovation group) were contacted during early Fall 1986 to request the participation of their units in our survey. The private firm had contacted the research team earlier for assistance in the planning of their new offices, and subsequently agreed to participate in our panel study. Employees from each of the six units received interoffice memoranda inviting them to participate in the proposed survey. Subsequently, orientation sessions covering the major goals and procedures of the study were presented by the research team to employees within each department. Survey packets were distributed to all members of each work unit during the orientation sessions. The packets contained questionnaires to assess employees' feelings about their jobs and work environments, physical and social conditions at work, illness symptoms and overall health status, and personal demographic information. The follow-up survey also included questions about the ways in which individual performance and work group effectiveness had been influenced by an office move or renovation. Employees were informed that participation in any or all of the survey was entirely voluntary, and that all data would be kept confidential. Unit managers gave varying amounts of staff time for completion of the survey. In most units employees were authorized to spend about 45 minutes of work time to complete the questionnaires and, in some instances, they finished portions of the survey during non-work hours. Those who volunteered to participate in the survey were also invited to have their blood pressure levels tested at their offices as part of the same study.

Members of the research team returned to each unit about a week after the questionnaires were administered to pick up the completed forms. A total of 166 employees within the six participating groups completed the initial survey,

and 107 completed the final survey. Surveys were completed at both time points by 80 individuals. They were distributed across the four levels of environmental change as follows: non-relocation/non-renovation, 16 participants; on-site renovations, 16 participants; short-distance relocation, 34 participants; and longer-distance relocation, 14 participants.

MEASURES AND ANALYSES

The major hypotheses were assessed through analyses of covariance (ANCOVAs) in which covariates and predictor variables measured during phase 1 were used to predict phase 2 measures of respondents' blood pressure, health status, job satisfaction and appraisals of social environment quality and changes in work activities. Standard covariates for employees' age, gender, job status and pre-change levels of the dependent variables (e.g. job satisfaction, health status, perceived quality of the social environment) were incorporated to control for individual and group differences on those dimensions at time-1. The predictor variables used in the ANCOVAs included levels of environmental change and either exploratory style or desirability of environmental change.

Predictor variables

The levels of environmental change index was formed by assigning a score of 1 to participants from the non-moving and non-renovation groups, a score of 2 to respondents from the renovation-only groups, a score of 3 to the short-distance relocation groups and a score of 4 to the longer-distance relocation group. Participants' ratings of their happiness about the upcoming move or renovation of their offices were assessed at time-1 on a five-point scale rating from very unhappy to very happy. This item was used as an index of change desirabilty. Participants in the non-relocation/non-renovation group were asked to estimate on a comparable five-point scale how happy or unhappy they would be if their offices were relocated. We incorporated this item as a control or baseline measure of receptiveness to change among participants in the non-change groups. Two additional five-point Likert scales measuring respondents' like or dislike for moving to new places, and their preference for being in familiar versus unfamiliar surroundings, were used to assess exploratory style. An internal consistency alpha of 0.69 was derived for these phase 1 survey items. The mean of each respondent's scores on the two items served as a summary index of exploratory style.

To check our assumption that higher levels of environmental change (i.e. relocations as compared with on-site renovations) would be associated with greater disruption of work, we asked members of the renovation, short-distance move and longer-distance move groups to estimate how much their work projects and tasks had been disrupted by preparations for the move (or renovation), on a

four-point scale ranging from not at all to a great deal. This item was included within both the initial and follow-up surveys.

Outcome measures

Physiological status was assessed by recording respondents' pulse rate and blood pressure levels during the phase 1 and phase 2 survey periods. Three separate recordings of each participant's pulse rate and diastolic, systolic and mean arterial blood pressure levels were taken over 15-minute intervals at each survey session using a Dinamap Vital Signs Monitor (model 1846P). During the blood pressure testing sessions, participants completed a 'physiological measurements' questionnaire which included items used as covariates in the blood pressure analyses (e.g. height, weight, alcohol and caffeine consumption, smoking habits, special medications taken, weekly exercise regimens and levels of activity just prior to the blood pressure recording sessions).

Personal health status was assessed using two five-point Likert scales which asked respondents to rate their overall health and spirits during the preceding three months on scales ranging from very poor to excellent, and from very low to very good, respectively. Additional health measures included the Global Stress Scale (Cohen, Kamarck and Mermelstein, 1983) and an index of physical health symptoms experienced while at work. The Global Stress Scale contains nine items that ask respondents to rate the frequency of certain stressful feelings or experiences during the preceding month, on five-point scales ranging from never to very often. Examples of the items are 'unable to control the important things in 'your life', 'nervous and stressed', 'down-hearted and blue', and 'could not cope with all the things you had to do'. Based on Cohen *et al.*'s report of high internal consistency among these scales, the mean of respondents' scores on the nine items was used as a summary index of global stress.

The index of physical health symptoms at work was derived from the Checklist of Work-Related Experiences (Stokols and Scharf, 1990). The symptoms index includes 10 four-point Likert scales that assess the frequency (never, rarely, sometimes, often) of various experiences at work (i.e. feeling energetic at work, being in good spirits at work, difficulties sleeping at night due to worries about work, headaches, eyestrain, soreness in neck/shoulders and arms/hands while at work, feeling overworked and feeling fatigued at the end of the day). Cronbach's alpha of inter-item consistency for these scales was 0.79 at phase 1 and 0.74 at phase 2. The mean of each respondent's scores on the 10 items was used as the summary index of physical health symptoms at work.

Job satisfaction was measured at phases 1 and 2 by an item which asked: 'All things considered, how satisfied are you with your current job', on a five-point scale ranging from not at all to very satisfied. Perceived quality of the social environment was also measured at both time-points using a nine-item index

derived from the Checklist of Work-related Experiences. Respondents were asked to rate the frequency of various experiences with co-workers and supervisors on a four-point scale ranging from often to never. These experiences included opportunities for open exchanges of ideas with supervisor, supportive interactions with co-workers, high levels of employee morale, conflict with co-workers about project priorities, insufficient guidance from supervisor, difficulties in contacting supervisor, opportunities to participate in decisions about work projects, opportunities to participate in decisions that affect the quality of the work environment and opportunities to be creative at work. Cronbach's alpha of internal consistency for these items was 0.70 at phase 1 and 0.78 at phase 2. Respondents' mean scores for the nine items were used as an index of perceived social environment quality.

Respondents' retrospective accounts of the behavioral and organizational changes prompted by the move or renovation of their offices were assessed at phase 2 using the Changes in Work Activities questionnaire. Participants in the renovation and relocation groups were asked to estimate the degree to which nine different categories of activities and experiences had changed as a result of the move or reconfiguration of their offices, on seven-point scales ranging from not at all to a great deal. For each of the nine activities and experiences they also were asked to indicate whether the change had been for better or for worse on a seven-point scale where 1 was scored -3 (for worse), 4 was scored as 0 (no change), and 7 was scored as $+3$ (for better). For each of the nine item sets, change$\times$valence product scores were computed, where highly negative products indicated a great deal of change for the worse and highly positive products indicated change for the better (cf. Stokols, 1979). The nine areas of change included: 'how efficiently I use my work time at the office; patterns of task-related communications within my department; the 'sense of community' in my department at work; my contacts with people from other departments; the convenience of my commute to work; the things I do during my lunchbreak; my feelings about the physical environment at work; the decoration of my work area with personal items; and my feelings about coming to work each day.' Cronbach's alpha of inter-item consistency were 0.77, 0.73 and 0.76 for the change, valence and product scores, respectively. A mean was computed for the nine change$\times$valence product scores and used as a summary index of perceived change in the overall quality of work activities following an office move or renovation.

RESULTS

INTERNAL VALIDITY

Random assignment of participants to different levels of environmental change was not possible in the present study. Several strategies, however, were used

in an effort to enhance the internal validity of the research. First, the survey was administered to panel groups on two different occasions about six to 12 months apart, thereby ensuring the temporal separation of major predictor and outcome variables. Second, the degree of interdependence among the predictor variables used in the analyses was assessed through a series of correlational tests, and statistical controls for intercorrelation were applied as necessary. The results of these tests are reported only in those instances where the predictor variables were found to be significantly correlated. Third, the internal reliability of newly developed survey measures was assessed as described above, and mean scores for multi-item indices generally were used to reduce the number of multiple statistical tests on closely related scales. Fourth, standard covariates for age, gender, job status and pre-change levels of the dependent measures were incorporated to control for these sources of variation in the phase 2 data. Finally, missing data were handled through a conservative deletion procedure in which respondents lacking any of the covariates, predictors or outcome measures included within an ANCOVA were omitted from that analysis. This approach avoids the extrapolation of missing data through mean-substitution or other estimation procedures, but it has the disadvantage of reducing the number of subjects available for the statistical analyses. Consequently, the degrees of freedom vary across the analyses reported below and, in some cases, reflect the unavailability of certain respondents on particular variables or instruments.

We had assumed that levels of environmental change and perceived disruptiveness of the move (or renovation) would be significantly correlated for the renovation, short-distance and longer-distance move groups. This assumption was not supported as the two variables were found to be unrelated, both at time-1 and time-2. As for correlations among the three major predictor variables, only desirability of change and exploratory style were significantly correlated, partial $r(53)=0.29$, $p<0.032$ (controlling for age, gender and job status). Therefore, each of these variables was entered as a covariate prior to the other in a series of additional ANCOVAs to assess the independent effects of change desirability and exploratory style on the dependent measures. The results reported below are consistent, both with and without the inclusion of these additional covariates, unless otherwise noted.

Analyses revealed a lack of the predicted interactive effects between the levels of change index and the change desirability and exploratory style factors, respectively. However, several predicted and unpredicted main effects of these variables were observed. These effects are reported below for each of the three predictor variables.

Levels of environmental change

Contrary to prediction, individuals whose work groups experienced higher levels of environmental change did not have higher blood pressure or

Table 13.1. Perceived quality of the social environment at work following office renovations, relocations or neither

		Perceived quality of social environment at work (time-2)*	
Levels of environmental change	*n*	M	SD
Non-relocation/non-renovation	16	3.00	0.48
On-site renovation	16	2.74	0.59
Short-distance move	34	2.96	0.41
Longer-distance move	14	3.23	0.40

Note: Larger means indicate higher ratings of social environment quality.
*Main effect of change levels on ratings of the social environment at time-2, $p<0.023$, controlling for age, gender, job status and pre-change ratings of social environment quality.

report more illness symptoms and stress at phase 2 than those whose groups experienced a lower level of change. Instead, the high-change participants (particularly those in the longer-distance relocation group) rated the quality of the social environment at work more positively at phase 2 than those in the lower-change groups, $F(3,72)=3.36$, $p<0.023$ (see Table 13.1). Also, individuals in high-change groups were more likely to report positive shifts in the overall quality of their work activities and experiences by phase 2 than those who experienced lower levels of environmental change, $F(2,48)=4.85$, $p<0.012$, on the summary (mean) measure of changes in work activities (see Table 13.2). Higher levels of environmental change were associated with more positive feelings about the physical environment at work, $F(2,47)=10.64$, $p<0.001$; and with marginally higher ratings of task-related communications among co-workers, $F(2,46)=3.11$, $p<0.06$, and sense of community at work, $F(2,46)=2.82$, $p<0.07$, on the individual change × valence product score comprising the overall index of perceived change. Also, the quality of workers' contacts with units outside their own work group changed most positively for members of the longer-distance relocation group and most negatively for members of the short-distance relocation group, $F(2,47)=6.44$, $p<0.003$. The reduced degrees of freedom for the Change in Work Activities scales is due to the omission of the Non-relocation/Non-renovation groups from these analyses, as they did not complete the Change in Work Activities questionnaire.

Desirability of environmental change

Respondents who were happier about an upcoming move or renovation of their offices rated the quality of the social environment at work more positively, $F(1,53)=4.53$, $p<0.038$, and reported themselves to be in better health, $F(1,51)=4.74$, $p<0.034$, during the follow-up survey than those who were less

Table 13.2. Perceived changes in quality of work activities following office renovations and relocations

Levels of environmental change		Overall change in quality of work activities**		Change in quality of the physical environment at work***		Change in quality of task-related communication*		Change in sense of community at work*		Change in quality of contacts with other units***	
	n	M	SD	M	SD	M	SD	M	SD	M	SD
On-site renovation	15	−1.03	4.54	−1.67	10.61	−3.47	9.61	−2.71	5.90	−0.93	4.83
Short-distance move	26	1.79	3.21	7.48	7.12	1.75	6.33	0.72	5.21	−3.12	6.42
Longer-distance move	14	3.47	2.93	8.29	7.02	4.50	6.20	4.36	6.02	2.64	4.77

Note: Larger means indicate higher scores on the attribute listed. Participants in the Non-relocation/Non-renovation groups are omitted since they did not complete the Changes in Work Activities Index.
Main effects of change levels, controlling for age, gender, job status and pre-change ratings of social environment quality: ***$p<0.003$; **$p<0.012$; *$p<0.070$.

Table 13.3. Post-change ratings of social environment quality and overall health in relation to time-1 appraisals of change desirability

Desirability of environmental change (time-1)		Perceived quality of the social environment at work (time-2)*		Level of overall health (time-2)**	
	n	M	SD	M	SD
Low	27	2.84	0.52	3.63	0.88
High	32	3.17	0.43	4.16	0.72

Note: Larger means indicate higher scores on the attribute listed. Participants in one of the short-distance relocation groups are omitted as they did not complete the change desirability scale at time-1.
*Main effect, $p<0.04$, controlling for age, gender, job status and pre-change ratings of social environment quality.
**Main effect, $p<0.06$, controlling for age, gender, job status and pre-change health symptoms.

favorable about the change (see Table 13.3). When the measure of pre-change illness symptoms is added as a covariate, the main effect of change desirability on overall health at time-2 is marginally significant, $p<0.06$.

Exploratory style

Individuals who scored higher on the summary index of exploratory style had lower scores on the Global Stress Index during the follow-up survey, $F(1,66)=5.16$, $p<0.026$, than those who were less inclined to explore new places and unfamiliar surroundings. When the index of change desirability and time-1 illness symptoms scores are entered into the ANCOVA analaysis prior to exploratory style, the effect of exploratory style on global stress remains significant, $F(1,64)=6.24$, $p<0.015$.

DISCUSSION

The present research reflects several of the limitations often associated with longitudinal field studies: non-random assignment of participants to different levels of environmental change, unequal numbers of respondents within the major levels of the predictive factors, and potential sampling biases with respect to certain demographic factors and the limited range of environmental change examined in this study (e.g. we did not include inter-county and inter-state relocation groups in our sample). In view of these constraints the findings from this study must be interpreted quite cautiously. Clearly, the present research raises more questions than it answers. But the questions posed by our data are intriguing and, we believe, worth pursuing in future extensions of this work.

The predicted interactions between levels of environmental change, desirability of change and exploratory style were not found. Nonetheless, the main effects observed for the three predictor variables are provocative in several aspects.

First, the effects attributable to levels of change indicate that major restructurings of the physical environment at work (especially relocations as compared with on-site renovations or no change at all) can prompt a variety of positive outcomes at personal and organizational levels. Earlier research on environmental relocation generally has emphasized the negative health and behavioral effects often associated with geograpic moves.

Our summary index of changes in work activities, however, reveals an overall pattern of improved functioning among individual employees and their co-workers subsequent to the relocation of their offices. Moreover, the higher levels of social environment quality reported among the relocated workers, *vis-à-vis* the on-site renovation groups, are consistent with the potentially positive and transformative influence of geographic moves, posited earlier. These results highlight the importance of using multiple and repeated measures to assess the mixed-valence outcomes of relocation experiences.

Also, the finding that on-site renovations, short-distance moves and longer-distance moves were not associated with different levels of perceived disruption at work suggests that higher levels of environmental change (at least within the spatial or geographic range of the transitions studied here) is not necessarily linked to experiences of greater upheaval and disruption, as we had assumed initially. Perhaps the process of planning an office reconfiguration is just as distracting as preparing for a move to different facilities altogether. Also, the positive opportunities afforded by a total change of one's work environment may offset the hassles and inconveniences of moving.

The global index of change levels used in this study does not specify the particular aspects of environmental transitions that are most directly promotive of positive and negative outcomes for individuals and groups (e.g. micro-level changes in the comfort and amenities of work areas associated with moves and renovations; or opportunities for workers to participate in organizational decisions about the relocation or reconfiguration of their workspace). Certain environmental alterations, such as the installation of new office furnishings, workstation dividers and lighting systems occurred both within the renovation and relocation groups. Workers' reactions to the relocation of their offices may be more directly tied to these proximal changes in their immediate work areas than to the geographic scope of the move itself.

It will be important in future studies of work group and residential relocations to identify the most pivotal or influential elements of environmental transition, with respect to their impact on personal health, performance and organizational effectiveness. The distinctive features of work environment relocations, for example, can be grouped according to certain taxonomic dimensions such as the 'micro' or 'macro' nature of the changes associated with such moves. Micro-level changes include those that are proximal to a single worker or small work group, such as shifts in the levels of physical enclosure, spatial density, ambient noise, illumination quality and overall comfort of one's immediate work area.

Macro-level changes include those that relate to more general features of the entire worksite and are less directly associated with particular workstations or work areas, such as the aesthetic quality, technological sophistication and locational amenities of an office building (e.g. its proximity to public transportation systems, parking facilities, restaurants and convenience stores).

The micro-level changes associated with office moves may vary considerably depending on employees' job status and work assignments (e.g. workstation comfort may increase for some groups but decrease for others as the result of a move). On the other hand, macro-level changes in the overall quality of the worksite are likely to be experienced similarly by all or most members of the organization. For example, individuals in the short-distance relocation groups reported that the quality of their contacts with people from other work units decreased following the relocation of their offices from UCI's central administration building to a new office facility located across the street from the UCI campus. For these participants (unlike those who experienced the longer-distance relocation), an important disadvantage of the move was that it reduced their physical proximity to colleagues in other campus departments, thereby making it more difficult for them to maintain pre-move levels of contact with employees in neighboring units. At the same time, however, these same individuals reported positive changes in the overall quality of their work activities and, especially, in the quality of the physical environment at work following their move from the administration building (see Table 13.2). Thus, participants were able to differentiate between the positive and negative consequences of changes in their work environments. Moreover, the pattern of relocation outcomes observed in this study seems more closely tied to the specific micro- and macro-level changes associated with a move than to the simple physical distance separating the old and new environments.

The most negative pattern of post-change outcomes was observed among members of the on-site renovation groups. These individuals reported the lowest ratings of social environment quality and the most negative impacts on their work activities during the phase 2 (post-change) survey. Interpretation of these findings, once again, calls for a situation-specific (rather than global) view of environmental transitions, and a more detailed assessment of the differences between office relocations and on-site renovations. One such difference concerns the timing and duration of environmental changes. Generally speaking, office moves are tightly scheduled events in which a wide range of micro- and macro-environmental features change simultaneously for virtually all members of the organization. For the groups in our study, office moves typically were implemented and completed within a period of a few days to one week. Although renovations of the new facilities often extended beyond the move-in period, the move itself, and most of the environmental changes associated with it, occurred relatively quickly.

On-site renovations, on the other hand, were typically implemented more gradually, since alterations of existing offices were not as dependent on fixed

moving dates and schedules. Because the renovations did not occur on a 'one-shot' basis they did not impinge on all members of the organization at the same time. Also, some participants in the renovations group were assigned to interim workspace while they awaited completion of the renovated areas. Perhaps the extended duration of on-site renovations makes them more difficult to cope with in certain respects than inter-facility moves. Also, on-site renovations tend to be more modest in scope than those prompted by full-scale moves and, consequently, may exert less positive impact on the perceived quality of work activities and experiences than do relocations to completely new quarters.

For those groups that experienced on-site renovations one of the major elements of environmental change involved the installation of new workstation dividers to create greater levels of physical enclosure and privacy. In two previous studies of employees' reactions to increased workstation enclosure (Brill *et al.*, 1984; Oldham, 1988), higher levels of perceived privacy, environmental satisfaction and self-rated quality of work performance were observed following the environmental change. In our study, however, post-change interviews with participants in the renovations and relocation groups revealed divergent opinions about the costs and benefits of greater workstation enclosure. The interview data suggest that the pattern of negative outcomes observed within the on-site renovation groups may have been linked to employees' preferences for lower levels of physical separation between their workstations. The installation of additional workstation dividers, which was a major facet of the on-site renovations, may have had the unintended effect of creating a more isolating and socially uncomfortable work environment. To assess these potential links between changes in workstation enclosure, employee performance, and perceptions of the social environment at work, additional analyses incorporating observational measures of workstation layout and design are planned.

The results of this study suggest that global categorizations of environmental transitions have relatively low explanatory power and utility. What seems to be needed as a foundation for future research are more fine-grained taxonomic analyses that differentiate among moves and other change events in terms of their distinctive qualities and their hypothesized effects on performance and well-being. Such analyses should encompass the various micro- and macro-level changes associated with environmental transitions and the major contextual factors that are likely to influence the desirability and behavioral consequence of those changes.

The unexpected main effects of change desirability and exploratory style also raise some interesting issues for future study. These findings suggest that a favorable orientation toward environmental change is predictive of better health, lower levels of stress and more positive ratings of the social environment at work over an extended period. We had expected these variables to qualify the effects of change levels on health and performance. It is not clear whether the lack of interactive effects is representative of the phenomena under study or,

alternatively, is attributable to methodological confounds (e.g. the small range of variation in our four-level index of environmental change). Nonetheless, the possibility that people who are favorably inclined toward the challenges and opportunities of environmental change are able to maintain higher levels of health and social functioning is an intriguing one. Further study of these personal orientations toward change may stimulate the development of organizational interventions to enhance employees' effectiveness in coping with significant environmental transitions at work.

Finally, an important methodological direction for future research pertains to the measurement of behavioral and health outcomes associated with environmental change. In the present study two major analytic strategies were used to identify the outcomes of environmental change at work. First, we combined pre-change and post-change measures of performance and health to assess shifts on these dimensions following one's exposure to environmental transition. Second, we asked participants directly about their experiences of environmental change and the perceived impact of these events on the quality and organization of their work activities. We have assumed that these methods are complementary, but we have not evaluated the specific advantages and disadvantages of the two approaches. The relative strengths and limitations of these alternative measurement techniques remain to be examined more closely in subsequent studies.

ACKNOWLEDGEMENTS

The reported research and preparation of the manuscript were supported by the Research Program on Work Environments and the Program in Social Ecology at the University of California, Irvine. The authors thank Janaea Martin and Renee Nishimoto for their assistance in this research.

REFERENCES

Aldwin, C. and Stokols, D. (1988) The effects of environmental change on individuals and groups: some neglected issues in stress research. *Journal of Environmental Psychology*, **8**, 57-75.

Altman, L. and Rogoff, B. (1987) World views in psychology and environmental psychology: trait, interactional, organismic, and transactional perspectives. In D. Stokols and I. Altman (eds), *Handbook of Environmental Psychology*, New York: John Wiley & Sons, pp. 7-40.

Brett, J. M. (1980) The effects of job transfer on employees and their families. In C. Cooper and R. Payne (eds), *Current Concerns in Occupational Stress*. New York: John Wiley & Sons, pp. 99-136.

Brett, J. M. (1982) Job transfer and well-being. *Journal of Applied Psychology*, **67**, 450-463.

Brill, M., Margulis, S. and Konar E. (1984, 1985) *Using Office Design to Increase Productivity*, Vols I and II. Buffalo: Workplace Design and Productivity.

Cohen, S., Kamarck T. and Mermelstein R. (1983) A global measure of perceived stress. *Journal of Health and Social Behavior*, **24**, 385-396.

Dohrenwend, B. S. and Dohrenwend, B. P. (1974) *Stressful Life Events: their nature and effects*. New York: John Wiley & Sons.

Holmes, T. H. and Rahe, R. H. (1967) The social readjustment rating scale. *Journal of Psychosomatic Research*, **11**, 213-218.

Kleeman, W. B. Jr (1986) The office of the future. In J. Wineman (ed.), *Behavioral Issues in Office Design*. New York: Van Nostrand Rinehold, pp. 251-291.

Krantz, D. S. and Schulz, R. (1979) Life crisis, control and health outcomes: a model applied to cardiac rehabilitation and relocation of the elderly. In A. Baum and J. E. Singer (eds), *Advances in Environmental Psychology*, Vol. 2. Hillsdale, NJ: Lawrence Erlbaum, pp. 23-57.

McMillan, L. (1987) Corporations relocate up to 63% of workers annually. *Facilities Design and Management*, October, pp. 88-91.

Minami, H. (1987) A conceptual model of critical life transition: disruption and reconstruction of the life world. *Hiroshima Forum for Psychology*, **12**, 33-56.

Oldham, G. R. (1988) Effects of change in workspace partitions and spatial density on employee reactions: a quasi-experiment. *Journal of Applied Psychology*, **73**, 253-258.

Pastalan, L. A. (1980) Relocation, mortality, and intervention. Paper presented at the Annual Convention of the American Psychological Association, Montreal, Canada, September.

Schulz, R. and Brenner, G. F. (1977) Relocation of the aged: a review and theoretical analysis. *Journal of Gerontology*, **32**, 323-333.

Snyder, C. R. and Ford, C. E. (eds), (1987) *Coping with Negative Life Events: clinical and social psychological perspectives*. New York: Plenum Press.

Stokols, D. (1979) A congruence analysis of human stress. In I. G. Sarason and C. D. Spielberger (eds), *Stress and Anxiety*, Vol. 6. New York: John Wiley & Sons, pp. 27-53.

Stokols, D. (1987) Conceptual strategies of environmental psychology. In D. Stokols and I. Altman (eds), *Handbook of Environmental Psychology*. New York: John Wiley & Sons, pp. 41-70.

Stokols, D. (1988) Transformational processes in people-environment relations. In J. E. McGrath (ed.), *The Social Psychology of Time*. Beverly Hills, CA: Sage Publications, pp. 233-252.

Stokols, D. and Scharf, T. (1990) Developing standardized tools for assessing employees' ratings of facility performance. In G. Davis and F. T. Ventre (eds), *Performance of Buildings and Serviceability of Facilities, ASTM STP 1029*. Philadelphia, PA: American Society for Testing and Materials. pp. 55–79.

Stokols, D. and Shumaker S. (1982) The psychological context of residential mobility and well-being. *Journal of Social Issues*, **38**, 149-171.

Stokols, D., Shumaker, S. and Martinez, J. (1983) Residential mobility and personal well-being. *Journal of Environmental Psychology*, **3**, 5-19.

Stokols, D., Martin, J., Scharf, T., Churchman, A. *et al.* (1988) Evaluating the links between facilities design, employee productivity, and organizational effectiveness. *Journal of International Facility Management Association*, **1**, 16-19.

Stokols, D., Scharf, T., Wright S., Nishimoto, R. and Carrere, S. (1989) Health and behavioral effects of changes in the level of physical enclosure surrounding employees' workstations. Paper presented at the National Heart, Lung, and Blood Conference on Work Environments and Cardiovascular disease, University of California, Irvine, April.

Wapner, S. (1987). A holistic developmental, systems-oriented environmental psychology: some beginnings. In D. Stokols and I. Altman (eds), *Handbook of Environmental Psychology*. New York: John Wiley & Sons, pp. 1433-1465.

Winkel, G. H. (1987) Implications of environmental context for validity assessments. In D. Stokols and I. Altman (eds), *Handbook of Environmental Psychology*, Vol. I. New York: John Wiley & Sons, pp. 71-97.

14 Becoming and Being Unemployed

ROY PAYNE
Manchester Business School

The publication, in the 4th issue of the 44th volume of the *Journal of Social Issues*, of the topic 'Psychological effects of unemployment' (Dooley and Catalano, 1988) is one of the latest reviews of this topic to appear in the 1980s. Jahoda (1982), Fryer and Payne (1986) and Warr (1987) also cover the research on unemployment in some detail. This present book has also been preceded by several reviews of the transitions literature during the decade: e.g. Bridges (1980), Allen and Van de Vliert (1984) and Nicholson (1987). At least two papers have brought the concepts of transitions and unemployment together; Warr (1984) and Latack and Dozier (1986).

Of the two literatures the transitions literature is probably the easier to understand, though it is less easy to evaluate. At its simplest a transition is 'A passage or passing from one condition, action or (rarely) place to another' (OED). A move from paid employment to unemployment (or even retirement) is obviously a transition. The concept has rarely been used in this narrow sense, however, though Stybel (1978) has focused specifically on the termination process. More usually the transition literature implies a process taking place over time, which occurs after some significant event such as bereavement, divorce or redundancy. A psychosocial transition is characterized by Parkes (1971) as: (1) lasting in its effects, (2) occurring over a short period of time, (3) affecting large areas of the assumptive world. The outcome state of this passage is thus not defined in the transition, and in transitions such as loss of spouse, job or life, is often very uncertain. The possibility of psychological metamorphosis is inherent in such disturbing events.

In the unemployment literature, and to some extent the bereavement literature, the emphasis has been on the negative consequences of the event. These have been named phase models, and one of the earliest ones in the unemployment literature is that of Zawadski and Lazarsfeld (1935), which describes seven stages, though is often more vividly remembered by the alliteration involved in 'shock, optimism, pessimism and fatalism'. The grief

On the Move: the Psychology of Change and Transition. Edited by S. Fisher and C. L. Cooper.

literature has been heavily influenced by Bowlby's (1960) description of the phases as shock, disorganization and readjustment. The more neutral term 'readjustment' might have been better applied to the unemployment experience, as we shall see, but the similarity of the two literatures is apparent.

Archer and Rhodes (1987) compare the two literatures with a focus on using the grief model to describe/explain the consequences of job loss. Their conclusions are

> that while many of the less specific components of grief are clearly apparent in accounts of reactions to job loss, the evidence on the central and specific features such as preoccupation and the urge to search is only suggestive, requiring further investigation. Existing evidence indicates little about the frequency of components, their interrelationship or changes over time (p. 218).

The evidence will require longitudinal, processual studies which are in short supply in these two literatures, and the transitions literature generally.

These authors reiterate the point made by others, but strongly made by Fryer (1985), that there is little empirical evidence in either literature that the majority of individuals experience the phases, or that the phases occur in the order in which they are supposed to occur. Furthermore, close examination of the descriptions of the various phase models reveals considerable contradictions about the psychological reactions which are expected to occur at each of the particular phases.

Despite these criticisms the search for common patterns of experience in response to major events continues, as does the attempt to create theories which may explain them and guide future empirical investigations. One of the more convincing attempts has been made by Nicholson (1987) and Nicholson and West (1989). Their empirical work has been aimed at understanding career changes such as promotions and downward mobility in employment, but the Nicholson paper (1987) offers a conceptual framework for the analysis of changes more generally.

I shall briefly outline this conceptual framework with the intention of applying it to the literature on unemployment. Before doing that I shall summarize: (a) the empirical literature on the transition from employment to unemployment, and back to employment; and (b) the theoretical explanations that have been drawn from it. It should then be possible to see if the transition cycle, as Nicholson calls it, can illuminate our understanding of being unemployed.

Nicholson's transition cycle

Phase 1. *Preparation:* expectations and anticipations before change/event.
Phase 2. *Encounter:* affect and sense-making of the event.
Phase 3. *Adjustment:* changes to self and situation.
Phase 4. *Stabilization:* settled connection between person and situation (I have slightly changed these definitions because the original ones

are couched in terms of work-role changes which don't necessarily fit all kinds of changes)

Phase 5/1. *Preparation for new cycle*

Nicholson emphasizes three points about this framework.

1. Recursion: the last stage of stabilization precedes and therefore influences the next transition cycle that occurs, though he suggests the cycles might overlap if transitions occur rapidly.
2. Interdependence: as the cycle suggests, preceding phases influence the stages that follow it.
3. Distinctiveness: the experiences at each stage are distinctive because they invoke different psychological and social systems.

The more innovative contribution that Nicholson has made is to identify nine dimensions of transition cycles which should facilitate comparison of cycles both across types of event/transition, and for different transitions experienced by the same person. These appear below:

Dimensions of transition cycles

1. Speed	how often cycle occurs
2. Amplitude	how radical is transition event
3. Symmetry	time adjusting versus time performing
4. Continuity	meaningfulness of connections between transitions
5. Discretion	autonomy in controlling process
6. Complexity	multiplicity of adaptations required
7. Propulsion	self versus system initiated
8. Facilitation	support for facilitating progress
9. Significance	change to person or situation.

Before applying these concepts to job loss it is necessary to review the empirical findings on the psychological consequences of becoming unemployed. As we shall see they present the difficulty that unemployment is by no means a homogeneous experience.

THE PSYCHOLOGICAL EFFECTS OF UNEMPLOYMENT

One of the largest data sets on unemployment has been collected by a number of researchers employed at the MRC/ESRC's Social and Applied Psychology Unit at Sheffield University. The list of cross-sectional and multi-phase longitudinal studies can be found in Warr, Jackson and Banks (1988). Using the General Health Questionnaire as the major measure of psychological distress (Goldberg, 1972)

they have shown convincingly that being unemployed raises the level of psychological strain symptoms by 100–200 per cent and that re-employment quite quickly returns symptom levels to those experienced by comparable employed populations. The same conclusion is drawn from the study immediately following the above article by Kessler, Turner and House (1988), who assessed anxiety, depression, somatic symptoms and physical illnesses, and the results apply to all four variables. Another excellent longitudinal study of a plant shutdown in Denmark also reports the same negative effects of unemployment and positive effects of re-employment, reinforcing confidence in these general trends (Iverson and Sabroe, 1988). This pattern is the same as has been found in the decades of the 1930s, 1960s and 1980s when rises in unemployment have occurred in many countries. What the more recent research has done is to use better measures, do larger studies and explore the major factors which influence this general pattern of results.

LENGTH OF UNEMPLOYMENT

This is particularly relevant to transitions approaches to unemployment, and the findings are that psychological distress increases quite severely in the first six to eight weeks of unemployment, remaining so for some months, and then by one to three years later (Warr and Jackson, 1985, 1987; Payne, 1988) has shown a slight improvement, though symptom levels are still about 100 per cent higher than when the same people were employed. Warr *et al.* (1988) suggest this is partly due to some unemployed people making a 'constructive adaptation' by developing their own interests and expanding social networks. More commonly, people achieve a 'resigned adaptation' by reducing aspirations, avoiding risk and making do with what they have got. As the authors point out: 'By wanting less, long-term unemployed people achieve less, and they become less' (p. 55).

A potential confounding factor in interpreting this fact is whether those who remain unemployed were more vulnerable to start with.

PERSONAL VULNERABILITY

Dupue and Monroe (1986) emphasize strongly the effects of four kinds of vulnerability factors which influence the reporting of symptoms of psychological distress. They are personality traits such as neuroticism, affective disorders, physical handicaps or chronic health problems and long-standing environmental threats. Elder (1974) studied children who grew up in the Great Depression of the 1930s, and has traced the long-term consequences of this experience. Elder and Caspi (1988) report how common major economic strain is, even in affluent

western economies, and show how this affects family adjustment and strain on different members of the family.

White (1985) and Warr and Jackson (1985) have shown that physical health problems before unemployment predicted the increasing severity of such problems during unemployment.

In a very impressive series of studies in Holland, Schaufeli (1988) found in a longitudinal study that those unemployed who become re-employed had lower psychological distress even when they were unemployed. He suggests the operation of a selection mechanism, resulting in more jobs for the relatively healthy unemployed, and less jobs for their less healthy unemployed colleagues.

No evidence of this kind was found by Payne (1988) in another longitudinal study, but he did show that trait neuroticism correlates strongly with symptoms of psychological distress in a group of long-term unemployed persons indicating its effects even in such a selected group: it is clearly in the nature of anxiety itself that people who are highly anxious will respond more negatively to threatening events. Schaufeli too reports that 'the level of distress [amongst the employed and the unemployed] was strongly determined by a stable vulnerability component, which explained about two-thirds of the variance of distress' (p. 264). The more distressed were characterized by low self-esteem, high anxiety and an external locus of control. Evaluation of much of what is claimed in this section on the effects of unemployment ought to take into account the fact that most studies in this area have not considered the effects of personal vulnerability.

Another factor which affects vulnerability to unemployment is the strength of desire/need to be employed, which has become conceptualized as 'employment commitment'. Warr *et al.* (1988) report several studies which have shown that those people with very high levels of employment commitment are more distressed if they are unemployed and less distressed if they are in employment than people whose employment commitment is merely strong or moderate.

Other variables which have been studied in unemployment research are not unconnected with vulnerability, such as gender, age, and social class. These are discussed below.

AGE

Traditionally the young and old are considered more vulnerable, but despite this potential vulnerability the young and old show fewer signs of psychological distress than do those aged between 20 and 59 years (Daniel, 1974; Warr and Jackson, 1985). It is worth recalling that the mental health of both young and old is still badly affected by unemployment. The explanation offered for this consistent finding is that the middle-aged groups have different role

responsibilities, different expectations and in fact are more seriously affected financially due to their greater responsibilities and needs.

GENDER

Differences in responsibilities, expectations and resources may also be expected to affect the mental health of males and females. In the population as a whole this appears to be true (Fletcher, 1988) but if circumstances are similar for males and females then there is no significant difference in the psycho-symptomatology they show, even when they are unemployed (Banks and Jackson, 1982; Breakwell, Harrison and Propper, 1984; Warr and Parry, 1982). The latter two authors found that social class may affect this general claim, since they found that working-class married women who were employed seemed to benefit more psychologically from their employment than did middle-class employed women.

SOCIAL CLASS

The psychological health of all social classes above the semi-skilled and unskilled (social classes IV and V) is not too dissimilar as measured in community health surveys using GHQ-12 (Finley-Jones and Burvill, 1977). About 11 per cent score 3 or more symptoms. For classes IV and V the proportion almost doubles (about 20 per cent). The proportion for the unemployed as a whole is something like 50–60 per cent and in a study of 399 long-term unemployed Payne, Warr and Hartley (1984) reported that the psychological distress scores of 196 semi-skilled/unskilled men, aged 25–39, were the same as those of 203 white-collar/professional men of the same age.

Schaufeli (1988) reports a study of 467 long-term unemployed professionals. Distress scores amongst the unemployed were higher than general population norms, though unemployment status accounted for only a small proportion of the variance in psychological distress within the professional group themselves. This is a different finding than in the British studies as indicated above. Schaufeli suggests that the difference may be due to the fact that in Holland the social security and unemployment benefits minimize the difference between the employed and the unemployed. Brenner and Starrin (1988) make the same point about the Swedish policies on unemployment, and show that only about 2 per cent of Swedish workers face unemployment and only a minority show any effects of it. An additional explanation Schaufeli offers is that the middle class are better able to cope with unemployment due to their education, skills and ability to be proactive in problem-solving.

It is worth noting here that sickness absence and mortality rates have a different distribution by social class than does psychological health. Sickness absence and mortality rates get systematically worse as social class gets lower. For the mortality rates this pattern holds for almost every category of disease including deaths from mental disease, and from the so-called 'executive's disease'—coronary heart disease (Fletcher, Gowler and Payne, 1979; Fletcher, 1988).

It is apparent from these studies that the effects of being unemployed depend on the context. If income is protected, or if there is a strong chance of getting work, then even remaining unemployed for long periods can have quite small effects on the people involved. On the other hand a threatened economic situation can have negative effects on the mental health of people even if they remain employed (Iversen and Sabroe, 1988). Whilst middle-class people start with the advantage of better mental health, and superior financial resources, they may have just as poor mental health as the unemployed working class if the employment position remains poor, as was the case in the Payne *et al.* study.

Reactions to unemployment also depend on personal factors such as age and personality, but for most people who become unemployed there are major negative consequences that for most of them have negative effects on their psychological health. On the whole a bad job is better than no job at all, unless people are cushioned from the financial effects of unemployment, or unless they are particularly resilient people. Fryer and Payne (1984) describe a small group of people who used their unemployment to pursue personal interests that had to some extent been frustrated whilst they were in paid employment. These were sometimes political, sometimes religious or sometimes just strong personal goals. Their personalities might be likened to those described by Kobosa, Maddi and Kahn (1982) as 'hardy personalities' or by Antanovsky (1987) as having a strong 'sense of coherence'. Despite their impressive resilience, however, they all said they would prefer to be employed, acknowledging the considerable difficulties of surviving materially on the support available in Britain in 1983.

CONCLUSION

Research during this century has shown that for most people being unemployed affects both their physical and psychological health in a negative way. More recent research has shown that there are many exceptions to this general picture. They arise from factors within the individual (health, age, social class, personality, etc.) and factors within the situation (state of the economy, financial support to the unemployed, social support from family and community). In applying the transition cycle to the experience of becoming unemployed I shall take the most common reaction to it, the negative one, but signal strongly that there are numerous exceptions which the transition cycle needs to deal with too. Before proceeding with this, however, it is necessary to consider the *explanations* that

have been offered to account for the negative (and some of the positive) consequences of losing paid employment.

EXPLANATIONS OF THE PSYCHOLOGICAL EFFECTS OF UNEMPLOYMENT

Jahoda (1982) is one of the few people who has offered an explanation for this widespread negative of unemployment effects. Jahoda claims that loss of a job deprives the individual of two sorts of supports. The *manifest* function of employment is the provision of an income to meet material and social needs. The *latent* supports are that regularly attending a place of employment provides a set of activities which the person is compelled to carry out, a time structure in which the work-related activities and others such as eating, arriving, leaving, etc. must be done, a role in the organization or group which provides a sense of personal identity, a task and purpose providing a sense of contribution to the community, and enforced social contacts with others involved in the achievement of the tasks. The function served by these latent supports is that they keep the person in touch with reality. If the supports are removed by job loss, then the person loses touch with reality, fails to keep busy doing things, loses any sense of purpose, withdraws from social contacts with others, resulting in loneliness, boredom, depression and anxiety. Jahoda claims that other institutions can provide these latent supports (e.g. crime or tribalism, but that in industrialized societies work is the main means by which individuals obtain these benefits).

A second candidate for an explanation of the effects of unemployment is a phase or stage model suggesting that job loss is followed by a series of psychological states, the final one being a negative one where the person becomes resigned to accepting poverty, low levels of activity, dissatisfaction and low status. The number of phases varies according to the author(s) but optimism, pessimism and fatalism are the minimum stages mentioned in this sort of model (see Fryer (1985) for elaboration) and many writers argue that optimism is preceded by shock (Archer and Rhodes, 1987). At first sight the phase model is a mere descriptive observation of what happens to people who have lost their jobs, and is no explanation at all. It is possible, however, to construct an explanation if the assumption is made that job loss leads to stress, and that continuing stress sets up a psycho-physiological chain reaction leading to lowered functioning. Such a process has been described by Hans Selye (1956) and named by him the general adaptation syndrome. The general adaptation syndrome (GAS) involves three broad stages, according to Selye. They are:

1. *The alarm reaction*, when the environment is perceived as threatening. In unemployment this reaction may well happen before job loss actually occurs

(Cobb and Kasl, 1972). This broad phase includes a *shock* phase where the body might be subjected to increased heart rate, loss of muscle tone, lowered body temperature and raised blood pressure. The psychological reactions are those of felt threat, tension and anxiety, and possibly fear. This shock phase is followed by a *counter-shock* phase when the body marshals various hormonal substances (e.g. cortisol, adrenaline and noradrenaline). Psychological defences come into play to mobilize the will to fight the threat, or to rationalize the possible negative impact of the perceived threat, etc.

2. *The stage of resistance* follows the counter-shock where both body and mind resist the threat, try and remove it or sit out the storm until it disappears. If this defensive strategy fails then phase 3 occurs.
3. *Stage of exhaustion*, where psychophysical resources are depleted, symptoms reappear and, ultimately, death ensues. Although there is some evidence that rises in the rate of unemployment lead to suicide and/or attempted suicide (Platt, 1984) it is not my intention to deal with that as an outcome of unemployment. I wish to focus on the more common experiences of cognitive, emotional and cognitive deterioration so widely reported. These appear to arise from a prolonged period in the stage of resistance (phase 2), for the problems created by unemployment worsen over two to three months and then seem to stabilize as people adapt to their circumstances (Warr *et al.*, 1988). Prolonged exposure to phase 2, however, almost certainly entails experiences of failure as various attempts to cope with financial, family and other difficulties founder, so that resignation to a world which is materially, socially and psychologically impoverished compared to when the person was employed eventually occurs. In learning theory terms, active striving goes unrewarded so that such striving behaviour is eventually extinguished or diminished in frequency. Resignation is the end-result.

A combination of the general adaptation syndrome and learning theory provides an explanation for the phases reputed to follow the loss of a job. What follows compares these two explanations, particularly by focusing on the assumptions that lie behind them.

As already indicated in the brief review of the empirical work on the psychological effects of unemployment there are various 'oddities' or exceptions in this literature where unemployed people do not appear to show these signs of deterioration (Eisenberg and Lazarsfeld, 1938). It is argued (see also Fryer and Payne, 1984; Jahoda, 1984) that these oddities have not been paid much attention because of the existence of a conceptual sieve or bias which has caused people to focus on data showing the negative outcomes of unemployment. This sieve is constituted by the latent functions thesis proposed by Jahoda. This filtering process led to an explanation which can be called the deprivation approach. The assumptions underlying this approach imply a model of man

that emphasizes dependence on the environment, passive behaviour unless moved by that environment, resulting in inactivity and separation from others. It is argued that this assumption is inconsistent with much other psychology as well as the oddities in the unemployment literature itself. The active striving inherent in the general adaptation syndrome is claimed to be a better explanation of the data, and its assumptions are spelt out in more detail emphasizing the choices that men/women make, the importance of imbuing situations with meaning and the orientation to the future which directs so much of present and future activity. This active approach is shown to explain the behaviour predicted by the latent functions thesis and how it predicts other sorts of problems for the unemployed.

THE DEPRIVATION APPROACH

Having recounted the dominant findings in the unemployment literature this section concentrates on the exceptions to this dominant picture.

Even in the 1930s, resignation was not the *only* response, merely the most manifest one. Amongst the classic Marienthal studies (Jahoda, Lazarsfeld and Zeisel, 1933) the authors describe families which were 'unbroken'. One family is described in some detail: the husband, who had a record of refusing 'to be pushed around' had held 'several different political posts', including head of the work council, still held an unpaid political job which kept him 'sufficiently busy'. The researchers comment on 'the atmosphere of contentment that still emanates from the family' and say: 'This is not a case of muddling through but still a rather purposeful existence'. These 'unbroken' families were not, however, as scarce as one might infer from the literature—the authors estimate that just under a quarter of all families in Marienthal were such, and this figure is already depleted, they suggest, by the emigration of some of 'the most active and energetic families'. They claim that the families who cope well are less noticeable: 'The unbroken and the broken elements, each for different reasons, have become less visible, giving rise to the impression of a community resigned.' Diamond (1936) also reported evidence that 'organized activity' helped unemployment radicals to become adjusted to their new state, and even the Pilgrim Trust (1938) discovered that 'There are unemployed men who not only enjoy their leisure but have found in unemployment the opportunity to develop aspects of their personalities which during employment have never had a chance'.

'The evidence for the 1970s . . . even repeats the occasional exception to the general picture of apathy and resignation' (Jahoda, 1979). Marsden and Duff (1975) mention an unemployed man who had taken up painting and both enjoyed it more and worked harder at it than at his previous employment. Harrison (1976) discusses some 'minority reactions' of people 'significantly less affected by some or all of the pressures of prolonged unemployment' because, he suggests, they

have 'low needs from paid work'. Hill (1978) admits that 'the various ill-effects described, however, are much less severe if a period of unemployment can be used constructively' (though his notion of constructive use is that which shortens unemployment and/or improves employability), and Fagin (1981), after interviewing an unemployed man who 'talked about his garden with such passion, we wondered whether he could ever have time over to keep a full-time job' was led to reflect that heavy involvement in activities outside wage-earning drastically affects the impact of unemployment.

Schaufeli (1988), as already reported, finds little effect of unemployment among Dutch professionals.

There are, then, numerous examples which contradict the general interpretation of the evidence that unemployment is bad for all or most people in most respects. These have not been given sufficient attention, partly because for many people unemployment *is* an unpleasant experience, but they may also have been ignored because they fall outside the dominant explanation contained in Jahoda's 'latent functions of employment' thesis (Fryer and Payne, 1984).

What I am trying to show is that the deprivation hypothesis about the negative effects of unemployment hides a more general hypothesis about the relationship between psychological experience and social institutions, and that the hypothesis is not refutable if stated in its present form since counter-examples can always be explained away by the latent functions thesis itself. These arguments also appear in Fryer and Payne (1984, 1986) but this particular elaboration of the thesis is unique to this chapter. The empirical findings from unemployment research (both those showing negative outcomes and those showing some positive outcomes) can be explained if it is assumed that environments differ in the degree to which they contain the latent functions. Indeed, if we turn to Henry Murray (1938) we find the concept of environmental press which was conceived to show how environments differ in the motives they arouse (e.g. motives for achievement, orderliness, growth, etc.), and the strength with which those motives are aroused. Thus the latent functions might be translated into need presses concerned with need for affiliation (enforced social contact); need for energy (enforced activity); need for orderliness or conjunctivity (time structure); need for ego achievement (status and identity); need for work or need for practicalness (purposelessness). Different environments (social institutions) vary in the nature and strength of the environmental press they create, and thus have differential effects on the psychological well-being of individuals. Employment creates more press than unemployment, rural unemployment creates more press than urban unemployment (Gore, 1978), mass unemployment creates more press than very low rates of unemployment, having three close friends creates more press than having one, etc., 'all other things being equal'. Stated in this form it is possible to refute hypotheses about the effects of differing degrees of environmental press. The hypothesis changes from 'unemployment leads to psychological deterioration' (because of removal of latent functions) to

'the lower the environmental press the lower the state of psychological well-being'.

The linear relationship implied in the above hypothesis may in fact be falsified. There is a long-standing tradition in the literature on stress that the relationship between environmental press and well-being is curvilinear. Too much press creates overload stress and too little creates boredom, inertia and deterioration. McGrath (1976) argues for a linear relationship between stress and work performance, and usefully reviews the evidence for both the linear and the curvilinear hypotheses. Nor must it be forgotten, when reviewing the latent functions of employment, that there is considerable evidence that employment is dissatisfying for at least 25 per cent of the workforce (Locke, 1976 includes references to many studies), that between 10 and 15 per cent of the employed population report levels of stress high enough to warrant some medical or psychological help (Fletcher and Payne, 1980), and that about 20 per cent identify work as the major source of their stress (Warr and Payne, 1982).

McGrath's findings of a linear relationship between stress and performance compared to a curvilinear relation between stress and anxiety suggests the idea that the relationship between environmental press and behaviour may alter for different psychological experiences. Let us, for example, hypothesize about the nature of the relationships between environmental press as represented by varying social institutions and each of the five latent functions attributed to employment. The five diagrams in Figure 14.1 plot press against psychological well-being. Press is held to increase from the situation where the individual is unemployed (U) through employed (E) through being employed and having busy social life (ES) on to being employed and having an active role in community affairs (EC). Temporary employment provided by government retraining schemes falls between unemployment and employment, and for most people appears to act more like employment (Davies, 1987). In reality this assumption may be false in particular cases, since some jobs are disliked intensely because they have an over-rigid time structure, and ones where well-being would be worse at work than out of work. Other jobs make the person very isolated, and the isolation at work may be worse than that out of work. In general, however, it is assumed that unemployment is lower on press than is employment.

Figure 14.1(a) presents the hypothesis that well-being improves as the press of the different institutional settings increases, until one arrives at the person who is employed in a job with a tightly defined time structure and who is also committed to a highly programmed schedule out of work as a result of community obligations. At this point well-being reduces, since the person ends up with hardly any personal time. Figure 14.1(b) presents the same argument for enforced social contacts—there comes a point where too many enforced social contacts create tension and anxiety. Figure 14.1(e) likewise implies that the environmental press to be active can become so great as to cause physical and psychological exhaustion. Karasek (1979) has empirically demonstrated such a relationship within jobs.

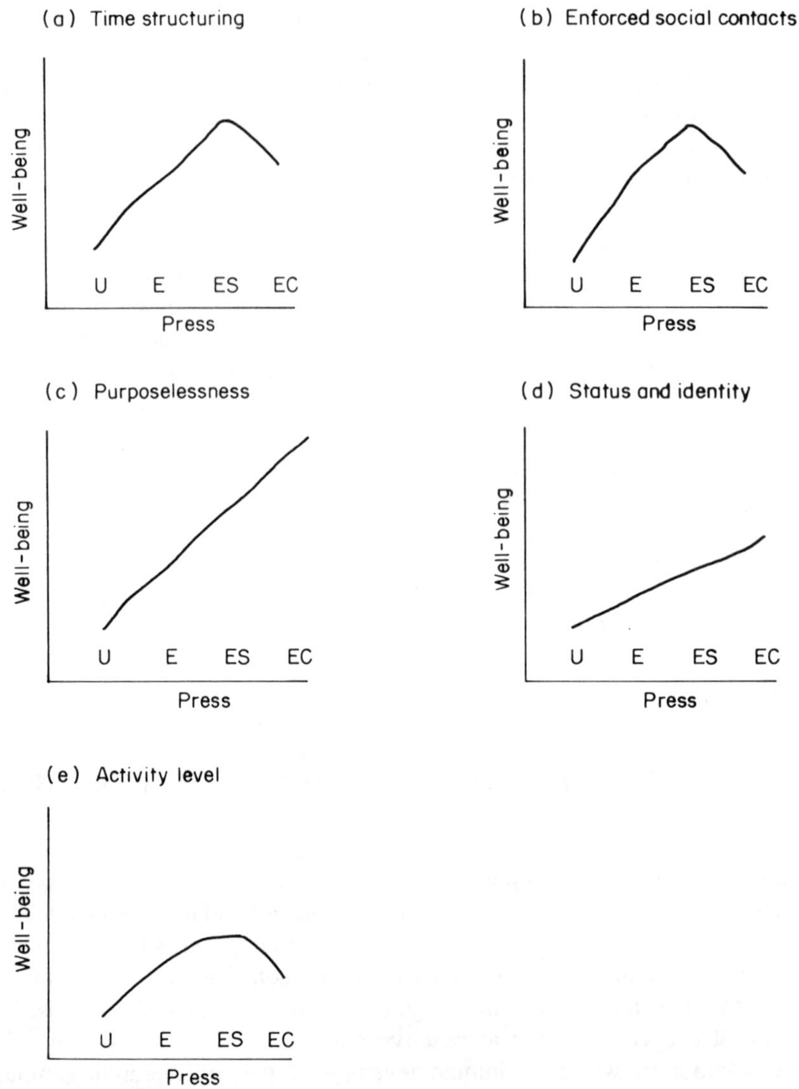

Figure 14.1. Environmental press and psychological well-being for each of the latent functions.

The hypothesized relationships in (c) and (d) are linear. At press increases so does a feeling of purposefulness and thus well-being, and the same applies to status and identity. Note that the angles of the slopes are hypothesized to differ between (c) and (d), which illustrates how theory-building can be further enhanced by this sort of analysis. All these are testable hypotheses. It even

becomes possible to conceive that unemployment differs in environmental press itself. For young people who have never worked, or old people who are near to retirement with well-established social networks and hobbies, etc., unemployment may still provide considerable press. For the middle-aged and highly committed careerist it may bring something akin to sensory deprivation. These hypotheses are not inconsistent with the findings already presented.

Apart from being inherently irrefutable the deprivation hypothesis invites categorical thinking which oversimplifies the situation of the unemployed and their means of coping with the problems unemployment presents. The sort of hypotheses and explanations generated here now suggest new approaches to empirical studies of the unemployed. They invite the conceptualization of environmental press in terms applicable to non-work situations. There has been considerable work on similar concepts in work organizations by Stern (1970), and much of the work on concepts like social support can be used in non-work situations, as has been demonstrated by Gore (1978). Payne *et al.* (1984), Payne and Hartley (1987) and Payne (1988) have based a study of the unemployed on a model of occupational stress called the Demands (Problems), Supports, Constraints model (Payne, 1979), and this provides measures which can be construed as measures of environmental press; low demand, high constraint and low support is low press; and high demand, low constraint and high support is high press. Focus on the concept directly, however, would inevitably improve its operationalization.

ASSUMPTIONS UNDERLYING THE LATENT FUNCTIONS THESIS

It is implicit in such a thesis that man is dependent on the external situation for enforcing activity, for imposing a structure on the pattern of the day, for providing a goal or purpose, for stimulating the individual into any activity whatsoever. The logical conclusion of such an assumption is that the person is moved only by outside forces. That is, the person does not initiate actions from within, and has no self-chosen goals which might provide purpose and direction. It is a view of man as reactive man.

Several important writers on human development propose hierarchical models where development is held to pass through a series of stages. Maslow (1954), for instance, proposes a hierarchical model of human needs in which behaviour is directed by the dominant need and where any need can become dominant only when the needs below it have already been satisfied. The needs in order of pre-potency are physical, safety, social, esteem and self-actualization needs. Even at the lowest level of need, physical, there is no suggestion that the person waits passively for the need to be satisfied. Indeed, the need can be so powerful that in dire circumstances normal behaviour is abandoned and murder or cannibalism can occur in the pursuit of the need's satisfaction. Loevinger (1976)

has a multi-stage model of ego development and even at the lowest of these levels, 'impulsive', where behaviour is characterized by lack of reflection, domination by immediate cues and/or body feelings and retaliatory fears, the behaviour pattern still implies an alertness and responsiveness absent from the reactive man implicit in the deprivation argument. Reactive man is inconsistent with most models of human behaviour. Even behaviourism would acknowledge the existence of a wide range of responses to a diminished stimulus situation based on the past history of reinforcement. It would certainly not predict the rapid extinction of responding implied in the deprivation approach. All these points suggest a more active man approach is consistent with other data and theory in general.

ASSUMPTIONS UNDERLYING THE ACTIVE MAN APPROACH

The basic assumption is that individuals who have no organic damage have the potential and the desire to make choices about what they want to do, and how, when and where they want to do it. This involves efforts to understand the physical and social world they inhabit, to predict what the future may hold, and to make plans for dealing with that future. This is not to say that individuals are all capable of doing these activities with the same level of competence. Nor is it to say that some individuals are not highly dependent on other people for helping them to ascribe meaning to the world, and for making novel choices about how to deal with it. As already indicated, both Maslow and Loevinger propose developmental steps leading towards behaviour which is more and more characterized by self-determined choices made to suit the individual's needs and perceptions of what will lead to his/her personal growth. Loevinger (1976) has carried out much empirical work in this area, and developed a taxonomy where the person is seen to develop from impulsive, through self-protective behaviour to behaviour characterized by conformity to prevailing norms and values, on through conscientious behaviour where the person makes the rules for himself and finally to a state of autonomy and integration where conflicts are recognized and tolerated, where ambiguity is accepted, and feelings freely expressed rather than hidden from the surrounding world. Loevinger has shown that very few people reach these high states of ego development and many people remain for most of their lives at the lower levels. This is partly attributed to differences in genetic capacity, but it has a lot to do with the social environment in which the person develops. Environments with low variety and a high demand for conformity are not conducive to producing autonomous-integrated behaviour. Maslow's theorizing is very similar to Loevinger's and his book *Eupsychian Management* (Maslow, 1965) shows how modern business organizations create conditions which inhibit psychological growth.

The point I wish to emphasize is that what people do and what they are capable of doing and wish to do are not the same thing. Given any freedom at all 'man' will strive to attribute meaning to his/her situation and act according to the sense s/he makes of it both in responding to the immediate situation and to the future as s/he would like it to be. The fact that Loevinger's empirical work has shown that many people have a very limited understanding of the world, do not try very hard to plan and execute those plans, is no argument for concluding that such sense-making and planning is not desired and important to all normally functioning persons. Long-term exposure to boring jobs and poverty, or to being out of work altogether, may suppress such behaviour, but they may do much less to suppress the *desire* to satisfy these sorts of needs. Kohn and Schooler (1982) have elegantly demonstrated how the complexity of the work environment affects intellectual complexity, in a 10-year longitudinal study. It is claimed (Fryer and Payne, 1984) that the behaviour so frequently found among the unemployed, and held to be a result of the withdrawal of the latent functions of employment, can be equally well, if not better explained, by the assumptions inherent in viewing man as active man.

Having summarized the evidence for the psychological effect of unemployment and the explanations offered, I will now consider how transitions theory might further illuminate understanding of these two aspects of the unemployment literature.

TRANSITIONS THEORY AND UNEMPLOYMENT

I have described briefly what is known about the effects of unemployment unaided by transitions theory, though it is obvious enough that the general adaptation syndrome bears some similarity to the stages of the transition cycle, as do other phase models describing the effects of unemployment. The question is: 'does the transitions cycle help to move unemployment theory forward?'

Interestingly, one of the few papers that links job loss to transitions concentrates on the potential that the experience has for improving career growth among managers and professionals: development derives from successfully coping with the threat (Latack and Dozier, 1986). The situational factors that determine success or failure, according to Latack and Dozier, are not unfamiliar: financial resources, social support and a flexible family structure, a professional approach to the termination on the part of the organization and the avoidance of prolonged unemployment.

Since Nicholson (1987) also starts from an interest in careers, it is noteworthy that he too tends to focus on the positive outcomes of transitions. In his figure 4 (p. 181), Nicholson describes the four stages of the cycle as follows:

Preparation: developing helpful expectations, motives and feelings.
Encounter: confidence in coping, enjoyment in sense-making.
Adjustment: personal development, role innovation and relationship building.
Stabilization: sustained trust, commitment and effectiveness with tasks and people.

Nicholson recognizes the negative aspects of transitions calling them pitfalls and problems (his figure 5) hypothesizing that being poorly prepared makes the encounter a shock, leading to poor adjustment strategies and stabilizing in failure or fatalism. This is, of course, a person–environment match model. Some very successful managers are quite unprepared for coping with unemployment, thus starting a negative transitions cycle.

Since the majority of people experience unemployment negatively, however, I wish to focus on that and explore its nature using Nicholson's nine dimensions, since they seem a potential contribution to our theoretical framework for describing and understanding both positive and negative transitions.

The derivation and meaning of the nine dimensions is illuminated by the recognition that they derive from the metaphor of the wheel. 'The motion of a wheel may be characterised by how fast it is turning (*speed*), its shape and size (*amplitude and symmetry*), how smooth its action (*continuity*), how it is regulated (*discretion*), whether it contains nested wheels (*complexity*), how it is initiated (*propulsion*), how it is assisted (*facilitation*), and where it is going (*significance*) (p. 190).

SPEED

Assuming the cycle is ended either by re-employment or retirement from the labour market then it would seem that the unemployment cycle would be a slow one for most people. There are differences in exposure to redundancy and unemployment by social class and occupation (Daniel, 1974), with the unskilled and semi-skilled being more frequently exposed, though managerial and professional redundancies have been increasing (O'Boyle, 1985). When cycles occur infrequently, it becomes difficult to learn how to deal with them, unless they are very simple, and Nicholson predicts such cycles will produce frustration and stuckness. This is consistent with unemployment research, but for job transition cycles which are slow Nicholson predicts a positive feeling of ownership of the cycle. This seems a most unlikely reaction to being unemployed where the dominant response is to attribute ownership to the 'system'. This slowness of the cycle would seem to encourage the fatalistic adjustment commonly reported by the unemployed.

AMPLITUDE

Unemployment is for most people a high-amplitude event and, as Nicholson predicts, such events produce shock, fear and defensiveness in all but the most

resilient. Few unemployed react with delight at the opportunity for self-discovery that high-amplitude events can generate according to Nicholson's theory.

SYMMETRY

This refers to the relative length of each of the four stages of the transition cycle. In unemployment the symmetry will be determined by the length of unemployment. As reported earlier, psychological distress increases rapidly in the first few months, and may be even higher if there is a period of anticipating the event (Cobb and Kasl, 1971). After that distress remains high but shows small improvements in the following one to two years. It would seem that for most people the preparation period is short, the encounter period moderately long, the adjustment period similarly moderate in length and the stabilization lengthy in duration, at least for the long-term unemployed. Except for this group almost any other symmetry pattern must be possible, depending on the length of the unemployment and the individual's subjective responses to it. There is evidence, however, that the encounter phase may be of very long duration even for those who get work: the effect of the event can be long-lasting (Fineman, 1983; Payne and Jones, 1987).

CONTINUITY

High continuity of transition cycles occurs when the cycles follow an orderly, connected sequence such as they do in some careers. For most individuals cycles of unemployment are, thankfully, unconnected, and presumably they are connected with either re-employment or retirement. Nicholson proposes that low continuity can bring a sense of novelty and optimism, though in unemployment a potentially negative cycle, outcomes of confusion and loss of purpose are clearly prominent. Being unemployed must feel like being on an island in the midst of the journey through life with the real problem being that one has no idea of how big the island is. This lack of continuity, or worse, its connections to other cycles such as divorce and sickness, make unemployment a potentially negative cycle.

DISCRETION

Most unemployed have become so involuntarily, and the level of control they have over the cycle remains low for many, though it varies according to the buoyancy of the local economy, personal resources and personal attitudes. Assuming low discretion as more typical, however, Nicholson predicts detachment and low self-esteem. In jobs he predicts positive outcomes of clarity and blamelessness. These seem unlikely for the unemployed, who are faced by uncertainty and considerable stigmatization from outside, as well as blame

from within themselves. Even in very high areas of unemployment the 'majority' are often still in employment.

COMPLEXITY

One of the central features of the latent consequences of unemployment involves the reduction in environmental challenge that unemployment brings. Except for the complexities of state bureaucracy and job-seeking the typical unemployed person's life space is narrowed at the same time as being made more threatening by financial and social insecurity. Boredom is a major problem for many unemployed people (Daniel, 1974; Warr and Payne, 1982), and whilst simplicity might bring clarity and contentment to some people in jobs, it rarely does so for the unemployed.

PROPULSION

Unemployment is for most people caused by the system rather than initiated by themselves. The unemployed tend to be pawns rather than origins (DeCharms, 1978). The powerlessness predicted by Nicholson is undoubtedly found amongst the unemployed, where it has been observed that they are difficult to mobilize politically even when there are large numbers of them concentrated in the same geographical area (Jahoda, 1982). Again, in employment Nicholson suggests system-propulsion enables the person to be detached and thus flexible, but it is almost impossible to detach oneself from the system when unemployed. One is dependent on it for sustenance, and for getting re-employed. Indeed, the financial dependence brings with it closer scrutiny of resources and activities, thus restricting flexibility even further.

FACILITATION

Unemployment causes, above all, a deterioration in resources. It also removes many people from social contacts which have been traditional sources of support. The stress it brings frequently has negative effects on family relationships, turning them from supportive and facilitative to provocations and problems (Elder and Capsi, 1988). Nicholson predicts high anxiety and loneliness from low facilitation cycles with the possibility of challenge leading to exploration and independence. Some unemployed do set up businesses (Fineman, 1983) as a response to unemployment, but even these start from a basis of resources and support. It is much more difficult to do this when unemployment has been prolonged and resources depleted. As Gore (1978) has suggested, lack of support does not just buffer one from the effects of stress, it becomes a stressor itself.

SIGNIFICANCE

The degree to which a transition cycle is significant for a person depends on the other strengths and interrelationships amongst the other eight dimensions. Taking a negative view of unemployment it is clear that the dimensions cohere around a negative and dehumanizing cycle of experience. The pain, grieving and strain that Nicholson predicts are the outcomes of highly significant events appear in abundance amongst the unemployed. He does, however, point out that self-actualization and growth also occur in significant, 'revolutionary' cycles. These acknowledged, but relatively rare reactions to unemployment have already been discussed here, though it needs to be added that Haworth and Evans (1987) report evidence that suggests the proactive reactions described by Fryer and Payne (1984) are more common than they believed.

It is apparent that it is possible to apply the dimensions of the transitions cycle to unemployment, though it is equally clear that it is not a homogeneous transition. Assuming a basically negative outcome, however, the dimensions proved to match up to the data quite well. One big difference was that the positive outcomes proposed by Nicholson when applying the transitions cycle to work transitions, rarely translated well to the unemployment cycle. This is not to deny they apply to some people, which is itself consistent with the current emphasis on proactive reactions to unemployment (Liem and Liem, 1988).

It would be over-reacting, perhaps, to claim that the transitions literature will revolutionize the study of unemployment, since that literature has alway contained a phases model within it. However, the increasing systematization of the transitions literature does offer a useful framework for dimensionalizing transition cycles and unearthing the roles of person versus situation in creating them. The dimensions also provide a useful way of studying the development of transitions over time, which might be very useful in the growing number of longitudinal studies emerging in the literature on unemployment.

REFERENCES

Allen, V. L. and Van de Vliert, E. (eds) 1984) *Role Transitions: explorations and explanations*. London: Plenum.

Antanovsky, A. (1987) *Unravelling the Mystery of Health*. San Francisco, CA: Jossey-Bass.

Archer, J. and Rhodes, V. (1987) Bereavement and reactions to job loss: a comparative review. *British Journal of Social Psychology*, **26**, 211-224.

Banks, M. H. and Jackson, P. R. (1982) Unemployment and risk of minor psychiatric disorder in young people: cross-sectional and longitudinal evidence. *Psychological Medicine*, **12**, 789-798.

Bowlby, J. (1960) Separation anxiety. *International Journal of Psycho-Analysis*, **41**, 89-113.

Breakwell, G. M., Harrison, B. and Propper, C. (1984) Explaining the psychological effects of unemployment for young people: the importance of specific situational factors. *British Journal of Guidance and Counselling*, **21**, 132-140.

Brenner, S-O. and Starring, B. (1988) Unemployment and health in Sweden: Public issues and private troubles. *Journal of Social Issues*, **44**(4), 125-140.

Bridges, W. (1980) *Transitions: Making Sense of Life's Changes*. Reading, MA: Addison-Wesley.

Cobb, S. and Kasl, S. V. (1972) Some medical aspects of unemployment. *Industrial Gerontology*, **12**, 8-16.

Daniel, W. W. (1974) *A National Survey of the Unemployed*. London: Political and Economic Planning Institute.

Davies, B. (1987) Coping with marginality. Paper presented at the BPS Section Conference, Oxford. SAPU Memo 874, MRC/ESRC, Sheffield University.

DeCharms, R. (1978) *Personal Causation: The Internal Affective Determinants of Behaviour*. New York: Academic Press.

Diamond, S. (1936) A study of the influence of political radicalism on personality development. *Archives of Psychology*, **29**, 203.

Dupue, R. A. and Monroe S. M. (1986) Conceptualization and measurement of human disorders in life stress research: the problem of chronic disturbance. *Psychological Bulletin*, **99**, 36-51.

Dooley, D. and Catalano, R. (1988) Recent research on the psychological effects of unemployment. *Journal of Social Issues*, **44**(4), 1-12.

Eisenberg, P. and Lazarsfeld, P. F. (1938) The psychological effects of unemployment. *Psychological Bulletin*, **35**, 358-390.

Elder, G. H. (1974) *Children of the Great Depression*. Chicago, IL: University of Chicago Press.

Elder, G. H. and Caspi, A. (1988) Economic stress in lives: development perspectives. *Journal of Social Issues*, **44**(4), 25-46.

Fagin, L. (1981) *Unemployment and Health in Families*, DHSS Publication. London: HMSO.

Fineman, S. (1983) *White Collar Unemployment*. Chichester: John Wiley & Sons.

Finley-Jones, R. A. and Burvill, P. W. (1977) The prevalence of minor psychiatric morbidity in the community. *Psychological Medicine*, **7**, 475-89.

Fletcher, B. and Payne, R. L. (1980) Stress at work: a review and theoretical framework. Part 1. *Personnel Review*, **9**(1), 19-29.

Fletcher, B., Gowler, D. and Payne, R. L. (1979) Exploding the myth of executive stress. *Personnel Management*, **11**(5), 30-35.

Fletcher, B. (1988) The epidemiology of occupational stress. In C. Cooper and R. Payne (eds), *Causes, Coping and Consequences of Stress at Work*. London: John Wiley & Sons, pp. 3-50.

Fryer, D. M. (1985) Stages in psychological response to unemployment: (dis)integrative review article. *Current Psychological Research and Reviews*, **4**, 257-273.

Fryer, D. M. and Payne, R. L. (1984) Proactive behaviour in unemployment: findings and implications. *Leisure Studies*, **3**, 273-295.

Fryer, D. M. and Payne, R. L. (1986) Being unemployed: a review of the literature on the psychological experience of unemployment. In C. L. Cooper and I. Robertson (eds), *International Review of Industrial and Organisational Psychology*. London: John Wiley & Sons, pp. 235-278.

Goldberg, D. P. (1972) *The Detection of Psychiatric Illness by Questionnaire*. London: Oxford University Press.

Gore, S. (1978) The effect of social support in moderating the health consequences of unemployment, *Journal of Health and Social Behaviour*, **19**, 157-165.

Harrison, R. (1976) The demoralizing experience of prolonged unemployment, *Department of Employment Gazette*, April.

Haworth, J. T. and Evans, S. T. (1987) Meaningful activity and unemployment. In D. Fryer and P. Ullah (eds), *Unemployed People: Social and Psychological Perspectives*, Open University Press, Milton Keynes, pp. 241–267.

Hill, J. (1978) The psychological impact of unemployment. *New Society*, 19 January.

Iverson, L. and Sabroe, S. (1988) Psychological well-being among unemployed and employed people after a company closedown: a longitudinal study. *Journal of Social Issues*, **44**(4), 141-152.

Jahoda, M. (1979) The psychological meaning of unemployment, *New Society*, 6.

Jahoda, M. (1982) *Employment and Unemployment: A Social Psychological Analysis*. New York: Cambridge University Press.

Jahoda, M. (1984) Social institutions and human needs: a comment on Fryer and Payne. *Leisure Studies*, **3**, 297-299.

Jahoda, M., Lazarsfeld, P. F. and Zeisel, H. (1933) *Marienthal: The Sociology of an Unemployed Community*. New York: Aldine-Atherton.

Karesek, R. A. (1979) Job demands: job decision latitude and mental strain: implications for job design. *Administrative Science Quarterly*, **24**, 285-308.

Kessler, R. C., Turner, J. B. and House, J. S. (1988) Effects of unemployment on health in a community survey: main, modifying and mediating effects. *Journal of Social Issues*, **44**(4), 69-86.

Kobosa, S., C., Maddi, S. R. and Kahn, S. (1982) Hardiness and health: a prospective study. *Journal of Personality and Social Psychology*, **42**, 168-177.

Kohn, M. L. and Schooler, C. (1982) Job conditions and personality: a longitudinal assessment of their reciprocal effects. *American Journal of Sociology*, **87**, 1257-1286.

Latack, J. C. and Dozier, J. B. (1986) After the ax falls: job loss as a career transition. *Academy of Management Review*, **11**(2), 375-392.

Liem, R. and Liem, J. H. (1988) Psychological effects of unemployment on workers and their families. *Journal of Social Issues*, **44**(4), 87-106.

Locke, E. J. (1976) The nature and causes of job satisfaction. In M. D. Dunette (ed.), *Handbook of Industrial and Organizational Psychology*, Chicago, IL: Rand McNalley, pp. 1297-1350.

Loevinger, J. (1976) *Ego Development*. San Francisco, CA: Jossey-Bass.

Marsden, D. and Duff, E. 1975) *Workless: Some Unemployed Men and their Families*. Harmondsworth: Penguin.

Maslow, A. H. (1954) *Motivation and Personality*. New York: Harper & Row.

Maslow, A. H. (1965) *Eupsychian Management*. Homewood, IL: R. D. Irwin.

McGrath, J. E. (1976) Stress and behaviour in organizations. In M. D. Dunette (ed.), *Handbook of Industrial and Organizational Psychology*, Chicago, IL: Rand McNally, pp. 1351-1396.

Murray, H. (1938) *Explorations in Personality*. New York: Oxford University Press.

Nicholson, N. (1987) The transition cycle: a conceptual framework for the analysis of change and human resources management. In J. Ferris and K. M. Rowland (eds), *Personnel and Human Resources Management*, Vol. 5. Greenwich, CT: JAI Press, pp. 167-222.

Nicholson, N. and West, M. (1989) Transitions and the concepts of careers. In M. B. Arthur, D. T. Hall and B. S. Lawrence (eds), *Handbook of Career Theory*. London: Cambridge University Press, pp. 181–201.

O'Boyle, T. F. (1985) Loyalty ebbs at many companies as employees grow disillusioned, *Wall St Journal*, July, p. 17.

Parkes, C. M. (1971) Psychosocial transition: a field for study, *Social Science and Medicine*, **15**, 101-115.

Payne, R. L. (1979) Demands, supports, constraints and psychological health. In C. J. Mackay and T. Cox (eds), *Responses to Stress: Occupational Aspects*. London: International Publishing Corporation, pp. 85–105.

Payne, R. L. (1988) A longitudinal study of psychological well-being of unemployed men and the mediating effect of neuroticism. *Human Relations*, **41**(2), 119-138.

Payne, R. L. and Hartley, J. (1987) A test of a model for explaining the affective experience of unemployed men. *Journal of Occupational Psychology*, **60**, 31-47.

Payne, R. L. and Jones, J. G. (1987) Social class and re-employment: changes in health and perceived financial circumstances. *Journal of Occupational Behaviour*, **8**, 175-184.

Payne, R. L., Warr, P. B. and Hartley, J. (1984) Social class and psychological ill-health during unemployment. *Sociology of Health and Illness*, **61**, 152-174.

Platt, S. (1984) Unemployment and suicidal behaviour: a review, *Social Science and Medicine*, **19**(2), 93-115.

Pilgrim Trust (1938) *Men Without Work*. Cambridge: Cambridge University Press.

Schaufeli, W. B. (1988) Unemployment and psychological health: an investigation among Dutch professionals. Rijksuniversiteit, Groningen.

Selye, H. (1956) *The Stress of Life*. New York: McGraw-Hill.

Stern, G. C. (1970) *People in Context*. New York: John Wiley & Sons.

Stybel, L. J. (1978) Managing human resource termination: the interpersonal conduct and organizational consequences of executive dismissal. Unpublished doctoral dissertation, Graduate School of Education, Harvard University.

Warr, P. B. (1984) Reported behaviour changes after job loss. *British Journal of Social Psychology*, **23**, 271-275.

Warr, P. B. (1987) *Work, Unemployment and Mental Health*. Oxford: Oxford University Press.

Warr, P. B. and Jackson, P. (1985) Factors influencing the psychological impact of prolonged unemployment and of re-employment. *Psychological Medicine*, **15**, 795-807.

Warr, P. B. and Jackson, P. (1987) Adapting to the unemployed role: A longitudinal investigation. *Social Science and Medicine*, **25**, 1219-1224.

Warr, P. B. and Parry, G. (1982) Depressed mood in working-class mothers with and without paid employment. *Social Psychiatry*, **17**, 161-165.

Warr, P. B. and Payne, R. L. (1982) Experiences of strain and pleasure among British adults. *Social Science and Medicine*, **16**, 1691-1697.

Warr, P. B., Jackson, P. and Banks, M. (1988) Unemployment and mental health: some British studies. *Journal of Social Issues*, **44**(4), 47-68.

White, M. (1985) Life stress in long-term unemployment. *Policy Studies*, **5**, 31-49.

Zawadski, B. and Lazarsfeld, P. F. (1935) The psychological consequences of unemployment. *Journal of Social Psychology*, **6**, 224-251.

15 Expatriate Stress: The Problems of Living Abroad

ADRIAN FURNHAM
University College London

INTRODUCTION

It is extremely difficult to ascertain the number of expatriates living in any one country. Figures are unreliable for a number of reasons: some countries can and do not attempt to keep reliable records; other countries are loath to disclose the precise number of the nationals living abroad; while others might be prone to exaggerate the number for political ends. Furthermore, expatriates are made up of a very diverse and heterogeneous population of individuals: businessmen and women, diplomats, military personnel, missionaries, students as well as a host of others who have left their country of birth for a wide variety of reasons. Hence research in the area is scattered and limited. Nevertheless, this chapter will consider various aspects of expatriate experience, focusing on the psychological problems associated with change and transition.

The first issue to be confronted will be to attempt to categorize or classify the many different types of expatriates that there are. The motives for movement inevitably relate directly to the personal experience of change, hence the issue is of fundamental importance. Secondly the concept of culture shock—a popular lay description of the experience of all sojourners—will be discussed from a psychological perspective. Adaptation to a new country, culture and environment clearly goes through different phases and the U and W curve hypothesis for adaptation will then be considered. Some of the more simple but important cultural differences that prove problematic for the expatriate will then be considered. The important issue of selecting and preparing expatriates for their move will be discussed penultimately. Finally, different methods for reducing expatriate stress will be considered.

On the Move: the Psychology of Change and Transition. Edited by S. Fisher and C. L. Cooper.

TYPES OF EXPATRIATES

Most scientific enterprise begins with initial classification and later refined taxonomization. The study of expatriates is no exception. Further, the dictionary is of little use as the term expatriate appears to have two related meanings: there is a neutral reference to one who lives, probably voluntarily, in a foreign country (specifically the one who has renounced his or her native country), but there is also a negative reference to someone banished and exiled to a foreign country, presumably involuntarily, and who subsequently withdraws his or her allegiance to that country. Hence the former definition simply implies change of status while the second stresses the change in affection, specifically patriotism or love of country. Curiously the term is frequently used by expatriates themselves, not to indicate disaffection from country of origin but the precise opposite—increased loyalty to one's home country. 'Expat' gatherings and entertainments are frequently characterized by affectionate nostalgia for the home country, its traditions and values.

Various attempts have been made to classify or categorize travellers using different dimensions. For instance, Bochner (1982) classified expatriates and sojourners according to their psychological response to the host culture. This is clearly a useful way of distinguishing expatriates but it tends to concentrate on reactions to migration rather than on motives for migration. However, motives are complex, numerous and not always explicit. Some have categorized them into *pull* and *push* motives—features of the second country or culture, like the climate or a higher standard of living that pulls one to that culture. On the other hand certain factors, like discrimination or political uncertainty, push one away from one's country of origin. Certainly it seems implicitly the case that expats who are pulled would adapt more readily than 'expats' who are pushed.

Furnham and Bochner (1986) suggest various dimensions on which groups of expatriates could be classified. These include:

1. Geographic distance—between 'home' and second culture, implying various climate and cultural differences.
2. Amount of change required—this is both qualitative and quantitative and suggests both behavioural and cognitive aspects.
3. Length of time spent—this could be categorized into meaningful time zones like five-year periods.
4. 'Voluntariness' of the move—the idea that the move itself may not be voluntary but may be the result of various constraints and prescriptions.

There are no doubt numerous other dimensions that could be used to categorize expatriates into quite different groups. One such is proposed by Gudykunst (1983) in his typology of stranger–host relationships. The point, however, is an

Table 15.1. Outcomes of cultural contact at the individual level: psychological responses to 'second culture' influences

Response	Type	Multiple-group membership affiliation	Effect on individual	Effect on society
Reject culture of origin, embrance second culture	'Passing'	Culture I norms lose salience Culture II norms become salient	Loss of ethnic identity Self-denigration	Assimilation Cultural erosion
Reject second culture, exaggerate first culture	Chauvinistic	Culture I norms increase in salience Culture II norms decrease in salience	Nationalism Racism	Inter-group friction
Vacillate between the two cultures	Marginal	Norms of both cultures salient but perceived as mutually incompatible	Conflict Identity confusion Over-compensation	Reform Social change
Synthesize both cultures	Mediating	Norms of both cultures salient and perceived as capable of being integrated	Personal growth Cultural preservation	Inter-group harmony Pluralistic societies

From B. Bochner, *Cultures in Contact: Studies in Cross-cultural Interaction*, Oxford, Pergamon, 1982.

important but simple one. Description usually precedes explanation, and taxonomization is frequently the first step to an adequate description. In order to understand the psychological perspectives, preferences and reactions of expatriates, it is first necessary to classify them into various groups or types. These taxonomies may differ according to the particular phenomenon considered. Thus, for instance, the taxonomy for looking at expatriate stress may be rather different from that concerning an expatriate–native interaction, though the two may be related. Hence no one exhaustive typology shall be offered here.

Yet there are a number of useful dimensions or factors that may be used to distinguish one type of expatriate move from another. These include: (1) *distance* (how far a person is transferred); (2) *country* (whether the move involves leaving one's own country, continent, linguistic area, or not); (3) *job* (whether the person is expected to do much the same or a different type of job, or at the same or different level; (4) *social support* (whether the person moves alone, with others from the workplace, with or without family); (5) *time* (how long are the persons likely to spend in this other place and when can they expect to return or move

on to another posting); (6) *returns* (benefits and costs of the move, including the possibility of being dismissed or demoted if not agreeing to the transfer); (7) *volunteering* (to what extent the individuals believe that they had a choice in the move).

These, and indeed other, factors may be important for the adjustment of the expatriate. For instance, a six-month sideways transfer, alone, to an unknown and distant country, is likely to have quite different consequences than a two-year sojourn in another part of the same country, accompanied by one's spouse and family, and provided with generous financial and social support. Stokols and Shumaker (1982) proposed that the health effects of location depend not only on the immediate circumstances surrounding a move but also on the broader context of the individual's residential history, current life situation, and aspirations for the future.

According to Torbiorn (1982), multinationals have *three* basic motives in posting people to foreign countries: *the control function* (to ensure that operations in other countries are being carried out as planned and to secure staff loyalty; *the know-how function* (to provide technological and administrative services); and *the contact/coordination* function (to evaluate and transmit salient information between company operations). Thus, business 'expats' have a difficult role in that they are required to act in accordance with the expectations of the parent company *and* also fulfil local expectations, the two often being incompatible. Problems with these professional roles include: unclear, ambiguous or even incompatible expectations on the part of the parent company; communication difficulties; a clash between company and personal interests and values; uncertainty about the future; and problems with the adjustment of the spouse and family.

In a large empirical study Torbiorn (1982) set out to establish the determinants of business expatriate satisfaction. In doing so he questioned over 1000 Swedish expat businessmen and women in 26 host countries. He looked at their personal circumstances (age, education, status); motives for moving abroad; who initiated the move; previous overseas experience; the nature of the country they came from and the country they moved to; their chosen lifestyle; and spouse satisfaction. He found that men more than women, and better-educated rather than less well educated people adapt better; that the motive for moving most strongly associated with adjustment was 'a special interest in the particular host country'; that previous overseas experience had no effect on adjustment; that expatriates who spent most of their free time with host country nationals were happier on average than those who turned to their own countrymen; and that the satisfaction of the spouse was a major factor in determining adjustment.

By and large, whichever variable was plotted against adjustment over time, (sex, age, previous experience, friends or attitudes to the host country), the pattern was much the same, showing a steady increase in satisfaction, though there was sometimes the indication of a flat U-curve (discussed later).

The study also covered variables such as the most popular countries to work in, knowledge and adoption of host country conditions, the adaptation of children, and the experience of work in other countries. Yet Torbiorn admitted to not being able to explain much of the variance in business expatriates' satisfaction and adjustment, the 30 variables he examined together accounting for between 25 and 50 per cent of the variance! Happiness of spouse was by far the most important factor, followed by various features of the external environment such as food and climate. Women tended to feel more isolated than men, which in turn greatly affected the man's satisfaction. A number of cultural barriers—religion, language and socioeconomic development—were good predictors of the business people's happiness, adjustment and lifestyle, and hence showed enormous variation between countries; the more the barriers the less the satisfaction.

Studies on expat businessmen and women who have moved from one area or country to another have revealed evidence of unhappiness, distress and poor adjustment. Of course, this is not always the case and, as research has shown, there is a large and complex number of variables determining the actual adjustment of particular individuals. At the same time it is probably safe to say that overall business 'expats' experience less difficulty than migrants, missionaries or other sojourners (particularly students) moving to new environments. There may be a number of reasons for this. Firstly, business people are usually posted elsewhere for a set, specific and relatively *short period of time* (two to five years). Hence they may see their move as relatively temporary and not requiring much adaptation and change. Secondly, businessmen and women are posted abroad for a *specific purpose*, usually to deal with particular technical and managerial problems. This is not to say that the problems are simple—indeed they are often complex and highly intractable—but rather that many of their problems are confined to work. They do not, as a rule have to worry about transportation, accommodation and other 'housekeeping' problems. Thirdly, business people usually have *strong sponsorship*. Many are given financial incentives for working abroad, and often their life overseas is an improvement on what they had left behind. Furthermore, the sponsorship is not only financial but may include social and political benefits that increase rather than decrease a person's social standing, political power and influence in the new society. Similarly a tour abroad often increases opportunities for *advancement on return*. Many business people travel specifically to enhance their chances for promotion; therefore any hardships on the trip may be seen as a small price to pay for the rewards to be gained later.

In contrast to students, military people, and some migrants, business 'expats' tend to be *older and are usually more mature*. Although the literature is equivocal on this point, it is generally the case that older, more experienced and better-educated people can cope with the problems of geographic movement (Furnham & Bochner, 1986). Businesses often provide accommodation enclaves, 'old-hand' guides and a *social support network* that insulate the foreigner against the initial

difficulties and surprises of movement. The long-term benefits associated with these 'ghettos' are, however, debatable as they reduce contact with the locals from whom the skills of intercultural communication are best learnt. Further, because businesses are primarily interested in the work their employees do, the employees' *time is carefully structured and scheduled.* This, as unemployment researchers have shown, is directly related to a reduction in mental illness. Finally the *social relationships* both inside and outside the workplace are probably more likely to be on an *equal footing for businessmen* than for students. Such equal-status peer-group interaction probably goes some way in accounting for the relatively better adjustment of business people compared to students, whose social relationships are more often asymmetrical with respect to status.

Clearly not all 'expats' are the same, and a full understanding of the psychological effect of change and transition depend on their individual or group circumstances.

CULTURE SHOCK

Experts, like other laymen and women, talk a lot about culture shock, which is a sort of shorthand for their early and profound experiences in the new culture. The concept implies that the experience of visiting or living in a new culture is an unpleasant surprise or shock, partly because it is unexpected, and partly because it may lead to a negative evaluation of one's own and/or the other culture.

The anthropologist Oberg (1960) was the first to have used the term. In a brief and largely anecdotal article he mentions at least six aspects of culture shock. These include:

1. *Strain* due to the effort required to make necessary psychological adaptions.
2. *A sense of loss* and *feelings of deprivation* in regard to friends, status, profession and possessions.
3. Being *rejected* by/and or rejecting members of the new culture.
4. *Confusion* in role, role expectations, values, feelings and self-identity.
5. *Surprise*, *anxiety*, even *disgust*, and *indignation* after becoming aware of cultural differences.
6. *Feelings of impotence* due to not being able to cope with the new environment.

The flavour of Oberg's observations may be gathered from this quote:

> Culture shock is precipitated by the anxiety that results from losing all our familiar signs and symbols of social intercourse. These signs or cues include the thousand and one ways in which we orient ourselves to the situations of daily life: when to shake hands and what to say when we meet people, when and how to give

> tips, how to give orders to servants, how to make purchases, when to accept and when to refuse invitations, when to take statements seriously and when not. Now these cues which may be words, gestures, facial expressions, customs, or norms are acquired by all of us in the course of growing up and are as much a part of our culture as the language we speak or the beliefs we accept. All of us depend for our peace of mind and our efficiency on hundreds of these cues, most of which we are not consciously aware. . . . Some of the symptoms of culture shock are: excessive washing of the hands; excessive concern over drinking water, food, dishes, and bedding; fear of physical contact with attendants or servants; that absent-minded, far-away stare (sometimes called the 'tropical stare'); a feeling of helplessness and a desire for dependence on long-term residents of one's own nationality; fits of anger over delays and other minor frustrations; delay and outright refusal to learn the language of the host country; excessive fear of being cheated, robbed, or injured; great concern over minor pains and irruptions of the skin; and finally, that terrible longing to be back home, to be able to have a good cup of coffee and a piece of apple pie, to walk into that corner drugstore, to visit one's relatives, and, in general, to talk to people who really make sense (Oberg, 1960, p. 176).

Cleveland, Margone and Adams (1963) offered a similar analysis, relying heavily on the personal experience of business and other travellers, especially those at two extremes of the adaptation continuum, individuals who act as if they had 'never left home' and those who immediately 'go native'. These descriptions are nearly always qualitative rather than quantitative and rarely attempt to explain *why* some expats experience it and others do not!

Researchers since Oberg have seen culture shock as a normal and expected reaction; as part of the routine process of adaptation to cultural differences and the manifestation of a longing for a more predictable, stable and understandable environment. Others have attempted to improve and extend Oberg's definition and concept of culture shock. Guthrie (1975) has used the term *culture fatigue*, Smalley (1963) *language shock*, Byrnes (1966) *role shock* and Ball-Rokeach (1973) *pervasive ambiguity*. In doing so different researchers have simply placed the emphasis on different problems—language, physical irritability or role ambiguity, but tend to have dealt with it in roughly similar ways.

Bock (1970) has described culture shock as primarily an emotional reaction that follows from not being able to understand, control and predict another's behaviour. When customary experiences no longer seem relevant or applicable, people's usual behaviour changes to becoming 'unusual'. Lack of familiarity with both the physical setting (design of homes, shops, offices) as well as the social environment (etiquette, ritual) have this effect, as do the experiences with and use of time (Hall, 1959).

This theme is reiterated by all the writers in the field (Lunstedt, 1963; Hays, 1972). Culture shock is seen as a stress reaction where salient psychological and physical rewards are generally uncertain, and hence difficult to control or predict. Thus a person is anxious, confused and apparently apathetic until he or she has had time to develop a new set of cognitive constructs to understand and enact

the appropriate behaviour. In the business world where, for instance, a manager has been successful and developed all the requisite skills for dealing with peers, subordinates, supervisors and clients in his/her culture, all or many of these skills, strategies and techniques may become ineffective or irrelevant in the new culture. Hence the anxiety and confusion until new techniques, skills and concepts are learnt.

Culture shock includes the individuals' lacking in points of reference, social norms and rules to guide their actions and understand others' behaviour. This is very similar to the attributes studied under the heading of *alienation* and *anomie*, which include powerlessness, meaningless, normlessness, self and social estrangements and social isolation. Certainly many poorly adapted expats react to their new environment like alienated people do in their native environment.

In addition, ideas associated with *anxiety* pervade the culture shock literature. Observers have pointed to a continuous general 'free-floating' anxiety which affects people's normal behaviour. Lack of self-confidence, distrust of others, and mild psychosomatic complaints are also common (May, 1970). Furthermore, people appear to lose their inventiveness and spontaneity and become obsessively concerned with orderliness (Nash, 1967).

Most of the investigations of a culture shock have been descriptive, in that they have attempted to list the various difficulties that sojourners experience, and their typical reactions. Less attention has been paid to explain for whom the shock will be more or less intense (e.g. the old or the less educated); what determines which reaction a person is likely to experience; how long people remain in a period of shock, and so forth. The literature suggests that all people will suffer culture shock to some extent, which is always thought of as being unpleasant and stressful. This assumption needs to be empirically supported. In theory some people need not experience any negative aspects of shock; instead they may seek out these experiences for their enjoyment. Sensation-seekers, for instance, might be expected not to suffer any adverse effects but to enjoy the highly arousing stimuli of the unfamiliar (Zuckerman, 1979). People with multicultural backgrounds or experiences may also adapt more successfully. For instance Adler (1975) and David (1971) have stated that although culture shock is most often associated with negative consequences it may, in mild doses, be important for self-development and personal growth. Culture shock is seen as a transitional experience which can result in the adoption of new values, attitudes and behaviour patterns.

> In the encounter with another culture the individual gains new experiential knowledge by coming to understand the roots of his or her own ethnocentrism and by gaining new perspectives and outlooks on the nature of culture. . . . Paradoxically, the more one is capable of experiencing new and different dimensions of human diversity, the more one learns of oneself (Adler, 1975, p. 22).

Thus, although different writers have put emphasis on different aspects of culture shock, there is by and large agreement that exposure to new cultures is stressful.

Fewer researchers have seen the positive side of culture shock either for those individuals who revel in exciting and different environments, or for those whose initial discomfiture leads to personal growth. The quality and quantity of culture shock has been shown to be related to the amount of *difference* between the visitor's (sojourners', managers') culture and the culture of the country they are visiting or working in. These differences refer to the numerous culture differences in social beliefs and behaviours.

Furnham and Bochner (1986) have offered eight different explanations for culture shock and evaluated the power of each 'theory' to explain the phenomena. Briefly the eight explanations are:

1. Culture shock is the psychology of loss and the phenomenon is akin to that of grief or grieving.
2. Locus of control type beliefs in fatalism or instrumentation best predict culture shock.
3. Social Darwinism or selective migration forces are some of the best predictors of culture shock.
4. Realistic expectations about what will be encountered are the most important factors in adaptation.
5. Culture shock should be seen as, and calculated by, negative life events such that the more actual change people experience and have to adapt to, the more likely it is they will experience culture shock.
6. The better, both quantitatively and qualitatively, one's social support network, the better will be one's ability to overcome culture shock.
7. Value differences between native and foreign culture are the most powerful predictors of adaptation and shock.
8. The actual social skills one possesses in dealing with people from the native culture are the best predictors of adaptation and shock.

Furnham and Bochner (1986) attempt to point out the insights and limitations of each 'explanation' favouring the latter four as having most explanatory power. Certainly each explanation has important implications for how one deals with culture shock and the psychological effects of change and transition.

THE U-CURVE HYPOTHESIS

Since Oberg (1960) it has been fashionable to describe the 'disease' of culture shock in terms of a number of stages (Smalley, 1963). These attempts have all been descriptive and tend to overlap. Oberg (1960) listed four stages of shock:

1. *Honeymoon stage.* An initial reaction to enchantment, fascination, enthusiasm, admiration and cordial, friendly, superficial relationships with hosts.

2. *Crisis*. Initial differences in language, concepts, values, familiar signs and symbols lead to feelings of inadequacy, frustration, anxiety and anger.
3. *Recovery*. The crisis is resolved by a number of methods such that the person ends up learning the language and culture of the host country.
4. *Adjustment*. The sojourner begins to work in and enjoy the new culture, though there may be occasional instances of anxiety and strain.

Others such as Adler (1975) have set out a much more elaborate 'theory'.

One of the consequences of these stage-wise theories is the debate on the U- or W-curve. The idea of the U-curve has been attributed to Lysgaard (1955). He concluded from his study of over 200 Norwegian Fulbright scholars in the United States that people go through three phases: initial adjustment, crisis and regained adjustment. Nowhere in the paper does Lysgaard describe the shape of the U, though he did imply that the period of adjustment took about 20 months with some point between six and 18 months being the bottom of the U. If one traces the sojourners' level of adjustment, adaptation and well-being over time, a U-shape occurs such that satisfaction and well-being gradually decline but then increase again. The W-curve is an extension by Gullahorn and Gullahorn (1963), who found that once sojourners return to their home country they often undergo a similar re-acculturation process, again in the shape of a U, hence the double U, that is W. Furnham and Bochner (1986) have pointed out various problems with this literature: the vagueness of the description and definition (when is a U not a U).

In a review of the U-curve literature, Church (1982) reports seven studies that found some evidence for the hypothesis but a similar number that did not. He concluded that support for the U-curve hypothesis is weak, inconclusive and overgeneralized. For instance, not all sojourners start off in the phase of supposed adjustment, elation and optimism—some are unhappy, depressed and anxious right from the start (if not before). Second, some never become depressed or anxious, enjoying the experience and adjusting to the culture right from the start. Third, where there are U-curves, they are of dramatically different shape—some are flat, others tall and all are fairly irregular. Church (1982) has noted that there are numerous problems with these simple descriptive theories:

> Is the order of stages invariant? Must all stages be passed through or can some be skipped by some individuals? In order to classify individuals, key indicators of each stage are needed, indicators that may vary with the culture or origin or be indicative of more than one stage, reflecting superficial adjustment in an early stage but a true 'coming to terms' with the new culture in a later stage (p. 542).

Bochner, Lin and McLeod (1980) argued that so-called adjustments entail the acquisition, over time, of behaviours, skills and norms that are appropriate to the social roles that expatriates are required to enact. In particular, this involves entering into new relationships with significant people in the host country and

Table 15.2. Adler's five-stage theory of culture-shock development

Stage	Perception	Emotional range	Behaviour	Interpretation
Contact	Differences are intriguing. Perceptions are screened and selected	Excitement Stimulation Euphoria Playfulness Discovery	Curiosity Interest Assured Impressionistic	The individual is insulated by his or her own culture. Differences as well as similarities provide rationalization for continuing confirmation of status, role, and identity.
Disintegration	Differences are impactful. Contrasted cultural reality cannot be screened out	Confusion Disorientation Loss Apathy Isolation Loneliness Inadequacy	Depression Withdrawal	Cultural differences begin to intrude. Growing awareness of being different leads to loss of self-esteem. Individual experiences loss of cultural support ties and misreads new cultural cues.
Reintegration	Differences are rejected	Anger Rage Nervousness Anxiety Frustration	Rebellion Suspicion Rejection Hostility Exclusive Opinionated	Rejection of second culture causes preoccupation with likes and dislikes; differences are projected. Negative behaviour, however, is a form of self-assertion and growing self-esteem
Autonomy	Differences and similarities are legitimized	Self-assured Relaxed Warm Empathic	Assured Controlled Independent 'Old hand' Confident	The individual is socially and linguistically capable of negotiating most new and different situations: he or she is assured of ability to survive new experiences.
Independence	Differences similarities are valued and significant	Trust Humour Love Full range of previous emotions	Expressive Creative Actualizing	Social, psychological and cultural differences are accepted and enjoyed. The individual is capable of exercising choice and responsibility and able to create meaning for situations.

From P. S. Adler, 'The transitional experience: an alternative view of culture shock', *Journal of Humanistic Psychology*, 15 (1975), 13–23.

resuming relationships with significant people after re-entry home. The sojourn U-shape can be derived from the distinction between observing a new culture and participating in it. When the sojourner's role as an observer shifts to that of a participant, a transition that is inevitable, the initial fascination with the new culture similarly shifts to having to cope with it, which in Bochner's terms means learning its salient features. Some sojourners never learn the new culture or develop reciprocal role relationships with their hosts. Other sojourners do acquire the social skills of the new society and develop genuine contacts with their hosts. Others again stand somewhere between the two extremes. Thus the rate of culture-learning is not uniform across sojourners, but depends on all the contact variables discussed elsewhere in this book. This may explain why the U-curve is not supported in some studies, since some individuals may not experience it, such as sophisticated culture travellers who immediately become full participants and hence their curve never drops. Likewise, there are some very poor culture-learners who fail ever to participate in their new society, and their curve of satisfaction would therefore never rise.

The re-entry U-curve can be derived from the notion of contradictory role demands. Bochner, Lin and McLeod (1980) have shown that returning 'expats' anticipate that they will be subjected to contradictory social expectations. In particular, they think that there will be some ambivalence in the treatment they will receive from their professional, peer and family groups. Again, the rate of resolving these role conflicts may vary with a number of circumstances and could account for the absence of a W-curve in some studies.

Furnham and Bochner (1986) have maintained that the advantage of the social psychological model of temporal adjustment is that it can predict and explain different 'adjustment' profiles as a function of quite significant determinants. Thus the successful culture-learner should exhibit a typical U-curve and, after re-entry, a W-curve. Experienced culture travellers should show a flat 'curve' and unsuccessful ones a declining curve during sojourn and a rising one after re-entry.

Figure 15.1 shows some of these possible relationships, all of which can be put to an empirical test. This model is not restricted to the adjustment patterns of sojourners but has general implications. For instance, the model predicts that all persons entering into new relationships or social situations can be expected to develop sequential feelings of satisfaction or dissatisfaction. The shape of these curves will depend on how well the persons acquire the relevant behaviours, to what extent they can clarify their new roles, avoid role ambiguity and resolve any contradictory role demands in their relationships with significant persons in these new situations. The model suggests that coping successfully with any life-event changes that have an interpersonal aspect (and most do) depends on processes similar to those involved in learning a new culture, and may explain why some people cope with change better than others.

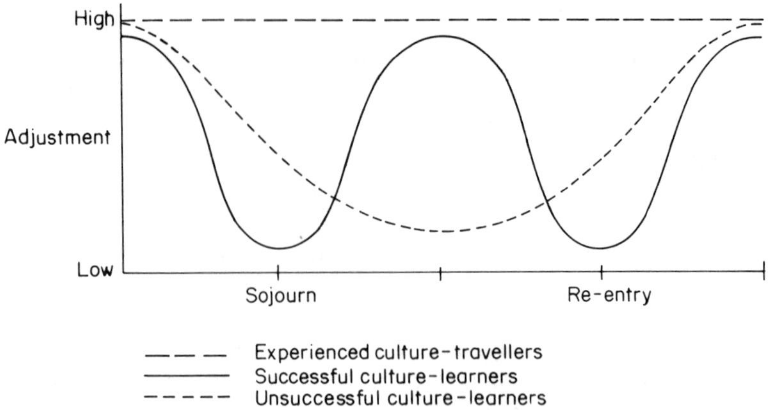

Figure 15.1 Different adjustment profiles of culture learners and travellers

COMMON (BUT IMPORTANT) CULTURAL DIFFERENCES

Expatriates of necessity are confronted with cultural differences at various levels: socioeconomic, organizational but also interpersonal. Essentially it is the sensitivity to these differences, and the way of coping with them, that is a major factor of adaptation. Hence the emphasis of various guidebooks, orientation manuals and cultural briefings on how social behaviour and expectations differ across cultures.

An essential part in any intercultural skills training is a comprehensive knowledge of cultural differences in social behaviour. Anthropologists, comparative sociologists and cross-cultural psychologists have documented in great detail some of the obvious, as well as subtle, cultural differences in social behaviour. These are frequently the cause of important misunderstanding. Argyle (1983) has divided these cultural differences into various categories: language, nonverbal communication; social rules; social relationships; motivation; and concepts and ideology; and has shown how these differ from culture to culture. A great deal has been written on verbal and particularly nonverbal differences between cultures. To illustrate the point, however, cultural differences in social rules will be briefly discussed. Argyle and Henderson (1985) have argued that social rules are developed so that people's goals in different relationships, groups or situations can be attained. That is groups find successful routes to their goals (the coordination of some behaviours and exclusion of others), which become collective solutions or subcultural goals. Rules work by coordinating the behaviour of a number of different people, or restricting their activities so that goals may be obtained. Different cultures have devised quite different social rules the infringement of which may cause both embarrassment and misunderstanding.

RULES ABOUT EXCHANGE

The essence of much of business is exchange: exchange of information, products, gifts and rules of exchange differ greatly from society to society. Indeed the very fact that certain, often pejorative terms exist in a society for certain acts of exchange, shows different cultures' attitudes to that behaviour. *Bribery* in one country where it is seen to be illegal and unethical is quite acceptable even expected in another where it is seen as a legitimate means of exchange. Similarly whereas *nepotism* may be an ordinary, everyday occurrence in some countries and seen to be a form of familial social welfare, in others it is thought of as being immoral. There are also elaborate and problematic rules for the exchange of *gifts* (Morsbach, 1977); buying and selling; rewarding hard work; settling disputes, etc. Recent studies on cultural differences in reward allocation (Leung and Bond, 1984) and perceptions of fairness (Berman, Murphy-Berman and Singh, 1985) have emphasized the *individualistic*, *equity* (performance management)-based schemes of industrialized cultures in North America and Europe do not become readily accepted elsewhere and are rejected in favour of the *societal*, *equality*-based schemes of Third World cultures in Africa and Asia. Related topics include advancement of managers (Rosenstein, 1985), the management of compliments (Barlund and Araki, 1985) and the management of the mixed-cultural work group (Anderson, 1983). Many of these rule differences occur because of differences in motivation and values in different cultures (Howard, Shudo and Umeshima, 1983; Hofstede and Bond, 1984).

RULES ABOUT SOCIAL RELATIONSHIPS

Argyle and Henderson (1985) have done fairly extensive work on the different kinds of rules for social relationships. These rules refer to such things as rewardingness (the amount, type and timing of rewards in different cultures); intimacy (the desired and appropriate level of intimacy); avoiding difficulties (preventing or minimizing interpersonal difficulties); third parties (dealing with problems of jealousy, keeping confidence etc.).

They studied the application of 33 rules in four cultures: Japan, Hong Kong, Italy and Britain. Overall the Eastern cultures prescribe fewer rules about expressing emotions, opinions and affection across all types of relationships. As Argyle and Henderson (1985) have noted:

> What do these findings tell us about relationships in general? First, they show that people share a consensus about what behaviours are appropriate in which relationships. Secondly, while certain rules apply across relationships in all four cultures, others are more specific to individual relationships—sometimes across cultures, but more often within particular cultures. Things we should not do in one relationship are strongly prescribed in others, and may not apply at all to a third relationship or to the same relationship in a different country. This

> This can obviously create difficulties and misunderstanding, as many Western businessmen have found, to their consternation, when dealing with non-Western cultures (p. 52).

RULES ABOUT TIME

Because 'time is money' at least in some societies businessmen and women are often very concerned with time constraints. Time-urgency which, along with competitiveness, drive and achievement appear to be characteristic of the business world, also appears to be related to coronary heart disease (Price, 1982). Expectations of how late it may be acceptable to arrive; how long a social or business function or meeting may last; how accurate 'time estimates' should be, etc., are culture bound. Perhaps this is best summed up by the following anecdote:

> One of the most deeply rooted, and largely unconscious, features of any culture is what the psychologists call the *time perspective*. Within the United Nations at least three different perspectives operate.
>
> '*Gentlemen, it is time for lunch, we must adjourn*', announces the Anglo-Saxon chairman, in the unabashed belief that having three meals a day at regular hours is the proper way for mankind to exist.
>
> *But why? We haven't finished what we were doing*', replies—in a puzzled manner that grows rapidly more impatient—an Eastern European delegate, in whose country people eat when the inclination moves them and every family follows its own individual timetable.
>
> '*Why, indeed?*' placidly inquires the Far Eastern representative, hailing from a country where life and time are conceived as a continuous stream, with no man being indispensable, with no life-process needing to be interrupted for any human being, and where members of electoral bodies walk in and out of the room quietly, getting a bite to eat when necessary, talking to a friend when pleasant; but where meetings, theatre performances, and other arranged affairs last without interruption for hours on end, while individuals come and go, are replaced by others, meditate or participate as the occasion requires, without undue strain, stress or nervous tension.
>
> As one or the other group persists in its own conceptions of the time perspective, as the Anglo-Saxons demand that the duration of meetings and conferences be fixed in advance and that meals be taken regularly at fixed hours, and as the Russians sit irritated and the Latins puzzled and the Secretariat frantic—as this condition continues, mutual friction grows, murmurs of 'unreasonableness' are heard around the room; and, when the issue under discussion is an important one, overt accusations are hurled across the room of 'insincerity', 'lack of a serious approach to the problem', and even 'sabotage' (Telber, 1950).

Even before a business man or woman moves into a new culture he or she should immediately become acquainted with local expectations about time both within and outside work. This may at first prove highly frustrating, particularly if he or she perceives the use and understanding of time in the other culture as wasteful. The problem with these rules, however, is that they are implicit and

not explicit; they are subtle and their infringment often has serious consequences. Yet they are clearly important and must constitute an important aspect of intercultural skills training.

No doubt various other cross-culture rules exist. Cultures have rules about eating and drinking; self-disclosure; touching, etc. Books on etiquette are the most useful guide to both the native and the expatriate. Many orientation courses attempt to spell out the most subtle and salient of these cultural differences and how to deal with them. Indeed, it is this sort of information that 'old hands' impart to new expatriates. The usefulness of such a task is discussed later.

PREPARING, SELECTING, TRAINING, EVALUATING AND REPATRIATING MANAGERS

Although somewhat scattered in the literature there are a number of references concerned with effective performance in overseas work assignments. Cleveland, Margone and Adams (1960) found that expatriates who performed well tended to be rated relatively high on technical skill, belief in their mission, a sense of politics, evidence of cultural empathy and clear organizational ability. In a smaller but more intensive study Stoner, Aram and Rubin (1972) studied over 50 men who had worked in Africa and Mauritius over an eight-year period. Using supervisor's and subordinate's ratings as the dependent measure of performance, they attempted to delineate the factors associated with high performance. Whereas previous overseas travel and work experience, age at the start of the overseas tour, academic education and reasons for going were not related to overseas performance, previous ability (at time of interview) and marital status (married as opposed to single) were positively correlated with success. Also the early reactions of the men to their new jobs appeared to be a powerful predictor of their subsequent success in developing a satisfactory working situation. Another predictor of success was the job-holder's rating of the similarity between his own and his organization's expectations about the job he would be performing. They conclude:

> In the staffing of overseas positions, in which the opportunities for direct contact between the new employee and the organizations are likely to be quite limited, the task of matching individuals to positions and helping establish constant expectations would seem to be both especially difficult and particularly critical for the subsequent evolution of the work situation (p. 318).

Others have concentrated much more significantly on how to prepare potential expatriates for overseas transfer. For instance, Lanier (1979) recommends seven steps to be taken in preparing personnel:

1. A well-planned, realistic, pre-visit to the site (country).
2. Early, prior to departure, language training.
3. Intensive study on issues such as history, culture, etiquette.
4. The provision of country-specific handbooks including useful facts.
5. Efficient, explicit provision of inter-company counselling facilities.
6. Meeting returnees for 'old-hand' tips.
7. Notification of personnel office and spouses committee on arrival.

Sieveking, Anchor and Marston (1981) stress the importance of orientation programmes prior to expatriation, which aim to do such things as:

1. Develop an understanding of personal and family values so that employees can anticipate and cope with the inevitably unsettling emotions which accompany culture shock.
2. Develop an appreciation of the important ways in which the host culture will differ from the employee's own culture so that the employee can guide his or her behaviour accordingly.
3. Show the expatriate how he or she can be rewarded in ways in addition to income and travel such as novelty, challenge and the opportunity to make an income.
4. To help expatriates anticipate and begin to plan for hardships, delays, frustrations, material inconveniences and the consequences of close living and working for others.
5. To help expatriates to anticipate that though they may have been superior employees in their own culture, they may need to gain greater satisfaction from experiences other than those which are work-related.

In a more considered and thoughtful paper on the selection of training of personnel for overseas, Tung (1981) outlines a contingency approach and notes four types of factors crucial to success in foreign assignments: technical competence on the job; relational abilities (social skills); ability to deal with environmental constraints (government, labour issues); and family situation. Tung argued that:

> This practice of basing the selection decision on technical competence criterion, regardless of the country of foreign assignment, may account for the high failure rate among expatriates. This practice should not be continued when research findings indicate that other factors may increase the chances of successful performance abroad (p. 30).

Tung outlines five types of training programmes: area studies (giving extensive background knowledge); culture assimilation (testing cross-cultural communication); language training; sensitivity training (focusing on affect); and

field experiences in a micro-culture. These programmes have very different emphases and can be costly and inefficient. A study of 26 organizations showed that many used language training and the environmental briefing (both non-psychological) and very few the culture assimilator (a training programme examining cultural differences in attributions), sensitivity training and field experience.

Instead Tung (1981) offers a way of coping with the process based on a sensitive selection process (see Figure 15.2). The flow chart is self-explanatory. It was agreed that organizations that experience lower expatriate failure rates adopt different criteria for selecting candidates, and sponsor different types of training programmes for personnel in each of the job categories. Clearly no one test selection criterion or training programme is appropriate for all job categories.

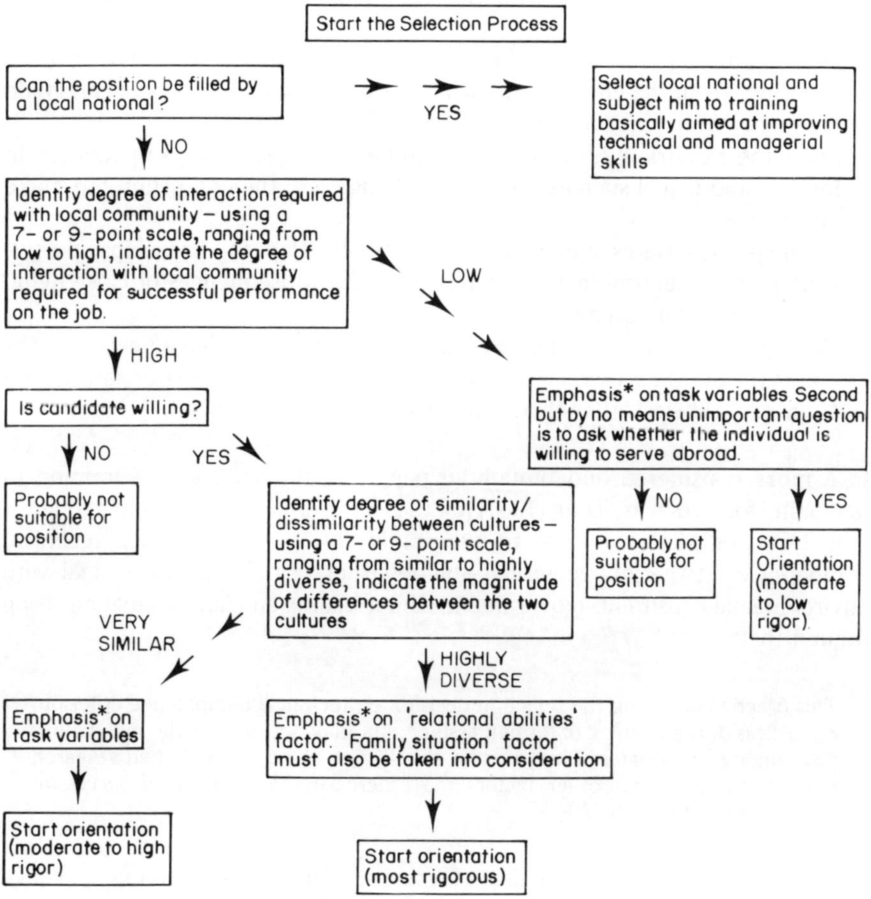

Figure 15.2. Flow chart of the selection–decision process

> A contingency framework states that in practice there is no one criterion that could be used in all situations. Rather, each assignment should be viewed on its own. In each instance, the selection of the 'right person' to fill the position should be made only after a careful analysis of the task (in terms of interaction with the social community) and the country of assignment (in terms of the degree to which it is similar/dissimilar to that of the home country), and the personality characteristics of the candidate (in terms of the candidate's and spouse's to live and work in a different cultural environment (pp. 77–78).

There has been something of an upsurge in this literature recently, with the establishment of various new journals (Kelley, Whatley and Worthley, 1987; Black, 1988). Many articles, however, have concentrated quite specifically on multinational corporate policies for expatriates. Many of these articles appear to accept, somewhat uncritically, lists of traits and abilities that supposedly distinguish successful expatriate managers. Thus for instance, Baliga and Baker (1985) accept *Business Internationals* list in Table 15.3, and the work of Howard (1974) shown in Table 15.4. These lists are interesting, and possibly correct, but

Table 15.3. Characteristics of successful expatriate managers

Basic Characteristics	
1. Zeal for work	8. Alertness
2. Ability to develop others	9. Foresight
3. Persuasiveness	10. Ability to learn foreign languages
4. Resourcefulness	11. Flexibility
5. Initiative and imagination	12. Adaptability to new ideas, new cultures and new challenges
6. Self-sufficiency	
7. Ability to make decisions	
Experience Factors	
1. Technical competence	5. Knowledge of job to which he or she is to be assigned
2. Professional, management and business experience	6. Open-mindedness to new ideas
3. Knowledge of company policies, markets, goals	7. Attitude toward foreigners
4. Resourcefulness	8. Lack of fixed prejudices
Environmental Factors	
1. Knowledge of firm's international operations	3. Knowledge of local language
2. Knowledge of foreign market	4. Contacts in foreign market
Personal Factors	
1. Motivation for seeking or accepting foreign assignment	5. Personal attitudes
2. Nationality	6. Emotional stability
3. Family status	7. Sociability
4. Personal appeal	8. Dignity and integrity

From Business International. *151 Checklists—Decision Making in International Operations*. (New York): Business International, 1974), pp. 145–146.

Table 15.4. Abilities of a successful expatriate manager

Position
1. Ability to handle programmed position responsibilities with ease
2. Ability to handle non-programmed position responsibilities with relative ease
3. Ability to perform diverse functional responsibilities
4. Ability to successfully perform with little or no expert advice
5. Ability to produce desired results without supervision
6. Ability to come up with a decision quickly

Management
1. Ability to plan effectively and economically
2. Ability to organize all factors of production at reasonable cost
3. Ability to lead and inspire confidence in people
4. Ability to motivate people
5. Ability to communicate effectively
6. Ability to control all factors of production

Personal
1. Character
2. Interest in overseasmanship
3. Understanding of mankind
4. Emotional stability
5. Open-minded and objective
6. Analytical mind
7. Tolerance and patience
8. Liking for people of varied backgrounds
9. Resourcefulness and diplomacy
10. Mental and physical health
11. Wife's cooperation and temperament

Environmental
1. Flexibility toward the American outlook and way of life
2. Flexibility to diverse cultural, economic, political conditions
3. Flexibility to solving business problems in a diverse cultural framework
4. Linguistic ability
5. Flexibility to moods

From C. G. Howard, 'Model for the Design of a Selection Program for Multinational Executives,' *Public Personnel Management*, Vol. 3 (March–April 1974), p. 143

it is uncertain to what extent there are research data to support them, or whether indeed they are simply hypotheses or 'hunches'. Other more obvious problems arise: how to measure these variables; the relationship between them; which are the most powerful predictors of which expatriate behaviour, etc. Nevertheless, such attempts to understand the problem do provide a rich source of hypotheses to test.

More recently, in an empirical study, Harvey (1989) looked at the problems in repatriating corporate expatriate executives. In his study of over 175 members, less than a third had repatriation programmes though over three-quarters had programmes before expatriation. Those programmes that did exist tended to

stress legal, organizational and economic issues rather than 'psychological' issues and problems. Some of the aspects of an 'ideal' patriation that executives and their wives wanted was family disorientation and dissatisfaction. Harvey recognizes that his survey provides more questions than answers, and himself poses various questions such as:

> To what degree does the lack of cultural 'signposts' increase the difficulty and stress upon repatriating? . . . Are the differences observed in Japanese, European and United States expatriates an indication or clue as to which nationalities might need more structured reentry programs? (p. 142).

The issue of selecting and preparing both expatriates and repatriates is, at last, meriting the attention and research it deserves for many reasons, not least of which is the cost of poor decision-making.

REDUCING EXPATRIATE STRESS

Attempts to reduce expatriate and repatriate stress and improve the skills and coping mechanisms of those preparing to move has been at the centre of research in this area. Opinions differ as to which is the most effective method. Few people would disagree with the idea that men and women working in culturally different environments require some sort of orientation programme. Many techniques are available which differ according to theoretical orientation, length and type of training and personnel involved. For instance, Brislin (1979) has listed five non-mutally exclusive programmes: self-awareness training (in which people learn about the cultural basis of their own behaviour); cognitive training (where people are presented with various facts about other cultures); attribution training (where people learn the explanation of behaviour from the point of view of people in other cultures); behaviour modification (where people are asked to analyse the aspects of their culture that they find rewarding or punishing) and experiential learning (where people actively participate in realistic simulation).

Furnham and Bochner (1985) have examined some of these in greater detail.

INFORMATION GIVING

The most common type of cross-cultural orientation usually involves providing prospective sojourners with specific information about their new culture. Prospective expatriates are presented with all sorts of facts and figures, either in written form or in lectures, or films about topics such as the climate, food, sexual relations, religious customs and anything else the trainer may consider important. However, the effectiveness of such illustrative programmes is limited because of four things. Firstly the facts are often too general to have any clear

specific application except when discussing tax or organizational structure; secondly the facts emphasize the exotic, yet tend to ignore the mundane but more commonly occurring happenings, such as how to hail or pay a taxi; thirdly such programmes give the false impression that a culture can be learned in a few easy lessons, whereas all that they mostly convey is a superficial, incoherent and often misleading picture, which glosses over the culture's hidden agenda; and finally, even if the facts are remembered they do not necessarily lead to action, or to the current action. It would be absurd to teach people how to operate a machine by *only* giving them information about how to do it. If the cognitive informational training is to be of any practical use it must be combined with some sort of practical experiential learning in the appropriate setting. Amusing lectures, helpful guidebooks and well-prepared videos are not enough.

CULTURAL SENSITIZATION

Programmes based on this approach set out to provide trainees with information about other cultures, as well as to heighten their awareness about the cultural bias of their own behaviour, and how the practices of their society differ from those of the host country. The aim is therefore to *compare* and *contrast* the two or more cultures, look at various behaviours from the perspective of each society, and thus develop a sensitivity to, and awareness of, cultural relativity. This view holds that very few human values, beliefs and behaviours are absolute and universal, and that what a particular individual believes to be true and good will depend on the norms prevailing in that person's society; norms that other societies may reject. Such programmes often operate at two levels: they aim to achieve self-awareness about the modal values and attitudes that are typically held by members of one's own society; and to gain insight into one's own personal traits, attitudes and prejudices. Culture sensitization and self-awareness programmes, being essentially cognitive techniques, suffer from many of the same limitations as information-giving. For instance, it is all very well for a westerner to accept intellectually that, in some cultures, ceremonies featuring ritual animal slaughter have the same socially cohesive function as, say, Trooping the Colour in England, but it is another matter to then willingly observe such occasions and regard them in the same light as indigenous spectators do.

ISOMORPHIC ATTRIBUTIONS

Many researchers have pointed out that a potential obstacle to effective cross-cultural communication is the inability of the participants to understand the causes of each other's behaviour, i.e. to make correct attributions about the other's actions. Effective intercultural relations require isomorphic attributions, which means observers offer the same cause or reason for actors' (others)

behaviour as they would for themselves. The likelihood of making isomorphic attributions decreases as the divergence between the subjective cultures of the participants increases, and explains why intercultural relations are often characterized by mutual hostility, misunderstanding and poor affect. One solution is to train the individuals to understand the subjective culture of the other group, which in practice means teaching them how to make 'correct' behavioural attributions. This is done through a device called the culture assimilator, which in effect is a programmed learning manual. The booklet contains descriptions of episodes in which two culturally disparate individuals meet. The interactions are unsuccessful, in that each incident terminates in embarrassment, misunderstanding or interpersonal hostility. The trainee is then presented with four or five alternative explanations of what went wrong, which correspond to different attributions of the observed behaviour. Only one of these attributions is 'correct' from the perspective of the culture being learned. The trainees select the answer they regard as correct, and are then instructed to turn to a subsequent page, where they are either praised if they selected the 'right' answer, or told why they were wrong if they selected an 'incorrect' answer. A great deal also depends on which particular critical incidents are selected to form the basic curriculum. Inevitably, exotic, strange and hence less common events tend to be given greater prominence than the less interesting but more frequently day-to-day problems that make up the bread-and-butter content of intercultural contacts.

LEARNING BY DOING

The limitations of information-based orientation programmes led to various attempts to expose trainees to supervised real or simulated second culture experiences. Most organizations do not have, or are unwilling to commit, such massive resources to experimental culture training. More typically, behaviourally based culture training programmes rely on role-playing encounters between trainees and persons pretending to come from some other culture, or if other-culture professional personnel are available, with such persons. In this respect the techniques are similar to those employed by social skills training. Some programmes also contain a behavioural evaluation component, which may take the form of a team of psychologists evaluating and training the performance of the candidates in the field.

Finally, the vast majority of sojourners, or those who come into contact with members of other cultures in their own societies, receive no systematic culture training whatsoever. The little 'training' that does occur is done informally by experienced migrants who pass on useful information to the new visitors. This in itself may not be such a bad thing. One of the requirements of a successful culture trainer is to be a mediating person, i.e. a person who is intimately familiar with both cultures and can act as a link between them, representing each to

the other. In theory, experienced sojourners should have that rare capacity, but in practice some may have highly specialized, distorted, or even prejudiced views of one or both of their cultures, and perpetuate these distortions in the informal training they impart to highly impressionable newcomers.

INTERCULTURAL (SOCIAL) SKILLS TRAINING

Although there are a number of different approaches to social skills training they share various elements in common. The first is an *assessment* or *diagnosis* of particular problem areas (e.g. assertiveness) of situations (e.g. chairing meetings) that the person has or is likely to encounter. The second stage is an *analysis* or *discussion* of the elements in these problem areas, possibly followed by a modelling exercise where a trainer enacts the role. This in turn is followed by a *role-play* by the trainee, with critical *feedback* in length following each practice. The number, range and variety of contexts in which the role-plays are enacted add to the generalizability of the training. Trainees are also encouraged to do homework exercises between role-play and feedback sessions. For Ellis and Whittington (1981) the following strategies may be useful in helping individual trainees to obtain maximum benefit:

> The programme should be carefully introduced to trainees and something of its rationale should be explained; trainees should be allowed ample time for 'practice' practices so that any cosmetic effect of video or other feedback can be got over; models should be as closely related to individual trainee characteristics as possible; trainees should participate as much as possible in the sensitisation phase and every effort should be made to accommodate individual learning differences in the activities provided; practice talks and situations should be readily comprehensible and should have validity for trainee; feedback should be at an appropriate intellectual level and should have a supportive emotional tone (p. 73).

The advantages of the intercultural skills approach include the following: Firstly the training procedures are based on a *specific theory*, which avoids vague statements about 'mutual understanding' and instead emphasizes behavioural skill deficits. Secondly the theory is '*practical*' in the sense that it has at its centre everyday, common, as well as business situations which nevertheless cause friction, misunderstanding and interpersonal hostility. This approach avoids vague statements about culture shock by attempting to quantify social difficulty on various dimensions and then reduce it. Thirdly the programme can be *tailor-made* to the trainee, in that a particular person's social skills deficiencies are diagnosed and the person is then given culturally appropriate remedial training aimed at removing those specific deficiencies. The training programme avoids general non-specific lectures and films about superficial and/or exotic aspects of the host culture, preferring to concentrate on those features of the culture that the clients find problematic. Fourthly the training uses well-tried,

behavioural techniques such as video feedback, role-playing, and modelling to realistically simulate real-life situations. The training does not rely exclusively on cognitive or information-giving procedures, partly because they do not generalize readily across to real-life situations, and partly because they are readily forgotten. Fifthly the training focuses on the *management* of interpersonal encounters. Its emphasis therefore is on the social psychology of the sojourner, and avoids vague assumptions about achieving personal growth and insight. The stress is on the acquisition and execution of skills. Sixthly the *evaluation* of the theory, training content, training techniques, and impact of the programme can be built into a project from the start, and not tacked on as an afterthought. At its completion it is possible to indicate if, and exactly how well, the various aspects of the project performed in accordance with expectations.

The disadvantages of this approach are that, because of the systematic nature of such programmes, they are likely to cost more, intrude into and disrupt the activities of the institution whose members are being trained, and require an interdisciplinary team of trainers, unless relevant bi-cultural mediating trainers (Bochner, 1982) are available.

SUMMARY AND CONCLUSION

The study of expatriates spans a number of different disciplines: psychology, sociology, management science and anthropology. Various attempts have been made to classify expatriates in the belief that, by identifying quite different groups, their beliefs and behaviours will be better understood. All expatriates are expected to suffer culture shock and that nebulous and multifaceted concept is discussed. Similarly stage-wise theories of adaptation to the new environment are described and evaluated. Some of the more important and common cultural differences in social behaviour are illustrated. Recent research on business expatriates was also reviewed, particularly that which attempts to isolate and specify the characteristics of successful and unsuccessful adaptors to the new culture. Finally some of the more common methods of helping prepare expatriates are listed, criticized and evaluated.

REFERENCES

Adler, P. (1975) The transition experience: an alternative view of culture shock. *Journal of Humanistic Psychology*, **15**, 13–23.

Anderson, L. (1983) Management of the mixed-cultural work group. *Organizational and Human Performance*, **31**, 303–330.

Argyle, M. (1979) New developments in the analysis of social skills. In A. Wolgang (ed.), *Non-verbal Behaviour*. London: Academic Press.

Argyle, M. (1983) Intercultural communication. In S. Bochner (ed.) *Cultures in Contact*. Oxford: Pergamon, pp. 61–80.

Argyle, M. and Henderson, M. (1985) *The Anatomy of Relationships*. London: Heinemann.

Baliga, G. and Baker, J. (1985) Multinational corporate policies for expatriate managers: selection, training, evaluation. *SAM Advance Management Journal*, **7**, 37–38.

Ball-Rokeach, S. (1973) From pervasive ambiguity to a definition of the situation. *Sociometry*, **36**, 133–145.

Barnlund D. and Araki, S. (1985) Intercultural encounters: the management of compliments by Japanese and Americans. *Journal of Cross-Cultural Psychology*, **16**, 9–26.

Berman, J., Murphy-Berman, V. and Singh, P. (1985) Cross-cultural similarities and differences in perceptions of fairness. *Journal of Cross-Cultural Psychology*, **16**, 55–67.

Black, J. (1988) Work role transitions: a study of American expatriate managers in Japan. *Journal of International Business Studies*, **8**, 277–294.

Bochner, S. (ed.) (1982) *Cultures in Contact*. Oxford: Pergamon.

Bochner, S., Lin, A. and McLeod, B. (1980) Anticipated role conflict of returning overseas students. *Journal of Social Psychology*, **110**, 265–272.

Bock, P. (ed.) (1970) *Culture Shock: A reader in Modern Anthropology*. New York: A. A. Knopf.

Brislin, R. (1979) Orientation and programs for cross-cultural preparation. In A. Marsella, R. Thorp & T. Civorowski (eds), *Perspectives on Cross-Cultural Psychology*. New York: Academic Press, pp. 287–305.

Byrnes, F. (1966) *Americans in Technical Assistance: A Study of Attitudes and Responses to their Role Abroad*. New York: Praeger.

Church, A. (1982) Sojourner adjustment. *Psychological Bulletin*, **91**, 540–572.

Cleveland, H., Margone, C. and Adams, J. (1963) *The Overseas Americans*. New York: McGraw-Hill.

Collett, P. (1982) Meetings and misunderstandings. In S. Bochner (ed.), *Cultures in Contact*, Oxford: Pergamon, pp. 81–89.

David, K. (1971) Culture shock and the development of self-awareness. *Journal of Contemporary Psychotherapy*, **4**, 44–48.

Dinges, N. and Maynard, W. (1983) Intercultural aspects of organizational effectiveness. In D. Landis and R. Brislin (eds), *Handbook of Intercultural Training*, Vol. I. New York: Pergamon, pp. 50–83.

Ellis, R. and Whittington, D. (1981) *A Guide to Social Skills Training*. London: Croom Helm.

Furnham, A. (1979) Assertiveness in three cultures: multi dimensionality and cultural differences. *Journal of Clinical Psychology*, **35**, 522–527.

Furnham, A. and Bochner, S. (1986) *Culture Shock: Psychological Reactions to Unfamiliar Environments*. London: Methuen.

Gudykunst, W. (1983) Towards a typology of stranger–host relationships. *Intermediate Journal of Intercultural Relations*, **7**, 401–413.

Gullahorn, J. & Gullahorn, J. (1963) Extension of the U-curve hypotheses. *Journal of Social Issues*, **19**(3).

Guthrie, G. (1975) A behavioural analysis of culture learning. In R. Brislin, S. Bochner and W. Lonner (eds), *Cross-Cultural Perspectives on Learning*. New York: John Wiley & Sons, pp. 15–34.

Hall, E. (1959) *The Silent Language*. Garden City, NY: Doubleday.

Hall, J. and Beil-Warner, P. (1978) Assertiveness of male Anglo and Mexican–American college students. *Journal of Social Psychology*, **105**, 175–178.

Harvey, M. (1989) Repatriation of corporate executives: an empirical study. *Journal of International Business Studies*, **10**, 131–144.

Hays, R. (1972) Behavioural issues in multinational operations. In R. D. Hays *et al* (eds), *International Business: An Introduction to the World of the Multinational Firm*. NJ: Prentice-Hall, pp. 27–47.

Hofstede, G. (1984) *Culture's Consequences: International Differences in Work-related Values*. Beverly Hills, CA: Sage.
Hofstede, G. and Bond, M. (1984) Hofstede's culture dimensions: an independent validation using Rokeach's value survey. *Journal of Cross-Cultural Psychology*, **15**, 417–433.
Howard, C. (1974) Model for the design of a selection program for multinational executives. *Public Personnel Management*, **3**, 143–152.
Howard, A., Shudo, K. and Umeshima, M. (1983) Motivation and values among Japanese and American managers. *Personnel Psychology*, **36**, 883–898.
Kelley, L., Whatley, A. and Worthley, R. (1987) Assessing the effects of culture on managerial attitudes: a three culture test. *Journal of International Business Studies*, **8**, 17–21.
Landis, D. and Brislin, R. (eds) (1983) *Handbook of Intercultural Training*, Vols. 1, II, III. New York: Pergamon.
Lanier, A. (1979) Selecting and preparing personnel for overseas transfers. *Personnel Journal*, **3**, 160–163.
Leff, J. (1977) The cross-cultural study of emotions. *Culture, Medicine and Psychiatry*, **1**, 317–350.
Lueng, K. and Bond, M. (1984) The impact of cultural collectivism on reward allocation. *Journal of Personality and Social Psychology*, **47**, 793–804.
Lundstedt, A. (1963) An introduction to some evolving problems in cross-cultural research. *Journal of Social Issues*, **19**, 3–19.
Lysaard, S. (1955) Adjustment in a foreign society: Norwegian Fulbright grantees visiting the United States. *International Social Science Bulletin*, **7**, 45–51.
May, R. (1970) The nature and anxiety and its relation to fear. In A. Elbing (ed.), *Behavioural Decisions in Organization*. New York: Scott, Foresman, pp. 113–131.
Morsbach, H. (1977) The psychological importance of ritualized gift exchange in modern Japan. *Annals of the New York Academy of Sciences*, **293**, 98–113.
Nash, D. (1967) The fate of Americans in a Spanish setting: a study of adaptation. *Human Organization*, **26**(Whole No. 3).
Oberg, K. (1960) Culture shock: adjustment to new cultural environments. *Practical Anthropology*, **7**, 177–182.
Price, V. (1982) *Type A Behavior Pattern: A Model for Research and Practice*. New York: Academic Press.
Rosenstein, E. (1985) Cooperativeness and advancement of managers: an international perspective. *Human Relations*, **38**, 1–21.
Sieveking, N., Anchor, K. and Marston, R. (1981) Selecting and preparing expatriate employees. *Personnel Journal*, **3**, 197–202.
Smalley, W. (1963) Culture shock, language shock and shock of self-discovery. *Practical Anthropology*, **10**, 49–56.
Stokols, D. & Shumaker, S. (1982) The psychological context of residential mobility and well-being. *Journal of Social Issues*, **38**, 149–170.
Stoner, J., Aram, J. & Rubin, I. (1972) Factors associated with effective performance in overseas work assignments. *Personnel Psychology*, **25**, 303–318.
Telber, I. (1950) They don't do it our way. *Courier* (*UNESCO*), **2**(4).
Torbiorn, I. (1982) *Living Abroad: Personal Adjustment and Personnel Policy in an Overseas Setting*. Chichester: John Wiley & Sons Ltd.
Tung, R. (1981) Selection and training of personnel for overseas assignments. *Columbia Journal of World Business*, **1**, 68–78.
Trower, R., Bryant, B. and Argyle, M. (1978) *Social Skills and Mental Health*. London: Methuen.
Weinshall, T. (ed.) (1977), *Culture and Management*. Harmondsworth: Penguin.
Zuckerman, M. (1979) *Sensation Seeking: Beyond the Optimal Level of Arousal*. Hillsdale, NJ: Lawrence Erlbaum.

Section III: Coping with Change and Transition

In this section there is consideration of major methods of coping with change and transition. Some of the coping strategies concern coping with stress in general and other approaches are specifically geared to change and transition.

In general, accepting the reality of change and adapting to it is the best approach because strategies are geared to the future. Reversing changes which are beneficial by giving up, dropping out, running away or deserting are not positive and may create regret. However, in cases of very high distress and unhappiness these may, for some individuals, prove to be the only acceptable solutions. Fortunately only a very small proportion of individuals are affected in this way.

16 Helping the Homesick: Attentional Management Strategy, Commitment and Adaptation

SHIRLEY FISHER
Centre for Occupational & Health Psychology, University of Strathclyde

IDENTIFYING THE PROBLEM

Those who have custodial roles in institutions, those who deal with young people and students in residence and those who have care-giving roles, have to find ways in coping with homesick students. Equally, companies and institutions who fund scholarships or bursaries, or who send employees away from home, are likely to incur financial penalties if homesickness is of sufficient intensity to cause a person to give up and return home.

There are multiple reasons why a person who leaves home might be worried and distressed. There may be on-going home problems with which the distant person has difficulty dealing. There may be problems created as a result of the move. Where possible an opportunity for these problems to be made explicit is important and, where feasible, help and support should be offered.

The biggest problem occurs when some form of homesickness affects the newly moved person. The symptoms will be likely to include depression, anxiety, social withdrawal, absent-mindedness, anxiety and phobic avoidance. Very often these symptoms will be accompanied by strong ruminative or contemplative activity centred on home. As described in Chapter 9, if homesickness is severe it may create total preoccupation, which swamps the mental resource and creates a state of total incompetence.

Since homesickness is generally not regarded as socially acceptable, there may be a tendency on the part of the victim to conceal the problem and to attribute distress to other more acceptable aspects of the job and working environment. Distress may occur for a number of reasons, including disappointment with features of the new environment. Whilst this is not synonymous with homesickness, it may nevertheless prompt it.

On the Move: the Psychology of Change and Transition. Edited by S. Fisher and C. L. Cooper.

Table 16.1. 'The Dundee Relocation Inventory'; a short diagnostic test of homesickness (from Fisher, 1989)

I forget people's names	Never	Sometimes	Often
When I do a job I do it well	Never	Sometimes	Often
I feel able to cope here	Never	Sometimes	Often
I miss home	Never	Sometimes	Often
I feel optimistic about life here	Never	Sometimes	Often
I miss having someone close to talk to	Never	Sometimes	Often
I feel happy here	Never	Sometimes	Often
I miss my family	Never	Sometimes	Often
I feel fulfilled here	Never	Sometimes	Often
I feel unloved here	Never	Sometimes	Often
I feel unsettled here	Never	Sometimes	Often
When I have problems I contact my family	Never	Sometimes	Often
I feel excited about work here	Never	Sometimes	Often
I feel needed here	Never	Sometimes	Often
I feel uneasy here	Never	Sometimes	Often
I would like to go home more often than I do	Never	Sometimes	Often
I regret having moved here	Never	Sometimes	Often
There are people here in whom I can confide	Never	Sometimes	Often
I feel secure here	Never	Sometimes	Often
I cannot stop thinking of home	Never	Sometimes	Often
I feel very satisfied here	Never	Sometimes	Often
I have many friends here	Never	Sometimes	Often
I feel threatened here	Never	Sometimes	Often
I wake up wishing that I were home	Never	Sometimes	Often
I made a mistake moving here	Never	Sometimes	Often
I feel lonely here	Never	Sometimes	Often

Table 16.1 illustrates the short diagnostic test for homesickness produced by Fisher and Murray. The test distinguishes homesick and non-homesick subjects and may be used as a quick method of determining whether this is the key problem for a subject. (For details on the development and reliability of the test see Fisher, 1989, Appendix I.)

THE EFFECTIVENESS OF HELP

Help may be more effective for some people than for others. It has been suggested by research that those with high self-esteem are more likely to benefit from constructive help than those with low self-esteem (see de Paulo, Brown, Ishie and Fisher, 1981). Also the mildly depressed are more likely to react adversely to negative feedback than are the non-depressed (see Loeb, Beck and Diggory, 1971). Some preliminary assessment of personality factors such as self-esteem might be a useful

prerequisite to determining timing and form of help to be given. More research is needed before these factors can be made explicit as part of training or coping programmes.

Help should focus on encouraging the restructuring of the qualities, opportunities and facilities offered by the new environment. As indicated by Cooper in the following chapter, changing features of the 'assumptive world' of the individual, in positive directions, should be an aid to coping. Creating opportunities for activities a person has always enjoyed doing can encourage this change as much as can deliberate training and instruction.

DEALING WITH THOSE WHO ABANDON THE ENVIRONMENT

For some the conflict between the commitment to stay and the wish to go home is protracted. Any perceived unpleasant or over-taxing qualities of the new environment may tip the balance towards abandoning the plan and returning home. This may be influenced by the perceived costs or penalties of returning home. 'I cannot let my parents know how unable I am to cope with this. They would be so distressed. So I cannot go home' (male, 18 years).

In cases where the same or similar educational or vocational opportunities can be obtained near home, transference to a location where a person can be home-based is an obvious solution in the short term. However, there may be long-term penalties because a person may fail to develop the resources to cope in new environments without home support, and may be unable to take opportunities in the future.

Nevertheless, some individuals will run away or abandon the venture. There is no research evidence which indicates whether or not the person should be encouraged to go back. Controlling life by avoidance of unwanted experience may be a very anxiety-provoking way of existing. Fisher argued that control by avoidance is particularly stressful because there is no evidence to suggest that control is possible; there is in effect no 'coping evidence'. The person behaves effectively and avoids encounters deemed unpleasant, but may well perceive personal helplessness because there is no evidence that the action was effective (because there is no way of knowing that the encounter would have occurred in the absence of action).

For adolescents at school or training centres, encouraging return with help for adjustment may be very important in encouraging the necessary adjustment skills. 'Looking back, I wish someone had encouraged me to go back and try again. I felt such a failure giving up so easily and I did actually miss a couple of things about the place when once I was back at home' (female, aged 29 years).

ENCOURAGING COMMITMENT

From research evidence it seems that those able to react to the new environment, by becoming committed to any of the range of physical and psychosocial interests it offers, can adjust more easily. It is those who withdraw or who react with helplessness that are more likely to be at risk for poor adjustment. The situation can become circular and recursive; the person who grieves for home fails to take note of the new environment, fails to become involved, and therefore fails to find that the new environment can have more positive qualities than originally perceived. This in turn enhances homesickness.

Klinger (1975) denotes 'current concern' as a state of sensitivity to a particular problem or task. The onset of current concern is commitment. The initiation of a concern (commitment) can be assumed to be an information-generator. The individual has new sources of mental activity and available sources of distraction.

In Chapter 4 the theoretical notion that change creates a period of perceived low control was introduced. It could be argued that those who have commitment are developing a form of control over the new environment. If the form of commitment involves pre-existing skills, then the individual is in effect establishing control over the new environment in a way that increases chances of success; in effect old but appropriate skills are brought into use in the new environment. A person skilled at, for example, badminton might make use of these pre-existing skills in the new environment. Thus a situation of high control is created in the post-transition situation. Seen in this way those who adapt quickly may be those who have a range of skills, some of which are relevant for the new environment. For sportsmen, for example, visiting new countries may not be at all threatening if the reason is to play and compete using the expert skill. Even a non expert may be less distressed if he or she spends time in a new country involved in a familiar leisure pursuit.

Encouraging the use of existing commitments and old skills as a means of becoming established in the new environment could therefore provide the basis of a programme to aid the adjustment of groups selected to move. Familiarity in ways of running a business operation or establishment might have positive implications for the adjustment of those expected to work for long periods in a new country. Military establishments may inadvertently offer this; ships and army bases abroad can provide sanctuaries of the parent country for conscripts abroad. Research is needed to see what benefits accrue from this.

ATTENTIONAL DISTRACTION

Findings reported in Chapter 16 suggest that for some homesick subjects the day's events may keep homesickness at bay, whereas for the severely homesick

the experience is continuous. One suggestion, expressed in the form of a conceptual model—'the competing resource model'—is that the commitment to the new (post-transition) environment helps to attenuate homesickness because the information generated by the new environment competes effectively for a limited-capacity resource (see Chapter 9).

The implication for the management of homesickness is that involvement with the new environment creates the potential for attenuation of the homesickness experience. There are two possibilities: one is to create the conditions for commitment as discussed above; the other is to enforce commitment by use of rules and regulations which minimize periods of lack of involvement. The latter technique may be particularly useful in schools where new pupils can be kept busy by fixed activities, regularly prescribed. The activities should be physical rather than mental (sports, games, walks, trips to museums, etc.) and active rather than passive. The day of a school pupil cannot be dominated by these kinds of activities because the main purpose of the school is to create and encourage learning and scholarship. However, periods at the beginning of the term, during the early and late part of the day and at weekends, could be directed in ways which will keep pupils busy, and if possible physically active.

In the case of groups who have more control over their life activities it may be necessary to train individuals to create commitment. This could be further targeted in that those who report homesickness can be detected prior to leaving home by raised levels of depression (Fisher and Hood, 1987). This might be important because of passivity and a lack of commitment to the new environment (Fisher, 1986, Chapter 7), and therefore lack of competing information which can effectively attenuate the ruminations caused by loss of home and by competition for the attentional resource.

The problem of encouraging commitment is that the individual concerned must participate and create the motivation. Whereas traditional theories have assumed that the depressed lack the volition for commitment (see Fisher, 1986), Kuhl and Kazen-Saad (1988) suggest that the depressed become over-committed to an existing task. The difference in emphasis in relation to homesickness seems to be that on the first analysis it would be argued that depression indicates *lack of ability* to become committed to any environment/task, whereas Kuhl's analysis would suggest that depression involves *strong commitment to the previous environment*. Therefore on the traditional analysis the depressed are assumed to fail to make use of the new environment for attenuating homesickness, whereas the non-depressed become committed and benefit accordingly. On the Kuhl model the commitment to home should create the preconditions for homesickness (greater distress because of greater home dependency and involvement) and might also create lack of ability to utilize sources of interest in the new environment for attenuating homesickness.

Encouraging commitment would be an important management principle. This may have paradoxical elements because features associated with the

homesickness reaction are withdrawal and depression. However, individuals can often be persuaded by rational argument to try behaviour which they do not necessarily favour and enjoy. The counsellor should instruct the sufferer to increase the proportion of time spent in active behaviour (including physical activity) and to take up interests and hobbies. The latter course of action might be encouraged by the provision of facilities which match with interests in the home environment. Students might be encouraged to indicate their hobbies, sports and interests in order of priority so that information about facilities could be provided and, where necessary, active encouragement to take up a high-preference hobby could be given.

Instructions about the importance of increasing level of commitment could be given to the homesick students in order to create efforts in that direction. An added possibility is to direct the person actively, by encouraged completion of a schedule. He or she could be instructed to create leisure periods during the week and to fill these leisure periods with desired activities of specified kinds decided in consultation with the counsellor concerned. An indirect spin-off will be the increased likelihood of social interactions which help to reduce loneliness and provide confiding relationships.

SELECTING THOSE FOR MOVING

In many cases selection for adjustment following a move is not feasible or desirable. The emphasis will be on educational standards, vocational skill and ambition, etc. However, in some cases it might be possible to consider response to new environments as a factor in selection. For example, a company wishing to have representations abroad for long periods might need to select from a range of appropriately qualified profesionals in the company.

There are some factors which should aid adjustment and reduce the possibility of protracted or intense homesickness. The list should be regarded only as providing indicators or possible resilience factors. These indicators are based not on direct research findings but on relevant findings from existing research.

PREVIOUS MOVES

In general, those who have moved away from home to reside in an institution are less likely to be homesick when making a second similar move later in life (Fisher and Hood, 1988). However, those who have moved frequently in life are not necessarily the best adapters (Stokols, Shumaker and Martinez, 1983).

EXPECTANCIES

Those with high expectancies of the new environment, and who have perfectionist tendencies, may not necessarily be the best choice in that disappointment following the move, may adversely affect adjustment and create distress.

EXPERIENCE OF CONTROL OVER THE MOVE

Those who are given decisional control over the move, and who accept and plan for it, are more likely to adjust positively than those who feel obliged to go, have pressure exerted, or who go because of dissatisfaction with the old environment. These are all reasons which create reduced control.

ADAPTABLE SKILLS

Those who have skills which will be of use in the new work and cultural environment should be able to fit in, become committed and adapt more quickly (see section above, on commitment). Thus all things being equal a person who enjoys mountain climbing in a country where mountain climbing is possible and a well-developed pursuit, might be expected to adapt better.

FOCUSED SKILLS

Those who have particular and valued expertise in a company or institution may use these skills to become committed and to be distracted from adverse effects of the new cultural environment. Thus the top scientist sent to work on a remote weather station may survive better if he or she is committed to his or her work. Interests which are intensely focused may keep the 'foreign' or 'institutional' aspects of the new environment in diminished perspective.

ENTHUSIASM AND COMMITMENT

Some individuals appear to react to change with energy and ambition. Whether this is because this represents a particular way of seeing the world, or because some people appear to be capable of tackling the world with energy, is perhaps of theoretical more than practical interest. Selecting people who have shown raised energy and the capacity for exploring the environment and making the best of resources could be advantageous. Those who are mildly depressed and react with passivity to events are less likely to adapt quickly—although little is known about long-term adaptive prospects. On the Kuhl model the depressed are those capable of forming very strong commitments (see above) and encouraging them to change commitments may be useful. Whilst this does not

favour adaptation in the immediate context, because previous commitments cannot be abandoned, when once a new commitment develops it should be very strong.

PERSONALITY FACTORS AND SEX DIFFERENCES

There is little evidence of sex differences in homesickness reporting, but females tend to report more symptoms of distress (Hood, MacLachlan and Fisher, 1987). This may be because they are more willing to discuss and report such symptoms. In general the available evidence supports the idea that females adapt better to moves in an educational context (e.g. see Fisher, 1989; Crombag, 1968).

Some limited evidence suggests that extroverts cope better with moves (see Fisher, Murray and Frazer, 1985), perhaps because of the sociability element which would enhance the involvement in the new environment and provide distraction against preoccupation with home. However, this has not been thoroughly investigated in the context of specific moves.

SUMMARY AND CONCLUSIONS

In this chapter there has been emphasis on methods of encouraging adaptation to the new environment following transition, and on possible features which appear to favour adaptation. These considerations have speculative elements but are linked to existing research evidence. However, specific research programmes designed to investigate the effects would be ideal.

REFERENCES

Crombag, H. F. M. (1968) *Studie motivatie en studie attitude.* Croningen: Walters.

de Paulo, B. M., Brown, P. L., Ishie, S. and Fisher, J. D. (1981) Help that works: the effects of aid on subsequent task performance. *Personality and Social Psychology*, **41**, 478-487.

Fisher, S. (1986) *Stress and Strategy*. London: Lawrence Erlbaum.

Fisher, S. (1989) *Homesickness, Cognition and Health.* London: Lawrence Erlbaum.

Fisher, S., Murray, K. and Frazer, N. (1985) Homesickness and health in first-year students. *Journal of Environmental Psychology*, **5**, 181-195.

Fisher, S. and Hood, B. (1987) The stress of the transition to university: a longitudinal study of vulnerability to psychological disturbance and homesickness. *British Journal of Psychology*, **78**, 425-441.

Fisher, S. and Hood, B. (1988) Vulnerability factors in the transition to university: self-reported mobility history and sex differences as factors in psychological disturbance. *British Journal of Psychology*, **79**, 1-13.

Hood, B., MacLachlan, M. and Fisher, S. (1987) The relationship between cognitive failures, psychoneurotic symptoms and sex. *Acta Psychiatrica Scandinavica*, **76**, 33-35.

Klinger, E. (1975) Consequences of commitment to and disengagement from incentives. *Psychological Review*, **82**(1), 1-7.

Kuhl, J. and Kazen-Saad, M. (1988) A motivational approach to volition: activation and de-activation of memory representations related to uncompleted intentions. In V. Hamilton, G. H. K. Bower and N. Frijda (eds), *Cognition, Emotion and Affect: a cognitive science view*. Dordrecht: Martinus Nijhoff.

Loeb, A., Beck, A. and Diggory, J. (1971) Differential effects of success and failure on depressed and non-depressed patients. *Journal of Nervous and Mental Disease*, **152**(2), 106-113.

Stokols, D., Shumaker, S. A. and Martinez, J (1983) Residential mobility and personal wellbeing. *Journal of Environmental Psychology*, **3**, 5-19.

17 Coping Strategies to Minimize the Stress of Transitions

CARY L. COOPER
Manchester School of Management

INTRODUCTION

Throughout the book we have focused on the stress of transitions, in one's career, personal circumstances and in life generally. There are, of course, a range of strategies that organizations can implement to minimize or attenuate some of the stressful consequences of occupational transitions, such as moving from education to work, relocations, career development and ultimately moving from work to retirement. But we, as individuals, can also do something to mitigate the adverse effects of transitions in our lives. This chapter will explore some ways in which individuals might learn to cope with the stresses and strains of the transitional phases in their life cycle.

There are a number of approaches to help people through these transitions. First, and probably most important, is to try and provide the individual with a sense of *control*. As we have seen earlier, transitions create situations in which individuals perceive they have little or no control. Second, it is important to help individuals structure their *lifestyle* in a way that minimizes stress—in this area we can draw from the work of Friedman and Rosenman (1974) in managing Type A behaviour, a pattern of living frequently implicated in and responsible for transitional situations. Third, many individuals in transitional situations could gain greater control of transitions by learning to unwind and relax, so that they can better assess their circumstances and plan more appropriately. Finally, it might be useful to help individuals to understand how they *could* perceive stressful transitions, by applying the principles of cognitive reappraisal, to minimize the stress of transitions in life.

MAKING CHANGES

Making changes can seem overwhelming at first. But remember, stress is not some all-powerful force in your life that cannot be resisted. Rather, your life is

On the Move: the Psychology of Change and Transition. Edited by S. Fisher and C. L. Cooper.

most probably full of small and large stress responses that either can be altered or, at the least, balanced with other, more positive experiences, such as relaxation. Before you consider the suggestions offered below it may be worthwhile to examine any feelings of resistance you harbour to the idea that your life can change. Sometimes it is helpful to consider someone else you know who is experiencing undue amounts of stress. Perhaps you have observed a family member or friend who is suffering from time pressures or other stress factors. It may be relatively easy for you to see how a few changes in that person's life, such as getting up half an hour earlier to get a better grip on the day, or learning to say 'no' when demands become too great, could improve the situation. You perhaps have even offered a suggestion to that person, only to be told, 'Yes, that's a good idea, but . . .'. Suggestions are often greeted with a variety of responses, all of which boil down to, 'I can't'. Depressed people, especially, may find it difficult to see options, even if they are pointed out by others. Psychologists recognize the inability to see options as a key characteristic of depression. When you consider the suggestions offered below, ask yourself if you are responding with, 'I can't'. Force yourself to consider each idea and seriously try to see if you can change your response to 'I will'.

REGAIN CONTROL—PLAN YOUR LIFE, DON'T LET YOUR LIFE PLAN YOU

Transitions frequently create situations in which the individual feels he or she has no control. It is important during these life phases to provide a person with the tools to help him or her regain control. Dyer (1976) believes an individual must be able to identify the problem areas or lifestyle patterns that are preventing him or her from achieving life goals, and then 'cut through the lifetime of emotional red tape' by changing behaviour and redesigning these patterns. What Dyer warns against—and this is a cardinal rule—is blaming any circumstances or other person for failures or an unsatisfying mode of living. People must 'own up', take responsibility and choose a more satisfying way to live. As George Bernard Shaw put it in his play *Mrs Warren's Profession*, 'People are always blaming their circumstances for what they are. I don't believe in circumstances. The people who get on in this world are the people who get up and look for the circumstances they want, and if they can't find them, make them.'

One exercise that might help people regain some control was developed by Pfeiffer and Jones (1970). There are three parts to this exercise. The first part is aimed at answering the question 'where am I now?' in three areas—your career, your personal life (friends and family) and your personal fulfilment, and it proceeds as follows:

1. Draw a graph or life-line, which can be straight or curved, that depicts the trend of the past, present and future of your career. Place an X to show where you are now. Then write a brief explanation of the career line you have drawn, highlighting the high points and the low points.
2. Repeat the procedure to create a life-line for your personal life with highs and lows.
3. Repeat again to create a personal fulfilment life-line.

This part of the exercise should give you some idea of where you've been, where you are now and where you are likely to go. The future aspects of each line may reflect either your hopes for where you ideally would like to go or where you think you are likely to end up (although you would rather not).

The second part of the exercise asks you to find out 'who am I?', by writing down up to 20 career adjectives which most accurately describe you in your work, such as ambitious, trustworthy, nonchalant and so on. Then write down a similar list of adjectives for your personal life and personal fulfilment.

Divide each group of adjectives into three categories: positive, negative and neutral. This regrouping can provide you with an awareness of your positive and negative traits in three major aspects of your life.

In the third part of the exercise, ask yourself 'where you want to be'. List up to 10 ideal attainments in each of the three main life areas—career, personal life and personal fulfilment. Goals might include 'I want to become self-employed', or 'I want to re-establish closeness with my husband', or 'I want to face my need for alcohol.'

Then assign priority values to the ideals within each of the three groups, using the following scale: 4=of very great importance; 3=of great importance; 2=of moderate importance; and 1=of little importance.

Finally, combine all the ideals into one group and rank them again, using the same scoring system. The combined list should reflect the relative importance of specific goals, whether they involve your career, personal life or personal fulfilment. This then gives you information about your ideal goals in life. You are now equipped with a launching-pad for life planning.

A way to begin your planning efforts would be to select five or so of the highest-rated goals and establish a programme to achieve them, one by one. You will need to think out the behavioural, emotional and practical strategies for each goal. Such an effort is not easy, but by writing out your goals and strategies you may see solutions you had not conceived before. This process may be easier if you work with someone else, with whom you could share your goals and eventual progress. If so, deliberately seek out a trusted colleague, relative or friend. In order to reward yourself for your progress, design specific strategies and objectives that can be measured, rather than just vague ideals. For example, if 'closeness with a spouse' is a goal, a strategy might be to plan one evening

out together each week. The initiation of small changes can one by one lead to the larger life goals established in your plan.

By analysing the life goals you have established in the three areas of career, personal life and personal fulfilment, you may see that the time and energy you have in the past given to one area is far greater than that given the other two. Many professionals, for example, may find they have developed their careers to the neglect of their home life, friendships and personal needs for health and creativity. The establishment of concrete goals in each of the three areas can be a first step towards restoring balance and wholeness to life.

The concept of life planning involves a basic idea: setting goals and objectives helps give direction and a sense of control of time, a precious and limited commodity. Once you have worked through the life planning exercises, the same process of setting specific goals and priorities can be applied to monthly, weekly and daily planning. Although the creation of a time-management programme is beyond the scope of this chapter, any such programme will grow out of the basic process of setting goals and prioritizing, as well as eliminating those tasks which are superfluous and learning to protect your time by saying 'no'. This should help you cope better with the stresses of many transitions. An excellent guide to time management can be found in *How to Get Control of Your Time and Your Life*, by Lakein (1973). He recommends using a written list of things to do, with every item on the list receiving a priority rating such as high, medium or low. By concentrating on the top-priority items first, and then dealing with the remainder in order, you can gain a better sense of accomplishment and control.

MANAGING YOUR LIFE STYE

In addition to trying to regain control in transitional situations, it is important to begin to manage your lifestyle. Lifestyles that are hard-driven, ambitious and time-conscious, create more circumstances for unnecessary and sometimes debilitating transitions (e.g. constantly moving to a more prestigious job regardless of family considerations; never saying 'no' to any status-enhancing activity, etc.). Friedman and Rosenman (1974) have done a great deal of research on the impact of lifestyle in creating stressful transitions in life. They make a number of valuable recommendations about what individuals can do to manage their stress-creating lifestye:

1. In order to put some of your Type A behaviour into perspective, carry out a number of exercises. Develop reflective periods in your self-created 'hectic programme for life', creating opportunities to assess the causes of your hurry sickness. One of the most important new habits to develop is a weekly review of the original causes of your present hurry sickness. Try to get to the

source of your problems and current obsessions. Is your time-dominated behaviour really a need to feel important? Is it designed to avoid some activity or person? Is it really essential to the success of a particular goal? Friedman and Rosenman offer this advice: 'Never forget when confronted by any task to ask yourself the following questions: (1) will this matter have importance five years from now? and (2) must I do this right now, or do I have enough time to think about the best way to accomplish it?'

2. Try to understand that the majority of your work and social life does not really require 'immediate action', but instead requires a quality end-product or a fulfilling relationship. Ask yourself, 'are good judgement and correct decisions best formulated under unhurried circumstances or under deadline pressures?'
3. Try not to make unnecessary appointments or deadlines. 'Remember, the more unnecessary deadlines you make for yourself, the worse your "hurry sickness" becomes.'
4. Learn to protect your time and to say 'No'. 'Try to never forget that if you fail to protect your allotment of time, no one else will. And the older you become, the more important this truth is.'
5. Try to create opportunities during the day or night when you can totally relax your body and mind.
6. Try to control your obsessional time-directed life by making yourself aware of it and changing the established pattern of behaviour. For example, 'whenever you catch yourself speeding up your car in order to get through a yellow light at an intersection, penalize yourself by immediately turning to the right (or left) at the next corner. Circle the block and approach the same corner and signal light again. After such penalization you may find yourself racing a yellow light a second, but probably not a third time.' You can help yourself in nearly all aspects of your life, including social situations, by seeking out opportunities to control your Type A behaviour. 'Purposely, with a companion, frequent restaurants and theatres where you know there will be a period of waiting. If your companion is your wife, remember that you spend far longer periods of time alone with her in your own home without fidgeting. If you and your companion cannot find enough to say to each other as you wait in a restaurant or a theatre, then you had both better seek different companions.'

RELAXATION TECHNIQUES

It is obvious that the body needs time to relax and recuperate from the effects of everyday stress. Some people can dissipate stress, while others 'bury it' deep within themselves. As Albrecht (1979) suggests,

> for these people life seems to be a series of crises. The chronically up-tight person seems to meet even a small problem as if it were a critical incident, as if somehow his survival were in jeopardy. A sudden call to come to the front office, a snag in a project schedule, a conflict with a co-worker, or a problem with a teenage son or daughter all take on the same apparent magnitude for the up-tight person. Such a person meets even the smallest problem situations with an unnecessarily intense reaction.

Relaxation can combat some of these adverse reactions. The evidence is mounting that relaxation techniques can provide the individual, through psychophysiological processes, with less damaging effects (Shaffer, 1983; Cooper, Cooper and Eaker, 1988). The positive bodily outcomes of deep relaxation as a means of coping with peak arousal situations have been highlighted by Shaffer (1983) (see Table 17.1).

DEEP RELAXATION TECHNIQUE

There is a deep relaxation technique which you can use to try to achieve the relaxation response described above. It is a simple technique, which anyone can practise. If you feel somewhat tense about the thought of adding such a technique to your daily life, we suggest you make a commitment to practise relaxation on a daily basis for one month before deciding if you want to continue.

Table 17.1. Relaxing activites

Pausing activities	Purposes	Effects
Smoking cigarettes, tobaccos	Pick-me-up, pausing, arousal, social activity	Increased energy, nutrient drain, poor sleep, indigestion
Drinking coffee or tea (non-herbal)	Pausing, arousal, social activity	Energy boost, nutrient drain, poor sleep, indigestion
Drinking hard alcoholic beverages	Pausing, social activities, central nervous system depressant	Energy drain, digestive imbalance, potential brain impairment
Drinking wines	Pausing, social activities, central nervous system depressant, muscle relaxant	Energy drain
Eating sugary or highly refined foods	Pausing, arousal, pick-me-up, social activity	Poor nutrition, possible low blood sugar, possible indigestion

From Shaffer (1983).

Following this technique is a brief description of 'progressive relaxation', an alternative technique for which training or further study is required. The two techniques which follow this are shorter relaxation practices which you can use in addition to deep relaxation.

For optimal effectiveness, deep relaxation is best done once or twice a day. It can help to assist your body in recovering from distress and prevent the build-up of tension, fatigue and anxiety. Nita Catterton of the University of Virginia uses the following techniques:

1. Sit in a comfortable position. (Support your back, neck, and head.) A quiet place where you will not be interrupted is best.
2. Slowly draw in and exhale a deep breath. Check your shoulders for stiffness or tense position. Allow them to fall naturally in a relaxed position. Take in a second deep breath and close your eyes.
3. Complete a body check to locate any areas of tension and tightness. Take each area and relax the involved muscles. Visualize the tension releasing and slipping away as warmth and relaxation flow into the area. You might imagine yourself basking in the sun and feeling the sun warm your area of tension. (If you are having difficulty evaluating whether or not you are relaxing a specific area try increasing the tension in the muscle and hold that tightness for a count of 10, then release.)
4. Starting with your feet, slowly work up through the body, relaxing muscle groups and areas of tightness and tension. Imagine warmth flowing into each area, muscles become heavy, and comforting relaxation replacing tightness or tension. Once you have progressed throughout your body, focus on your hands. (You can focus on any area of tension you would like to work on.) Create a sentence that you can repeat to yourself emphasizing warmth, heaviness, and relaxation, such as, 'My hands are warm, heavy, and relaxed.'
5. Do not be discouraged if at first your mind tends to wander away to other thoughts. Once you are aware that you have wandered to other thoughts simply come back and focus again on the area you are relaxing. Try to notice how good it feels to have some quiet time to yourself and how comfortable it is to let go of any tightness or tension you may have.
6. Deep relaxation is most effective when practised for a period of 20 minutes. If you find that sitting still for that long is more stress-inducing than stress-reducing then start with a period of five or 10 minutes and gradually build up to 20 minutes.
7. Always end your relaxation session with several deep breaths. Then, after slowly opening your eyes, maintain your relaxation position for a few minutes before resuming your next activity.

Make a commitment to practise deep relaxation on a daily basis for one month before determining if you want to continue with this stress-reduction technique.

PROGRESSIVE RELAXATION

Progressive relaxation, as developed by Jacobson (1958), aims at reducing anxiety by emphasizing physical relaxation. Jacobson combines psychological awareness of stress factors with physiological manifestations and treatment. As it is currently taught, progressive relaxation consists of first tensing, then releasing, all 16 major skeletal muscle groups into which Jacobson has divided the body. As Quick and Quick (1984) describe it,

> the muscles are tensed for five to seven seconds and then relaxed for about thirty seconds. This process begins with the arms, progresses to the face, neck and throat, and then through the chest, abdomen, legs, and finally, the feet. . . . The whole process lasts thirty to sixty minutes. With experience, the subject learns to combine muscle groups into first seven and then four groups. It may take thirty hours or more to master the skill.

Two shorter relaxation exercises which take a maximum of 10 minutes to practise can also be helpful. The following exercises, developed by Dr Cary McCarthy, are aimed at allowing an individual to evoke a feeling of peace and relaxation whenever desired.

Mental relaxation (five to 10 minutes)

1. Select a comfortable sitting or reclining position.
2. Close your eyes and think about a place that you have been before that represents your ideal place for physical and mental relaxation. (It should be a quiet environment, perhaps the seashore, the mountains, or even your own back garden. If you can't think of an ideal relaxation place, then create one in your mind.)
3. Now image that you are actually in your ideal relaxation place. Imagine that you are seeing all the colours, hearing the sounds, smelling the aromas. Just lie back, and enjoy your soothing, rejuvenating environment.
4. Feel the peacefulness, the calmness, and image your whole body and mind being renewed and refreshed.
5. After five to 10 minutes, slowly open your eyes and stretch. You have the realization that you may instantly return to your relaxation place whenever you desire, and experience a peacefulness and calmness in body and mind.

Number count down (three to 10 minutes)

1. Select a comfortable position.
2. Close your eyes, and breathe deeply and rhythmically several times.
3. Take another deep breath and, while exhaling, mentally visualize the number three (3); 3 is your symbol for complete body relaxation. (Relax any tension in your body, remembering the state of deep relaxation felt after the tensing muscle exercise.) Mentally repeat to yourself, '3, complete body relaxation'.

4. Take another deep breath, and while exhaling mentally visualize the number two (2); 2 is your symbol for complete brain and nervous system relaxation. (Any thoughts, fears, concerns, worries—let them all go. Relax all thought processes, feeling a sense of mental stillness and harmony.) Mentally repeat to yourself, '2, complete brain and nervous system relaxation'.
5. Take another deep breath, and while exhaling mentally visualize the number one (1); 1 is your symbol for complete 'oneness' within yourself, for complete attunement and harmony of mind and body. Mentally repeat to yourself, '1, oneness, mind-body harmony'.
6. In this deep state of mind-body relaxation you are filled with calmness, peacefulness. You are at one with creative forces to bring about positive changes and benefits in your daily life and health. (At this time give yourself positive health suggestions you wish to hear. If there is a particular part of your body that needs healing, imagine that your own health energies are flowing to that part. Create a tingling sensation, and imagine the body area bathed in pure light energy, restoring and renewing every cell and tissue.)
7. When you are ready to continue with your daily activities, say to yourself, 'I have been in a deep, renewing state of mind-body relaxation. I will maintain the perfect attunement I have experienced, and will be in perfect health, feeling better than ever before, I will count from one to five, and at the count of five I will feel wide awake and in perfect health'.
8. Then begin counting, '1, 2, 3, 4, 5'. Open your eyes and say out loud (or repeat mentally with your eyes open), 'I am wide awake, in perfect health, feeling better than ever before'.

MEDITATION

Although a wide variety of meditation practices exist, transcendental meditation (TM) has been the most widely analysed in terms of its relief of stress. TM has been reported to help work adjustment through the reduction of tension. Researchers (Benson *et al.*, 1973; Kuna, 1975) who have evaluated TM, indicate it has lowered anxiety, increased job satisfaction and improved work performance. TM has been shown to have long-term benefits as well, such as the reduction of high blood pressure levels. Although TM is increasingly being used in the treatment of hypertension and anxiety, there are those (Benson *et al.*, 1973) who contend it also has positive biochemical effects directly linked to stress-related illness. Although such contentions will need confirmation through further research, it appears clear that TM can help the individual prepare his bodily processes for the pressures of everyday life. Approved TM instructors teach meditators to spend two daily 20-minute sessions in a quiet, comfortable place silently repeating their mantra, the sound or word given to the trainee by the instructor. The trainee aims at developing a passive attitude and peaceful view of life.

AUTOGENIC TRAINING

Profound muscle relaxation is achievable through hypnosis, research has shown. Hypnosis is defined as 'induced state of altered consciousness, characterised by extreme relaxation and a heightened susceptibility to suggestion' (Sach, 1982). A trained expert can induce a hypnotic trance by focusing an individual's attention on a mental or visual image; for example, by suggesting they think of something peaceful or repetitive. Many individuals can be trained to induce a hypnotic state in themselves through self-hypnosis. Self-hypnosis is best learned from an experienced practitioner, but can then be practised continually without further reinforcement.

Quick and Quick (1984) describe autogenic training as a method of self-hypnosis which 'emphasises the development of individual control over physiologic process through organ- and symptom-specific exercises'. In a training process which usually takes between two and three months, the subject learns six standard training exercises aimed at inducing a general feeling of well-being and high coping ability. From this point an individual goes on to learn 'organ-specific' exercises, which deal with particular psycho-physiological dynamics, such as breathing, blood flow and skin temperature. Once again, autogenic training succeeds best with the help of a trained therapist (Jencks, 1979).

SLEEP

Anyone who has experienced a sleep disturbance or insomnia can testify to the importance of sleep to overall functioning and mood. Sleep provides the body with a chance to recuperate and rebuild. As Shaffer (1983) describes it,

> the brain, which controls biological survival, needs rest to maintain its equilibrium . . . the brain, without adequate rest and sleep, cannot maintain the biochemical and electrical balances needed for effective functioning. Furthermore, when the brain is in such a state of disequilibrium, a person cannot cope effectively.

Difficulty falling asleep, insomnia and early morning awakening can all reflect depression or anxiety. Individuals who rely on alcohol to unwind and fall asleep in the evening may often find they awaken in the early morning when the body responds to an alcohol-induced adrenalin surge (Quick and Quick, 1984).

Obviously, we all differ in the amount of sleep we need. Some people need few but continuous hours of sleep, while others need more hours (say eight to 10). The ability to fall asleep quickly and sleep deeply appears to be improved by becoming relaxed before retiring (through a relaxation exercise or personal routine such as taking a warm bath); resolving, or consciously putting aside, emotional conflicts; avoiding overeating in the evening hours; and creating a sleeping environment that is comfortable in terms of light and temperature levels.

Resting during the daytime has also been shown to benefit bodies and minds. To be truly restful, a break must involve a real withdrawal from the day's activities. Often even a brief change in scenery can be refreshing. Many people who work in a tight space find that lifting their eyes and gazing out of a window, or at a pleasant painting or poster several times a day, can be restful. Some research is available which suggests that daytime resting or breaks can moderate illness.

COGNITIVE REAPPRAISAL

There are a range of techniques available to help cognitively reappraise many stressful situations. One such technique has been referred to by Quick and Quick (1984) as 'constructive self-talk'.

They describe this as 'intermittent mental monologue' that most people conduct about the events they experience and their reactions to these events. This monologue or self-talk can range from being gently positive to harshly condemning. When people engage in 'negative self-talk' they achieve nothing and just maintain the stress, dissipating their emotional energy. If you are involved in constructive self-talk it can achieve more positive psychological results. Quick and Quick (1984) provide a range of examples of situations, 'mental monologues' and alternative strategy for constructive self-talk, which is shown here in Table 17.2.

Another technique one could use is what Albrecht refers to as a 'quick recovery', that is, the ability to bounce back from an upsetting experience. Learning to recover quickly takes little more than an awareness of how you actually do recover. As Albrecht (1978) describes it, 'once you begin to think about your emotional responses, you can recognise the process of returning to emotional equilibrium after a provocation has passed.' For example, if you find yourself drawn into a personal confrontation you will very probably experience anger and a full-blown stress response. 'Your higher level mental processes will probably not be functioning very well', Albrecht explains. 'However, at a certain point, your emotions will begin to subside and you will realise that you are angry. That is, you will experience your anger as an intellectual concept as well as a physical feeling.' Albrecht states that, at this point, you have the option to continue and aggravate your angry feelings by 'rehashing the provocation, rejustifying your position, re-opening a new attack on your adversaries, and becoming newly outraged by their unreasonable behaviour'. A quick recovery approach would suggest you stop this 'negative circular approach', become more rational and less conscious of your need to 'win'.

The final two approaches which may prove helpful are what Quick and Quick (1984) refer to as 'thought-stopping' and 'mental diversion'. Thought-stopping means recognizing non-constructive thoughts, attitudes and behaviours and

Table 17.2. Constructive self-talk

Situation	Typical mental monologue	Constructive self-talk alternative
Driving to work on a day which you know will be full of appointments and potentially stressful meetings.	'Oh boy, what a day this will be!' 'It's going to be hell.' 'I'll never get it all done.' 'It'll be exhausting.'	'This looks like a day.' 'The day should be very productive.' 'I'll get a lot accomplished today.' 'I'll earn a good night's rest today.'
Anticipation of a seminar presentation or public address	'What if I blow it'? 'Nobody will laugh at my opening joke.' 'What if they ask about . . . ?' 'I hate talking to groups.'	'This ought to be a challenge.' 'I'll take a deep breath and relax.' 'They'll enjoy it.' 'Each presentation goes a bit better.'
Recovering from a heart attack	'I almost died. I'll die soon.' 'I'll never be able to work again.' 'I'll never be able to play sports again.'	'I didn't die. I made it through.' 'The doctor says I'll be able to get back to work soon.' 'I can keep active and gradually get back to most of my old sports.'
Difficulty with a superior at work	'I hate that person.' 'He makes me feel stupid.' 'We'll never get along.'	'I don't feel comfortable with him.' 'I let myself get on edge when he's around.' 'It will take some effort to get along.'
Flat tyre on a business trip	'Damn this old car.' (Paces around car, looking at flat tyre.) 'I'll miss all my meetings.' 'It's hopeless.'	'Bad time for a flat.' (Begins to get tools out to start working.) 'I'll call and cancel Jenkins at the next phone. I should make the rest of the appointments.'

From Quick and Quick (1984), p. 221.

stopping them immediately—by visualizing, for example, a large STOP sign. Then one uses 'mental diversion' to divert the topic, issue or crisis to one that is manageable, until one has resources to cope with it. Or as Quick and Quick suggest, one way to stop a thought pattern is to divert yourself to a more positive topic. For instance, once you have prepared yourself adequately for a coming event, such as a presentation or interview, obsessive worry can only drain your emotional resources. Diverting your thoughts to a more pleasant, restful subject can stop a negative thought pattern. It is often helpful to develop several topics as substitutes, such as memories of a favourite vacation, plans for a hobby project or the words to a favourite song or poem.

CONCLUSION

These and other techniques may help alleviate the strains of transitions; at the very least they may provide one with the feeling of *control*, an essential characteristic of managing stress.

ACKNOWLEDGEMENT

Most of this material is derived from Cooper, Cooper and Eaker (1988).

REFERENCES

Albrecht, K. (1979) *Stress and the Manager: Making It Work For You*. NJ: Prentice-Hall.

Benson, H. *et al.* (1973). Decreased systolic blood pressure in hypertensive subjects who practiced meditation. *Journal of Clinical Investigation*, **52**, 8.

Cooper, C. L., Cooper, R. D. and Eaker, L. (1988) *Living with Stress*. Harmondsworth: Penguin.

Dyer, W. W. (1976) *Your Erroneous Zones*. New York: Avon Books.

Friedman, M. D. and Rosenman, R. H. (1974) *Type A Behavior and Your Heart*. New York: Knopf.

Jacobson, E. (1958) *Progressive Relaxation*. Chicago, IL: University of Chicago Press.

Jencks, B. (1979) *Exercise Manual for Autogenic Training*. IL: American Society for Clinical Hypnosis.

Kuna, D. J. (1975) Meditation and work, *Vocation Guidance Quarterly*, **23**(4), 342-346.

Lakein, A. (1973) *How to Get Control of Your Time and Your Life*. New York: Wyden.

Pfeiffer, J. W. and Jones, J. E. (1970) *Structural Experiences for Human Relations Training*. Iowa City, IA: University Associates Press.

Quick, J. C. and Quick J. D. (1984) *Organizational Stress and Preventive Management*. New York: McGraw-Hill.

Sachs, B. S. (1982) Hypnosis in psychiatry and psychosomatic medicine, *Psychosomatics*, **23**, 523-525.

Shaffer, M. (1983) *Life After Stress*. Chicago, IL: Contemporary Books.

Index